THE
BALTIMORE
SABOTAGE CELL

THE
BALTIMORE
SABOTAGE CELL

GERMAN AGENTS, AMERICAN TRAITORS, AND THE U-BOAT *DEUTSCHLAND* DURING WORLD WAR I

DWIGHT R. MESSIMER

Naval Institute Press
Annapolis, Maryland

This book has been brought to publication with the generous
assistance of Marguerite and Gerry Lenfest.

Naval Institute Press
291 Wood Road
Annapolis, MD 21402

Library of Congress Cataloging-in-Publication Data
Messimer, Dwight R., 1937-
  The Baltimore Sabotage Cell : German agents, American traitors, and the U-boat
Deutschland during World War I / by Dwight R. Messimer.
      pages cm
  Includes bibliographical references and index.
  ISBN 978-1-59114-184-6 (hardcover : alk. paper) — ISBN 978-1-61251-869-5 (ebook)
1. Deutschland (Submarine) 2. World War, 1914-1918—Naval operations—Submarine. 3.
World War, 1914-1918--Naval operations, German. 4. Baltimore Sabotage Cell. 5. Espio-
nage, German—United States—History—20th century. 6. World War, 1914-1918—Secret
service—Germany. 7. World War, 1914-1918—Secret service—United States. 8. United
States Bureau of Investigation—History. 9. Sabotage—United States—History—20th century. 10. World War, 1914-1918—United States. I. Title. II. Title: German agents, American
traitors, and the U-boat Deutschland during World War I.
  D592.D4M48 2015
  940.4'8743—dc23

                                                                                2014046356

♾ Print editions meet the requirements of ANSI/NISO z39.48-1992 (Permanence of
Paper).
Printed in the United States of America.

23 22 21 20 19 18 17 16 15   9 8 7 6 5 4 3 2 1
First printing

DEDICATED TO JACK KEANE,
A NAVAL AVIATOR, A GENTLEMAN,
AND A VERY GOOD FRIEND

CONTENTS

Photos

Maps

Preface and Acknowledgments

When I did the research for *The Merchant U-Boat* (Naval Institute Press, 1988) in 1985–87, I focused on the *U-Deutschland* exclusively, because I was unaware of her connection to the Baltimore sabotage cell. During the intervening twenty-eight years the great information highway known as the World Wide Web came into existence and grew into an unimaginably rich lode of information on the *U-Deutschland*. Previously inaccessible archives in Germany and the United States opened up online, making it possible to literally travel the globe and never set foot out of my house. The amount of new material that became available was, and still is, staggering.

During the same period a number of scholarly works appeared that touched on various aspects of Germany's cargo submarine project. Those new works focused on the British blockade and its financial and social effects on Germany, on the role of Deutschebank in German-American relations, and on Germany's intelligence agencies—the navy's Etappendienst and the army's Geheimdienst, with its special sabotage unit, Sektion Politik.

The Web also provided a huge amount of material that had been effectively out of my reach in 1986 and '87. Postwar congressional hearings on *Brewing and Liquor Interests and German Propaganda,* the findings of the Mixed Claims Commission with regard to the Black Tom Explosion and the Kingsland Fire, the records of the Bureau of Investigation (forerunner of today's FBI), and the records of the Department of State for World War I are a few in the hoard of documents that became available on my computer screen.

And the Web made it possible to join an online forum for collectors of war relics that put me into contact with several people who have an interest in the submarine *U-Deutschland*. During nearly two years on the forum several of the members provided me with photographs of the boat, various artifacts from it, and bits and pieces of information that helped add "color" to the account. Nearly all of those contributors are named in connection with the items they contributed. The discussions we had about the *U-Deutschland* also produced interesting tidbits that I have incorporated into the text. Those people are Luke Lutton (USA), Steve Zukowsky (USA), Howard Hirsch (USA), Gary McGee (New Zealand), Fritz Lohmann (Germany), Jøn Jensen (Norway), and Claas Stöckmeyer (Germany). One archivist in particular was very helpful—Jonathan Eaker, at the Library of Congress.

Comparative Table of Ranks in World War I

KAISERLICHE-MARINE	U.S. NAVY	ROYAL NAVY
Admiral	Admiral	Admiral
Vizeadmiral	Vice admiral	Vice-admiral
Kontreadmiral	Rear admiral	Rear-admiral
Kommodore		Commodore
Kapitän zur See	Captain	Captain
Fregattenkapitän		
Korvettenkapitän	Commander	Commander
Kapitänleutnant	Lieutenant commander	Lieutenant commander
Oberleutnant zur See	Lieutenant	Lieutenant
	Lieutenant (junior grade)	
Leutnant zur See	Ensign	Sub-Lieutenant

Sources: Harrison S. Kerrick, *Military and Naval America* (New York and Garden City, N.Y.: Doubleday, Page, 1916); *Jane's Fighting Ships of the Great War* (n.p.: Jane's, 1919); U.S. Naval Academy Department of Languages, *Naval Phraseology* (Annapolis, Md.: Naval Institute Press, 1934).

1

The Blockade

Karl Wilhelm Frölich sat at the head of the kitchen table, his sixteen-year-old son Heinz-Wilhelm on his right and his twelve-year-old daughter Brigitte on his left. His wife Helga was still in the kitchen. It was 18 August 1915, three weeks into the second year of the Great War. Karl was an international accounts clerk at the Handelsbank Berlin, and he was worried.

His wife entered the room carrying a steaming bowl in one hand and a bread-basket in the other, set them on the table, and turned to the china cabinet for bowls. Karl spoke as she distributed the bowls. "The new ration allowances were released today."

Helga pulled back her chair and sat down. "What have they cut back on this time?"

Her husband stirred his soup as he answered, "Meat and bread. Starting on Monday the allowance is 350 grams a week for meat and two hundred grams daily for bread."

Helga spooned soup from the bowl. "It's not the end of the world," she said, spooning another mouthful.

"Not yet," Karl responded, "But it's going to get a lot worse very quickly."

Helga stopped eating and looked at her husband. The children continued to eat, paying no attention to the adult conversation, in which they were not included. "What have you heard?" She asked, a frown darkening her face.

"The British have announced their intention to seize any goods made in Germany or bound for Germany regardless of where they are coming from or where they are going," he answered, tearing a bread roll in half.

"How do you know that?"

He sopped up soup from his bowl as he replied, "They announced it last March. The War Office sent a notice to all the banks today telling us about it. It won't be released to the public anytime soon, because they don't want a panic."

Helga shrugged and went back to eating her dinner. Between mouthfuls she said, "I don't think this will really have any effect on us. At least not a serious effect. The war will be over before anything can come of it."

Karl ate his soup silently. Finally he stopped eating, laid down his spoon, and looked directly at his wife. "I hope deeply that you are right, but I don't believe that you are. This is going to be a long, long war, and we are in for very hard times."

"You're a pessimist." His wife chuckled as she spoke.

Karl shook his head wearily. "Not a pessimist, a realist. I have worked daily with the numbers for the past six years. We import a third of our food supply and more than two-thirds of our chemical fertilizers, specifically nitrogenic and phosphatic fertilizers."

"And what does that mean?" Helga asked, sounding put off by what he had said.

"It means, my dear, that without chemical fertilizers Germany will be unable to raise enough food to feed the people." Karl saw no reason to elaborate on what to him was an obvious conclusion. German agriculture was absolutely dependent on chemical fertilizers. Without them, the crop yield would shrink to the point that the nation, being unable to make up the losses through importation of whole food, would starve.[1]

"I don't think the kaiser will let that happen, Karl."

"I don't see how he can stop it," Karl answered and resumed eating.

Now, it was Helga who stopped eating and laid down her spoon. "Our U-boats will force the British to lift the blockade," she said with conviction.

He waited a moment before answering, "Unless we can win the war soon, it will happen."

"Karl," she said, with a strong positive tone to her voice, "before we all starve, the war will end." She resumed eating.

"There is one other thing," he said as he tore another roll in half. "The priorities for imports now are raw materials for the arms and munitions industries. Not food."

Helga spoke between mouthfuls, "I'm sure that's true, Karl. But we will always have the potato, and that will keep us alive."

At the time that hypothetical conversation was taking place in Berlin, the British blockade was already very effective, and the German people were just beginning to feel the effects. But unlike the populace, German industry was already feeling the effects and was approaching a crisis. The first sign of the impending crisis appeared in October 1914, when the German army used up its reserves of artillery ammunition and had to rely solely on new production for replenishment. The munitions manufacturers, notably Friedrich Krupp AG, were so starved for raw materials that on 14 November German artillery on the western front was down to a four-day supply of ammunition. The Germans slapped a patch on the problem by creating the Kriegsrohstoffabteilung (War Raw Materials Agency), under Walter

Rathenau, responsible for distributing what raw materials Germany had on hand according to priority need. The supply of munitions increased, but the long-term problem of how and where to obtain more raw materials did not go away.[2]

The strength of the British blockade came from two sources. One was the ability of the Royal Navy to enforce the blockade, and the other was Britain's favorable geographic position, which made the Royal Navy the gatekeeper of the seaborne trade routes to Europe. There are only two bodies of water across which seaborne trade to and from Germany can be carried—the North Sea and the Baltic. The North Sea was, and is, Germany's aorta. Seal off the North Sea in wartime, and Germans will starve. And starve they did from 1917 to 1919. Germany depended on access across the North Sea for something between a third and a half of its imports of all commodities, and it still does. The Baltic route satisfied less than 30 percent of Germany's needs.

There are only two ways into the North Sea for traffic coming from anywhere in the world except parts of Europe. One is to enter the English Channel from the western approaches, pass up the Channel, transit the Dover Strait, and turn right into the German Bight to reach Bremen, Bremerhaven, or Hamburg. The British easily closed that route on the day the war started and kept it tightly closed for the duration. The other route, called the Northern Route, was considerably longer. It came out of the North Atlantic, hooked around Scotland, and passed down and across the North Sea to the German Bight, and then to Bremen, Bremerhaven, and Hamburg. By the beginning of 1915 the British 10th Cruiser Squadron had virtually closed the northern route. In fact, the 10th Cruiser Squadron became so effective that the commercial traffic that did slip through was miniscule and eventually nonexistent.

The British had a more difficult time shutting down commercial traffic between Germany and the Nordic states—Norway, Denmark, and Sweden. The problem was a practice called "continuous voyage," by which commodities would be landed in a neutral port before going on to their final destination, which was often Germany. The British solution was to issue an Order in Council on 11 March 1915 that made all cargoes consigned under continuous voyage subject to seizure.[3] The British also blacklisted companies that did business with Germany or provided front destinations for goods en route to Germany. And they coerced, by threatening to withhold coal, the neutral Scandinavian states into not shipping their own commodities across the Baltic to Germany. The dual policies did not completely shut down trade between the Scandinavian countries and Germany, but the trade was measurably reduced.[4]

During the first months of the war, the blockade had only a marginal effect on Germany, because it was still able to draw on existing supplies, and also because the British did not immediately prevent neutral shipping from reaching German ports. Nevertheless, 36 percent of Germany's entire merchant fleet was bottled up in German ports. The other 64 percent was interned in neutral ports throughout the world or already seized by the Entente powers. The merchant ships that were in Germany's harbors could be used only for coastal traffic, operating between Germany and Dutch ports through the inland passage, or trading with Scandinavian ports in the Baltic. Though Germany's merchant tonnage represented only about 15 percent of the world's total, German ships carried 60 percent of all German imports.[5] Thus, the instant loss of three-quarters of Germany's merchant fleet was a major blow, compounded by the virtual end of neutral deliveries. The most damaging loss was the end of Germany's ability to trade with the United States.

In the first months of the war, the Germans were largely unconcerned about the blockade's effect, because they confidently expected the war to be over by Christmas 1914, and they did not see as a problem the fact that they had no strategic reserves of food and only a six-month supply of raw materials.[6] It was a shortsighted view for a country that imported a third of its food and nearly all its industrial raw materials. But the Germans fully believed that they could make up the loss by relying on neutral shipping to bring in the needed supplies.

Though Germany's scientists made great strides in developing synthetic substitutes for some of the nation's war needs, they were not able to assure a sufficient supply of the synthetics for a protracted war. There was, moreover, little or nothing the scientists could do to mitigate the growing food shortage, which became a crisis when the potato crop failed in 1916, leading to the 1917 potato famine. But in the summer of 1915 those hardships were still over a year away.

At the same time that the supply of artillery ammunition to the western front was resuming, food prices on basic foodstuffs were rapidly going up, due to shortages caused by the blockade. The government imposed price ceilings in November 1914 and in January 1915 nationalized wheat production. In February 1915 the individual meat allowance was down to eighteen ounces per week, and two days a week were declared meatless. By June bread was being rationed throughout Germany.[7] In the absence of chemical fertilizers, wheat and rye production fell by from 30 to 50 percent in 1915.

As the war ground on, the British blockade became increasingly efficient and effective, so much so that on 24 January 1916 General Erich von Falkenhayn, Chief of the General Staff, told the kaiser that time was against Germany and that he expected the Austrians and Turks to drop out of the war not later than the autumn of 1916. He repeated that warning on 9 February 1916 during a war council in Berlin. On 4 March 1916 the German chancellor, Theobald von Bethmann-Hollweg, told the kaiser and his advisors that he did not believe Germany could hold out through the 1916–17 winter. Though these gloomy predictions were premature, they reflect the deteriorating situation in Germany, and they underscore the historical truth that the blockade was the most powerful weapon in the Allies' arsenal and was the primary cause of Germany's defeat.[8] By mid-1915 it was obvious to the Germans that a way to break the blockade had to be found.

But 1915 made another serious threat to Germany's war effort painfully apparent. Germany lacked the ability to conduct a similarly effective blockade against the British, which left the British and French free to conduct unrestricted trade with the United States. Not only was Britain able to feed its people with grains and meats from America, but it could import virtually unlimited amounts of raw materials needed for its war industry, as well as millions of tons of ready-to-use munitions.

Germany was faced with two related, but somewhat dissimilar, problems: how to break the blockade and how to stop or seriously disrupt the British supply line across the Atlantic. The solution to breaking the blockade was to find a way over it, through it, or under it. Aircraft in those days were too primitive, underpowered, and short-ranged to accomplish the first option, and Germany lacked the naval strength to force a passage through the blockade. But if a fleet of cargo U-boats could be built that were large enough to carry meaningful loads and had the range to make a round trip between Germany and the United States without having to refuel, the blockade might be broken. Responsibility for implementing this solution rested with a section of German Navy Intelligence known as the Etappendienst, about which there will be more later.

The Germans also lacked the naval strength to effect the solution to the other problem, cutting Britain's supply line to America. The German navy could not defeat the Royal Navy in a slugfest, and there were not enough U-boats to effectively block Britain's transatlantic sea trade. The answers were to blow up the munitions factories, depots, and ships at the western end of the supply line—that is, in the United States—and to infect horses and mules that were bound for Europe with anthrax and glanders.

Responsibility for carrying out sabotage of all types in the United States rested with a newly established subsection of German Army Intelligence called Sektion Politik that fielded an army of trained saboteurs in the United States beginning in 1915. Before America's entry into the war on 6 April 1917, German agents carried out more than fifty successful attacks involving fire and explosion—a figure that does not include the spread of anthrax and glanders on the East Coast.

One of the two solutions to Germany's problems, sabotage, was incompatible with Germany's primary diplomatic goal to keep the United States out of the war, whereas the other, breaking the blockade, provided the least danger of bringing the United States into it. The two solutions were widely dissimilar, but the fact that the cargo U-boat project and the sabotage campaign were both run by intelligence agencies (the Etappendienst for the navy, the Geheimdienst for the army), through the agency of one man (Paul Hilken), and in one U.S. city (Baltimore, Maryland), makes them inseparable. Those separate solutions created the dichotomy that produced the U-boat *Deutschland* and the Baltimore sabotage cell.[9]

2

The Beginning

It was Sunday, 18 May 1915, when Paul G. L. Hilken answered the phone in his upscale Roland Park home in Baltimore. The caller identified himself as Franz von Rintelen and told Hilken that he had a letter of introduction from Frederick Henjez, a New York freight forwarder. Hilken recognized Henjez's name and asked the caller his business. Von Rintelen told Hilken that Philipp Heineken, general director of Norddeutsche Lloyd (NDL), and Captain Bartlett, the chief of navigation for NDL, had suggested he call. Paul Hilken and his father were the Baltimore agents for NDL, and von Rintelen's call suddenly became important. "Can you meet me in New York at the Astor Hotel?" von Rintelen asked. Hilken immediately agreed and told von Rintelen that he would take the next train and be in New York that evening. Hilken hung up, having agreed to meet von Rintelen in the hotel lobby, where von Rintelen would have him paged.[1]

Kapitänleutnant (lieutenant commander) Franz von Rintelen—whose full name was Franz Dagobert Johannes von Rintelen—was an Imperial German Navy officer who had come to the United States to carry out acts of sabotage on "all kinds of factories for war material deliveries." The people who sent von Rintelen to the United States did not intend that he should personally carry out the sabotage; he was simply to organize and fund the operation in the United States, for which he had a half-million dollars and virtually unlimited bank credits. Paul G. L. Hilken was going to be his Baltimore paymaster.[2]

◄ Paul König and Paul G. L. Hilken on board the *U-Deutschland* in Baltimore, 10 July 1916. Paul König was a former NDL captain, a German naval officer, and the captain of the *U-Deutschland*. Paul G. L. Hilken was an American citizen, a wealthy Baltimore businessman, and the head of Germany's most successful sabotage cell in the United States. *Library of Congress*

Henry and Paul Hilken, father and son, owned a tobacco export company in Baltimore called A. Schumacher and Company. They were also the Baltimore agents for NDL, and Paul was the Swedish vice consul in Baltimore. Though both Henry and Paul were American citizens, they harbored a fierce loyalty to the *Vaterland,* and both men were outspoken about their support of Germany during World War I.

The elder Hilken had immigrated to the United States in 1866 when he was nineteen, married an American woman, and had become an American citizen. Before World War I, Henry Hilken had been the subject of a glowing public tribute.

> There is, perhaps, no citizen of Baltimore upon whom the consensus of opinion would unite with more unanimity as to the possession of ability, integrity and general trustworthiness, than upon Henry G. Hilken, of the widely known firm of A. Schumacher & Company. For more than forty years Mr. Hilken has been prominently identified with the commercial and social interests of Baltimore, and throughout that period his influence has been invariably and powerfully exerted in favor of every enterprise tending to promote the welfare and advance the prosperity of our city.[3]

His son, Paul, was less commendable. Paul Hilken was born on 13 February 1878 in Baltimore. He attended Lehigh University in Bethlehem, Pennsylvania, a four-year technical school for men, where he majored in mechanical engineering, and was active in several clubs and groups, including the Mustard and Cheese, a theatrical group. In 1897 it staged *Ulster,* in which Paul played "Agnes." He was also a Delta Phi fraternity member.[4]

He entered the Massachusetts Institute of Technology (MIT) in 1900 in the class of 1904. He again majored in mechanical engineering and took a difficult, yearlong study of naval architecture known as "Course XIII." In 1900 those who had survived the rigors of the course founded the Naval Architecture Society at MIT, and Paul was an early member.[5]

In June 1903 he applied for a passport and listed his occupation as "marine architect," which might offer a clue to his character, since at the time he was not working in that capacity and had not yet graduated from MIT, where his major was still mechanical engineering.[6] On 2 June 1906, in New York, he married Helen Frances Parsons. From 2 November 1906 to 15 December 1909 he worked as a draftsman in the Marine Department at Maryland Steel's Sparrows Point plant. In December 1909 he joined his father's business in Baltimore.[7]

By 1915 Paul was effectively running the NDL operations in Baltimore, while his father continued to head A. Schumacher and Company. By that time Paul was the stereotypical upper-middle-class success, with an attractive wife, three children, and a comfortable two-story home. Paul was five feet, eight inches tall, slightly built, and had a small face with a mustache. He looked intelligent, and he was, but his prominent ears, which stuck out from his head, and his small face and head gave him a mouse-like look. He was not a flashy dresser, but he wore obviously expensive, well-tailored clothes that suited his slight figure. One would say that he dressed for success, and he *was* a success.

But he was not a person whom everyone liked or thought well of. He was described as "ruthless," "a weakling and degenerate," and a "liar, not presumptive but proven."[8] The last allegation is absolutely true, although Paul probably would not have judged his character quite so harshly. He had an eye for women, as the Bureau of Investigation files reveal and his later divorce proved, and a proclivity for making himself out as something he was not, as evidenced by his claim to be a naval architect in 1903. Twelve years later he was impressing the women he dated by hinting at dark secrets and intrigues in which he was involved—claims that were not entirely false but were exaggerated.[9] He apparently changed later in life, but during World War I he was not a nice person.

The Hilkens' headquarters was the Hansa Haus at the corner of Charles and German Streets, a three-story building that reflected sixteenth-century Hanseatic League architecture. The Hilkens' A. Schumacher Company, Norddeutsche Lloyd, and the German consul shared the building.[10]

When von Rintelen and Hilken met on the evening of 18 May 1915 in the Astor, von Rintelen introduced himself as "Hansen" and produced the letter of introduction that Henjez had written for him. Hilken read the letter and returned it to von Rintelen without asking why "Hansen" had been given a letter of introduction in the name of von Rintelen. The absence of any inquiry reassured "Hansen" that Paul would be agreeable to the proposition he was about to make. He was right.

He then told Hilken that he was in the United States to instigate strikes among stevedores and railroad workers, an activity in which Hilken had already been involved, and to place explosive devices on board munitions ships.[11] He described a time-delayed explosive device that he could provide to Hilken, but he did not say a word about the fact that during the three weeks he had been in the United States he had already created and put into action a sizeable sabotage group in New York City. In fact, von Rintelen was creating three sabotage cells, one in New York, one in Baltimore, and one in New Orleans, each cell to be separate and unknown to the other two.

Von Rintelen wanted Hilken to be the paymaster of a Baltimore sabotage group that would plant the time-delay explosives on ships that were carrying supplies to the Allies, with ammunition ships the priority. Von Rintelen would supply the devices, which were already being manufactured in New York City in a place that he controlled. Hilken readily agreed, his extreme pro-German attitude making it easy for him to justify any effort to aid Germany, even sabotage that might cause loss of lives, possibly American. Hilken told von Rintelen that at their next meeting he would introduce him to Captain Friedrich Hinsch, who, Hilken assured him, was perfectly suited to organize and direct the Baltimore-based sabotage crew. Hinsch was indeed the right man for the job.[12]

Before the war Friedrich Hinsch had been the first watch officer on board the NDL passenger-freighter SS *Neckar*. Like all German merchant marine officers, he held a reserve commission in the Imperial German Navy, in his case as a *Leutnant zur See,* equivalent to enisgn in the U.S. Navy. On 1 August 1914, the SS *Neckar* entered Havana Harbor to avoid being captured by British warships in the West Indies and came under the control of a German naval intelligence cell known as Etappe Westindien, headquartered in Havana.

On 26 August *Neckar* and three other vessels were dispatched to a point east of Trinidad to await the German light cruiser SMS *Karlsruhe* and provide her with coal and supplies. But before the *Karlsruhe* arrived, the British cruiser HMS *Berwick* arrived; during the ensuing chase she captured three German ships, SS *Spreewald, Thor,* and *Lorenzo.* The *Neckar,* with Hinsch in command, escaped and went into Baltimore for internment on 21 September 1914.[13]

The second meeting between von Rintelen and Hilken took place on the weekend of 29–31 May in Baltimore, where von Rintelen was Hilken's week-end houseguest. On 29 May he and Hilken had lunch at the Baltimore Country Club, where von Rintelen used the alias "Edward Gates." (The frequent name changes never bothered Hilken, who later told Justice Department investigators that he never asked von Rintelen about the aliases.) It was during this weekend visit in Baltimore that Captain Hinsch joined the undertaking and von Rintelen explained how the time-delay explosive worked.[14]

One meeting with Hinsch that weekend took place on Sunday, 30 May, in Hilken's third-floor office in Hansa Haus. During this meeting von Rintelen produced an example of the incendiary device he called a "cigar," which was made by rolling a thin lead sheet into a tube about the length and diameter of a large cigar. A copper or aluminum divider disc was pushed halfway down the tube and sealed so that the barrier between the two halves of the tube was tight. One end of the tube was filled with sulphuric acid, the other end with either picric acid or a mixture of potassium chlorate and sodium peroxide. The ends were sealed with wax. The acid, or acids, ate their way through the divider from each end and ignited on contact with each other. The thickness of the center divider determined how much time would elapse—always several days—before the device erupted in flame. The flame that was produced was intense and under the right conditions would cause a major fire.[15]

The incendiary devices had been developed by Dr. Walter T. Scheele, a German chemist who was the president of the New Jersey Agricultural Chemical Company in Hoboken, New Jersey—a front for bomb making and other activities related to German espionage in the United States. German crewmen assembled the pipe-bomb casings in the engine room of the NDL liner *Friedrich der Grosse,* which was interned in New York Harbor. The assembled casings were then filled in

Scheele's lab in Hoboken, capped at both ends with wax, and distributed to groups of stevedores who would plant the bombs on board ships. Von Rintelen told Hinsch that he could supply fifty bombs a day.[16]

The following day, Monday the 31st, von Rintelen gave Hilken ten thousand dollars in cash to pay Hinsch and his men for planting the bombs and causing strikes among stevedores and railroad workers. At this point von Rintelen had said nothing about attacking targets on land, focusing entirely on destroying ships. Von Rintelen was not keen on blowing up factories, believing instead that merchant ships carrying munitions and supplies to the Entente powers were better targets. His rationale was that sinking heavily laden freighters was easier than blowing up factories and accomplished the same thing. The land jobs would come later.

Hinsch hired J. Edward "Eddie" Felton to be his crew leader.[17] Felton was an African-American stevedore who had worked for NDL since 1908. He was bright, clever, and reliable. Felton hired two assistants to be his crew chiefs, George Turner and John Grant, both African-American NDL stevedores whom Felton knew and trusted. The men who worked under Turner and Grant would vary in number depending on the nature of the job and would receive their pay from them. Felton and the men he hired took the jobs for money alone and had no feelings one way or the other about what was happening in Europe. The only effect the war had had on them had been to take away their livelihoods by effectively shutting down NDL, leaving them to scramble for any work they could find. The arrangement with Hinsch provided a regular source of income, with better wages than they had earned as stevedores.

The organization that Hinsch put together was efficient, and it was virtually immune to exposure, because the men under Felton did not know who was in the chain above Felton. If arrested they could expose only Felton, who could be relied on to keep his mouth shut, since in the event of his arrest Hinsch would see to the financial needs of his family. Hilken paid Hinsch, who in turned paid Felton, and Felton paid his part-time workers according to a scale that he devised. Being an NDL employee, Felton could go to the Hansa Haus or later the Eastern Forwarding Company (EFCO) warehouse whenever he needed to meet with Hinsch, but he never met with Hilken.

Hinsch first tackled the job of fomenting strikes, by setting up a dummy union called the Union of Russian Workers, with a headquarters at 36 East Montgomery Street in Baltimore. The union had no members, and the name, being generic, could apply to stevedores and railroad workers. The union building was a two-story structure, the nonexistent union occupying the second floor. The front was complete with a "singing and reading room." in which songbooks and sheet music were stacked on tables and shelves of books in Russian and English lined one wall. There was a meeting room, complete with chairs and a podium. Hinsch had flyers printed by the Mechanics' Press in New York City calling on workers to strike and had the flyers delivered to the East Montgomery Street address, where Felton's men picked them up and distributed them in Baltimore and to Newport News and Norfolk, both in Virginia.[18]

For the business of planting bombs on ships, Eddie Felton, Turner, and Grant each hired four or five day-labor stevedores on the docks. Working in units of two or three men per ship, they had ready access to the holds and the cargos themselves, which made it a relatively easy task to plant a half-dozen of the incendiary bombs within the grain, cotton, and munitions.[19]

Hinsch was never directly involved in any of the sabotage activities, his job being limited to directing the operations and paying the men with money he received from Hilken. Because only Hinsch and Eddie Felton knew about Hilken, he was safely insulated from discovery. And because Hilken and Hinsch knew nothing about the cells in New York and New Orleans, those cells could not be compromised if the Baltimore cell were exposed. Hilken and Hinsch enjoyed the same security should one of the other two cells be exposed, which in fact happened.

Hilken had very few contacts with von Rintelen after the 29–31 May meeting. They met in New York on 23 June and had lunch at the Lawyer's Club, where von Rintelen was again using the name "Gates." On 26 and 27 June 1915, von Rintelen stayed at the Belvedere Hotel in Baltimore as "Hansen," but the only contact Hilken had with him was a phone call on the 27th. Von Rintelen had more frequent contact with Hinsch, who ran the day-to-day field operations in Baltimore, than he did with Hilken, the paymaster.[20]

On the surface it does not appear that Hinsch's bomb crew was very active in Baltimore, since the thirty-seven ships that are known to have been damaged or sunk by Doctor Scheele's bombs were out of New York. There were several mysterious fires on board ships in May, but they were written off as accidents, and they occurred before Hilken's group became active.[21] Between 2 June and 27 August 1915 ten vessels were bombed, and some of these attacks might be attributed to the Baltimore cell.[22] There is no solid evidence that Hinsch's crews were attacking land targets, though there were unexplained explosions and fires in New York, Pennsylvania, and Delaware in July that his group could have caused. A more likely example of a fire set on land was one that destroyed two grain elevators in Connecticut in 1915, about which Hilken bragged to two of his girlfriends.

Eddie Felton, John Grant, and Arthur Young told the Mixed Claims Commission that they were also active in Newport News and Norfolk "starting fires," but they did not provide specific details because the commission was looking only at the Black Tom explosion and the Kingsland fire, both of which were the work of Hilken's cell. Other than Hilken's diary, which recorded only what he was personally involved in or privy to, there are no records of what the Baltimore cell did. The only large-scale, sustained sabotage documented as having been carried out by Hinsch's people was the spreading of anthrax and glanders (infectious diseases that attack primarily the lungs) beginning in the autumn of 1915.

In any event, von Rintelen's activities were cut short when Sektion Politik ordered him to return to Berlin. Before von Rintelen left for Germany he provided Hilken with ample money to continue sabotage activities while he was gone. The bombing attacks on merchant ships sailing from the East Coast and out of New Orleans continued without letup until 13 April 1916, when von Rintelen's man in charge of the New York cell was arrested and the entire ring in that city was smashed, without revealing a hint of another sabotage cell in Baltimore.

On 3 August 1915, von Rintelen left New York on board the Holland-America liner SS *Noordam* using a Swiss passport in the name of "Emile V. Gasché." When the ship put into Ramsgate for inspection, the British arrested von Rintelen and held him as a prisoner of war. By the time he was cooling his heels in a British prison, powerful businessmen and government officials in Berlin and Bremen were working on a plan to break the British blockade.[23]

The solution to the blockade problem reached in Berlin and Bremen brought the Baltimore sabotage cell and the commercial submarine project together. Though both operations had shadowy backgrounds that included both German army and navy intelligence organizations, they were not operationally joined.

What came to be a joint civilian and government commercial submarine project had its start in both the civilian and government sectors. Whether the idea of building a cargo submarine was original to the promoters or came from a dinner conversation between Simon Lake and Alfred Lohmann in Berlin in 1909 is not known. What is known is that the idea was born because of the increasing raw materials shortages caused by the British blockade.

➤ Gustav Krupp von Bohlen und Halbach, whose company had stored in New York warehouses 1,200 tons of nickel and raw rubber that the British blockade prevented from being delivered. Krupp planned to build his own cargo submarine to get the materials.
Author's collection

◄ Rudolf Erbach, the Krupp engineer who with Hans Techel designed the *U-Deutschland* on the cheap.
Author's collection

The June 1915 munitions crisis in Germany underscored the shortage of critical raw materials.[24] Friedrich Krupp AG, one of the first munitions makers to feel the crunch, had huge stores of nickel in the United States but no way to get them. Beginning in November 1914, the German commercial attaché in Washington, Dr. Heinrich Albert, acting for Krupp, had acquired over a thousand tons of refined nickel stored in a warehouse belonging to the Nassau Smelting and Refining Company in New York City. Krupp desperately needed that nickel, but the British blockade made it impossible. Gustav Krupp von Bohlen und Halbach, the chairman of the board of the Krupp industries, directed Rudolf Erbach, senior engineer at Germaniawerft, the Krupp shipyard in Kiel, to design a cargo U-boat capable of carrying the nickel from the United States to Germany. Another talented Krupp engineer, Hans Techel, was assigned to work with Erbach on the project.

It appears that Friedrich Krupp was at this point acting independently, but even the most powerful industrialist in Germany could not have carried out the building of a cargo submarine on his own. He certainly had the shipyard, the workers, and the steel mills, but the government, through Walter Rathenau's War Materials Department, had the say as to how those resources were used. In any case, Krupp was not the only one thinking along those lines.

At about the same time that Erbach and Techel were designing a cargo U-boat, the state secretary of the treasury, Karl Helfferich, spoke with Admiral Eduard von Capelle, state secretary of the navy, about using frontline U-boats to carry "essential supplies" from the United States to Germany. Part of his plan included transferring rubber from cargo ships into U-boats at sea; Admiral von Capelle rejected that scheme as impractical in all respects but endorsed the concept. Exactly what was said between the two men is not known, but Admiral von Capelle thought the idea of using U-boats to carry freight should be pursued.

Helfferich's idea was not entirely new to the Imperial German Navy. In the fall of 1914 Theodore Reitz, who was the Prussian senior naval architect and director of engineering operations *(Marine-Oberbaurat und Maschinenbau-Betriebsdirektor Preussen)*, suggested to Hamburg businessmen that they finance the building of cargo U-boats. The people he talked to were not interested, and in the spring of 1915 he submitted a memorandum to Admiral von Capelle's Reichsmarineamt (RMA) suggesting the same idea.

Reitz's memorandum landed on von Capelle's desk at about the same time that the transportation of military supplies by sea in the Mediterranean had become necessary and the RMA had directed that interchangeable, modular, cargo-carrying forward sections for UB- and UC-boats be built to replace their torpedo- and mine-equipped forward sections. So when Helfferich discussed using war boats as make-do cargo carriers, Admiral von Capelle was already aware of the concept.[25] Enter Alfred Lohmann, a forty-five-year-old Bremen businessman with powerful business and government connections.

A reference to a dinner that Lohmann had with Simon Lake in Berlin in 1909 has already been made, and it is very possible, even probable, that Lake did bring

▲ Alfred Lohmann, the Bremen businessman who acted as the front man for the Deutsche Ozean Reederei, a dummy company created by the German navy's secret Etappendienst. *Claas Stöckmeyer collection*

up the subject of commercial submarines. The subject was one of his favorites.[26] Just three years after his dinner with Lohmann, Lake tried to interest the Canadian government in using specially built cargo submarines to carry freight and passengers from the mainland to islands off Canada's west coast that were inaccessible to surface ships during the winter.[27] If so, it is equally possible that Lohmann, who in 1915 was working with Karl Helfferich in the State Treasury, said something to him about Lake's idea. The Lake-Lohmann dinner in 1909 would explain the source of the idea that Lohmann put to Helfferich in 1915, who in turn suggested it to Admiral von Capelle.

Alfred Lohmann, the son of a former Norddeutsche Lloyd director, was the chairman of the board of three major companies and president of the Bremen Chamber of Commerce. His own importing firm, Lohmann and Company, had offices in Bremen, Sydney, and Melbourne. In addition to having worked with the state secretary of the treasury, Lohmann's brother, *Kapitän zur See* (Captain) Walter Lohmann, was a member of the Etappendienst, which became a major player in the commercial submarine project.[28]

Buried within the Intelligence Section of the Imperial German Navy, the Etappendienst was primarily responsible for providing coal and provisions to Germany's far-flung ocean commerce raiders. To accomplish that mission, the Etappendienst had established prewar cells in nearly all the world's major ports. The cells were composed of men who were either German-born or German sympathizers and were involved in some way in the shipping business. German diplomats were also involved in Etappendienst activities, primarily providing funds and directing cells. An example is the New York Etappendienst cell, which had been active since the declaration of war in Europe.

The New York Etappendienst cell received its funds, direction, and bogus documents from *Kapitänleutnant* Karl Boy-Ed, the naval attaché in Washington. The cell, headquartered in the Hamburg-America Lines office, was headed by Dr. Karl Gottlieb Bünz, a career diplomat who in 1914 was assigned as the American director of Hamburg-America Lines. Under Bünz the New York cell actively provisioned German surface raiders operating in the Caribbean and off the east coast of South America until federal agents broke it up in 1915 and arrested the five principal operatives, including Dr. Bünz.

Each cell was part of a larger district called an *Etappe*. The U.S. Atlantic coast was the *Etappe* New York, which in addition to New York included the ports of

Baltimore, New London, and Boston. Given the nature of its contacts and organization, the Etappendienst became the natural conduit through which the German navy controlled the development and implementation of the commercial submarine project. And Alfred Lohmann, with his experience in shipping and international business and his connections to finance and government, including the Etappendienst, was the ideal choice to play the role of the public front man for the project.[29]

In June 1915 Karl Helfferich met with Alfred Lohmann to discuss the commercial submarine idea, including an organizational plan. The discussion led to a plan centered on establishing a limited-liability company, to be known as the Deutsche Ozean Reederei (DOR), to build two cargo U-boats and operate them between Germany and the United States. From the start, the businessman and the state treasurer recognized that to succeed the commercial submarine project would have to be a joint civilian and government venture.

On the civilian side, the DOR would be a subsidiary of NDL, backed by the Deutschebank with a capital investment of two million reichsmarks, one and a half million from NDL and a half-million from Alfred Lohmann. The German government would guarantee the total investment and pay an annual 5 percent return on the investment. All profits would be shared 80 percent for the government and 20 percent for the investors.

The boats would be insured through the Deutsche Versicherungsbank for 2.7 million marks each, which meant the government would cover any loss and provide all financing beyond the two-million-mark initial investment. The government would supply the building materials, and the crews would come from active naval personnel, most of them from the U-boat service.[30]

Though the government provided the major part of the financing and the German navy controlled the project—the boats belonged entirely to the navy, despite the titular private investment—the navy made it clear that there was not to be even a hint in public of any government involvement. The commercial submarine project was to look like and function as an entirely private capital venture headquartered in the NDL offices in Bremen. The subterfuge was so successful that even today virtually everything written about the *U-Deutschland* and *U-Bremen* describes Germany's cargo submarine project as a civilian capital venture.

On 2 October 1915 Admiral von Capelle's RMA awarded a contract to Krupp AG for one cargo submarine (to be charged to the Deutsche Ozean Reederei) and on 15 November another for the second boat (to be charged to Krupp), both to be built to Rudolf Erbach's and Techel's design. The pressure hulls for both boats were ordered from Flensburger Schiffbau AG, while the Krupp Germaniawerft was responsible for the machinery and fitting out. The RMA assigned naval construction numbers U-200 and U-201 to the *U-Deutschland* and the *U-Bremen,* respectively.[31]

At the time, the Deutsche Ozean Reederei did not officially exist, but on 8 November 1915 it was established as a subsidiary of NDL, with NDL director, Karl

Stapelfeld, listed as general director. The following day the *U-Deutschland's* keel was laid, followed by the *U-Bremen's* on 12 December 1915.

During the time that the commercial cargo submarine project was taking shape in Bremen, a saboteur more dangerous than von Rintelen arrived in the United States. Dr. Anton Dilger arrived in New York on board the SS *Kristianiafjord* on 7 October 1915, bringing with him cultures to produce anthrax and glanders.[32] Though he had been born in Virginia in 1884, he had spent most of his childhood in Germany and been had been trained as a surgeon at Heidelberg, as well as at Johns Hopkins University in Maryland. As a freshly minted physician, he volunteered to serve in the Bulgarian army in 1912 as a surgeon during the Serbian-Bulgarian War. He was back in Germany when the European war broke out in August 1914 and immediately joined the German army's Medical Corps, which assigned him to a hospital in Karlsruhe.

Somewhere along the line, he came to the attention of the German Army Intelligence Unit and was transferred to Sektion Politik, where he worked on biological-warfare cultures of anthrax and glanders. In the autumn of 1915 Sektion Politik sent him back to the United States along with the cultures needed to produce the toxins. Together with his brother Carl, he established a lab in Maryland at the corner of Lexington and 33rd Streets in Chevy Chase for that purpose and contacted Paul Hilken for help in spreading anthrax and glanders. Since von Rintelen had left Hilken with adequate cash to pay for the work, he agreed, and Hinsch assigned Eddie Felton and his men to the mission.[33]

Since many of the attacks would be against corrals at or near shipping centers, the stevedores were the ideal choice. The dockworkers fanned out across the country, carrying out their assignments in inland stockyards, waterfront holding pens, and occasionally on ranches that raised horses. "They carried the Germs in glass bottles about an inch and a half long and three-quarters of an inch in diameter and stoppered by a cork through which was stuck a long needle extending into the liquid culture. Felton and his band did the work by walking along the fences which enclosed the horses and mules, and jabbing the animals with the needles. The germs were also spread on the food they ate, and in the water they drank."[34] The spreading of anthrax and glanders went on continuously from October 1915 until the United States entered the war on 6 April 1917.

At the time when Hinsch's crews were spreading anthrax and glanders, Paul G. L. Hilken came to the attention of the Bureau of Investigation, the forerunner of the FBI. The first instance occurred on 17 November 1915 during a Bureau of Investigation interview with Frederick Henjez Jr., who had written the letter of introduction for von Rintelen to Hilken. The interview was part of a federal case being prepared against Franz von Rintelen.[35]

The second instance occurred a few days later, when the bureau's agent in charge, William B. Mathews, read a report from the Secret Service about its investigation of Dr. Karl Bünz and his Hamburg-America Lines employees. In his initial report concerning the Henjez interview, Special Agent Mathews described Hilken as "one of the most active pro-German agitators in Baltimore" and noted that "the Hilkens were prominently connected with the investigation that resulted in the arrests of Dr. Karl Bünz and his coconspirators.[36]

At the time, the recently established Bureau of Investigation was not authorized to handle espionage cases, which was the Secret Service's job. The Secret Service and the Bureau of Investigation did not work closely together, and there was very little information sharing.

Mathews did some background work on Hilken, but all he learned that seemed to be of interest was that J. Kronacher was the Baltimore agent for Hamburg-America and there had been friction between Kronacher and Paul Hilken. Mathews filed an informational report, but the bureau did not pursue an investigation of Paul Hilken until its interest was renewed in May 1916. At the time Mathews filed his report, the bureau was completely unaware that Hilken had been involved with von Rintelen, and it remained unaware as he became increasingly involved in sabotage over the next six months.

While the Bureau of Investigation was becoming interested in Paul Hilken, Friedrich Hinsch was off recruiting saboteurs. On 3 January 1916 he met a twenty-three-year-old Austrian-Czech, Michael Kristoff, in the Pennsylvania Railroad station at 33rd Street in New York City, where Kristoff was waiting for a train to Columbus, Ohio. Hinsch, who was using the name "Graentor," offered Kristoff a job for twenty dollars a week, which Kristoff accepted. Hinsch took the man to his hotel, the Hotel York, and got him a room for the night. The next day they set off by car.

During the next several weeks they visited Philadelphia, Bridgeport (Connecticut), Cleveland, Akron (Ohio), Columbus, Chicago, and Kansas City, Missouri, before returning to New York. Kristoff later said that they stayed two or three days in each city and that his job was to carry two large suitcases that Hinsch had with him, one of them filled with plans and blueprints of bridges and factories, the other with money. Hinsch made several stops in each city, leaving Kristoff in the car. During their travels Hinsch learned that Kristoff worked for Tidewater Oil Company and sometimes for a smaller company, Eagle Oil Company, which was adjacent to the Black Tom munitions depot. At the time it was just a trivial piece of information picked up during idle chit-chat, but a few months later it became useful.[37]

In January 1916 the Germans called Anton Dilger back to Berlin, and he departed on 29 January on board the SS *Kristianiafjord*. In his absence his brother Carl continued to grow new anthrax and glanders cultures for Hinsch's crew to spread. Anton had taught Carl how to grow the cultures that produced the diseases, and in time Carl became reasonably proficient. Deliveries were made to Hinsch using an A. Schumacher employee, Carl Ahrendt, as the courier. Ahrendt was Hinsch's "gofer" and sometimes a stand-in for Hilken, providing Hinsch with cash when Hilken was away. Ahrendt was aware of what the Hilken cell was doing, but other than delivering anthrax and glanders to Hinsch and doling out cash he did not have an active role.

In addition to Dilger's production lab in Chevy Chase, Maryland, the Baltimore cell was operating its own bomb factory in Hinsch's house. Von Rintelen's departure and arrest meant that Hinsch's crew no longer had a supply of incendiary devices from Doctor Scheele's lab, but Hinsch made up the loss by opening a factory in his house in Baltimore and having the bombs assembled under the direction of the *Neckar's* doctor, Bernard Sombolt.[38] The incendiaries produced in Hinsch's house were essentially the same as those made in Scheele's factory, but instead of being tubular they were egg shaped—and Hinsch called them "dumplings." They were terribly unreliable.

Although spreading anthrax was the cell's principal undertaking in 1915, Hinsch was also fomenting strikes among dockworkers and railroad men and starting fires. For the moment, it was business as usual in Baltimore, but in Bremen things were moving forward quickly. The general plan having been agreed and the boats ordered, the crew selection process was under way.

Sektion Politik and the Eastern Forwarding Company

The Baltimore Etappendienst cell was activated on 15 January 1916 by a telegram from Karl Stapelfeld, director general of Deutsche Ozean Reederei, asking Paul Hilken to come immediately to Bremen. Hilken left on 2 February on board the SS *Noordam,* traveling to Norway and then into Germany through Denmark, arriving at the NDL offices in Bremen on the morning of 14 February. In Bremen he learned that he and his father were being given responsibility for preparing a Baltimore station for the merchant submarine *U-Deutschland* and all subsequent merchant submarines. Stapelfeld directed Paul to acquire waterfront property in Baltimore and at another port of his choice for landing and loading cargo. He also directed him to form a new company, to be called the Eastern Forwarding Company, to handle the U-boat cargo business in the United States. Stapelfeld gave him authority to draw workers from the crews of NDL ships that were interned in Baltimore and to make use of whatever NDL assets were available. He also briefed Hilken in detail about the nickel that Dr. Heinrich Albert had already purchased and stored in a New York warehouse and directed him to buy several tons of crude rubber. The meeting concluded with Stapelfeld telling Hilken

▲ The *U-Deutschland* on her acceptance trials in May 1916. The black skirt that covered the exhaust ports is visible on the port quarter. The *U-Bremen* did not have that black exhaust skirt.
Author's collection

to go to the Deutschebank in Berlin to arrange credits for funding the Baltimore operation.[1]

Hilken arrived in Berlin on the evening of 14 February 1916 and completed his business with the Deutsche Bank the next day. On Wednesday, 16 February, he met with several government officials, including Franz von Papen, the former military attaché in Washington, whom the United States had declared persona non grata on 28 December 1915. This meeting had nothing to do with the cargo submarine project. Two days later, on 18 February, Hilken showed up at the German Army Intelligence headquarters at Molkestrasse 8, where *Hauptmann* (army captain) Rudolf Nadolny, chief of the sabotage section, Sektion Politik, introduced him to his second in command, *Hauptmann* Hans Marguerre and several others as "a German-American who can be useful to us."[2]

It is unlikely that Karl Stapelfeld knew anything about Hilken's connection to Sektion Politik or the meeting Hilken attended. Had he known or suspected such a connection, he would have been duty bound to report it to the Etappendienst director, *Fregattenkaptitän* (Commander) Walter Isendahl. The commercial submarine project was entirely separate from anything associated with army intelligence, and the navy was adamant that nothing be done to compromise it. In that respect, Hilken was on his own when he got involved with Sektion Politik.

German Army Intelligence, known as the Geheimdienst (Secret Service), was a section within the Army General Staff. It had two subsections—Abteilung IIIb, which was the espionage section, and Sektion Politik, which dealt in sabotage. It was during the meeting of the 18th that Hilken was given the responsibility of paying saboteurs that Sektion Politik would send to the United States in the future. He was not going to be responsible for paying every agent the Germans sent, only those that Sektion Politik directed him to pay. As things worked out he ultimately became responsible for funding sabotage operations in the United States and Japan and the spreading of anthrax and glanders on the East Coast and in Argentina. In Mexico, the primary target was the Tampico oil fields.[3]

Nadolny gave Hilken a large sum of money and made credits available to him through the Continental Bank, the Corn Exchange Bank, and the Guaranty Trust Company in New York. For immediate access, an account was also set up in the Baltimore Trust Company. When Hilken returned to Baltimore in late March he had about $30,000 immediately available, the rest to be available in the next two or three months. There was no requirement to account for how the money was spent, and other than checkbook stubs, there are few records of payments, most having been made in cash.[4]

The scope and volume of the sabotage operations he oversaw are hinted at by the known amounts he spent. Von Rintelen left him $10,000 when he left for Germany, all of which went to Hinsch before March 1916. From April 1916 until the United States entered the war, Hilken gave at least $50,000 to Hinsch and Fred Herrmann in Baltimore, $50,000 to an unidentified agent in Japan, and $100,000 to an agent named John A. Arnold in Buenos Aires. After 6 April and over the period until the end of the war, he sent at least $100,000 to Herrmann and Dilger in Mexico, not including $24,000 that went with Hinsch when he fled in May 1917. And those are only the recorded amounts. He kept a locked box in his house containing $20,000 in cash, which he regularly replenished, from which he regularly withdrew cash payments. To put these figures in perspective, the wartime median income in the United States was from $4,600 to $6,299 annually.

But there was more to the meeting with Sektion Politik than just talk about money. Two other American citizens were also present—Anton Dilger, whom Hilken already knew, and Fred Herrmann. Herrmann was a twenty-year-old from Brooklyn who had relatives in Germany. He was six feet tall and slender of build, with blond hair and blue eyes. In January 1915 he took passage on the SS *Ryndam* to visit his grandmother in Germany. On board the ship he met a German naval agent, Wilhelm Kottkamp, who recruited him into the German Naval Intelligence Service. From March to December 1915 Herrmann was a spy in England and Scotland. He performed his tasks well until December 1915, when the British became suspicious and deported him to the United States.[5]

He remained in the United States for just two weeks before boarding the SS *Kristianiafjord* to Bergen, Norway, in January 1916. By coincidence, Dilger had been called back to Germany, and he and Herrmann were on the same ship. They became friends without either confiding in the other about their shared espionage activities. After their ship reached Norway they separated, only to meet by chance in the office of the German commercial attaché in Copenhagen, *Kapitän zur See* (Captain) Wilhelm Bartling. The office doubled as the army intelligence office in Copenhagen.[6] There they revealed their true identities and set off together for Berlin. Dilger was in Berlin to get a new assignment, Herrmann to effect a transfer from naval intelligence to Sektion Politik. In a statement Hilken made before the Mixed Claims Commission about the 18 February meeting he said,

> Sabotage against munitions and supplies in the United States was fully discussed by us all. The incendiaries were handled and discussed by us at the time and our instructions were to get busy on this work immediately on our return to the United States. Fred Hinsch was discussed by us and his activities were known to Nadolny and Marguerre at that time. Herrmann was not under the authority of any one of us and I distinctly remember the high recommendation with which Herrmann had been sent to the General Staff of the army by the Admiralty Department. In addition to the general sabotage activities in the United States, Nadolny and Marguerre urged the destruction of the Power House at Niagara Falls and also the Tampico Oil Fields. The Tampico Oil Fields were quite a sore spot to Germany as Britain was obtaining large supplies from Mexico. It was urged upon me that an effort should also be made to set fire to these wells.[7]

The incendiaries Hilken mentioned were slender glass tubes that were "drawn to capillary dimensions in the center." The top part of the tubes contained sulphuric acid and the bottom half a mixture of sugar and chlorate of potash. The two halves of an ordinary pencil were separated by splitting the pencil lengthwise, the lead was removed, and the explosive glass tube was placed in the channel previously occupied by the lead. The two halves of the pencil were then glued together. The incendiary pencil was fired by breaking off the tip, which was hidden under the eraser, and placing the pencil writing end down. This forced the sulphuric acid down onto the mixture of sugar and chlorate of potash, creating a white-hot flame. The pencils had a fifteen-to-thirty-minute delay before igniting.[8]

Following the meeting, Hilken spent an additional two weeks in Berlin enjoying the sights and nightlife before returning to Baltimore by the same route he had taken to Germany. When he arrived home in late March his principal task was to set up the Eastern Forwarding Company, but first he had to put the sabotage operations in order. His first task was to go to each of the banks to which the Germans had sent credits in his name and set up accounts.

Paul Hilken found himself in the odd position of representing the two solutions to the two most pressing problems Germany faced—the blockade and Britain's transatlantic supply line. His position was unique in that, on one hand, he was engaged in breaking the blockade without endangering German-American relations and, on the other, he was engaged in activities that would utterly destroy those relations. He was probably the only person in such a position in World War I, though he probably failed to recognize that, since he lumped both activities under the heading of aid to Germany.

Fred Herrmann arrived in Baltimore in early April with a hollow-bottom suitcase filled with the improved incendiary devices. On Sunday, 9 April, he, Hilken, and Hinsch met in Hilken's office on the third floor of the Hansa Haus to discuss Herrmann's role in the operations. Herrmann showed them the new devices and turned them over to Hinsch. Herrmann explained that he was an independent operative but would work cooperatively with Hilken and Hinsch. Hilken suggested that a good place for Herrmann to start would be working with Carl Dilger in Chevy Chase making glanders toxins.

Since Anton Dilger had returned to Germany in January, Carl had been working alone in the lab. Hilken had grown uneasy about Carl, who was a heavy drinker and prone to make to outsiders statements that Hilken feared would jeopardize the Baltimore cell. He hoped that having Herrmann on-site in Chevy Chase would put a leash on Carl. Before the meeting ended all three agreed that they must be discreet in their activities so as not to "jeopardize the submarine work" but that there would be no letdown on sabotage. In fact, Hilken later told the Mixed Claims Commission, after Herrmann arrived "sabotage was carried on with greater intensity."[9]

Less than two weeks after Herrmann went to work in the Dilger lab in Chevy Case, on 13 April 1916, a joint federal and New York Police task force smashed von

Rintelen's New York City bomb ring. The bomb-assembly factory in the engine room of the *Friedrich der Grosse* was raided, and four German sailors were arrested, together with several other figures who were active ring members. It was virtually a clean sweep that effectively ended the bombing of ships sailing from New York Harbor. Dr. Walter T. Scheele, the operator and owner of the bomb lab in the New Jersey Agriculture and Chemical Company, escaped the dragnet, fleeing to Cuba, where he remained until 1918.

The headlines that appeared in the *New York Times* on 14 April 1916 probably alarmed Hinsch and Hilken, if only because the Baltimore cell was a part of the three-cell operation von Rintelen had set up in 1915, but it soon became evident that the authorities were not looking for them. And the arrests had no effect on Hilken's supply of incendiary devices, because in addition to what Hinsch had produced in his home shop, he had what Herrmann had brought with him. It was about this time that Hinsch and Herrmann made up a list of bomb targets and made trips to the more important ones. Two of those targets were the Black Tom munitions depot, in Jersey City, and the Kingsland munitions factory, in what is now Lynnhaven, in Bergen County, New Jersey.

First they looked at Black Tom, originally a small island in New York Harbor close to the New Jersey shore. During the last half of the nineteenth century the island was connected to the mainland by a causeway and rail lines terminating at a freight facility with docks. After the turn of the century, the Lehigh Valley Railroad filled in the area between the island and the mainland, making it a part of its Jersey City facility. By the start of World War I Black Tom was a major munitions depot; at any given time there were dozens of railroad cars loaded with explosives sitting on the spur tracks. Other than a half-dozen poorly paid night watchmen whose primary responsibility was to watch for fire, the place was wide open.

The second place they visited was Kingsland. Whereas Black Tom was not even properly fenced, Kingsland was another matter and required considerably more planning and preparation. Kingsland was actually an assembly plant, to which over a hundred different factories shipped munitions components, shells, fuses, shrapnel, and powder. It was an enormous factory, producing three million assembled shells per month, all of which went to Russia. The operator, which was the Canadian Car and Foundry Company, decided not to take any chances with security and constructed a six-foot fence completely around the plant. In addition to twenty-four-hour security patrols around the perimeter, there were guards at the gates to search and check the numbered identity badge of each of the 1,400 workers entering the plant. Matches were forbidden. When Herrmann and Hinsch finished their inspections, they cut the list into two parts. Hinsch got the list that included Black Tom, and Herrmann got Kingsland.

Another new player appeared on the scene in May. His real name was Curt Thummel; he was German-born and had come to the United States in 1907. In

1913, after working at odd jobs for several years, he had changed his name to
Charles E. Thorne and joined the U.S. Coast Guard. In late 1914 he met Hinsch
in the bar of the Emerson Hotel in Baltimore, where Hinsch told him he was
involved in working for Germany. The two men remained in contact, and when
Thorne's enlistment expired in May 1916 he went to work for Hinsch as a courier
between New York and Liverpool.[10]

With the sabotage business in hand, Hilken's next task was to rent or lease
property to use as the terminal for the submarine freight line. Initially, he and
Hinsch looked for sites in Norfolk and Newport News, but did not like the idea of
being so close to active navy facilities. Instead, he found what he was looking for
in Baltimore, during the last part of April. It was a city-block-size piece of property on Locust Point that featured a large two-story, brick warehouse and a three-
hundred-foot pier, and he rented it from the McLean Construction Company.[11]

The property was on the south side of the point, between the Western and
Maryland Railroad marshalling yards at Port Covington to the west and the
Baltimore and Ohio (B&O) freight yards to the east. The B&O main line ran
along the property's north boundary; between the railroad tracks and the brick
warehouse was a treeless, open field. At the east end of the field, and separated
from the McLean warehouse by about fifty yards, was a two-story brick building
that housed the American Agricultural Chemical Company. Andre Street formed
the east boundary of the property and ran north and south across Locust Point
from the edge of the Patapsco River to B&O Piers 8 and 9, a distance of five or
six blocks. NDL maintained an office on Pier 9, and the NDL passenger freighter
SS *Rhein* was interned at Pier 8. Hinsch's ship, the *Neckar,* was anchored a short
distance downriver, off Pennsylvania Elevator No. 3, at Canton. As a maritime
freight terminal, the Locust Point property was ideally located.

On 5 May, shortly after signing the rental agreement with the McLean
Construction Company, Hilken filed a Certificate of Incorporation for the Eastern
Forwarding Company (EFCO) with the Maryland State Tax Commission. The
document showed that the subscribers were Henry G. Hilken, Charles W. Field,
and Paul G. L. Hilken. Charles Field was a Baltimore attorney whose sole purpose
was to provide EFCO with legal advice and, if necessary, legal representation. The
total capital stock was $50,000, divided into five hundred shares at a par value of
one hundred dollars. The document listed the three directors as Henry Hilken,
Paul Hilken, and Charles W. Field. The document said nothing about what sort of
business the Eastern Forwarding Company was going to do, and Hilken released
no information to the press.

Though he was not mentioned in the document, Friedrich Hinsch would
be the general manager. There were two reasons for that choice. On one hand,
Hilken needed a reliable straw boss to run the company's day-to-day operation,
and Hinsch was both qualified and dependable. Hilken also wanted to provide a
solid cover for Hinsch's sabotage activities, and the Eastern Forwarding Company

was the ideal cover. As general manager, Hinsch would be able to travel freely to any port or harbor in the greater Baltimore area without attracting attention, and EFCO had a New York office, overlooking the Hudson River, run by Paul Hoppenberg. The arrangement made it possible for Hinsch to meet openly with dockworkers and anyone else whom he needed for his sabotage activities.

When Hilken rented the property, the previous renter, the Sagax Wood Fiber Company, was still on the property but in the process of moving out. There were also three subtenants: the Marden Orth Hastings Company, dealers in linseed oil; the Maryland Aeroplane Company, owned by Otto Janis, an early Baltimore aviator; and the Coastwise Shipping Company, a freight forwarding company. Given Hilken's concern about security and his insistence on secrecy, it is odd that he let those companies remain on the premises as long as he did.

Hilken's work to prepare the property for the *U-Deutschland*'s arrival was briefly interrupted in early May by a personnel problem. Anton's brother, Carl Dilger, had become a security risk, and Hinsch wanted to get rid of him. Hinsch's main complaint was that Carl was a heavy drinker who was always demanding money and he was concerned that in an inebriated state would say something that would compromise all of them. Hilken, who had never been comfortable with Carl, agreed. Carl in any case was no longer vital to the operation, because Herrmann had been shown how to produce the anthrax and glanders, which ensured that the supply would be uninterrupted even with Carl gone.

Hilken and Hinsch told Carl that they needed to send him to Germany with an important package for Nadolny and Marguerre. Carl, anticipating a reunion with his brother in Karlsruhe, eagerly accepted the assignment. The package that Hilken gave him contained a letter telling Nadolny and Marguerre that Carl was a security risk and asking them to detain him in Germany indefinitely. The plan misfired, unbeknownst to Hilken and Hinsch, when Carl panicked on learning that British naval officers would inspect the ship and question the passengers in Kirkwall. Worried that the package he was to deliver contained "reports of fires and other things that Hinsch and his men had been doing," Carl threw it overboard.[12]

Believing that he had seen the last of Carl Dilger, Hilken returned to the job of preparing the EFCO property at the McLean Pier. Using crewmen from the interned *Rhein,* Hilken immediately started to increase security. The first step was to erect two heavy wire fences eight feet high around the property and the warehouse. The outer fence followed the property line; the inner fence was in close proximity to the warehouse. The fences were followed by the installation of powerful arc lights along the warehouse roofline that flooded the area around the building with intense illumination at night and the mounting of two searchlights on the roof facing the river, that constantly swept the river and the grain elevators on the opposite shore throughout the night.

Similar steps were taken to secure the interior of the warehouse. Walls were erected between the areas the three subtenants occupied, separating each from the others and sealing off all from the main floor of the warehouse. Each subtenant was provided a separate entrance in the front wall of the building. Guards, again crewmen from the *Rhein* and the *Neckar,* were stationed inside and outside the building around the clock. Their job was to keep everyone, even government agents and police, out of the building. They were so enthusiastic about their job that they prevented the resident McLean Company night watchman from making his rounds and turned away a Baltimore police officer at the main gate.

As the days passed, more security measures were put in place. Barbed wire was added to the enclosure, and a seven-foot-high board fence was put up on the east side of the pier, with burlap bags at the top to block any view of the dock where the *U-Deutschland* would tie up. Floating obstacles, including a high fence on floats that could be drawn across the river side of the berth, were begun.

Early in the process of getting the property ready to receive the *U-Deutschland,* Hilken sent Hinsch to New York to buy a tugboat. The vessel he bought, the *Thomas F. Timmins,* actually belonged to the NDL New York office, so the sale was really an intracompany transfer. Previously named *George H. Allen,* the *Thomas F. Timmins* was a wooden, single-screw steam tug built in 1904. Hinsch and his crew took her to the Arundel Sand and Gravel Company plant at Fairfield, New Jersey, for overhaul. In addition to a new color scheme, including a black stack adorned with the white letters "E.F.C.O.," she was equipped with a powerful searchlight atop the wheelhouse and a spark-gap radio transmitter and receiver. The latter was an unusual piece of equipment for a tug the size of the *Thomas F. Timmins,* and coupled with Hilken's public statement that the craft was for "general towing," it caused a storm of rumors about what the tug would really be used for.[13]

The ongoing construction at the McLean pier attracted the attention of Capt. John Danton, the B&O police supervisor in Baltimore. Danton was worried that whatever was going on at the newly acquired EFCO property might not be in the best interests of the B&O. He knew that Hilken was involved with EFCO, and he knew that several months earlier Hilken had been caught instigating strikes among B&O employees. Company officials had declined to call the police and had handled the matter themselves, confronting Hilken directly in his Hansa Haus office. Caught flat-footed, Hilken had shrugged off the charge, mumbling something about it not being a secret and everyone being aware of his efforts. Nevertheless, he had ceased all direct efforts to foment strikes and in May 1915 had given the job to Hinsch.

A string of strikes started on 24 April 1916 with a series of wildcat actions that seriously hindered the movement of freight at the B&O Locust Point Terminal. In the first strike, all the B&O employees who worked on the grain elevators walked out. In Captain Danton's words, "The strikes could not have been arranged in a more effective manner. . . . No sooner was this strike practically overcome by the B&O police than the car repairers and car builders struck, which seriously hampered the B&O in moving freight for export. When B&O hired men to take the strikers' place, all the B&O employees who handle freight for export struck."

Increasingly concerned that EFCO was a growing threat to the B&O, on 9 May 1916 Captain Danton sent a lengthy report describing his concerns to his supervisor, Edmund Leigh, general superintendent of police for the B&O. Leigh, in turn, sent the report to the chief of the Bureau of Investigation, A. Bruce Bielaski, who passed it down to the agent in charge in Baltimore, Billups Harris. In his covering memorandum Chief Bielaski directed Harris to meet with Captain Danton.

Harris arrived at Danton's office on 13 May, the same day that a fifth strike was called, involving seven hundred freight handlers. Danton told Harris that he did not know what sort of business EFCO was going to be doing but that he "strongly suspected that it had to do with crippling shipments of munitions to the Allies, and general German propaganda." His suspicions were based on his prior knowledge of Hilken's activities and the fact that Hinsch was frequently seen going from the EFCO warehouse to the interned SS *Rhein* at Pier 8, where he spent time with the skipper, Captain Myers.

Like Danton, Harris was suspicious of EFCO's intentions, but instead of focusing on the threat to the B&O he assumed that EFCO was going to be used as a supply base for German warships operating in the western Atlantic, off the South American coast, and in the Caribbean. He saw the problem as a neutrality violation, a crime with which his office was much concerned. His assumption was based on what he knew about Hilken's openly expressed pro-German attitude, his unspecified connection to the Karl Bünz and von Rintelen cases, and the fact that the German consul in Baltimore, Carl A. Luderitz, whose office was in the Hansa House together with A. Schumacher and Norddeutsche Lloyd, had been indicted on 6 April for supplying a fake passport to a German agent. The German agent had been Franz Wachendorf, who called himself "Horst von Goltz."

Agent Harris' focus on EFCO and the possibility of neutrality violations rather than possible sabotage against B&O property was the result of law, or rather the absence of law. Prior to 15 June 1917, espionage, in whatever form, was not a federal crime. Acts of sabotage certainly violated state laws, but no federal statutes prohibited it or exacted penalties. Acts of sabotage, particularly bombings, were handled by the local police. Even though acts of sabotage occurred in and around Baltimore during the EFCO investigation, they were not within the bureau's jurisdiction. As a result, the intense scrutiny under which the Bureau of Investigation placed EFCO was not only misdirected but entirely unnecessary, because EFCO was as clean as a whistle and existed solely as a freight terminal for the Deutsche Ozean Reederei. Hilken and Hinsch, in contrast, were up to their eyes in criminal activity.

During the evening of 12 June, George Turner, who was working for Eddie Felton, set two incendiary devices in the grain elevators in the B&O's Canton yard, burning both to the ground. Two days later Fenton paid Turner twenty dollars for the job. The Bureau of Investigation office in Baltimore did not investigate the fire, which was attributed to spontaneous combustion. But in his 13 June daily report Harris wrote, "It seems probable the fire was of incendiary origin."

On 14 June, Hilken's father wrote his son a letter: "Unfortunately I must bring you bad news, the Canton elevator burned up here. Two steamers were also lost. The Englishman had munitions aboard and I'm not sorry for him. But the elevator will do much damage to Baltimore and it is to be regretted because several lives were lost."[14] One wonders why Henry Hilken wrote to his son to tell him about the fire. Paul Hilken was in Baltimore and for many reasons would have known about it. And he saw his father almost daily at the A. Schumacher office in the Hansa Haus. The best explanation might be that the letter was a cover in the event that the authorities became suspicious of Paul.

One of the odd facts about the situation in Baltimore was that though the sabotage cell and the cargo submarine operation were separate entities, everyone involved with EFCO and nearly everyone in the Baltimore NDL office knew about the sabotage. Some, such as the NDL clerk Carl Ahrendt, were at least peripherally involved in some aspects of the cell's operations.

Throughout the time that the Bureau of Investigation was focused on discovering neutrality violations, EFCO was preparing for the *U-Deutschland's* arrival. On 31 May the company started dredging along the east side of the pier to make a berth deep enough for the *Neckar,* which was going to act as the accommodation ship for the submarine's crew. But the most obvious sign that something big was going to happen was the delivery of trainloads of nickel, tin, and rubber to the EFCO warehouse from 1 to 27 June.

Among the purchases that Dr. Heinrich Albert had made on Krupp's behalf in November 1914 were 740 tons of nickel, 480 tons of raw rubber, and an unspecified amount of chromium and vanadium, used to make hardened steel. The purchases had been made through the International Nickel Company at Communipaw, New Jersey, using American agents as the buyers.

The nickel purchases were the trickiest part of the purchases, because in 1914 the world's nickel supply came from Canada, which had an agreement with the big American nickel houses not to sell nickel to the Central Powers or their agents. Albert convinced the International Nickel Company in New Jersey that the consignees were all U.S. citizens who had placed orders before the war started and so were exempt from the agreement. Both parties agreed that regardless of the consignees' pedigrees, the British would kill the deal, so the sale was carried out in secret.

Albert broke the nickel purchase into lots, which he consigned to cooperating German-Americans who lived in the New York–Baltimore area and who in turn sent the shipments to the Nassau Smelting and Refining Company's storehouses at the foot of 25th Street in New York City. During the next several months, the nickel was moved in batches to the New York Dock Company in Brooklyn and stored in Warehouse 104.

Beginning on 1 June 1916, Hilken moved the nickel in quick shipments to various places and to different consignees in order to conceal the true source of the nickel. As of 27 June the Eastern Forwarding Company had received fourteen cars of nickel in barrels, four carloads of tin in pigs, and six cars filled with crude rubber. The total weight of the nickel was 529.2 tons. In every case but one the deliveries were made by a circuitous route that took the cars to dummy stops before going to Baltimore. The one exception was a carload of nickel, B&O car V-62186, that came directly from New York to Baltimore.

To handle these deliveries, B&O laid a spur track directly to the EFCO ware-house. Nickel that arrived in Baltimore to go on board the *U-Deutschland* was dumped out of the barrels and was shoveled by African-American workers into hundred-pound bags, which were easier to handle than barrels and allowed more nickel to be carried in the U-boat's cramped holds. The *U-Deutschland* took on nine carloads of nickel, averaging forty tons per car.

The mystery about the nickel's origin caused the Bureau of Investigation to launch an investigation that required the resources of its offices throughout the United States. Its agents finally traced the shipments back to the New York Dock Railway Baltic Terminal, but the fact that the metal was in the charge of the B&O foreign freight agent indicated the nickel had been imported.

The Bureau of Investigation focused on all the people whose names were connected with the shipments. One by one the men named were determined to be innocent of any wrongdoing. But the name Charles W. Field, with an office in the First National Bank Building in Philadelphia, remained a mystery and would be the cause of a blind-alley investigation that gave Baltimore's Bureau of Investigation office a red face. Warning flags went up when the bureau office in Philadelphia reported that after a thorough investigation it had determined that there was no Charles W. Field in the building and never had been. Several days and many man-hours were wasted searching for the mysterious Mr. Field, only to dis-cover that he was named on the EFCO Certificate of Incorporation as subscriber and officer of the company. His office was in Baltimore, about three blocks from the local Bureau of Investigation office.

Rumors about what EFCO was going to do with all that metal were rife in the days following the first delivery. The earliest rumor started on 5 June, when a B&O informant inside the EFCO warehouse told Captain Danton about a sub-marine that was to arrive at the EFCO pier. The informant added that the tug *Timmins* was going to "handle" the boat. Though the information lacked specific details, it and that which the man later provided were surprisingly accurate. On 10 June the *Baltimore News* ran an article about EFCO mentioning a rumor that a submarine would arrive at the EFCO pier. Again there were no particulars. The rumor came up again in a slightly different form when Pascual Bellizia, the owner of a small Mexican-flagged freighter, SS *Fontera,* told Agent Chalmers about a sub-marine that would take on cargo from EFCO offshore.

On 30 June the *New York Times,* following up on a story about "the reported arrival of a super submarine," reported that the *Timmins* was "cruising off the

Virginia Capes, waiting to convoy a submersible into Baltimore." On 1 July, Harris sent a report to his chief saying that the New York papers were reporting the submarine was "hiding somewhere in the Chesapeake Bay." On 5 July, the B&O informant told Danton that the submarine had "left her base twenty-one days ago and was overdue." That particular piece of information was 100 percent accurate—the *U-Deutschland* had left Helgoland on 14 June. Danton was also told that the boat was bringing several tons of dyestuffs, which was correct. Obviously, despite all Hilken's attempts to keep the boat's arrival a secret, people inside the warehouse were talking.

By 1 July the Baltimore newspapers were running daily stories about the imminent arrival of the supersubmarine, most of which simply repeated the latest rumors. On 6 July there was a report that an outbound steamer, SS *Stanley,* had sighted a German submarine near the Azores headed toward the U.S. coast. By that time the *U-Deutschland* was already in the Gulf Stream and nearing the United States. The only substantial information the press had was that the *Thomas F. Timmins* had been going out to sea daily since 26 June. The *Timmins* was making daily trips out past the Capes watching for the *U-Deutschland,* though the official story that she was there waiting for a tow. The only noteworthy event of the first week in July never made it into the papers. On 7 July, Billups Harris wrote in his report that it appeared that EFCO was ready to receive the submarine. He concluded, "It appears the company is all it claims to be."[15]

The Crew and the Boat

15 SEPTEMBER 1915–13 JUNE 1916

The man who strode through the main entrance of the Adlon Hotel and across the expansive lobby to the front desk did not attract any attention from the expensively dressed guests scattered throughout the opulent *Saal*. *Kapitän zur See* Paul Lebrecht König was a fifty-two-year-old sea captain who would be invisible in a crowd. He was five-eight, 155 pounds, often described as "elfin," and wholly unassuming. His purpose for being in Europe's premier hotel on 15 September 1915 was to discuss with Alfred Lohmann his assignment to the command of the *U-Deutschland*.

At the time König was selected for the position he was serving as a watch officer on the old battleship SMS *Brandenburg* and had seen action against the Russians

▲ Hansa Haus in Baltimore on the corner of Charles and German Streets. The building housed the A. Schumacher Company; the Eastern Forwarding Company, another dummy company associated with the cargo submarine project; the German consulate; and the offices of the Norddeutsche Lloyd. The operations of the Baltimore sabotage cell were directed from Hilken's third-floor office. *Author's collection*

◄ The *U-Deutschland* under final construction at Germaniawerft, showing her tank deck and the struts that support the casing deck. Photo taken in December 1915. *Author's collection*

for which he had received the Iron Cross 2nd Class. His service in the Imperial Navy and his participation in combat operations against the Russians counted heavily in the decision to give him command of the *U-Deutschland*. But the more important reasons for his selection to command the boat, besides his long service with NDL, were that he had made several trips to the American East Coast and that he spoke excellent English. Following the interview, König was assigned to the 2nd *Matrosen*-Division in Wilhelmshaven, a training establishment for new sailors and the clearinghouse for specialty schools. There he selected his officers.[1]

His first watch officer was Franz Krapohl, who was thirty-seven years old, came from NDL, and like all German merchant marine officers held a reserve commission in the Imperial German Navy. He too had seen combat against the Russians and had been awarded the Iron Cross 2nd Class. He was considered to be a reliable, steady officer who showed good judgment.[2]

The second watch officer was Paul Eyring, a twenty-nine-year-old reservist who had been on board the SMS *Karlsruhe* during her commerce-raiding cruise in the West Indies off Brazil in 1914. On 4 November 1914, without warning, she suddenly exploded and went to the bottom like a rock. Eyring was among the few survivors. Plucked from the sea, he was on board the SS *Rio Negro* when she slipped through the British blockade and returned to Germany in December 1914. He had remained on board the ship as a watch officer and was with her when she again broke the blockade, carrying supplies to German troops in Africa. From September 1915 to January 1916, he had commanded a minesweeper out of Ems. Eyring was also rated as a "reliable" officer.[3]

The fourth officer selected was *Leitende Ingenieur* (Chief Engineer) Helmut Klees, who, next to König, was the most critical member of the crew. *Leitende Ingenieur* was a position, not a rank. It was held either by a *Marine Ingenieur* (which was a commissioned rank) or by the senior engineering-rating petty officer on the boat, which is what Klees was. On the U-boats the position was usually filled by a *Marine Ingenieur* or a *Marine Oberingenieur,* both of which were commissioned ranks that corresponded to the German officer ranks of *Leutnant zur See* and *Oberleutnant zur See* (ensign and lieutenant).

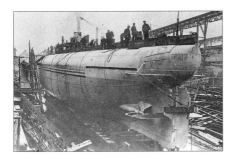

▲ On the ways and ready to be launched, 28 March 1916. The rudder is locked in place to protect it during the launch. *Author's collection*

➤ The *U-Deutschland* ready to slide stern first into the water, 28 March 1916. Her forward diving planes were permanently rigged out. Among the yard workers the boat was known as *"die dicke Frau,"* the fat lady. *Author's collection*

In the smaller UB– and UC–boats the *Leitende Ingenieur* was often an enlisted man, usually an *Obermaschinist,* a chief petty officer like Klees, or occasionally a rated senior machinist. Whether the man filling the position was a commissioned officer or a chief petty officer, his name sometimes came immediately after the commanding officer's name on crew rosters, especially on casualty lists, which is why the position is often misrepresented as the second in command. In the case of the *U-Deutschland's* muster roll, Klees is listed as the fourth-senior man in the crew, behind the purser, Wilhelm Kassel. It was done that way to conform to the practice used on commercial vessels.

The *Leitende Ingenieur,* regardless of his rank, was not a watch officer. In addition to being fully in charge of the engine room he was the boat's diving officer, exclusively in charge of the boat during dives, while running submerged, and surfacing. The captain told him how deep to go and directed the boat's movements, but the *Leitende Ingenieur* directed how those orders were fulfilled.

On 18 October 1915, five weeks after König had his interview with Alfred Lohmann, another long-service NDL captain, Karl Schwartzkopf, was called in. Schwartzkopf was serving as a watch officer on board the SMS *Braunschweig* when his name came up, and like König he had seen action against the Russians for which he too had received the Iron Cross 2nd Class. Schwartzkopf, who was also familiar with the American East Coast and spoke excellent English, was given command of the *U-Bremen.*[4]

The *U-Bremen's* first watch officer was *Leutnant zur See* Hermann Liebermann von Sonnenberg, an aristocrat whose father had served in the German army during the Franco-Prussian War and had served in the Reichstag before World War I.

Leutnant zur See Liebermann von Sonnenberg was thirty-two years old and a former NDL watch officer who before the war had been on board the SS *Grosser Kurfürst* with Schwartzkopf. At the time he was selected for the merchant submarine project he was serving on board the torpedo boat *S-137,* based in Helgoland.[5]

Schwartzkopf's second watch officer, *Leutnant zur See* Gerhard Posse, came directly from NDL, where he had been a junior officer on board a freighter in the service of the German navy, as were many NDL ships during World War I. Of the six officers selected for the merchant submarine project, Posse is the biggest mystery. His military service file, held in the Deutschedienststelle in Berlin, is empty except for a card that provides his name, rank, and the date on which he was declared dead, 1 October 1916.[6]

The man who was selected to be the *U-Bremen's Leitende Ingenieur* was *Obermaschinist* Walter Dähn, a chief petty officer. Other than that he was a long-service veteran of the Imperial German Navy, we know nothing about him.[7]

In January 1916, the six commissioned officers selected for the *U-Deutschland* and *U-Bremen* entered an abbreviated, twelve-week U-boat commanders' school in Kiel. One of their instructors was *Kapitänleutnant* Hans Rose, who plays a cameo role in this history of the commercial submarine project. While the six officers were learning how to command and operate a U-boat, the 2nd *Matrosen*-Division was selecting the enlisted men to man the *U-Deutschland,* which was another example of the navy's involvement in, and control over, the project.

The men selected were not the bottom of the barrel but were among the best the German navy had to offer. In November 1916 several American naval officers who had the opportunity to observe Klees and three of his engine-room crew working on an engine described them as "well educated," adding that they "corresponded to the attainments of a lieutenant, a lieutenant (jg) and two ensigns in our service." The four men, in the order the Americans rated them, were Klees and three *Obermaschinisten* (petty officers) Otto Wegener, Karl Früchte, and Johann Kissling.[8]

The *U-Deutschland's* twenty-five enlisted crewmen arrived in Kiel alone and in groups of three to seven men between 11 and 25 April 1916. The last to arrive were the steward, Adolf Stucke (who at fifty-six was the oldest man in the crew), and Wilhelm Karl Gotthold Prusse, the only true civilian on the boat and the twenty-eighth man on the *U-Deutschland's* crew roster. Prusse was listed as "supercargo," which was really an abbreviation for cargo superintendent, or in German, *Lademeister.*

➤ Afloat on 28 March 1916. From here she was towed to a long pier to be completed and fitted out. *Author's collection*

He was forty-five and a highly trained, experienced Krupp engineer whose presence on board the boat was never fully explained to the American public.[9] In press stories about the *U-Deutschland* in Baltimore he was described as the loadmaster, the man who had supervised the building of the *U-Deutschland,* and a technician who possessed unnamed but extraordinary knowledge. However, his enigmatic presence on board the boat and occasional disappearances from Baltimore caused speculation that he was something more than just a civilian engineer.

The average age of the enlisted *U-Deutschland* crewmen who had been drawn from active U-boats was 25.2 years. The youngest was Engine Mechanic Karl Steen, age nineteen, and the oldest was Machinist's Mate Erhard Hultsch, forty-six. With the exception of six stokers who were relatively new to the U-boat service, the enlisted crewmen were all experienced U-boat veterans. In fact, the only exception was the steward, Adolf Stucke who had been a steward on board the NDL liner SS *Kronprinzessin Cecilia.* At the time König handpicked Stucke, the steward had been recently released from a French internment camp.[10]

When the *U-Bremen* vanished at sea, the personnel records listing the men's ages and the dates they reported on board were lost with her. We do know that the entire crew was officially mustered on board the *U-Bremen* on 11 August 1916, and it is reasonable to assume that its makeup was, with regard to experience and age, very similar to that of the *U-Deutschland*'s.

The boats that the crews boarded were not the giants they were made out to be, but they were the largest U-boats the Germans had built up to that time. The *U-Deutschland*-class boats were 213.2 feet long (65 meters), their outer beam was 29.2 feet (8.9 meters), the pressure-hull beam was nineteen feet (5.8 meters), and the distance from the keel to the rim of the conning tower fairwater was thirty feet. They displaced 1,575 tons on the surface and 1,860 tons submerged, and their maximum rated depth was 164 feet (50 meters). Their gross registered tonnage was 791 tons, and the net tonnage was 141 tons.

Rudolf Erbach and Hans Techel had produced a design for a completely unarmed cargo submarine that drew on existing technology, parts, and labor skills, which meant that the boat could be built in the minimum time at the lowest possible cost. There were no innovations involved. Erbach and Techel's design also borrowed heavily on drawings of U-boats then in production, sections and parts of which were adapted to the *U-Deutschland*-class boats. An example of this were the forward and after diving planes, which were adapted from the *U-46* class.[11]

Similarly, the ballast-tank vent valves were designs already in production. During the spring of 1915, the Germans developed a "rapid vent valve" that reduced diving time (the time it took for the boat to reach periscope depth) to one minute for boats the size of the *U-19,* compared to three to five minutes previously. But even with the improved valves, the *U-Deutschland*'s dive time was one and a half to two minutes under optimum conditions. In heavy seas it could take up to five minutes to get the boat under.

Simon Lake was probably right when he said that the *U-Deutschland* embodied many of his design characteristics. Like Lake-designed boats, the *U-Deutschland* submerged "practically on an even keel, seldom more than a couple degrees inclination," and when she was submerged she ran down by the head one-half to one degree with the forward diving plane set in the neutral position. She was particularly difficult to get under in heavy seas. Commander Yates Sterling talked to Captain König about the problem.

> In speaking of submerging in heavy weather the Captain said that he placed the vessel in the trough of the sea, then flooded tanks and gave her twelve to fourteen tons of negative buoyancy to get her deck under, maintaining even trim. As soon the deck was under, he went ahead at slow speed, about two knots, on motors and began to pump out superfluous water.[12]

Commander Sterling added, "This looks like a dangerous method, but he claims it is the only way to submerge in Heavy weather." The boat was "under" when she reached periscope depth, which in the *U-Deutschland*-class boats was forty to forty-five feet, measured at the keel. At those depths the conning tower's rim was ten to fifteen feet below the surface.

The periscopes were production models, with one small change. The range-finding reticule was removed in both periscopes, leaving the optic with a single vertical line. The deletion was a brilliant example of forward thinking, because the presence of a periscope capable of determining a target's range would have raised serious questions about the claim that the boat had no military application. Otherwise the periscopes were standard Zeiss, two-power, housing, walk-around types.

The primary periscope was in the conning tower, and the secondary periscope was located in the control room, offset four feet to starboard of the keel line. The secondary periscope was difficult to operate, because it was raised and lowered by hand, with a crank and wire-reel system, and it was rarely used. The optics in both periscopes were described as "excellent and wonderfully clear."

As in all German U-boats, there were three steering stations: the outside steering station, on a platform that formed the forward portion of the conning tower outside the fairwater. The central control-room steering station; and an emergency steering station in the tiller room, which was all the way aft in the stern. The outside steering station was used whenever the boat was in a harbor or narrow waterway, and the central control-room steering station was the primary steering station and was used whenever the boat was under way but not in a harbor. The after steering station was used only if the other two stations were out of commission.

Each steering station was provided with a gyro repeater, the master three-axis gyro being in the central control room. The emergency steering station was equipped with a magnetic compass, "mounted in a special receptacle above the hull," apparently meaning outside the pressure hull. "By means of a light and mirror this reflected down onto a ground glass in front of the helmsman in the after steering station." The image was only a small section of the compass card, but it was "highly magnified" and "very clear."

Interior voice communications, including from the bridge to the control room, were done with voice tubes. Diving commands were given visually and audibly. On the starboard side of the central control room's after bulkhead was a light panel with red and blue lights representing each ballast and trim tank. The red light meant that the tank was to be flooded, and the blue light meant "close the valve." Several green lights on the panel represented hatches and through-hull openings in the boat's five watertight compartments. As each hatch and opening was closed a green light came on and remained on. A light that was off indicated a hatch or through-hull opening in that compartment that was not closed. The dive alarm was a gong-type bell that could be activated from the bridge or the control room. When the dive alarm sounded, all the hatches and through-hull openings were immediately closed, and the corresponding green lights on the panel in the control room came on. When all the panel lights were lit a klaxon sounded to initiate flooding, and the various red indicator lights came on.

The diesel engines used in the *U-Deutschland* and all her sisters were not designed to be main propulsion engines instead they were diesel generators, of the type used on board large ships for auxiliary electrical power. Those smaller, less powerful engines were installed instead of much the bigger Mann Diesels because those diesel generators were readily available and could be delivered immediately. They also took up less space than the regular U-boat diesels, making more room for cargo.

On 2 November 1916 in New London, the naval inspectors noted that with one engine running there "was no engine or hull vibration, and little if any noise." They also noted that the temperature in the engine room was eighty degrees Fahrenheit. The *U-Deutschland*'s engines were air-started and nonreversible, meaning that the boat could go astern only on its electric motors. This arrangement was found in many submarines built in countries other than Germany but was used here only to save costs and speed construction.

◄ The control room, looking aft. The helm is the wheel in the front center of the photo, and the forward and after diving-plane wheels are on the left. *Author's collection*

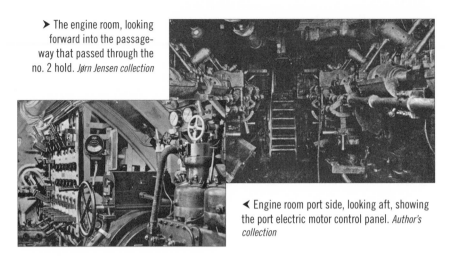

> ➤ The engine room, looking forward into the passageway that passed through the no. 2 hold. *Jørn Jensen collection*

◀ Engine room port side, looking aft, showing the port electric motor control panel. *Author's collection*

The electric motors in the boats were, like the diesel engines, of a type not designed as propulsion motors for U-boats. They were commercially produced dual-armature motors used in merchant ships for a variety of shipboard uses. Since they were already in production and were used throughout the merchant fleet, the motors were readily available and relatively inexpensive, but they were underpowered.

König told the American naval officers who inspected his boat that the *U-Deutschland* could "run submerged for ninety-six hours at 1.5 knots," which led one of them to comment, "The radius of action submerged was not great in miles, but very large in time." Before accepting that figure one must keep in mind that König was prone to exaggerate the *U-Deutschland*'s capabilities for the propaganda effect. A more realistic figure is sixty-five nautical miles at three knots, which would give a duration of a little over twenty-one hours.

Another cost-cutting feature was a conning tower much smaller than normal, with only one periscope. The *U-Deutschland*-class boats had a miniscule, five-foot-diameter conning tower crammed full of controls, a rack of speaking tubes, a compass repeater, and the periscope. The conning tower was also equipped with "all apparatus or signals" needed to enable trimming down from the conning tower. When the boat was trimmed down, the chief engineer was in the conning tower and the captain was on the bridge.

The *U-Deutschland* was equipped with a 1.5-watt, spark-gap radio that had a useful range of about a hundred nautical miles under favorable conditions. The radio could send and receive messages over the high antenna or the jumper antenna, depending on which antenna the radio was connected to. The high antenna provide the greatest range, while the jumper antenna was limited to about fifteen nautical miles at the absolute maximum range. The jumper antenna ran from the bow, over the conning tower, across a short mast and yardarm arrangement, and down to the stern. The high antenna was strung between the two tall radio masts.

The boat's two radio masts were of a standard design and material. They were hollow, made of iron, and started tapering three feet up from the base. They were forty-feet tall and equipped with counterweighted, electrically powered quadrants at the base so that they could be quickly and effortlessly raised and lowered from inside the boat. When lowered, the masts were housed in recesses cut into the casing.

The crew quarters, which were located aft of the forward hold, were paneled with wood; the beds had steel pipe frames, wire springs, and cork-filled mattresses. Every man had a locker for his clothing. The crew's head was in the bow on the starboard side. The officers' quarters were on the starboard side forward of the control room. The captain's cabin was on the port side squeezed between the control room and the officers' head. The officers' quarters were identical to the crew quarters except that the beds were made entirely of wood and had better springs and mattresses. Regardless of his rank, the *Leitende Ingenieur* was considered an officer and shared the officers' quarters. No bath or shower was provided for anyone.

Provisions consisted of canned soups, vegetables, and meat. "Marmalade, jellies, and conserves were plentiful, and crackers, bread, cheese, and butter, together with tea, coffee, and sugar were stocked in the galley." Absent was anything that required refrigeration, which meant no fresh meat, milk, or juices; there was no fresh fruit, and there were no eggs. Meals were taken in shifts in the galley, located on the starboard side, aft of the officers' quarters. Metal trays and mugs were used to eat from, but the ship's china was used on occasion.

"Wet cargo," meaning cargo that could withstand immersion, was carried outboard between the pressure hull and the casing. A perforated deck was built over the ballast tanks with a six-inch clearance. The perforated deck allowed water to quickly drain from the cargos spaces down onto the tank deck and out through long openings in the casing. Cargo that could not stand immersion was stored in four interior holds, two forward and two aft. The forward holds, near the bow, were slightly smaller than the after holds. The two after holds were just aft of amidships, between the control room and the engine room. The port and starboard holds were separated by a narrow passageway.

The boat's paint scheme on both trips was dark green on the upper casing and light green on the hull. The periscopes were painted dark sea green with splashes of white, "much as an artist's attempt to create waves."

Despite the use of proven technology, the *U-Deutschland* was not a problem-free design. One of the drawbacks was the boat's displacement, which was much greater than that of existing U-boats of about the same length. This made the *U-Deutschland*-class boats slower to dive, as noted, and more difficult to control when submerged. But Krupp's engineering estimates and experience indicated that the relatively long diving time and poor submerged characteristics would be "acceptable for the intended purpose."[13]

Her acceptance trials ended on 5 May, the same day that Hilken filed the Certificate of Incorporation for the Eastern Forwarding Company in Baltimore.

▲ This is an example of the merchant marine identification booklet that each *U-Deutschland* crewman received to establish that he was not a member of the German navy (Kaiserliche-Marine). The ID was a stiff-back, pocket-size booklet. The photo on the left is the front cover, and the two photos on the right are the first two pages inside the booklet. The three photos appear to be separate pieces of paper because they were photographed individually and cropped. This identification was issued to Ludwig Schwarzschild, who had just graduated from the navy's *U-Bootschule* in Kiel as a mechanic, the lowest engine-room rating, before being assigned to the *U-Deutschland* on 14 April 1916. His pay was set at 100 marks a month, considerably more than he had received before he was "civilianized." The document shows that Schwarzschild remained on board the *U-Deutschland* as a crewman until 8 February 1917, for a total of nine months and twenty-five days. The date of his last day as a *U-Deutschland* crew member was the date on which the *U-Deutschland* was commissioned as the *U-155*. Schwarzschild remained on board the *U-155* until the end of the war. *Courtesy of Howard Hirsch*

That same day the Deutsche Ozean Reederei accepted the *U-Deutschland* as the first of a small fleet of commercial U-boats, and the next four weeks were spent training intensively for the transatlantic trip. The business of taking on fuel, stores, and cargo began on 7 June; when it was complete the crew conducted several full-load diving and trim tests under Prusse's supervision. The *U-Deutschland* was carrying 348 tons of dyestuffs, valued at over one million dollars. She was also laden with 598 tons of cast-iron ballast, 354 tons carried in her internal holds and eighty-one tons between the casing and the pressure hull.

On the evening of 12 June, Captain König gave his crew a pep talk that focused on the vital importance of the *U-Deutschland*'s getting through to Baltimore and back to Germany with the raw materials the *Vaterland* so desperately needed. On 13 June, the U.S. consul in Bremen, William Thomas Fee, issued the *U-Deutschland* a bill of health and certified invoices. But at the request of DOR officials, he did not report the *U-Deutschland*'s departure to the U.S. embassy in Berlin, a direct violation of State Department regulations. He withheld the information because he agreed with the DOR officials that any public announcement of the boat's movements would pose a threat to the boat's safety.[14] The paperwork was completed, and the boat was fully fueled, loaded, and ready for sea. The crew was experienced and thoroughly versed in handling the tubby U-boat.

5

The First Crossing

T he *U-Deutschland* lay port side to at the long Germaniawerft pier, wedged between the *U-67* and *U-68,* which were nearing completion. It was early evening, and the only well-wishers on the pier were Alfred Lohmann, Karl Stapelfeld, and Philipp Heineken, who shook hands with König, after which the captain stepped back, touched his cap, and hurried up the gangplank. The moment he set foot on the deck, dockhands withdrew the gangplank. The boat's diesel engines were already running, evidenced by grayish diesel smoke rising from the port quarter. König climbed into the conning tower and looked quickly around. Line handlers were standing by fore and aft on the pier, ready to cast off the mooring lines when told to. The harbor tug *Charlotte* was standing off the submarine's starboard quarter, a heavy towline running from her bow to a cleat on the submarine's stern.[1]

▲ Germaniawerft in 1914. The long pier is the one with the battleship under construction, in the berth the *U-Deutschland* occupied two years later. *Jørn Jensen collection*

König took a quick moment to study his maneuvering problem. The *U-Deutschland* was 213 feet long and, had she been a car, would have been said to be parked bumper to bumper between the war boats ahead of and behind her. But that was just half of the problem. The other half was that the *U-Deutschland* was facing the wrong direction to get out of the Krupp turning basin, and the turning basin was too small to allow her to go forward and make a U-turn. It was a classic "ship-in-a-box problem."

König's solution was to have the tug pull the *U-Deutschland*'s stern away from the pier while the bow pivoted on its bow lines. Once the stern had swung far enough into the turning basin to allow him to back out, he would cast off the tow and the bow lines and go astern on the electric motors, performing a tricky maneuver called "twisting." If he did it exactly right, the submarine would rotate without moving forward or backward. But at the same time he had to compensate for the wind and current, which meant he had to control the engine and rudder movements deftly to prevent the boat from moving laterally.

The thirty-year-old helmsman, *Matrose* (Seaman First Class) Anton Born, was standing on the steering platform that formed the front of the conning tower, both hands resting on the twenty-eight-inch-diameter wheel.

König turned to face forward and spoke to him. "Rudder amidships."

"Aye, sir. Rudder amidships," Born answered, unconsciously feeling the king-spoke knot at the top of the wheel's steel rim and lightly touching the midline of his torso with his thumb. Without even glancing down, he knew that the knot and the midline of his torso were exactly aligned. The simple but effective method of ensuring the rudder was in line with the keel went back to the days of sail, which in 1916 had not completely vanished.

König leaned forward and shouted down the speaking tube, "Stand by to cast off!"

From the control room Franz Krapohl immediately replied, "All stations manned and ready."

König turned around completely and faced aft, directing his attention to the three crew members standing by the stern line. Then, cupping his hands around his mouth, he shouted to the civilian line handlers on the pier, "Cast off aft!" He paused for a moment as the lines splashed into the water, watched as the boat's crewmen quickly hauled the wet lines onto the submarine's stern. He shifted his attention to the tug, his hands still cupped around his mouth. "Haul away, *Charlotte!*"

The jangle of the tug's engine telegraph was clearly audible across the water. The tow line went taut and snapped up out of the water as it took up the load. The *U-Deutschland*'s stern slowly swung away from the pier as two sailors and a petty officer on the bow paid out line, allowing the bow to pull away, hinging on the dock and swinging left. König cast quick glances fore and aft, checking on the boat's changing attitude in relation to her surroundings. It was working.

Cupping his hands around his mouth again, he shouted to the sailors on the submarine's stern, "Cast off the tow!" The line splashed into the water, the tug crewmen hauling in the line as the tug backed away. He straightened up and shouted down to the men on the bow, "Cast off forward!" He then quickly bent forward to the speaking tube. "All astern one-third!"

The *U-Deutschland* was now clear of the two war boats that had been her neighbors and was moving backward. Momentum caused the bow to continue swinging slowly to the left until it pointed directly at the pier.

"All stop!" König ordered through the speaking tube. "Port astern half, starboard ahead half!" The boat shuddered and accelerated its swinging motion to the left. He looked up and spoke to Born. "Port twenty points."

"Port twenty, aye," Born responded, turning the wheel.

König made another quick survey of his surroundings, gauged the swing, and bent forward as the hull swung parallel to the pier sixty feet away. "All ahead half!" He stood erect again and told Born, "Keep to starboard in the channel." Born said "Aye," as he nodded and made necessary adjustment with the wheel.

Kiel Harbor is actually a narrow inlet from the Baltic, about eight nautical miles long and one nautical mile wide at its widest point. The Germaniawerft was at the extreme southern end of the inlet in a district called Kiel-Gaarden,

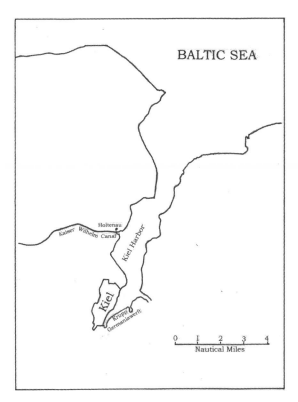

Map 1. Kiel and the area around it, including Germaniawerft and the entrance to the Kaiser Wilhelm Canal

▲ The *U-Deutschland* entering the German naval base at Helgoland on her first outbound voyage,
14 June 1916. *Author's collection*

approximately four nautical miles from the entrance to the Kaiser Wilhelm Canal
at Holtenau, which at eight knots would take the *U-Deutschland* thirty minutes to
reach. The boat would pick up a canal pilot before entering the locks and passing into the Kaiser Wilhelm Canal, which ran fifty-three nautical miles through
Schleswig-Holstein to the locks at Brunsbüttel. About twelve hours later the boat
would emerge into the Elbe Estuary and then proceed into the North Sea and on
to Helgoland, fifty nautical miles away. The estimated time of arrival in Helgoland
was 1100 on 14 June 1916.

The plan was to stay only a few hours in Helgoland, where König would
receive briefings from recently returned U-boat captains about British patrol lines
and threats along the northern route. Publicly the Germans avoided any mention
of the stop in Helgoland, instead creating the official myth that the boat had made
the first crossing from Bremen to Baltimore nonstop. However, because of the
unexpected lengthy time of the first crossing, and König's slips of the tongue in
Baltimore, the story was changed to the boat's having remained in Helgoland until
23 June "to keep the British guessing about the boat's movements." The real reason
for the cover story was to hide the fact that the *U-Deutschland* was a very slow boat.[2]

The Germans were convinced that the British had spies in and around Kiel
who reported to London regularly about the *U-Deutschland*. Actually, there were
no British spies in Kiel, and with regard to the *U-Deutschland* they were not necessary. British diplomats in neutral countries kept London reasonably well informed
about the development of Germany's cargo U-boat program. The press, both
German and international, was the source of most of the information about the
boat, most of it from loose-lipped yard workers in bars on the waterfront. The
information was not always accurate, but there was enough that in April 1916 a
Dutch newspaper published a story about the Germans building a fleet of cargo
U-boats. The British consulate in Stockholm passed that and other stories on to
London. And diplomatic parties in Berlin provided more information, which
made its way to London.[3]

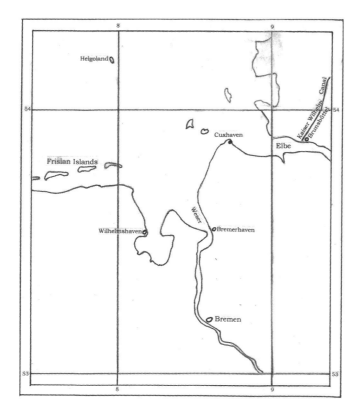

Map 2. Bremen and the area around it, including the Kaiser Wilhelm Canal exit at Brunsbüttel on the Elbe and the position of Helgoland

In late June 1916, Alfred Lohmann had articles placed in the *Weserzeitung* and *Bremer Tageblatt,* drafted to appear as if the newspapers' own editorial staffs had written them. Carefully avoiding even a hint of navy involvement, the articles put forth the claim that the venture was entirely a civilian undertaking.[4] This claim became the official German position in 1916 and is still repeated today. So, by the end of June 1916 the fact that Germany was building at least two cargo U-boats was well known to the British. What the British lacked were the details about the boats, their probable sailing schedules, and their U.S. destinations. There was also the question of whether or not the boats were armed, which the British assumed they were.

The two biggest security threats to the Germans were not spies but two experienced reporters in Berlin, one American and the other German. Carl W. Ackerman, the foreign correspondent for United Press Associates in Berlin, knew that the cargo submarines' crewmen had been selected from experienced U-boat crews and that the Deutsche Ozean Reederei was a front. But he was wrong in believing that the *U-Deutschland*'s officers came from naval intelligence and that Krupp controlled the operation on behalf of the navy. Luckily for the Germans, Ackerman sat on the story, because he was afraid he would be arrested as a spy if he released it.[5]

The German reporter was Dr. Emil Leimdörfer, editor of the *Berliner Zeitung,* which was better known by its initials, *BZ.* He had learned about a plan to operate a U-boat freight service to the United States but incorrectly assumed it would be run by the Hamburg-America Steamship Company. He submitted a story to the censors in March 1916; the censors immediately spiked it.

His suspicions fully aroused, Leimdörfer went on a hunt for facts, and by July 1916 he had developed an accurate picture of the whole operation. On 6 July 1916, two days before the *U-Deutschland* would arrive off the Virginia Capes, he met with Alfred Lohmann in the *BZ* offices and laid out what he knew. All Leimdörfer wanted was the date that the *U-Deutschland* was supposed to arrive in the United States and exclusive use of the story. Lohmann was appalled by the obvious security breach. To pacify Leimdörfer he agreed to give *BZ* an exclusive story *after* the boat arrived in the United States and after the kaiser had been told of the arrival. Lohmann did not want Wilhelm II to learn about the success from *BZ*.[6]

While the boat was in Helgoland, Captain König was briefed on the three northern routes around Scotland, and it was then that he selected his route. Because the boat's logbooks were destroyed by the Allied bombing during World War II, we have no way of knowing for sure what route he selected. But we do know that he did not pass through the English Channel, as was claimed in the book *The Voyage of the* Deutschland, because on 10 April 1915 *Fregattenkapitän* (Commander) Hermann Bauer, the High Seas Fleet's U-boat commander, ordered the U-boats under his command not to use the English Channel to reach their patrol areas.[7] Despite being ostensibly a commercial vessel, *U-Deutschland* fell into the category of boats covered by the order, and so she went "north about," which was through the North Sea and then around Scotland's northernmost point. The High Seas U-boats used three routes to go "north about."

The lowest route passed Fair Isle, north of the Orkney Islands, along about latitude 59° 40' north and then turned south near North Rona, taking a course to pass about forty-three nautical miles west of St. Kilda, off the Hebrides. The last leg on this route, from North Rona to St. Kilda, passed the southern end of a patrol barrier of 10th Cruiser Squadron cruisers, designated the "C" line. This is the route that König probably used. The central route passed between the Shetlands and the Faeroe Islands along about 61° 30' north before turning to a southerly course that passed directly through the 10th Cruiser Squadron's "C" line. The third route went around the Faeroe Islands as high as 62° 50' north and passed through the gap between the 10th Cruiser Squadron's "C" and "F" lines at about 62° 30' north latitude, 12° west longitude. This most northerly route was probably safest, but it took longest, and König was on a schedule.[8]

The immediate threat was a British minefield that lay five nautical miles north of Helgoland and bore 315 degrees (true) from the entrance. The Germans swept the field regularly, and the British replanted the mines just as regularly, and in the process the size and position of the field varied somewhat, so that the possibility of

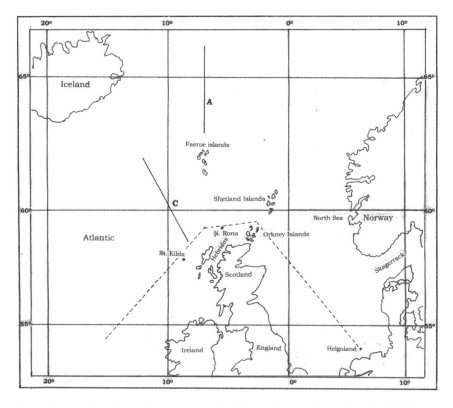

Map 3. The probable north-about route taken by the *U-Deutschland* on both her trips to the United States and the *U-Bremen* on her fateful trip

hitting a mine in an unexpected spot was always present. Mitigating the threat was the fact that the British Service Mine was notoriously unreliable and often failed to explode. Despite the mines' spotty performance, U-boat captains did not develop a cavalier attitude toward them, and the Germans always provided a minesweeper escort for U-boats leaving and returning to Helgoland.

The *U-Deutschland* left Helgoland at about 2000 on 14 June, following a mine-sweeper through a German defensive minefield and south along the British mine-field until the two vessels reached a point fifty-three nautical miles northwest of Helgoland.[9] Her escort turned around, the crew waving and the officers on the bridge throwing a final salute, and disappeared astern. Alone, König took a good look around before carrying out a test dive. Everything went according to plan, and after fifteen minutes running at just below periscope depth he brought the boat back to the surface and proceeded northeast toward Fair Isle, some 385 nautical miles distant.

Early in the trip the *U-Deutschland* experienced a diving accident that was very nearly fatal. According to the only account available, the lookout spotted what was believed to be a destroyer and König ordered what later came to be called a "crash dive," which for the *U-Deutschland* would be something of an oxymoron. In the haste to get under the surface the boat became uncontrollable, took an extreme down angle, and rammed the bottom in about 110 feet of water. The *U-Deutschland*'s bow was buried in the seabed at a thirty-six-degree angle, her stern, after diving planes, and both propellers several feet above the surface. She swayed like a pendulum every time a wave passed over, so the still-spinning propellers alternately raced in the open air and dug into passing waves.

Chief engineer Klees was able to shut down the motors and after a six-hour ordeal of flooding and using the motors managed to fully extract the *U-Deutschland* from the bottom and returned her to an even keel. Given König's propensity to tell sea stories that made good propaganda, one must ask, did it really happen? Probably it did, though maybe not quite as it was described in *Voyage of the* Deutschland. In any event, the *U-Deutschland*'s uncontrolled dive offers a possible explanation for the *U-Bremen*'s unexplained disappearance in September 1916.

The *U-Deutschland* was an unwieldy boat to handle under the best conditions and in heavy weather almost impossible. König later said, "To attempt to dive with such a sea running was sheer madness, as experience had taught us." What went wrong? There probably were two causes, each the result of haste. The first problem was that König ordered the dive when the *U-Deutschland* was still pushing head on into heavy seas. The second cause was probably either error on the part of the sailor who was responsible for flooding the after dive tanks or that Klees gave the order to flood the after tanks too late in the dive.

In the usual sequence, Chief Engineer Klees would have started with the order, "Bow planes maximum down angle," followed immediately by an order to flood the forward tanks. A few seconds later he would have ordered the after tanks flooded, in order to prevent the bow-down angle from becoming so extreme that the boat's stern rose out of the water, which is what happened. Assuming that Klees, an experienced *Leitende Ingenieur,* followed the prescribed sequence, the fault lay with the sailor whose job it was to flood the after tanks but apparently delayed carrying out the order.[10] In his book König wrote, "It was possible that the tanks, owing to the haste induced by the presence of the destroyer, had not been quite freed of air."

A subject that is prominent in all accounts of the first crossing is the seriousness of the threat posed by the "lines of British cruisers" across the boat's track. How serious were the threats he was facing from them? The answer is, not very. The British 10th Cruiser Squadron, eighteen armed passenger liners and freighters that were now auxiliary cruisers, was stationed along three patrol lines within a rectangle between 10° east and 20° west and between 57° and 68° north, an area greater than 400,000 square nautical miles. The greatest threats to the *U-Deutschland* came from the nine-ship "C" line, which ran northwest from the Hebrides to a point about 180 nautical miles off Iceland, as well as from ships assigned to that line going to and from the British coaling base in the Shetlands.

The armed merchantmen were primarily concerned with maintaining the blockade of the North Sea, not antisubmarine warfare, for which they were not equipped. Short of being terribly unlucky and being caught on the surface within gun range or being rammed, either deliberately or accidentally, the *U-Deutschland* had little to fear from 10th Cruiser Squadron. Nevertheless, though in practical terms the threat was extremely limited, König correctly did his best to avoid being detected by any ship he encountered, since a sighting could easily result in a radio warning that would bring warships that were equipped for antisubmarine warfare.

But the auxiliary cruisers of 10th Cruiser Squadron were not the only British warships operating in that area. The British deployed drifters and trawlers of the Auxiliary Patrol in two separate commands in the waters north of Scotland as far as 68° north, and Royal Navy sloops, corvettes, and destroyers were also operating in those waters. Those vessels were equipped for antisubmarine warfare.

The other question is, did the British know the *U-Deutschland* was at sea and going north about? Maybe, but there is no indication that they acted on it. British naval radio intelligence, known as Room 40, copied all German naval radio traffic, especially U-boat traffic. Since the first weeks of the war the British had been in possession of the three codebooks that the German navy used throughout the conflict—an intelligence coup equal to the breaking of the Germans' Enigma code in World War II. One of the codes was called the *Handelsverkehrsbuch* (HVB), which the German navy used to communicate with German merchant ships. This was the code that the *U-Deutschland* used to contact the radio station at Nauen, using its high antenna, and to contact Helgoland, on the jumper antenna.[11]

The boat's radio call sign was AKPV. König might have sent two noon positions before he got out of radio range, which was standard procedure for the war boats. If he did send his noon positions, Room 40 might have copied the transmissions. The British were probably unaware that AKPV was the *U-Deutschland*, but they would have recognized it as a merchant ship's call sign, and since there were no German merchant ships operating in the North Sea in 1916, it would not be much of a reach to conclude that AKPV must be the merchant U-boat about which there were so many rumors flying about. And since the British knew the routes the High Seas Fleet U-boats used when going north about, and they knew the *U-Deutschland*'s general destination, it would not have been difficult to move warships into her estimated path. Given the outcome, it does not appear that any of that happened, but for König the threat was no less real at the time. In an interview he gave in 1931, König told *New York Times* reporter T. R. Kennedy Jr. that when they left Helgoland, "we were careful not to transmit, for that might have given away our position. Instead we listened and avoided both friend and foe."[12]

We now enter a period about which very little is known for fact, the time during which the *U-Deutschland* crossed the Atlantic. The only sources available about the conditions on board the boat during the first crossing are König's ghostwritten book, *Voyage of the* Deutschland, and whatever he told the press. The problem with those sources is that they are for the most part propaganda. In this case, I have used those sources but compared them to existing logbooks from other U-boats that traveled the north-about passage during the same period.

One point about which König was consistent was that he experienced several days of extreme weather in various places along his route. He described the waves as huge and winds as approaching and occasionally reaching hurricane force. König described seas as "a waste of white-crested waves racing along," and he spoke of the need to "spare the nerves" of his men and "husband their strength" in view of the long voyage ahead. He decided to steer a more southerly course, believing that he would find better weather there. But the boat continued to make very slow headway against heavy seas and her motion was "jerky." He told Commander John Rogers that in the heavy seas the boat developed a vicious snap roll that was "so quick that if a bottle were standing on the table and it started to fall on the roll to starboard, it would be caught by the return roll to port before it could finish the fall."[13]

Though much in *Voyage of the* Deutschland about the weather can be confirmed from other sources, the most dramatic account is probably fabricated. It was after the decision to move south that he ran into heavy weather that included winds reaching Force 11 and 12. Force 11 on the Beaufort Scale is described as a violent storm with "high waves" reaching thirty-seven to fifty-two feet high and winds from fifty-six to sixty-three knots. Force 12 is a hurricane, with "huge waves" exceeding forty-six feet and winds above sixty-four knots. König said the heavens were "converted into a bellowing chaos."

The boat supposedly encountered this storm as she was approaching the North American coast. But according to the National Oceanic and Atmospheric Administration's North Atlantic Hurricane Database (HURDAT2), for 1851–2013, the only storm of that magnitude during the time the *U-Deutschland* was on her last leg of the crossing was Hurricane Number 2, which formed in the Caribbean on 29 June 1916, passed across the Gulf of Mexico, and made landfall near Gulfport, Mississippi, on 5 July. The hurricane's track was nowhere near the *U-Deutschland*. So why include it in his book? The answer is that it was propaganda to make it appear that the *U-Deutschland* could withstand any weather and that her captain and crew were master mariners, capable of dealing with any emergency, mechanical or natural.

But if König might have exaggerated the weather for propaganda reasons, the fact is that the logs of other U-boats along the *U-Deutschland*'s early track record similarly extreme weather. It is also true that upon arrival in Baltimore, and before the crew was allowed ashore, König made it clear to them that nothing was to be said about the abominable conditions on board caused by violent movements, unbearable heat, foul air, and widespread motion sickness. He himself described that part of the trip as "Hell with a lid on." Was the bottle story he told Commander Rogers fact or fiction? It was probably fact, because telling it violated the policy of saying only "good" things about the boat's behavior.

Before questioning König's accounts of heavy weather too critically, keep in mind that *The Voyage of the* Deutschland was ghostwritten. Another factor to keep in mind is that from the bridge of a relatively low-lying U-boat, one that had very poor sea-keeping qualities, the appearance and effects of the wind and sea would seem much worse than they were. But there is another, more important point to consider when trying to determine the effect the weather had on the boat and its first crossing—the formula Time x Rate = Distance. The *U-Deutschland's* top speed was ten knots, and anything that slowed her down lengthened the time it took for her to cross the Atlantic. Those things included the amount of time she ran submerged, the number of times she encountered heavy seas, especially oncoming seas, and problems she developed that either slowed or stopped her. Given her slow average speed during the crossing, it is reasonable to assume that the boat did encounter heavy weather frequently and for extended periods.

In the early morning hours of 26–27 June, the *U-Deutschland* reached the northern end of the Gulf Stream, which put her at about 42° north, 50° west and 1,020 nautical miles from the Virginia Capes. She was thirteen days out and only two-thirds of the way across, a slow passage mostly attributable to unfavorable, even extreme, weather.

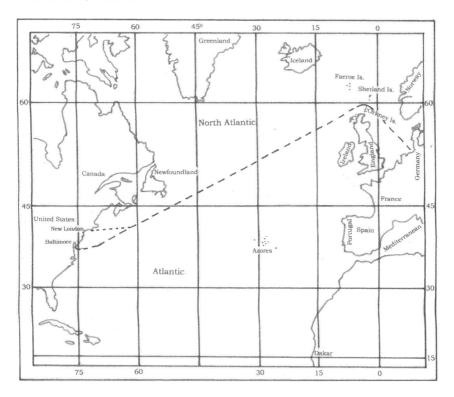

Map 4. The route the *U-Deutschland* followed across the Atlantic to Baltimore and New London

Though König later played heavily on high seas and fierce winds, he also described conditions inside the boat after she entered warmer waters in the Gulf Stream, which drove the temperature inside the boat to over 100 degrees Fahrenheit. As noted above, he graphically described conditions inside the pressure hull, where all the ventilation system could accomplish was to move hot, oily air throughout the boat. The humidity inside the hull rose to the point that the men could barely breathe and sweat from condensation ran down the sides of the hull and the bulkheads. The dense moisture soaked everything, causing wooden drawers and locker doors to swell shut. Off-watch crewmen lay naked on their berths in a futile attempt to find relief from the brutal heat. It was impossible to sleep, and those on watch fell into a dull stupor. In the engine room the heat was so ferocious that the men on watch wore only undershorts and tied rags across their foreheads to keep the sweat from running into their eyes. Blood hammered in their temples, and any exertion was a test of willpower.

But relief came as the boat worked her way closer to the North American coast, and there were several good days during which the hatches were opened and the crew came out on deck. It was during this time that König allowed his narrative to take on a more pleasant note. He described a "sea bath" that allowed the crewmen to bathe by standing atop the tank deck, "washed" by the saltwater flowing through the casing openings and down the pressure hull. There also an account of disguising the *U-Deutschland* as a single-stack freighter, complete with smoke coming from the stack, and of enjoying music from five gramophones. The weather was undoubtedly much improved in this stage, but the rest is almost certainly fabrication.

The *U-Deutschland* arrived twenty-five miles offshore of the Virginia Capes on 8 July at dusk. König called Krapohl and Eyring to the bridge to discuss the best way to approach the coast and cross the three-mile limit. Krapohl and Eyring suggested that they wait for total darkness. König wanted to close to a point ten miles out, dive, and wait in deep water for dawn. Then they would make a periscope sweep and, if they saw nothing, surface and run toward the three-mile limit. The unknown factor was the weather; would it hold or turn worse?

The decision was made to move in closer and see what the weather did. As they moved toward the coast the wind picked up and blew away the summer haze, leaving the air clear and visibility exceptional. But the wind also kicked up a short, sharp chop that made the boat's motion "extremely disagreeable." König decided then, "upon the basis of exact astronomical calculations," to remain surfaced and steer toward the shore lights of Cape Henry and Cape Charles. Because of the exceptional visibility, he ordered Klees to trim the boat down until the decks were awash and only the conning tower was visible above the surface. With two lookouts with him on the bridge, König conned the boat at half speed toward their goal.

Just after dark they spotted a pale glow on the horizon that repeatedly flared up and went out. König recognized it as the revolving light at Cape Henry. Moments later a white light appeared off the starboard bow, remained on for a short while, and then went out. The on-and-off appearances of the light occurred several times. Moments later another white light flashed up to starboard, and after what seemed to be a brief exchange of signals, both lights went out. The *U-Deutschland* continued her slow approach to the Capes entrance, her conning tower lookouts alert and the crew below at diving stations.

A small steamer, displaying only a light at the masthead, passed well astern of them, followed several minutes later by a three-masted schooner that displayed only a handheld lantern on the quarterdeck. König realized he was encountering coasting vessels that were running without their sidelights, displaying only a white stern light from time to time. He cautioned his two lookouts to keep a sharp eye out for darkened ships.

König next encountered the Cape Henry fixed light, as it grew brighter and brighter on the horizon. Soon the Cape Charles intermittent-blinking light became visible, and König knew that he was on the right course for the entrance between the Capes. His opinion was confirmed sometime later when the *U-Deutschland* encountered the first channel lantern buoys. The next waypoint was a whistling buoy with which König was very familiar from his prewar voyages.

Once past the whistling buoy, König had Klees bring the boat all the way to the surface, ordered the diesel engines cut in, and went full ahead on both. The boat was still running without lights, and König was aware of the lights of several outbound passenger steamers. He took the *U-Deutschland* in close to Cape Henry, still without lights, and crossed the three-mile limit at 2330, on 8 July.

At 0145 on the 9th, the *U-Deutschland* was in the lee of Cape Henry, where the weather observer at Fort Story saw the U-boat and logged the sighting. König held that position until 0400, when he finally passed the Capes and entered the Chesapeake Bay as dawn was breaking. Shortly after he made out the white top lights of a pilot ship, brought the *U-Deutschland* to a stop, and ignited a blue flare, the international night request for a pilot.[14]

A searchlight on board the pilot boat snapped on and swept along the U-boat's hull. From behind the light came a shout, "Where are you bound for?"

König lifted a megaphone to his lips and replied. "Newport News."

"What ship are you?"

"The *U-Deutschland,* sixteen days out of Bremen." The answer was not entirely accurate, but it was in keeping with the need to portray the boat and its mission as an entirely civilian venture. It would have hardly been in keeping to have said that she was sixteen days out of the Imperial German Navy base at Helgoland. The crossing had actually taken twenty-six days, five hours, but for propaganda reasons sixteen days was the official count.

Moments following the exchange, a rowboat came alongside, and the pilot, Fred Cocke, stepped onto the tank deck. "I'll be damned," he said with feeling. "Here she is." They had officially arrived, having traveled 3,510 nautical miles at an average speed of 5.6 knots.

6

Baltimore, Part I

With the pilot Fred Cocke on board, the *U-Deutschland* headed toward Norfolk up the Thimble Shoal Channel at eight knots, arriving in an area known as Lynnhaven Roads, off Norfolk, at about 0630. The *Timmins* was waiting for them. It was now that König learned that Baltimore was his destination, not Norfolk. The change in destination necessitated a change in pilots, because Cocke was a Virginia pilot and not licensed to pilot vessels into Baltimore. After about an hour's delay, a Chesapeake pilot, Samuel Coleman, was taken on board and the two-vessel convoy, *U-Deutschland* and *Timmins,* started toward Baltimore.[1]

As the two-vessel convoy made its way up the Patapsco River on 9 July the trip began to look and sound like a victory parade, as neutral and American commercial vessels sounded raucous salutes with their steam whistles and sirens. The *U-Deutschland* respond in kind until her compressed-air whistle drew down the boat's compressed-air supply to a dangerous level, after which the *Timmins* picked up the slack with its steam whistle. At 1600 the *U-Deutschland* slowed as the *Timmins* came alongside to deliver a block of ice and several bottles of champagne. König later commented, "What this first iced drink meant to us can only be appreciated by one who is able to picture to himself what it means to have lived day after day in a temperature of 53 Celsius. We merely regretted that it was only the corks which popped over to Captain Hinsch."[2]

Shortly after the crew's moment to enjoy a victory glass of champagne, the first of a fleet of powerboats began to appear. Their numbers grew steadily as the convoy continued toward Baltimore, each boat loaded to the gunnels with gawkers, reporters, and movie cameramen. Even when the sun started to go down the powerboats stayed with them, finally pulling away and vanishing in the growing dusk as the day ended.

At 2300 the *U-Deutschland* slowed, stopped, and dropped her anchor in the Quarantine Area, where she spent the night. At 0500 on 10 July, the deputy health officer, Dr. John C. Travers, came on board, and Captain König led him down into the boat through the forward hatch. Starting in the bow, the doctor found that the

◄ This postcard shows the *U-Deutschland* (misidentified as the *U-Bremen*) leaving Helgoland on the evening of 14 June 1916 en route to the United States. The black skirt on her port quarter identifies her as the *U-Deutschland* rather than the *U-Bremen*; the *U-Deutschland* was the only boat of the class that had the black skirt. *Claas Stöckmeyer collection*

crew's quarters were "nothing more than bunks on both sides of a narrow passageway." Moving aft he came to the captain's quarters, which were "barely six-feet square and furnished entirely in metal except for an oak desk." He was surprised to see that there was "hardly room inside for a man to stand." While he was in the captain's quarters he examined the boat's health certificate that the U.S. consul in Bremen, William T. Fee, had issued on 13 June. As they moved aft he was shown the forward hold, which he estimated was seventeen feet deep. The officers' wardroom was "scarcely larger than their staterooms and equipped with a galley built with all the economy of space of a Pullman dining car and kitchen."

He was awed by the "mass of machinery" in the central control room and was allowed to look through one of the periscopes, which he described as "having amazing clearness." While in the central control room König told him that when they were running on the surface, the noise from the diesels was "deafening" and the heat was at times "unbearable." He also examined the ship's larder and found that "canned meats and fruits were the crew's staple." He concluded that with the exception of weight loss, which he attributed to the "oily atmosphere" below decks, the "men and officers were physically fit."[3]

One wonders if the doctor had the opportunity of talking to the civilian engineer who was listed as "supercargo," Prusse. As we will see later, there are strong indications that Wilhelm Prusse had active tuberculosis and was in very bad shape by the time the boat docked in Baltimore. Prusse told a reporter who asked him about the trip over that the ordeal had nearly killed him and that he would not be returning to Germany on board the U-boat. In any event, Doctor Travers, clutching two loaves of German war bread that König had given him as a souvenir, declared that he was satisfied with what he saw and cleared the boat for entry. The *U-Deutschland* upped anchor and got under way again, arriving at the EFCO pier at 0630, thirty-one hours after crossing the three-mile limit.[4]

It was raining when the *U-Deutschland* was eased into her berth on Monday, 10 July, but despite the early hour and miserable weather a crowd of several hundred had already gathered in front of the warehouse and along Andre Street. Security at the EFCO site was very tight and included not only the usual German seamen but

➤ The *U-Deutschland* anchored in the quarantine area in Baltimore on the morning of 10 July 1916. Standing on the foredeck are left to right, Paul Eyring (second officer), Captain König, and Paul Hilken in civilian clothes. The man in the straw hat is probably the Chesapeake pilot, Samuel Coleman. The other crewmen are not identified. *Author's collection*

➤ The *U-Deutschland* approaching her berth in Baltimore at about 0630 on 10 July 1916. The tug, *Thomas F. Timmins,* belonged to the Eastern Forwarding Company. The portly man standing on the tug's starboard side, outside the wheelhouse, is Captain Friedrich Hinsch, the field supervisor and chief operative for the sabotage cell. *Author's collection*

also hired security men and Baltimore police. In addition to the large number of NDL employee security guards, and police personnel, the barbed-wire fence kept the crowd away from the warehouse.

The Germans had also taken measures to ensure that the U-boat would be all but completely hidden from view. The *U-Deutschland* was berthed starboard side to the pier, with her bow pointing at the warehouse. The warehouse and the high fence along the pier covered her from two sides, and the *Neckar,* berthed on the other side of the pier, formed an additional barrier. The 150-foot steel barge *George May* was made up on the port side of the U-boat and a smaller barge across her stern with its hatch covers up, forming an effective screen from the river. A heavy log boom was positioned a hundred feet from the boat's port side to prevent anyone in a boat from reaching the *U-Deutschland.*

The *U-Deutschland's* arrival in Baltimore presented the U.S. Department of State with a political hot potato. Was the boat really just a merchant vessel, or was she a U-boat disguised as one? Who actually owned and operated the boat; the Deutsche Ozean Reederei or the Imperial German Navy? Captain König had already slipped twice, the first time when he told a boatload of reporters off Sandy Point that his departure had been made from Helgoland, and the second on arrival at the EFCO pier, when he announced, "My orders are from my home government." Both slips were published in the newspapers. E. Mitchell Ferriday, of Waterbury, Connecticut, spotted them and fired off a telegram to Frank L. Polk, acting Secretary of State.

IN NEW YORK TIMES OF TODAY CAPTAIN KOENIG OF
THE GERMAN SUBMARINE IS QUOTED AS SAYING MY
ORDERS ARE FROM MY HOME GOVERNMENT—STOP—
THE STATUS OF THE WARSHIP NOW HARBORED IN OUR
NEUTRAL PORT IS CLEARLY THAT DEFINED—STOP—
OUR GOVERNMENT TAKE HEED.[5]

As early as 3 July, six days before the *U-Deutschland's* arrival in Baltimore, the British and French governments had begun putting pressure on the Department of State to declare the *U-Deutschland* a war boat. The submarine's ability to submerge became a key issue. If the U-boat was a freighter, then under the law the British had to stop and examine her for contraband before taking any action against her. But how could they do that if the boat simply vanished beneath the surface? On the other hand, if they treated the *U-Deutschland* like any other U-boat and sank her on sight, they would be violating international law in the same way that many German U-boats were—not that the British would have been too concerned about that.

The British conveniently overlooked the legal fact that under the law their armed merchant ships could be considered warships and could legally be sunk on sight. It was a point that the British wanted to avoid discussing at all costs, because the Prize Regulations worked overwhelmingly in their favor, especially in the field of propaganda. But to the British and French the *U-Deutschland* was a U-boat whether she was armed or not, and they wanted her classed as a warship.[6]

In 1916, the term "U-boat" evoked a picture of a submarine armed with torpedoes and, sometimes, deck guns. Submarines by any name were a new sort of warship, and a cargo submarine was an entirely new use of the type. The *U* in U-boat is the German abbreviation for *Untersee*, meaning under sea. In Germany the *U-Deutschland* was also called *das Untersee-frachtschiff-Deutschland* (undersea freighter *Deutschland*), *das Handels-U-Boot Deutschland* (commercial undersea boat *Deutschland*), and *U-Schiff-Deutschland* (undersea ship *Deutschland*). Terms like that made it easy for Germans to recognize the difference between a war boat and a commercial vessel. But the usual connotation of the term "U-boat" made nearly every one automatically assume that the *U-Deutschland* was a sort of warship.

In the minds of most Americans, and apparently most of the nation's reporters, the question of whether or not the *U-Deutschland* was a merchant ship or a warship rested on the simplistic question of whether or not she carried a deck gun. For some reason, the people who were the loudest about the deck-gun question ignored the fact that armed British, French, and Italian merchant ships were to be found in any American harbor on any day of the week during the time that the *U-Deutschland* was in Baltimore. Three examples taken from State Department records illustrate the point: SS *Celtic* (British) arrived in New York on 7 July 1916 armed with a 4.7-inch gun and departed with war materials; RMS *Saxonia* (British) arrived in New York on 19 July 1916 armed with a 4.7-inch gun and was cleared loaded with war materials; and SS *Georgia* (French) arrived in New York on 16 July 1916 armed with a 65 mm gun, remained several days, and departed with a cargo of war materials. But a U-boat, armed or not, presented an entirely new set of issues. The U.S. government's solution was to have the U-boat carefully inspected to determine if she was in fact a merchant vessel or a cleverly disguised warship.

At 0630 on 10 July, four U.S. Treasury officers, Boarding Officer P. J. Curran, Deputy Surveyor F. Sydney Hayward, Chief Clerk Wynde, and Acting Deputy Collector Thalheimer, went on board to examine and certify the boat's manifest. They were also supposed to look for any signs of armament, whether guns or torpedoes. Even though these men had never been inside a submarine before, they had no problem seeing that the boat was unarmed. They were finished and gone before the next officials boarded the boat.[7]

The second visitors were Agent Billups Harris and Lt. Jacob H. Klein Jr., USN, who arrived just after 0800. Lieutenant Klein, who was not in uniform, was a member of naval intelligence, and his presence on board the boat was not part of the State Department inspection for armament. Klein was there to see what he could learn for the navy about the boat's construction and technology. Harris had received a phone call that morning from his boss, Chief A. Bruce Bielaski, telling him to get the lieutenant on board without attracting any attention, which he accomplished by telling the Germans that Klein was his assistant and that his name was Kelly. Not realizing that the Bureau of Investigation had no business on board, the Germans greeted them warmly.

Klein spoke fluent German with a slight Berlin accent, but when he first went on board he intended to keep his language ability a secret, hoping to pick up information from unsuspecting crewmen as they conversed with one another. He quickly abandoned that plan when he found that the Germans were surprisingly chatty, and he soon discovered that the men were surprisingly well informed on the construction, features, and operation of U-boats.

When he mentioned that he had recently read an article on U-boats, they unhesitatingly added to, and corrected the errors in, what he had read. One would think that the depth of knowledge that the "civilian" crew exhibited would have raised a red flag. But either Klein ignored the obvious or he simply failed to recognize it. Still, it was his job to gather naval intelligence, not assess the crew's true nature. The only oddity he mentioned was that the "Mates' caps looked quite new." Having gotten the information he was after, he returned to his headquarters to report his findings.[8]

The next to arrive were also not entirely what they purported to be. Deputy Surveyor Guy W. Steele was certainly there on official business, but Steele's friend Ary J. Lamme was a civilian stockbroker. Steele was there to "make an extended examination of the vessel, and to interrogate the master, officers, and crew." He brought Lamme along because he spoke German, which Steele thought might be useful, but he did not mention that to Paul Eyring, letting the boat's second officer believe that Lamme was just another Treasury official. The two men remained on board until nearly noon while Lamme made sketches of the boat's interior spaces and Steele questioned the crew and officers about their status as merchant seamen. They all produced their newly issued merchant marine identification and swore that they had never been in the Imperial German Navy. The identification was certainly official, and it was the Treasury Department's routine practice to accept verbal affirmations that no crew members were serving servicemen, so Steele was satisfied. When the two men walked back down the gangplank, Lamme became the first, only, and last unauthorized civilian who ever went on board the *U-Deutschland*. His sketches were later published in the *Baltimore Sun* and *Popular Mechanics*.[9]

That afternoon, at 1330, Department of Commerce radio inspector R. Y. Cadmus went on board to inspect the boat's radio to see that it complied with both U.S. and international law with regard to range and power. He found that the *U-Deutschland* was equipped with a 1.5-watt Telefunken quenched-gap set, which he estimated had a sending range of about a hundred nautical miles at sea, depending on atmospheric conditions. He satisfied himself that the radio complied with all laws and regulations and noted in his report that the high antenna was not rigged. The radioman, Arthur Geilenfeld, asked that he be allowed to raise the high antenna in order to receive the time from the Arlington, Virginia, naval radio station, so that they could correct the ship's chronometer if necessary. Cadmus said he could, since the law allowed the radio to remain unsealed for ten days, until 20 July. But it was not until 24 July, two weeks after she arrived, that a navy radioman, accompanied by Cadmus, came on board and sealed the radio.[10]

Late in the morning of 10 July, Acting Secretary of the Treasury Frank L. Polk forwarded a telegram to Secretary of State Robert Lansing from Collector of Customs William Ryan stating that there were no guns on the *U-Deutschland*. Lansing called Polk and observed that the telegram mentioned only guns and said nothing about torpedoes. Both men realized that the reports the Treasury officials had submitted would have little weight with the British and French governments, because the men were not technically competent in the construction of submarines or questions of armament. The solution was to have qualified U.S. Navy officers inspect the boat. Lansing called the secretary of the Navy, Josephus Daniels, and asked him to assign three officers to conduct the inspection. Lansing then called Polk again and gave him the names of the three officers whom Daniels had assigned, which Polk immediately passed on to Ryan.[11]

Late that afternoon, William Ryan notified Paul Hilken and Captain König that three naval officers were going to inspect the boat the following day. Hilken did not like the idea but was realistic enough to know there was nothing he could do about it. Ryan released the information to the press shortly after he informed Hilken, and the first thing the reporters wanted was Hilken's reaction. He told them, "I do not think a naval officer should be allowed to examine the boat to learn the secrets of her construction." His clincher was a statement making it clear where his loyalties lay. He said, "We do not permit anybody but our own naval

men to go aboard our submarines." Captain König was more agreeable. He told
the reporters, "I was ordered by my owners in Bremen to permit no one to board
the vessel. But if Captain Hughes has government credentials he may go aboard
her. We have no secrets. He won't find anything."[12]

On 11 July Collector of Customs Ryan and three navy officers—Capt. Charles
F. Hughes, representing the General Board of the Navy, and Naval Constructor
Herbert S. Howard and Lt. Joseph O. Fisher, representing the Bureau of Steam
Engineering—went on board at noon to conduct a thorough technical inspection
"to ascertain if the ship was fitted to mount guns, if she carried ammunition for
guns, was she fitted with torpedo tubes, were there any torpedoes on board, could
she lay mines, and was she designed and built for ramming?"[13]

From the point of view of impeccable qualifications, Captain Hughes was
an excellent choice to be the officer in charge of the official inspection. He was
a member of the General Board and a member of the Board of Inspection and
Survey. In 1914 he had been the chief of staff to Rear Admiral Charles F. Badger,
the commander of the Atlantic Fleet, during the occupation of Vera Cruz.

In the course of their three-hour inspection they went into, or looked into,
all parts of the boat except the cargo holds and the fuel and oil tanks. They even
inspected the central ballast tank. They found nothing to support a claim that
the boat was anything other than a merchant vessel. They also concluded that
she could not be converted to a war boat "without large structural changes," and
they remarked on the cooperativeness of the crew, especially *Leitende Ingenieur*
Klees. What was not included in their report was the beastly temperature inside
the boat. Reporters who watched them emerge from the after hatch told their
readers, "Captain Hughes and his aides were damp and dirty when they emerged
from their stay of over three hours in the *U-Deutschland*. They had removed most
of their outer clothing and had stripped to the waist, but their appearance told of
the temperature below."[14]

Based on the reports the Treasury officials submitted, and giving heavy weight
to the Hughes report, the Department of State on 13 July classified the submarine
as an unarmed merchant vessel, forwarding all the reports to the Joint State and
Navy Neutrality Board, which would officially give the *U-Deutschland* the government's stamp of authenticity. On 14 July 1916, the Neutrality Board issued its
five-page findings and the final decision. The *U-Deutschland* was a merchant vessel.

It has been written and said that the decision was the result of German diplomatic pressure to force the United States to demonstrate that its neutrality was
genuine and not a partial neutrality that favored the Allies. That might be true, but
the Neutrality Board's advice to the Wilson administration indicated that future
impartiality could be conditional. The board advised that each future visit be examined separately, no matter how many times the boat came to the United States, and
went on to say, "In view of the novelty and importance of the question at issue, the
Board suggests to the Department of State the advisability of accompanying any

decision with a statement to the effect that its decision is subject to revision at a later date, should experience suggest the propriety of such revision."[15]

On 17 July 1916, the Department of State sent a telegram to the U.S. ambassador in London, Walter Hines Page, directing him to advise the British government of the decision and the reasons for making it. But the last line of its instructions reflected the Neutrality Board's suggestion, so as to reassure the British: "Inasmuch as a merchant submarine presents [a] new problem, [the] Department [was] careful to create no precedents." In other words, the Germans might not be so lucky next time. Nevertheless, the British and French were not pleased, and they protested the decision. The Allied protest focused on three points. The *U-Deutschland* could be armed outside the three–mile limit, by some sort of "mother ship." The second point was that the nature of the boat's design and construction made it a warship. The third point was that she could not be stopped and searched like a surface merchant vessel, because at the first hint of trouble she would drop beneath the surface. The State Department rejected the first two points for lack of merit, based on the official reports. The third point was simply ignored.

But the issue still was not dead. On 12 July, Samuel H. Hoppin, a New York attorney, sent a letter to Polk questioning the status of the *U-Deutschland's* crew:

> Can the United States safely give clearance to a type of vessel heretofore considered exclusively a war-vessel, unless the owners show affirmatively that the crew of twenty-nine men are definitely discharged from all present and future duty to the German empire during this war? Let them produce their discharges from the German navy. It is not enough to masquerade in uniforms of the North German Lloyd S. S. Co. It is inconceivable that there are twenty-nine able bodied seamen of military age, expert in submarine operation, who are not attached to the colors.[16]

Mr. Hoppin had a very good point.

Two foreign newspapers illustrated the viewpoints of the two sides in the war. *Le Temp* of Paris railed against the Neutrality Board decision, telling its readers, "It goes without saying that the Powers of the Entente are in no way held to conform to the opinion of the administration in Washington, and are free to have the *U-Deutschland* sunk when their cruisers encounter it."[17] The Constantinople daily *Tanin* said that the arrival of the *U-Deutschland* in Baltimore

> forms a new happening with respect to international law. In fact, until now there has been no mention of submarine merchant vessels in the dispositions of international law, and in like manner there has been no mention of the name submarine in the portions of the provisions of international law dealing with questions of marine commerce. Consequently, the position of merchant submarines

with respect to international law will now be determined for the first time, and the first principle, if not the first law, will be laid down.[18]

Others also raised questions about the boat's real purpose and true capabilities. On 10 July a *New York Times* editorial, titled "Deutschland's Mission," had asked, "And is it possible that the Germans have sent this U-boat over with the deliberate intent to veil their entire submarine operations in a protecting cloud of ambiguity, putting their enemies under obligation to visit and search every U-boat before opening fire?"

Gabriel Hanotaux, a former French foreign minister, saw the *U-Deutschland* as a sinister threat that the Germans would use to "intimidate neutral powers," clearly meaning the United States. He was not far off the mark when he argued that the German message was, "The sea no longer is an obstacle; here we are, and beware our coming again." But the most prescient observation was made by a U.S. Navy constructor, Dr. Franz E. Junge, who commented, "By far the most important and revolutionary features of the new craft consists in its possibility as an auxiliary war vessel. For this harmless submarine can be readily transformed into a formidable fighting unit."[19]

There was truth in what Hanotaux and Junge said, but the fact at the moment was that the *U-Deutschland* was in Baltimore to take on rubber and nickel, both of which were critical to the German war effort. Anything else achieved by her visit, such as implicit intimidation or veiling the "entire submarine operations in a protecting cloud of ambiguity," would be unintended profits.

While the Neutrality Board was reading the State Department decision and the supporting reports, Carl Ackerman in Berlin explained how important the State Department's decision on the *U-Deutschland*'s status was going to be: "Berlin is anxiously awaiting a decision by the American State Department on the status of the submarine *U-Deutschland*. A formal finding that the *U-Deutschland* is a merchantman, in the face of protests of allied diplomats, will go a long way toward convincing Germans that America really is neutral."[20]

Ackerman's observation was on the mark. To most Germans, both in the United States and in Germany, the United States was anything but neutral; they perceived it to be providing enormous material aid to the Entente powers while strangling Germany. That attitude was to persist far beyond the end of the war, as shown by a postwar best-selling book, *Sperrfeurer um* Deutschland (Curtain of Fire around Germany), by Werner Beumelburg, a World War I veteran and a popular interwar author in Germany: "Sometimes the ammunition for German artillery was rationed. Some might think that the French would have also liked to conserve ammunition and would follow the German example. In fact, they never considered conserving ammunition. They had more rounds than they could shoot because all of America worked for them."[21]

While the Germans were celebrating in Berlin, Bremen, and Baltimore, the French and the British clung to the faint hope that Simon Lake would file a suit against the *U-Deutschland* that would keep her in Baltimore. On 9 July, Lake held a press conference in which he said, "If it has any of my devices on it . . . I will libel the boat." For a brief moment the British and French were ecstatic at the possibility that the *U-Deutschland* would be tied up in a lengthy legal battle, because Lake had good reason to suspect that the Germans had used some of his patented designs in the *U-Deutschland*.

Lake had entered into an agreement with Krupp AG in 1909 for the Germaniawerft to build submarines of his design, but the deal fell through. Krupp, who still had possession of Lake's plans and information, built U-boats without consideration for Lake by refusing to recognize the validity of Lake's international patents. As a result, German U-boats included several of Lake's ideas, including the double-hull design. Six years later Lake had patented a design for a cargo submarine that was remarkably similar in appearance to the *U-Deutschland,* and by the time the *U-Deutschland* arrived in Baltimore Lake was publically talking about building a fleet of large cargo submarines to supply England with food and war materials.[22]

But there would be no lawsuit. On the morning that the *U-Deutschland* docked at the McLean Pier, Lake was one of the few people to gain access to the EFCO office inside the warehouse. After waiting for König, Hilken, and Hinsch to finish a meeting, he had a private conversation with König and asked several questions about the U-boat, one of them whether the *U-Deutschland* was equipped with wheels that allowed her to roll along the ocean floor. Lake told a reporter, "When I mentioned their utility to Captain König, he merely smiled." König discussed his boat with the famous inventor in only general terms. But he did turn the conversation around, by suggesting that Lake build cargo submarines for Germany. From that point forward Lake dropped all interest in filing suit for patent infringement.

That same day Lake held a press conference in the Norddeutsche Lloyd offices in New York City and announced that he, the Hilkens, and the munitions firm Friedrich Krupp AG would form a company to build cargo U-boats in the United States for delivery to Germany.[23] The British and French were appalled. If the scheme actually materialized, Germany could have a steady supply of new U-boats, which could leave the United States carrying cargo and be converted to long-range war boats in Germany. The British had every reason to take seriously the idea that Lake would build submarines for Germany: Charles Schwab had done essentially the same thing for the British in 1915.[24]

Beyond the fact that the *U-Deutschland* had demonstrated that the British blockade could be broken and had driven home the message that no ocean in the world was too distant to be reached by U-boat, the focus of attention was on her cargo of dyestuffs. The U.S. dye industry was suffering what it called "a dyestuff famine," caused by the complete shutdown of deliveries from Germany. Before the war Germany had supplied the American dye industry with 75 percent of its concentrated dyestuffs requirements. No other country produced dyestuffs that equaled the quality of the German products, and no other country could match German production.[25] The Americans were working on developing their own dyestuffs, and while there were signs of improvement, output was low and quality even lower.

In May 1915 there was hope that two large German chemical companies would be able to build branch plants in the United States. If that happened, the problem would be largely solved, because the U.S. petroleum industry, the world's largest producer of coal tar, could supply the necessary coal-tar materials with which to make the dyes. The problem was how to get German technicians and equipment through the British blockade. That same year, the U.S. State Department tried to broker a deal with the British government to allow 15,000 tons of German dyestuffs through the blockade and thereafter permit the delivery of enough American cotton to Germany to pay for them. The British refused, since it was their policy "to keep all of Germany's goods out of the world's markets while the war is on."[26]

Another option the Americans tried was to buy Switzerland's entire dyestuffs output, which represented about 60 percent of America's annual requirements. But the Swiss refused the deal, because they depended entirely on Germany for the necessary coal-tar materials, which Germany threatened to withhold if the Swiss sold to the United States.[27] In the meantime, the U.S. government continued its efforts to get the British to allow German dyestuffs through the blockade.

Finally, on 3 July 1916, just seven days before the *U-Deutschland* put into Baltimore, the Americans learned that the British would not agree to the deal. The *New York Times* headlined, "Despair of Getting German Dyestuffs." But despair sprang to hope with the *U-Deutschland*'s arrival in Baltimore, only to be clouded in confusion and a rapidly growing prospect of serious price gouging and opportunism on the part of Henry and Paul Hilken.

Herman A. Metz was the head of the dye-importing firm H. A. Metz and Company, which did business in the United States as Farbewerke-Hoechst US, one of the six big American dye companies. His company had placed a large order with Farbewerke-Hoechst in Germany before the war shut off all deliveries from Germany, and Metz desperately needed those dyes. Metz told a reporter that six weeks prior to the *U-Deutschland*'s arrival in Baltimore he had been told by a "concern in Germany" that a consignment of dyestuffs had been sent to Bremen for shipment to the United States. Since the *U-Deutschland* was the only vessel capable of making the delivery, Metz felt he had every reason to believe that all or part of his order would be on the boat.

The six big American dye companies—Farbewerke-Hoechst, Casella Color, Geigy Company, Badische Company, Berlin Aniline Works, and Bayer & Company—were also expecting previously placed orders to be on board the U-boat, and after the *U-Deutschland* docked they bombarded the Baltimore office of the Eastern Forwarding Company with phone calls asking about the cargo and to whom it was consigned. What they did not know, but would soon learn, was that the entire dyestuffs cargo had been consigned to the Hilkens' firm, A. Schumacher and Company, making Henry and Paul Hilken sole owners.[28]

The cargo was unloaded on 11 and 12 July and placed in the general-order store on McLean's Wharf, but none of the dye companies received any word about how the cargo was to be divided up. The absence of any information created widespread speculation as to the cargo's market value. Prices for the rarest colors were already estimated at being 300 to 400 percent above normal. Estimates of the cargo's value ranged from six million dollars to a hundred million. Adding to the speculation was a report that the dyestuffs on board the *U-Deutschland* were in a "highly concentrated form," which substantially increased their value.[29]

Some of the rumors were reasonably accurate. The *U-Deutschland*'s marketable cargo consisted entirely of 3,042 cases of concentrated aniline dyestuffs, having a net weight of 163 tons.[30] Prewar prices for aniline dye had been roughly twenty-five cents a pound, which would make the *U-Deutschland*'s cargo worth about $62,500. But the war had changed that dramatically. Domestically produced dyes sold for $1.05 a pound in 1915 and were up to three and four dollars a pound in 1916. If the *U-Deutschland*'s cargo was sold at four dollars a pound, its total value would be a million dollars. But everyone knew the price would be much higher, because they correctly assumed that the Germans had sent only the "rarest colors." The range of educated guesses ran from ten to fifteen dollars a pound, which would raise the cargo's value to $2,500,000 at the low end and $12,500,000 at the high end.[31]

On 17 July, seven days after the dyestuffs arrived in Baltimore, the American dye companies got the bad news that Schumacher and Company was the sole consignee. The *New York Times* said that "the fact the title of the dyestuffs rested in Schumacher & Company came as a surprise to the half-dozen big color firms, which in normal times, handle the output in this country of the plants in Germany." It was more than just a surprise. One insider noted that the big companies in the dye trade would have to pay "enormous advances over regular rates." If anyone doubted that the cargo would go for top dollar, those doubts vanished on 25 July when Paul Hilken told reporters, "The cargo was consigned to us, and none of it to any individual dealer in dyes or any company"—and, asked what Schumacher and Company would do with the cargo, he answered, "We shall sell it." Asked if he expected any difficulties selling something with which his company had no experience, Hilken replied, "Difficulties in selling it? If you could see the pile of letters we have from dealers all over the country making inquiries about it, you would not suppose there would be any difficulty about selling it."

Actually, there was more to it than that. The reality was that the firms who had placed orders would have to stand in line to buy whatever they could get at whatever price the Hilkens chose. Herman Metz said, "We will have to buy them at the same price as anyone else. The whole thing is a big speculation." To whom the dyestuffs would be sold remained a secret until 10 August, eight days after the *U-Deutschland's* departure from Baltimore. On that date the *New York Times* reported that Schumacher and Company had sold the dyestuffs, some of which were twelve times their normal strength, to the six biggest dye companies at "war prices."

So, what were the final numbers? The Hilkens sold 163 tons of dyestuffs for $6,180,960.00, as compared to the entire year 1913, in which the American dye companies had paid a total of $10,071,008 for 23,000 tons of imported German dyestuffs. Since the Hilkens had paid $332,000 for the dyes in Germany, they made a fortune.[32]

While the big dye merchants stewed, the U.S. government's 14 July decision that the *U-Deutschland* was a commercial vessel had positive effects in Germany. The most significant was the boost in civilian morale brought on by the widespread belief that the blockade was finally broken. The euphoria was heightened when Philipp Heineken announced that six more cargo U-boats were already under construction and that the *U-Deutschland's* sister, *U-Bremen,* was preparing to go to sea. The Berlin stock exchange, the Berlin Börse, experienced "a lively demand for shipping stocks, particularly those of Norddeutsche Lloyd and the Hamburg-America Line." There was also hope in financial circles that the return of regular trade between the United States and Germany would strengthen the reichsmark, which had lost over 25 percent of its value since the war started.

Also, the news undercut the people who were pushing for a resumption of unrestricted submarine warfare, which had been waged for several months in 1915 until suspended in the face of protests from, especially, the United States, after the sinking of the British liner *Lusitania*. Ackerman had earlier predicted that a State Department decision classifying the *U-Deutschland* as a merchant vessel would "be a blow to the von Tirpitz supporters who have been urging a disregard for American opinion and the resumption of former submarine policies."[33] Ackermann's opinion was proven correct when Ernst Graf zu Reventlow, a political writer and advocate of ruthless submarine warfare, wrote, "The submarine freight line to America is by no means freedom of the seas," and added that even if submarine freighters did establish regular service they would provide only "negligible assistance in Germany's economic offensive and be of no use at all for inflicting direct injury on England."[34]

The State Department's decision also generated euphoria among the people associated with the *U-Deutschland* and her cargo. The German ambassador, Johann Heinrich Graf von Bernstorff, told reporters, "I have heard there will be a boat each month," and Paul Hilken, with the Lake agreement in his pocket, was already predicting "weekly" arrivals of the DOR's future cargo submarines. Adding to the speculation, Captain König told Baltimore city officials that Zeppelin freighters were being built for regular transatlantic service. "In the not distant future one or more of them will sail through the air to the United States," he predicted.[35] Milton Ager and Jack Yellen should have written "Happy Days Are Here Again" in 1916 instead of 1929.

7

Baltimore, Part II

On 10 July, at 1000, the German chief counselor to von Bernstorff, Haniel von Haimhausen, arrived at the EFCO warehouse and office. He was there to pick up the three diplomatic mail pouches that the *U-Deutschland* had brought. But the local customs officials refused to release the pouches, on the basis that only mail addressed to agents of the shipping line, in this case the Hilkens, could be delivered without first passing through the U.S. Post Office.

Von Haimhausen was dumbfounded, since he knew that international protocol required that diplomatic mail be turned over on demand to representatives of the embassies for which it was intended. The diplomat protested, citing the protocol, but got nowhere, other than a grudging agreement from the official to send the problem up the line for a decision. Faced with bureaucratic intransigence, the diplomat decided to go to lunch, inviting Krapohl to join him.[1]

Late in the afternoon, the answer arrived from Washington, informing the local customs office that there was not only a protocol covering the issue but also a postal regulation stating that embassies could send and receive mail without going through the Post Office. At 1800 Krapohl and von Haimhausen left the EFCO warehouse with three diplomatic pouches and three sealed envelopes, which they delivered to von Bernstorff at the German summer embassy in Rye, New York.[2]

The brief flap over the status of diplomatic mail raised what was to many people a vastly more important question: Would the boat carry regular mail between the United States and Germany? As soon as the speculation and rumor that a cargo submarine was coming to a U.S. port became a reality, people began asking if the boat would carry mail. By April 1916 the British blockade had become essentially airtight, and the British resolve to deny all cargoes into or out of Germany, including mail, was a reality. The only way the new policy could be evaded was to send the mail by submarine.[3]

The exchange of regular mail was a very important issue to Germans on both sides of the Atlantic. Until the advent of the new British practice of searching and seizing mail, some Germans living in America had sent letters to addresses in Sweden, Denmark, or Norway, from which they were forwarded to Germany.

A very few with good connections gave their letters to sailors on board neutral ships that were bound for Amsterdam. The make-do solutions had become wholly inadequate even before the new British policy went into effect, which meant that communications were effectively ended for families in Germany and the United States who were desperate for news from and about their relatives.

The issue of mail service was equally important to American and German businessmen, as was their ability to send money in both directions. If the Germans were in fact going to operate a submersible freight line that could transport merchandise in both directions, there would have to be a mail service to go along with it. Banks especially needed a mail service, so that they could transfer money and send credits as needed.[4]

But operating a submarine mail service would entail high operating costs and high prices for postage.[5] The absence of an agreement between Germany and the United States was the real sticking point. Transoceanic mail routes were negotiated between the United States and countries that shipping lines represented. Countries that had transoceanic shipping lines had made international postal agreements covering every shipping line that carried mail to any place on the globe. But in 1916 there was no mail agreement between the United States and Germany for mail being carried on board ships belonging to the DOR. Therefore the *U-Deutschland* and the *U-Bremen* could carry diplomatic mail but not regular mail.

Many businessmen felt that lengthy negotiations to reach an agreement could be avoided by simply transferring the existing agreements covering Hamburg-America and Norddeutsche Lloyd to the DOR. The argument for such an emergency agreement was that all other German shipping lines were unable to fulfill the agreements because of the British blockade. It was a good idea, but that is not how it was done.[6]

In early October 1916, Germany and the United States opened negotiations for an agreement allowing the DOR to provide once-a-month mail runs, with a limit of eight hundred pounds for first-class mail. An agreement on those two points, frequency and weight, was quickly reached, but then the negotiations stalled on the issue of price. The United States was willing to pay the standard price of eighty cents per pound, but the Germans wanted eight dollars a pound and the right to carry the mail in specially made, hermetically sealed packages. This was because of the extreme dampness inside the boat, which would damage the mail, but the Americans said no. The Germans dropped the special packaging and upped the price to ten dollars a pound. The Americans said no. Finally both sides agreed on one dollar per pound, with the agreement to go into effect on 1 January 1917.[7]

Related to the subject of mail was the question of taking passengers, directly to Germany, on one of the U-boats. In principle it was a fair question, since many freighters were actually passenger-freighter ships. But if the question was fair, the application was entirely impractical. In the first place, there was no room on the *U-Deutschland* or the *U-Bremen* for a passenger. Prusse, although classed as a supercargo on the trip to Baltimore, had been a sort of passenger, but he was needed in Baltimore and so room had been made for him. Neither was there room for the mountains of luggage that transoceanic passengers typically took along.

And then there were the abominable conditions inside the boat—temperatures over 110 degrees, foul air, terrible food, and very little water. Despite anyone's wildest imaginings, the *U-Deutschland* was no luxury liner. Without enumerating all the drawbacks, Paul Hilken emphatically made the fact known that there would be no passengers taken on board the boat: "Under no circumstances will passengers be carried on the *U-Deutschland*. Not at any price." But people applied for passage anyway.

The first to get in line for seats on the boat were reporters. The EFCO office was "besieged with requests" from metropolitan newspapers that they be allowed to send representatives to Bremen on board the U-boat.[8] The requests were directed not only to EFCO but also to A. Schumacher and Norddeutsche Lloyd, since all three companies were closely associated with one another and the *U-Deutschland*. The Hilkens were the common factor. Norddeutsche Lloyd received requests from people who were willing to pay anywhere from $5,000 to $50,000. Karl Ahrendt, a clerk at NDL, told a *New York Times* reporter, "We have had letters from some persons who said they would pay any price we wanted."[9] The applicants fell into two categories, Germans who wanted to join the crew to return to Germany to serve the *Vaterland* at the front and well-heeled adventurers who wanted the thrill of travel by U-boat. It was the latter who were offering the huge sums of money for the privilege.

The fact that many people were asking for places on board the boat got back to Germany, where the kaiser suggested to Admiral Eduard von Capelle that accepting an American citizen as a crewman or a passenger might be a good idea. He believed that if an American were on board, the United States would extend protection to the U-boat. In a lengthy reply, Admiral von Capelle pointed out all the reasons that the kaiser's suggestion would not work. In the first place was the fact that the United States did not extend protection to Americans who crewed on board foreign ships.

Somehow the British learned about the kaiser's suggestion and, unlike Admiral von Capelle, they thought it was a great idea—from their viewpoint, that is. If an American, or anyone else for that matter, was taken on board as a passenger, that would give the British grounds to insist immediately that the boat's departure be blocked under the Lafollette-Seams Act, which required all ships carrying passengers to be equipped with lifeboats and davits, without which they would not be permitted to sail from a U.S. port. That would have been a clever ploy, but it would not have worked, because the Lafollette-Seams Act applied only to U.S.-flagged ships.

While the weighty issues of mail and passengers were being addressed, the mundane administrative tasks and the backbreaking work of off-loading cargo went on. König took the ship's manifest to the Customs House shortly after the

U-Deutschland had been made fast to the pier. While he was there he gave a prepared statement to the reporters who crowded the customs office. The prepared statement had nine points, the first of which was that the *U-Deutschland*'s visit was the first of many more to come; then followed assertions of the boat's peaceful and purely commercial nature. He told the crowd that the cargo consisted of "badly needed dyestuffs," and then rolled smoothly into the theme that Britain's "illegal" blockade violated the cherished principle of freedom of the seas. The voyage across the Atlantic was in the Hansa League tradition and demonstrated the fallacy of Britain's claim that it ruled the waves. He told the reporters that for security reasons he could not disclose any details about the trip across the Atlantic, but he assured them that in the future the DOR boats would carry mail.[10]

That afternoon, Captain König met with a *New York Times* reporter for an exclusive interview. The resulting article, which had no byline, was headlined, "Subsea Perils Bring Joy to Skipper; Wine Flows, Music Blares under Waves." Below that schmaltzy headline was a lightweight question-and-answer session in which the questions were tame and the answers were heavily laced with propaganda, both overt and subtle. There might even have been a fact or two. The interview demonstrated that Lohmann and company had picked the right man for the job, one who could charm, impress, and mislead with the smoothness of a maestro. The opening paragraph in the published article shows the effect that König had on the reporter.[11]

> Only the flashing lights that played in his clear blue eyes and the laughter that bubbled from his lips ordinarily stern-set gave a hint of Captain Koenig's tremendous feeling over the exploit of the submarine *U-Deutschland* which he commanded. . . . Discussing Shakespeare with facility as great as that with which he explained the workings of the deep-sea microphone. Speaking in excellent, carefully chosen English and gesturing hardly at all, Captain Koenig loomed large as the typical modern ocean adventurer.

Following a rundown of his career with Norddeutsche Lloyd, König sidestepped a question about his route across the Atlantic by answering, "I'm not in a position to give you full details. . . . Needless to say that we are quite unarmed and only a peaceful merchantman." When asked about conditions in Germany in light of the British blockade, he said that all Germans were confident of victory and that under Germany's "peaceful rule" thousands of acres in Poland and Kurland "had been put under the plow" and that the harvest would be the best in over a century.

When asked to tell "in detail" the extent of his "undersea" experience before he had been selected to command the *U-Deutschland,* he answered honestly, "But you see, I have not had any." The rest of the answer—which included, "We practiced after we went aboard"—made it sound as if his transition from commanding an ocean liner to commanding a U-boat had been accomplished through a sort of on-the-job training, provided by the company that hired him. The vague, rather general answers he gave were intended to conceal the truth that he had been trained in the Imperial German Navy's U-boat commanders school.

Next the reporter wanted to know when he had left Germany. He said, "We left Bremerhaven at noon on 18 June and proceeded quietly to Helgoland, and there we stayed for four days." Up to that moment, the official story had been that the boat had started her trip from Bremen on 23 June and had never entered Helgoland. It was a potentially embarrassing and trouble-provoking slip, but he got away with it.

In answer to the question "How many times did you dive?" he replied, "Once each day we submerged as a practice drill, and five times in the North Sea, six in the English Channel, and four in the open water." To make the story better, he told the reporter that they rested on the bottom of the Channel for ten hours, "snug and comfortable," listening to *Peer Gynt* and drinking champagne. Continuing, he said the *U-Deutschland* could run submerged for four days before having to surface and recharge the batteries. But if they simply rested on the bottom, they could remain down for "as long as our provisions held out." He was quoted as saying that the *U-Deutschland* could dive to fifty-fathoms (330 feet) "but [that] as a matter of fact we never went nearly that deep and probably never shall." It is possible that he said fifty meters (164 feet), which was the actual rated maximum depth for the boat, and the reporter wrote "fathoms."

One might ask why it was so important to convince people that they had passed through the English Channel and even rested on the bottom there for ten hours. Again, the reason is one word—propaganda. Going north about was obviously much safer than trying to pass through the Dover Straits and the English Channel, at the time the most heavily patrolled and netted waters in the world. Claiming to have safely taken the shorter but more difficult route drove home the assertion that Britain did not rule the waves—not even the Dover Straits and the English Channel.

Off-loading cargo started at 0820 on 11 July, using the boat's own cargo-handling equipment—two mast derricks, a type of hoist that consisted of a ten-foot mast and a twenty-three-foot boom with an electrically powered hook and was capable of hoisting up to 2,200 pounds. The dyestuffs were packed in 3,042 wooden boxes each measuring twelve inches square by fifteen inches high and weighing about 107 pounds. Because of the limited lifting capacity of the boat's derricks, each cargo net brought out twenty boxes, setting them on the pier.

African-American stevedores on the pier stacked the boxes on dollies and rolled them into the warehouse, where more African-American workers stacked them according to type. All the work on the pier and in the boat's two holds was done by African-Americans, while the boat's crewmen operated the derricks supervised the off-loading in the holds and the stacking inside the warehouse. Because the work was hard, the loads heavy, and the hours long, there were from

100 to 150 stevedores working in relays in the warehouse, on the pier, and in the holds handling, moving, and stacking boxes. It was an efficient operation, and the off-loading was finished on Thursday, 13 July, at 1100.[12]

While the stevedores and the *U-Deutschland*'s crewmen were moving cargo on 11 July, Captain König, together with the Hilkens and "several ladies," went to lunch at the Hotel Belvedere, where the Elks were holding their national convention. If, as is probable, the timing and place for the luncheon were picked to provoke a "spontaneous" ovation for König, the plan worked. As the König-Hilken party walked through the lobby, someone shouted, "There's the Captain. It's Captain König!" Suddenly the lobby was jammed with people trying to get close enough to shake the captain's hand. As the crowd pressed in, König backed into the dining room, where the band immediately struck up *Die Wacht am Rhein* and the crowd applauded. Obviously pleased with the reception, he sat down, only to leap back to his feet when the band struck up *The Star-Spangled Banner.* Throughout the anthem König stood at attention, and saluted when the band finished. The crowd loved it, and König scored one of the many public-relations victories that the *U-Deutschland*'s arrival and stay in Baltimore produced.

That same day, multimillionaire and philanthropist August Heckscher delivered a check for $10,000 to the home of Charles von Heimolt, the New York NDL manager. A letter accompanying the check asked Heimolt and his NDL associates to distribute the money among the entire *U-Deutschland* crew. The letter closed with Heckscher's "admiration for their gallantry, their seamanship, and their matchless courage." The check was made out to Norddeutsche Lloyd, so that evening Von Heimolt delivered $10,000 in cash to König, who gratefully accepted it, knowing that neither he nor any of the crew could accept the money, because they all still belonged to the Imperial German Navy. The solution to the problem was to turn Heckscher's generosity into another public-relations victory. That same night, the crew voted "unanimously" to turn the entire amount over to the German Red Cross to be used for "war relief work."[13]

On Wednesday 12 July, two more derricks were set up on the port side to start removing the boat's cast-iron ballast, which had been stowed in wet storage, between the casing and the pressure hull. The ballast would not be needed for the trip home, and the wet storage space was needed for the crude rubber that would go on board after all the dyestuffs were landed. The cast-iron ballast was loaded into the barge *George May.*

On 13 July the Baltimore Germania Club hosted a luncheon for the German ambassador, Count von Bernstorff, and Paul König. Von Bernstorff brought Hugo Schmidt (the American representative of Deutsche Bank in New York), Dr. Heinrich Albert (financial attaché to the Germania embassy), and Carl A. Lüderitz, the German consul in Baltimore—who at the time was under federal indictment for passport fraud. Paul and Henry Hilken were also in the party, as were Mayor James Preston and several of his fellow city officials.

As was to be expected, the luncheon was a media event, with König prominently featured in all the photographs. After lunch at the Germania Club the guests were loaded into cars and driven to the municipal pier, where they boarded the launch *Baltimore* for a trip across the harbor to the *U-Deutschland*. Press photographers were allowed to go along, but "only on the condition that they would not get off the launch," which anchored so that they had only a distant view of the submarine.

While the press fumed, Ambassador von Bernstorff and the others trooped down into the *U-Deutschland,* where the temperature was around 110 degrees. When von Bernstorff came up through the after hatch onto the casing deck, he was sweating profusely. He mopped his brow and said, "It must be a 110 down there. I pity those men who had to come across on her." But it appears that more came out of that luncheon than just good press for Captain König.[14]

An item appeared in the *New York Times* on 14 July that had all the earmarks of a deliberately planted story intended to whip up American outrage against the British but that might have had some truth to it. Its factual basis was a British investigation into the sources and buyers of the nickel waiting to go on board the *U-Deutschland*. Unknown to the public in general, but known to the Hilkens and the German embassy, was the fact that the Bureau of Investigation had also made an investigation into the suppliers of the nickel to determine if there had been a violation of the Neutrality Law.

The fact that the British wanted to know who the nickel suppliers and buyers were came as no surprise, because Canada was virtually the world's sole supplier of nickel, which gave Britain the ability to control who got it. Because the American steel industry bought nickel in huge quantities, the British and Canadian governments had pressured the American steel industry into an agreement with Canada at the start of the war not to allow American metals agents and factors to sell nickel to any of the Central Powers. But as we have seen, money talks, and the German commercial attaché, Dr. Albert, had been able to buy enormous amounts of nickel using dummy companies and domestic storage locations.[15]

But it was not just nickel that had the British upset; they did not want the Germans getting rubber, either. Though Britain essentially controlled the world's crude rubber trade, they had no direct control over the sale of South American rubber, and the possibility that a fleet of cargo U-boats would be able to supply Germany with all its rubber needs via the United States represented a serious threat. American businessmen who were in the business of selling rubber on the international market were fully aware of that, and they had well-founded concerns that Britain might do something to block America's trade in South American rubber.[16]

The fear among American rubber dealers was increased when the *New York Times* ran a story on 14 July claiming that the "allied nations" intended to carry out "relentless reprisals upon every American manufacturer, miner, or merchant who supplies cargo to a freight-carrying German transatlantic submarine." The source of this warning was reportedly a "responsible member of Mayor James Preston's official party" who had attended the luncheon at the Germania Club. The unidentified source told the reporter that his information had come to him "authoritatively," and that an "English official" had "vouched for its correctness." According to the anonymous source, the dealers who had sold the rubber that was going on board the *U-Deutschland* would be the first to suffer the reprisals.

The story sounded plausible, based on public knowledge that the British did maintain a growing blacklist of companies that did business with Germany or acted as fronts for other firms doing business with Germany. But it seems unlikely that the British would do something that was so obviously directed at the United States, since the last thing they wanted to do was shove the Americans into the German camp.[17]

The British had repeatedly rebuffed American requests to allow German dyes through the blockade to relieve American dye companies, which were "suffering from the want of dyestuffs."[18] Blocking trade with Germany was one thing, however; interfering with trade between neutral countries was something else, and there is no evidence that Britain ever considered interrupting America's rubber trade with South America. In any event, the story quickly faded, to be replaced by more pressing issues.

On Friday evening, König was the chief guest at yet another dinner, at the Baltimore Country Club, hosted by Paul Hilken and Mayor Preston. Also invited were Carl Lüderitz, German consul, a Swedish businessman, Sir John Hammer, and Axel von Eckermann, engineer of construction for the Swedish navy. For once, however, the dinner was not the high point of the day's news.

The event that overshadowed the dinner was a surprise visit by Vice President Thomas R. Marshall's wife, Lois, on board the *U-Deutschland* while the dinner was in progress. Lois Marshall and her parents, accompanied by a sizable contingent of friends and Secret Service, arrived unannounced in three cars at the EFCO warehouse after dark. The importance of the uninvited guests was immediately apparent to the gate guards, who summoned Hinsch to handle the problem. Hinsch was very affable and invited everyone on board the *Neckar,* where he ushered them into the promenade deck bar and had drinks and finger food served. He explained that he would be pleased to give Mrs. Marshall a tour of the boat but that the rest of the party would have to remain on the *Neckar.* They could, however, view the *U-Deutschland* from the promenade deck's railing.

While the parents and the others remained on board the *Neckar,* Hinsch gave Mrs. Marshall a tour of the *U-Deutschland,* inside and out. Hinsch said that despite the 110-degree temperature inside the boat Mrs. Marshall "expressed amazement at almost every turn." He told a reporter the next day that Lois Marshall was the only woman ever allowed on board the boat. Shortly after her visit, Lois Marshall sent Hinsch a signed photograph of herself, thanking him for "his courtesies."[19]

The next day, Christine Langenhan presented König with an inscribed silver loving cup, causing an uproar that dwarfed whatever outrage the *Times* article about possible British reprisals against American rubber merchants might have provoked. Christine Langenhan was a soprano who had been a member of the Royal Opera in Berlin before she married an American, Hugo Boucik, and moved to Philadelphia. When the *U-Deutschland* arrived in Baltimore she apparently felt the need to do something to express her German patriotism—and garner publicity at the same time. She had a sixteen-inch-high silver loving cup mounted on an ebony base inscribed with, "Presented to the conqueror of English prestige on the sea and to the commander of the first merchant submarine, the *U-Deutschland,* the Captain Paul König and his crew in commemoration and appreciation of their service by Christine Langenhan, Royal Opera singer, 15 July 1916."[20]

The inscription was not the cause of the uproar but the fact that the American flag provided its background. In 1916, Americans were very touchy about how their flag was used, especially pro-British Americans when the flag was used on something that was pro-German. On 18 July, a New York landscape artist, Frederick T. Blakeman, wrote to Secretary of State Robert Lansing quoting the inscription and pointing out that the "inscription sat in an American flag." He demanded to know, "Is not this an illegal use of this country's flag (the flag of a neutral country) and a direct slight to a friendly nation? Must this overt act be classed with the countless other unneutral acts by the Germans, violating the statutes of this country?"[21] He closed with an acknowledgment that Lansing was a busy man, but he strongly felt that "the misuse of our flag certainly should not be overlooked." Many Americans shared Mr. Blakeman's opinion and outrage.

The loading of the cargo started at 0915 on 14 July, while the last of the ballast was still being taken off. The first to go on board was 401 tons of crude rubber, stowed in the space between the hulls, followed by ninety tons of nickel on 17 July. On 19 July all loading was stopped so that two railroad tank cars could be rolled onto the pier and pump twenty-eight tons of diesel fuel into the *U-Deutschland's* fuel tanks.

That prompted an immediate howl from the pro-Allies faction that the boat was going to be an offshore gas station for U-boats. The proof was that König had said that he had fuel enough to get home without refueling; why did he need twenty-eight extra tons? König said that he took on board the extra fuel because American diesel oil was of a higher grade than he was getting in Germany. To make his point and to stifle the criticism he had twenty-eight tons of the German diesel pumped out of the *U-Deutschland's* fuel tanks and into the *Neckar's* on the 24th. The claim that American diesel was better than German diesel was pure public relations and showed König at his best when it came to flattering his hosts.

The real reason why *U-Deutschland* had taken on twenty-eight tons of fuel she did not need was because those twenty-eight tons were going into war boats when the *U-Deutschland* returned to Germany. And the real reason the extra fuel was pumped back into the *Neckar* was that Prusse had determined that the extra fuel was too heavy and negatively affected the boat's trim when added to the weight of the cargo.[22]

By 19 July there was already an expectation of imminent departure in the air; one headline declared, "Subsea Trader's Dash for the Sea Only Hours Away." There was also a burst of events that featured the crew. One gains the impression that these were farewell gestures. On 18 July Mayor Preston entertained half the crew with an outing that included "a long automobile ride through the environs of Baltimore and dinner at the Suburban Garden, where the band played *Die Wacht am Rhein.*" The mayor did the same for the other half of the crew the next day. At the same time eight members of the crew, including the steward Stucke, went to Washington, where they got a "tour of the White House." They did not meet President Wilson, but they were "allowed into the Oval Office, where they took turns sitting in the president's chair."[23]

The last of the nickel went on board at 2140 on Tuesday, 25 July, bringing the total nickel stowed to 376.3 tons. The boat was fully laden with 876.8 tons of cargo and ready for sea, but the *U-Deutschland* showed no signs of preparing to leave the McLean Pier. König had already overstayed the ten days he had said he would be in Baltimore, and the assumption was that the *U-Deutschland* was on the brink of leaving. She had been repainted, and the only other work observed was the shifting of some of the cargo to trim the boat.

The end of cargo handling opened the EFCO gate to a special visitor for whom Paul Hilken had made special arrangements. The visitor was Henry Reuterdahl, considered at the time the nation's foremost marine and naval artist. John N. "Jack" Wheeler had contacted Hilken about a special feature article on the *U-Deutschland* for Wheeler's newly established Bell Syndicate. Wheeler had asked Hilken if Reuterdahl could be allowed to sketch the interior of the *U-Deutschland* for a short technical article to be run in *Scientific American,* and Hilken agreed. Reuterdahl had a thorough understanding of naval construction and engineering, and the *U-Deutschland* article, which appeared in the 10 February 1917 issue of *Scientific American,* reflected that knowledge. Among the technical points he mentioned was the fact that German periscopes were far more advanced than what was being used in the American navy's submarines. He also reported, correctly, that the *U-Deutschland* required two minutes to get completely under. He also explained the details of the engine's air supply and described the onboard cargo-handling system, which featured "sockets in the casing at regular intervals." The amount of accurate technical information he provided the *Scientific American* readers exceeded by a wide margin anything that had been made public up to then.[24]

In contrast to Reuterdahl's factual report, the press had been running daily stories since 20 July on the fate that awaited the *U-Deutschland* outside the three-mile limit. If what the reporters said was true, the threat started in Baltimore and extended to the Capes in the form of an army of spies "so placed as to report the passage of the *U-Deutschland*" to the warships offshore.

The offshore threat was described as a "cordon of hostile warships estimated at eight to ten miles out." The offshore fleet was supposed to be not only huge but equipped with airplanes, submarines, and high-speed patrol boats. According to several accounts, the cruiser armada waiting out of sight was kept advised of the *U-Deutschland's* status by light signals from a flotilla of small craft that hung around the Capes at night. Some were of the opinion that the cruisers that could be seen from shore were scouts for the much larger, out-of-sight fleet farther out to sea, which somehow confirmed for the press that the unseen fleet was equipped with fast patrol boats, submarines, and airplanes.

As for the cruisers that were seen, only two were ever named, the French light cruiser *Condé* and the British auxiliary cruiser HMS *Caronia*. The reporters might have been right about the *Condé,* whose odd four-stack arrangement was easily recognizable, but in July 1916 the *Caronia* was in Liverpool being disarmed and readied for return to Cunard.[25]

On 21 July, Ambassador von Bernstorff, apparently believing that where there is smoke there is fire, asked the State Department to "give the *U-Deutschland* protection within the three-mile limit." He wrote that "it is to be expected that our enemies will attack her within this limit unless protection is given by the American Navy." The State Department declined to provide a convoy, on the grounds that it was unnecessary.[26]

Though the press was overstating the threat to the *U-Deutschland,* some of the newspaper reports caught the State Department's attention, especially one that several fishermen had ordered large, heavy nets that they were going to use to snare the submarine. On 26 August the State Department asked the Treasury Department to look into a report that the British warships had hired American fishermen to "assist them in apprehending the merchant submarine *U-Deutschland*." The investigation that followed lasted until 29 September and concluded that the whole affair had been media hype. There were no offshore signalers, no trackers, and no fishing boats equipped with nets to snare the U-boat.

But on 26 July there was a report that a British cruiser had actually entered the Capes and steamed into the Chesapeake.[27] The battleship USS *Louisiana* (BB 19) was anchored in Lynnhaven Bay when an unidentified ship passed her at 0230. The weather was "thick," and the strange ship was not clearly seen, but she was displaying "two man-o-war lights aft." The *Louisiana* challenged the vessel, which replied by blinker "British cruiser" and disappeared, "apparently standing up the channel toward Hampton Roads." A search the following morning revealed nothing, and the *Louisiana's* captain believed that the ship had gone back out through the Capes in the dark.[28]

The Navy Department passed the *Louisiana's* report to the State Department, which asked the Treasury Department to look into the matter. The Norfolk collector of customs, Norman R. Hamilton, contacted the Virginia pilots who had been on duty during the night. They replied that an American warship had entered at about 0200 but had not requested a pilot. The only other ship they had seen was the U.S. transport *Sumner,* which entered later.

Though the investigation proved inconclusive, the fact was that since the start of the war in Europe British and French warships had frequently violated U.S. territorial waters. While it is a matter of record that British warships repeatedly crossed the three-mile limit to stop ships or to check them out, it is difficult to believe that a British cruiser captain would take his ship through the Capes and head toward Hampton Roads. In doing so, he would have to pass the Norfolk Naval Yard and the naval base at Newport News.[29]

So, what was out there, waiting for the *U-Deutschland?* In terms of a serious antisubmarine threat, there was very little. The British 4th Cruiser Squadron was assigned to the North America and West Indies Station, commanded by Vice Admiral Sir George Patey, with his headquarters at Halifax, Nova Scotia. The squadron consisted of five armored cruisers—HMS *Suffolk, Lancaster, Essex, Berwick,* and *Bristol*—and two light cruisers. The squadron was divided into two divisions, one operating out of Halifax and the other out of Jamaica. The French had provided two cruisers to the force, *Condé* and *Descartes.* The 4th Cruiser Squadron's task was to protect shipping against German surface raiders and enforce the blockade.

Those eight ships covered the Caribbean, the Gulf of Mexico, and the waters off the Eastern Seaboard from Key West to Halifax. The force available to intercept the *U-Deutschland* consisted of two cruisers stationed three to six miles southeast of the Ambrose Channel Lightship to monitor ships approaching and leaving New York. The station ships rotated in and out of Halifax every two weeks.[30]

Despite the daily reports that the *U-Deutschland* was only moments away from leaving, nothing about her or the people associated with her changed. On 22 July Prusse, Klees, and Machinist Johann Kissling started a three-day job of removing and replacing all the boat's alloy engine bearings and steel machinery gears with American-made bronze bearings and gears. While they worked through the weekend the radioman, Geilenfeld, had the masts raised so that he could set the chronometer, and on Saturday night König and eighteen of the crew attended a Red Cross bazaar at the Cannstatter Park that attracted a crowd of "more than 10,000 Germans and Austrians." The day after the bazaar a Baltimore group associated with a Bremen-based group called *Verein für das Deutschtum im Ausland* gave each member of the crew an Iron Cross ring.[31]

When König requested clearance for departure on 26 July he told Ryan that he would have an American in the crew, but he did not provide a name. Why he said that is not known, because even if he really was going to sign on an American, there was no opening available. And anyone he did sign on would be untrained in operating something as complex as a submarine. Maybe, like the kaiser, he thought that having even an unqualified American as a crew member would afford an extra level of protection to the boat and avoid any issues stemming from carrying a passenger. In any event, it did not happen, and on the evening of 27 July König caught Ryan in the customs office after hours and told him there would be no American on board.[32]

The day after the clearance papers were issued, a gaggle of politicians—a delegation of the congressional Rivers and Harbors Committee, led by Representative J. Charles Linthicum of Maryland—showed up at the pier wanting a tour of the boat. They met with König and Hinsch at the front gate, where König told them that no visitors were being admitted to the pier or on board the U-boat but that if Hinsch agreed they could go on board the *Neckar* and look down at the submarine from the rail. He then gestured to Hinsch, who stepped forward and politely told them no, explaining that he regretted the decision but that "circumstances would not allow it." Disappointed, they left, the last applicants for admission to the boat.

Even with his clearance papers in hand, König did not put to sea, and the press worked overtime trying to figure out why the boat was still tied up to the McLean Pier. Some thought he was waiting for the *U-Bremen* to arrive, because it had been widely reported on 16 July that "Captain König had said, or rather intimated, that he would be here when the *U-Bremen* . . . arrived." On the 18th it was reported that the *U-Bremen* was due "anytime," and on 20 July it was stated positively that the *U-Bremen* was bound for Baltimore. Four days later König was described as "waiting anxiously for word of the safety or arrival in Boston or some other Eastern port of the long expected submarine *Bremen*." On the 25th König and the crew were reported to be displaying "ill-disguised anxiety over the non-arrival" of the *U-Bremen*. In fact, however, at the time the press was describing Koenig's "anxiety" about the absence of the *U-Bremen,* she was undergoing her acceptance trials in the Baltic.

On Saturday 29 July it was reported that the cruisers had moved farther out to sea because of heavy weather. The crew's personal gear was back on board the *U-Deutschland,* the cargo was stowed, her freshwater tanks were filled, and the machinery was in perfect shape. The *U-Deutschland* was, as she had been since the 25th, in all respects ready for sea. But literally in a flash, the anticipation of her departure was put on hold. The Baltimore sabotage cell struck again.

The Black Tom munitions depot on the New Jersey shore exploded with a force equivalent to that of an earthquake measuring between 5.0 and 5.5 on the Richter Scale. The blast was heard ninety miles away, and shrapnel and debris was hurled over a mile. Windows were shattered up to twenty-five miles away, and some Marylanders were shaken awake by what they thought was an earthquake. Freight cars, warehouses, barges, tugboats, and piers were completely destroyed. *Johnson Barge No. 17,* loaded with 100,000 pounds of TNT, was vaporized, along with its captain, who was sleeping on board. Remarkably, only two other people were killed, though hundreds were injured. Property damage was estimated at $20 million, which today would be about $422 million. Initially it was believed that a fire was started by smudge pots that two of the night watchmen had lit to keep mosquitoes away. The two were arrested but soon released when it became evident that smudge pots had not caused the explosion.

Michael Kristoff, who had been Hinsch's traveling companion and flunky in January, soon came under suspicion. At the time of the explosion he had been working for Tidewater Oil Company and living with his aunt, Anna Rushnak, in Bayonne, New Jersey. After the explosion she heard Kristoff asking himself, "What I do? What I do?" Concerned, Anna consulted her daughter, Lulu Chapman, who had been Kristoff's landlady at one time and thought he was strange. They decided to tell their friend Captain John J. Rigney, of the Bayonne Police. Lulu Chapman told Rigney that when Kristoff was living in her house she had seen a letter that he was writing to someone named Graentor, demanding money he was owed. Graentor was, of course, Hinsch, though neither the women nor the police knew that. The police arrested Kristoff, who told them that his only contact with Germans had been some time earlier when he carried bags for them. In the end the Bayonne police decided that Kristoff was either dimwitted or crazy but in either case harmless, and they released him.[33]

Was Michael Kristoff the man who caused the Black Tom explosion? Probably, but there is some doubt. He was slow-witted to the degree that the judges on the Mixed Claims Commission did not believe he could have done it alone. But they did believe that it was probable that Hinsch and Kristoff had been involved, and Kristoff always maintained that he had done it with two other men. For many years, and still today, there are people who believe that the other two men were Kurt Jahnke and Lother Witzke, both of whom were experienced saboteurs working for Sektion Politik. At one point Witzke supposedly told an American undercover agent that he was involved, but he later denied it. The Mixed Claims Commission determined that neither Jahnke nor Witzke had been on the East Coast when Black Tom blew up.

The fact that Kristoff was asking for money owed by Graentor would lead one to believe that there was a connection to Black Tom. In any event, Michael Kristoff died of tuberculosis at Staten Island Hospital in 1928. When his body was exhumed in connection with the Mixed Claims Commission investigation the authorities found that the clothing and identification were his but that the corpse's teeth did not match Kristoff's prison dental records.[34]

On 30 July, while the fires were still burning at Black Tom, the Baltimore collector of customs, Ryan, agreed to assign the Coast Guard harbor tug *Wissahickon* to "supervise the submarine's departure under the same authority that it provides patrols for yacht races." The decision undercut the State Department's decision not to provide an escort, but Ryan was acting in response to König's concern about the horde of press, camera, and tourist boats he expected when he made the trip down the Chesapeake Bay.[35]

8

The Triumphant Return

1–24 AUGUST 1916

A small crowd had gathered at the EFCO warehouse just after sunup on Tuesday, 1 August, to watch the *U-Deutschland* leave Baltimore. On the water there were two press boats, the yacht *Valiant* and the speedboat *Esperanza,* tied up at the nearby Page Engineering Company pier, and a half-dozen private powerboats anchored near the dolphin at the entrance to the *U-Deutschland's* berth. The people in the boats had a good view of the *U-Deutschland,* because the barge *George May* had been towed away to a new location, leaving the boat fully exposed on her port side. Only the log boom remained in place to keep boats away. The *Timmins* was alongside the pier in the space between the *U-Deutschland's* bow and the inland end of the pier.[1]

At 0630 the company launch, *EFCO,* and the tug *Timmins* rigged a heavy net between them and steaming abreast proceeded to "drag the river leading out into the channel for a mile from the moorings of the *U-Deutschland.*" The precaution underscored the fact that Hilken and König took the threats they had read about in the papers seriously. König was also convinced that British sympathizers in boats would attempt to harm the boat in some way.

As the day dragged on, the shore crowd changed as new people arrived and the early birds left. Downriver there were other small groups waiting along the banks of the Patapsco, and a few more powerboats joined those anchored off the dolphin. Many of the hopeful sightseers had brought lunches or snacks, and as the sun passed noon the open field behind the warehouse looked like a picnic ground. As the afternoon lengthened, the crowd grew and pressed closer to the water, hoping for a better view.

Around noon the reporters and cameramen from Washington and New York who had chartered the yacht *Valiant* got a shock when Acting Deputy Collector Thalheimer told the owner of the yacht, Edward Toulson, that he could not carry passengers for pay because his vessel was not registered at the customshouse. Toulson exploded. He said that he had tried to register the boat several years earlier and had been told it was not necessary, and he had been carrying passengers ever since. Thalheimer was adamant—no paying passengers.

The New York and Washington reporters were panicked; it was too late to charter another boat, and without a boat they were literally "up a creek." The worst part of the situation was that owner of the speedboat *Esperanza,* Dr. R. T. Somers, had five local reporters on board as his guests, and they were going to scoop the out-of-towners unless another boat could be found. Toulson called his attorney, and the reporters "burned up the wires" trying to get the *Valiant* released.

By midafternoon, the order still stood and things looked bleak for everyone on board the *Valiant* until Toulson was struck with a brilliant idea. He would not take paying passengers, he would take guests. He told the reporters, "All I ask is you will sign an affidavit that I did not accept money from you." The reporters rushed to sign the paper; Toulson told them, "I'll even buy the gas."

Finally at 1600 there was activity on board the *Neckar;* men carrying what looked like seabags were coming on deck and descending the ladder to the pier. A few minutes later the Coast Guard harbor tug *Wissahickon* arrived and stood off, using her engine to maintain position. Ashore and in the small-craft fleet expectations rose. But there was still doubt that the actual departure was about to begin. Several minutes later the Harbor Police patrol launch *Lannan* was seen approaching the berth, and the odds got better. But the time dragged on, and the presence of several "ladies" on the *Wissahickon* led many to believe that the Coast Guard tug and the police boat were just sightseers. Expectations dropped.

The opinion spread that Captain König was waiting for the sun to set so that he could make his getaway under cover of darkness. They were close to being right, but the real reason was that he was waiting for the onset of the flood tide. The wind was out of the north, which worked against the tide coming up the Patapsco, and König felt that he needed the high water to get safely across the shoal where the river joined the Chesapeake.

As the afternoon turned to evening, the shore crowd began to thin, and one or two motorboats fired up and left. The time dragged until a few minutes before 1700, when the *EFCO* pulled into the berth, passed a line to the log boom, and towed the barrier clear of the berth. Expectations soared. As soon as the log boom was clear, the *Wissahickon* moved into the berth and was warped alongside the *Timmins,* to which she rafted. The police boat quickly backed in and rafted to the *Wissahickon.* The Coast Guard officers, customs men, the *Timmins'* captain, Hinsch, König, and Hilken held a discussion on the tug's quarterdeck.

At 1730 the police boat pulled away from the Coast Guard tug and moved out of the berth into the stream. The *Wissahickon* took a line from the *U-Deutschland,* shoved off from the *Timmins,* and moved across the berth, paying out the line to keep it slack. The *Timmins* left the pier, moved past the *U-Deutschland,* and took a line from her stern. The *Wissahickon* took up the slack and pulled the *U-Deutschland's* bow away from the pier, while the *Timmins* did the same with the stern. When the *U-Deutschland* was clear of the pier, the *Wissahickon* cast off her line and the *Timmins* pulled the boat stern first into the stream. Accompanied by the cheers from a small crowd at the foot of Andre Street and the blasts and hoots of steam whistles and sirens, the *U-Deutschland* engaged her engines, swung her bow downriver, and got under way.

One reporter noted, "It was an impressive sight. The sun was setting in a clear western sky and the twilight silhouetted the ships against the waters as the little craft was started on its way." Adding to the display was the *Neckar,* fully dressed, the imperial German flag flying from her trunk, and the international code flags for "Homebound, Good Luck" flying from the signal halyard. The *Neckar* crew lined the rails shouting good wishes.

As expected, the trip down the Patapsco started out looking like a river parade. The Baltimore police boat was an early dropout, because it soon reached its jurisdictional limit, and most of the small boats dropped off before they reached the river mouth, leaving only the two press boats and the *Wissahickon*. At 1900 the *Valiant* and the *Wissahickon* turned back, leaving only the *Timmins* and the press boat *Esperanza* to continue. König later remarked on the speed and agility of the speedboat, which he described as "a sort of overgrown racing boat." Despite efforts by the *Timmins* to run the boat off, it stayed, making frequent circles around the tug and the U-boat. As night fell the press boat "hung out its lights" and followed astern. Despite the darkness, the press boat persisted and was still with the *U-Deutschland* when the little convoy passed the Severn River mouth at 2045.

By 2200, as they approached Sharp's Island, the wind had risen and a "pretty neat little sea was underway." At that point the press boat broke away and vanished into the night. It was now just the *Timmins* and the *U-Deutschland*. They passed Sharp's Island at 2245 and were off Cove Point an hour later. If the times of the reported sightings at those positions are correct, König had been making about ten knots since leaving Baltimore. Approaching Sharp's Island, the two vessels encountered "a great number of fishing trawlers," which raised concerns in König's mind that he might be running into a trap. He was still spooked by the dire warnings the press had made about fleets of pro-British fishermen. Instead, his passage was greeted with cheers and whistles, which he soon discovered were coming from a group of well-wishers.

At 0600 on 2 August the *U-Deutschland* was alone, and König took the opportunity to make two test dives in a spot where his chart showed a depth of thirty meters, about ninety-eight feet. He later wrote that he did it "to get the crew and the boat once more well in hand." Given that he was in a busy traffic lane, one wonders why he felt the need to do it. The U-boat had already conducted six test dives at the McLean Pier to ensure that the boat was in proper trim, which it was. He was going to do, as he had alongside the pier, what was called a "stationary dive," or as Simon Lake called it, an "even keel dive." The boat had no forward way and simply went straight down like an elevator. The first dive was shallow, just deep enough to get the boat completely under.

The second dive was intended to set the boat on the bottom, "to see that everything else was tight and in good order." He already knew the boat was tight and in good order, and setting her on the bottom would not reveal any problems that a normal full submergence would not have revealed, unless he was testing the pressure hull at its maximum rated depth. The dive started normally, but at thirty meters, where he expected to feel a "slight bump" telling him they had touched bottom, there was nothing. The boat continued to sink, passing forty, and then forty-five meters, causing König to wonder aloud, "The depth of the Chesapeake Bay must have some limit." The limit was reached at fifty meters, about 164 feet, which was the hull's rated limit.

König went down the ladder into the central control to discuss the situation with his two watch officers and Klees. The consensus was that the hull was tight and that surfacing from fifty meters was no different than surfacing from thirty meters. So König climbed back into the conning tower, where according to his book he saw the dial on a magnetic box compass spinning madly on its axis. He immediately concluded that the boat was actually rotating around its vertical axis. One must ask three questions at this point. What was a magnetic box compass doing inside a steel conning tower on a boat equipped with four three-axis gyro-compasses? How could the boat, with its hull sunk into the mud, rotate on its own vertical axis? And if it was rotating, what was making it rotate?

In any event, the next problem was that the pumps, though they ran as they should, ran dry and were not pumping water out of the ballast tanks. The boat "continued to stick in the mud and did not move an inch." Now they discovered that they were "sinking deeper into the mud, but the revolving motion had ceased and the boat lay perfectly quiet." Finally, Klees fixed whatever the pump problem was, and the boat started to rise. But the depth gauge showed forty-nine meters one moment and then twenty meters another. Despite the severity of their situation "a stony calm prevailed in the boat." At that critical moment, Klees suddenly saw the solution and "darted for a lever." Compress air hissed, and the dial "made a wild kick to 120 meters" and resettled on forty-nine. The compressed air had blown out a plug of mud from the "opening in the manometer." For good measure, Klees blew out the exhaust pipes too.[2]

Is the account given in his book, *Voyage of the* Deutschland, fictitious? To some degree yes, but he probably did make the shallow test dive. The only spot that deep in Chesapeake Bay is near the Bloody Point Light, a position that he should have reached at about 2330 on 1 August. So, in addition to the fantasy of the stuck-in-the-mud episode, his book's timing is off, in that he puts it at 0600, about seven hours after he passed Bloody Point.[3] To be fair to König, he did not actually write the book that bears his name as author. The writer was Dr. Ernst Bischoff, a journalist whom the German foreign office assigned to ghostwrite the book based on newspaper stories, a talk with Paul König, and the boat's log. It was Bischoff's job to add the drama and heroic parts to the story.

By the time she passed Solomon's Island at 0200 on 2 August, the *U-Deutschland's* speed was down to about seven knots. It was dusk as she approached the south end of the Chesapeake Bay, and the sea was building outside the Capes. As the boat passed the channel lightship, eighteen nautical miles from the Cape Henry light, crew members moved about the deck securing the radio masts and making a final inspection. Then they all disappeared below. The *Louis Feuerstein,* a press boat with two *New York Times* reporters and two movie cameramen on board, had been waiting eighteen hours for the *U-Deutschland* to come into view and had nearly given up when its passengers spotted her at 1900. One reporter opined:

> The *U-Deutschland,* through accident, through some superior calcu-lation, or through some mysterious design on the part of her allied enemies had a clear gateway to the Atlantic. . . . [W]hile the sea grew more menacing it was evident that the submarine had cho-sen the most ideal night for her going. It was after eight-o-clock and the *U-Deutschland* was still moving seaward. From that direction there still came not the slightest intimation of any lookout for the out-coming submarine. There was neither sight nor sound of the motor patrol boats or the aeroplanes the Allies had repeatedly been declared to have in evidence.

And there was no offshore armada. The previous day, passengers on board the coastal steamer SS *Fair Wind* told reporters in Norfolk that they had seen only one warship off the coast. By the time the U-boat started through the Capes, the storm outside had become a howling northeaster that had forced many outbound vessels to turn back. At 2035 the *U-Deutschland,* trimmed down so that her decks were awash, her running lights off, vanished into the storm.

On the day that the *U-Deutschland* passed through the Capes, a Royal Navy spokesman told a *Washington Post* overseas reporter in London that though it was the intention of the Royal Navy to "to arrest her if we can, we are not making any extraordinary plans to catch the *U-Deutschland,* although the Germans would like to believe so."

In a practical sense, the British were helpless to stop the U-boat from return-ing to Bremen unless they got awfully lucky and the *U-Deutschland* got awfully unlucky. Like the flap over the claim that the British had hired American fish-erman to help trap the *U-Deutschland,* the tales of an offshore armada equipped with airplanes, fast motorboats, and submarines was pure media hype concocted to sell papers. The story has, however, become one of the enduring myths about the *U-Deutschland.*[4]

The moment he crossed the three-mile limit, König ordered the boat down to sixty feet. According to his book, "the most dangerous moment of the entire voyage was approaching." He was sure that American fishermen were out there with their nets deployed, hoping the *U-Deutschland* would foul them and so be halted. It's even been suggested that the Germans' paranoia, and the press' need for drama, caused both groups to overlook a more plausible reason for the

American fishermen's behavior. Maybe the Americans were not intent on netting the *U-Deutschland* to stop her; it could be that all they wanted was to snag her so they could put in claims for damaged nets. In the end the whole thing was pure hyperbole, because there was no one out there waiting for the *U-Deutschland* with or without nets. Despite what was written in *The Voyage of the* Deutschland about nets and "English ships racing up and down jerking their searchlights across the waters," while the *U-Deutschland* was at times "within the radius of their shadows," the boat was never in danger of being sunk by an enemy warship or an American fisherman. There simply was no one out there.

The news that the *U-Deutschland* had left Baltimore reached Germany on 2 August and appeared in the papers the following day. The nation was elated; there was almost universal confidence that she would make the crossing safely. The international news agency Reuters, which had sent the report, erred by saying that the *U-Deutschland* had left on 30 July, two days earlier than she did. Based on the reported departure date, the German navy notified Helgoland to expect the boat on or about 19 August. On the day the Reuters report appeared in Germany's newspapers, the *U-Bremen* was nine days away from being accepted for service. Nevertheless, plans were made for her to meet the *U-Deutschland* in Helgoland so that König could brief Schwartzkopf on what to expect during his Atlantic crossing and arrival in the United States.

The *U-Deutschland*'s departure from Baltimore released Hilken to resume his direct involvement in the cell's sabotage operations and to catch up on matters that had been ignored. One of the more pressing Sektion Politik matters that needed his attention was the expansion of sabotage activities into Argentina. On 7 August he cabled John A. Arnold in Havana. Arnold was a German national whom Sektion Politik had assigned to Argentina for the purpose of spreading anthrax and glanders among horses and cattle being shipped to the Allies. Hilken was to be his paymaster. On 7 August Arnold was passing through Havana, and there Hilken's cable reached him. The cable told Arnold that Hilken was unable to meet him in Havana but would send Fred Herrmann in his place, describing Herrmann as "a trustworthy representative . . . who has been in the employ of our friends abroad." The friends abroad were Nadolny and Marguerre at Sektion Politik in Berlin.

The cable and subsequent communications between the two German agents show that handling the American end of the submarine freight line was taking more time than Hilken could afford and still devote full time to sabotage. While the boat was in Baltimore, he had been forced to rely heavily on Herrmann and Hinsch to keep the sabotage operations moving along.[5]

The trip back across the Atlantic was without incident. König remarked again about being in the "hot, humid atmosphere and turbid air of the Gulf Stream," and the stifling heat it caused inside the hull. Toward sundown on an evening while they were still in the Gulf Stream, the lookouts became complacent and allowed a steamer to come down on them on a reciprocal course. The ship was rapidly approaching, bow on, when the lookouts woke up and shouted the alarm. The helm was put over hard to port, the rapid ventilating valves were opened wide, and the *U-Deutschland* wallowed down into the deep without a moment to spare.

They stayed down an hour, and as they rose toward the surface, König peered through the glass ports to see "an incandescent medium of luminous transparency." When they came to the surface it was already dark. König told of experiencing a "sea-illumination of dæmonian unreality," adding that "we had gone down in the depths in dark water and emerged in a sea of flames." Looking aft, the men on the bridge saw the steamer "slipping like a great dark shuttle through this flaming element." From the conning tower they looked out over a phosphorescent glow of an intensity no one on the bridge had seen before.[6]

The blessing was that the heavy seas eased as they approached the outer limits of the Gulf Stream, but the respite did not last long. Once out of the Gulf Stream they ran into a "stiff northwester and a heavy sea" that lasted two days and put the crew through all the miseries that they had experienced on the trip over. It was the same old story of "turret-high" seas that swept over the boat and made life inside the pressure hull pure hell. Fortunately the bad weather was short-lived, and on the third day they had fair skies and reasonably smooth seas. Life returned belowdecks, and the crew came out on deck.

They enjoyed fair weather for several days, and they saw, on the evening of 13 August, only one other ship, which turned out to be the White Star liner RMS *Olympic,* the *Titanic's* sister ship, rushing westward. König changed course to move away from the liner's path but remained on the surface while the crew took turns coming on deck to watch the giant pass by.[7] It was a sight to behold. The *Olympic* was slightly shorter than the ill-fated RMS *Titanic* but almost identical in appearance. After the *Olympic* faded from view the trip settled into a "peaceful, uneventful mercantile voyage" that allowed König the opportunity to read Jules Verne's *Twenty Thousand Leagues under the Sea* for the first time. A friend he made in Baltimore had given him the book, which turned out to be an edition for "young people."

The good weather continued as the U-boat came closer to the British Isles, and outbound traffic increased. She remained outside the regular shipping lanes, so that the ships they did see were in the distance. Nevertheless, the ever-cautious König changed course each time to give the ships wider berths. The only notable event he recorded was a day on which the U-boat entered a debris field littered with floating fifty-gallon oil drums. "Everywhere, as far as the eye could reach, the sea was covered with a field of black oil-barrels, through which we were forced to worm our way." The similarity to a minefield was obvious, causing Krapohl to comment, "This is fine practice," referring to the constant course changes that König was making as they passed through the barrels.

The fine weather ended as they drew closer to St. Kilda; dense fog that lay heavily on the surface forced the *U-Deutschland* to reduce speed to a crawl. Because the boat was now in the area that was heavily patrolled and visibility was greatly reduced, the crew was kept at diving stations, and the boat was trimmed down in readiness for a quick dive. They did see what they thought was a British light cruiser, and König had the boat trimmed down lower, but the cruiser was never a serious threat. As soon as the enemy ship moved away, König brought the boat up so that just the decks were awash. Not long after seeing the cruiser, they saw another patrol vessel that was much closer and forced them to dive. An hour later König brought the boat to periscope depth and extend the periscope for a look around and saw still another patrol vessel. He took the boat down to fifty feet and settled in for a long submerged run.

The fog persisted as they rounded Scotland, adding more time to their passage, which raised concerns in Helgoland that the *U-Deutschland* might have run into trouble. On 15 August naval headquarters in Berlin radioed to Kiel asking if *U-200* would pass through the Kattegat between Denmark and Sweden and wanting to know when she was expected in German waters. Apparently the *Admiralstab* believed that the *U-Deutschland* was going to return to Kiel instead of Bremen. Room 40 intercepted and decoded the message but probably did not associate it with the *U-Deutschland,* because of the *U-200* identification, which had been the *U-Deutschland's* hull number during construction. But the British analysts must have known something was up, because at the time the highest-numbered U-boat in service was *U-81*.[8]

They surfaced at noon to find that they were alone under overcast skies and facing a building sea. They had a messy, uncomfortable trip down through the North Sea, but they made better time, because they were able to remain on the surface and run at about ten knots. Based on the incorrect departure-date information, Berlin believed the *U-Deutschland* was now six days behind, causing concern and doubt to grow in the capital and Helgoland, a state of affairs that was kept out of the press. It was then 21 August, the *U-Deutschland* was two days out of Helgoland, when König and his crew had their scare.

Eyring was the officer of the deck, and after one look to confirm the sighting he whistled down the speaking tube for the captain to come to the bridge. It was about 2000, and König had been working on the report he would submit to the navy about the cruise. He hurried up onto the conning tower and saw through the mist and rain "a whole circle of white lights surrounding the horizon." He ordered a turn to starboard and saw more lights ahead. His immediate thought was that they had blundered into a trap and were surrounded. He was on the verge of ordering a dive when one of the lookouts said that some of the vessels were getting closer. All the bridge glasses were trained in the new direction, and there was a collective sigh of relief. The lights were the masthead lights of a fleet of Dutch herring loggers.

At 0600 on 2 August the *U-Deutschland* was approximately 210 nautical miles northwest of Helgoland when she encountered the outbound *UB-35,* under the command of *Oberleutnant zur See* Rudolf Gebeschus. The *UB-35* was a newly commissioned Type II UB-boat assigned to the High Seas Fleet and based at Helgoland. She was on her first war patrol. When the two boats saw each other, each initially assumed the other to be an enemy submarine; König started to dive while Gebeschus prepared to torpedo the *U-Deutschland.* Fortunately Gebeschus ordered recognition signals hoisted as he maneuvered the *UB-35* into firing position. König recognized them and had his own recognition flags hoisted in the nick of time. The two boats came alongside one another and exchanged greetings, information, and small talk before going their separate ways—"we to our homecoming and they to their work," König later said.

Nearly fourteen hours later, when the *U-Deutschland* was west of Sylt, in the Friesen Islands, and about ninety nautical miles northwest of Helgoland, she reported her position to the naval base. During the three-minute transmission, she asked about minefields and requested an escort. Room 40 copied the lengthy transmission, but it was much too late for the British to use the information. Nine and a half hours later, at 0500 on 23 August, she entered Helgoland and went alongside the *U-Bremen.*[9]

The stop in Helgoland was made so that König could brief Schwartzkopf on what to expect during the Atlantic crossing and on his arrival in the United States. With Schwartzkopf fully briefed and the writer Ernst Bischof on board, the *U-Deutschland* cast off and proceeded to the Hoheweg Light, just outside the Weser mouth in what the Germans call the *Ausserweser,* where she dropped anchor for the night.[10]

In the meantime, the news of the *U-Deutschland's* arrival was telegraphed to the Bremen City Hall, setting in motion the plans for a grand reception. Messengers were sent out to individually contact the families of the crewmen so that they could be at the dockside when their sons, husbands, and relatives stepped off the boat. The city's bells rang throughout the afternoon of 23 August, announcing to the entire city that the *U-Deutschland* was returned and would arrive in Bremen any day. Special editions of the newspapers went to press with the glad news and a schedule for the official homecoming. The news spread quickly beyond the city limits, attracting thousands from the surrounding countryside to Bremen.[11]

On 25 August at 0500 the pilot came on board, bringing mail for the crew. But there was more to getting under way that morning than simply hoisting the anchor. The plans for the *U-Deutschland's* triumphant return had been made with all the effort and attention to detail of a major campaign. The timetable called for the boat to arrive in Bremen's Free Harbor II at Shed 18 precisely at noon, but the boat had to be readied first. From about 0600 to 0900 the crew was occupied with dressing ship and hoisting various signal flags, raising the radio masts, and hoisting the DOR company flag and the American flag to the tops of the masts, the U.S.

➤ The *U-Deutschland* arriving in her berth 10 July 1916. It was raining lightly when she arrived. *Author's collection*

flag forward and the DOR flag aft. In truly German fashion, a large bouquet of roses was fastened to the mast beside the American flag. The crewmen then went below to don clean uniforms and foul-weather gear.

The sky was lead grey and it was raining when the boat started its fourteen-nautical-mile trip upriver. For the first two miles of the trip the *U-Deutschland* had the river largely to herself, in part because of the relatively early hour but mostly because the "decorated fleet of press and official steamers" was assembled two miles upriver. But even at this early point there was the "usual assortment of holiday river traffic of rowboats and canoes" that would be a feature along the entire route. But once the *U-Deutschland* reached the twelve-mile point and picked up her welcoming escort, the riverbanks were packed with cheering crowds.

There were thousands of people lining the shores along the twelve-mile route. All the schools in the Bremen area were closed for the day, and the crowds were enormous. The press reported "that many bare-legged boys stood knee-deep in water to see the *U-Deutschland* pass" and that the bridges spanning the Weser were "black with humanity." Once under way, with the *U-Deutschland* in the lead and her escorts trailing, the parade took on the air of a Roman triumph. That probably was not the planners' intention, but that is how it worked out.

König was standing on the bridge in the chariot-shaped conning tower, the helmsman directly in front of him, and the pilot to his left. As the parade moved upriver the crowds roared, "*Hoch* König, *Hoch* König" and chanted "*Deutschland, Deutschland, Deutschland*"—meaning the boat, not the nation. An assortment of local brass bands blared out an assortment of German marches, and any vessel on the river that had a horn, whistle, or bell was hooting, screeching, and clanging in a collective expression of utter jubilation. The din was deafening. One reporter wrote, "It was *Deutschland, Deutschland über Alles* for twelve miles."

At one point the press boat *Gazelle,* containing the foreign press, moved in close to the U-boat in an attempt to get an underway interview with König. In response to the shouted request, König gestured "with a flourish of his mega-phone" toward the American flag and called for three cheers for the press, to which his "trained and weather-beaten crew responded lustily." The crowd ashore heard the cheering and enthusiastically joined in.

The steady rain did nothing to dampen the excitement and joy of the people who stood on the banks or drifted on the river in open boats as the parade passed slowly by. Farther up the river, the excitement was becoming even more pronounced, because the waiting crowds could hear the noise from downriver but could catch no sight of the *U-Deutschland*. At one point several town bands became so overcome with the moment that they all struck up *Die Wacht am Rhein* in ragged succession so that the discordant noise was spread over a large area. Fortunately, it did not last long.

Some of the people who were waiting exercised initiative and tried to find positions with better downriver views. One of them was a nine-year-old lad, Franz Eichberger, who was unusually tall for his age. He found a fifteen-foot-high stone tower at the water's edge and clambered up it. There was an iron pole at the top, which he grabbed as he leaned out over the water to get a better look. Amid the delirium below him stood a policeman who was not caught up in the moment and had not forgotten his duty. "Get down from there!" he ordered. A quick glance over his shoulder and down convinced Franz that this was not a voice to be ignored. He shot one more look downriver, and there she was. There was no doubt about it. "I see the *U-Deutschland!*" he hollered and pointed downriver with his free hand. "I can see him. He's coming!" The announcement electrified the crowd but did not faze the policeman, who again ordered the boy down.[12]

Cannons along the river fired salutes as the parade glided past in the rain, a sea of sodden white handkerchiefs were waved, and hats were lifted. König, much to the crowd's pleasure, responded by lifting his cap, returning salutes, and waving back. He was the man of the hour, a true national hero. At one point someone started yelling *"Vive le Roi!"* and the crowd took it up. The crowd's size and reaction underscored the degree to which the German people were suffering under the ever-tightening British blockade and the degree to which the *U-Deutschland's* accomplishment represented salvation and hope of relief to them.[13]

Exactly on schedule, the *U-Deutschland* entered Bremen's Free Harbor II and was warped alongside a barge that had been especially prepared for the boat's arrival. Directly behind the *U-Deutschland* lay the NDL liner *Frankfurt,* with a military band on her stern playing "patriotic airs." Beneath a brightly colored canopy rigged over the barge's recently added deck were the dignitaries selected to meet the captain and his crew as they came ashore. They were also there to make speeches and hand out awards. Notably absent was the kaiser or any member of his government except for the minister of the interior, Karl Helfferict, who had been in on the original planning for the commercial submarine project. The kaiser's absence was not a snub; it was intended to prevent any hint of government interest in the *U-Deutschland,* which was supposed to be an entirely private capital venture. But even without the kaiser, there were plenty of bigwigs to go around.

▲ The *U-Deutschland* headed up the Weser to Bremen on 25 August under overcast skies and in steady rain. In this photo she is approaching the entrance to Bremen Harbor. *Jørn Jensen collection*

The barge had seating for 240 people, which included all the members of the DOR board of directors, military representatives of the garrisons from Bremen and the neighboring cities, and a host of other members of the elite in uniforms of one sort or another. The front row was reserved for *Grossherzog* (Grand Duke) Friedrich August von Oldenburg, Magnus Freiherr von Braun (whose son is known to the world as Wernher von Braun, the rocket scientist), *Graf* Ferdinand von Zeppelin, the Bremen mayors Clemens Carl Buff (1915) and Carl Georg Barkhausen (1916), the president of the Bremen-Bremerhaven legislative body called the Bürgerschaft, Rudolf Quidde, and Princess Eitel-Friedrich, whose name was Sophie Charlotte von Oldenburg, the daughter of the duke and married into the royal family, and whose presence thus eased the disappointment over the kaiser's absence.

Alfred Lohmann made a short speech lauding the crew and their accomplishment while putting some digs into the British for their illegal blockade and their assault on the freedom of the seas. The Bremen garrison band played *Die Wacht am Rhein* and *Deutschland Über Alles,* and everyone trooped into the Bremen city

▲ The *U-Deutschland* laid alongside the covered barge where the reception party and VIPs greeted her homecoming. *Author's collection*

hall for the start of "a series of wearisome official luncheons and receptions" that opened with the entire *U-Deutschland* crew receiving medals. Everyone in the crew received a medal specifically for civilians or that could be used for either civilians or military personnel, again to underscore the boat's civilian nature. But there was a lone exception, missed by the press—the Knight's Cross of the Hohenzollern House Order with Swords that went to Paul König. It was an award that held equal rank with the *Pour le Merit,* the so-called Blue Max, and was awarded only to serving officers.

There were other prizes, gifts, and awards made to the crew, and the Universities of Kiel and Halle made König an honorary doctor of philosophy. Following the awards and more speeches, König, *Graf* Zeppelin, and Alfred Lohmann, followed by a press of city dignitaries, went out on the second-floor balcony and greeted an enthusiastic crowd that was literally jammed cheek to jowl in the street below. König lifted his hat, waved to the crowd, and finally brought the appearance to an end by saying, *"Gute Nacht. Ich bin Furchtbar müde"* (Good night, I am terribly tired). The evening ended with a state banquet, more speeches, and several toasts.[14]

The *U-Bremen*

Celebrating the Black Tom explosion with a party in the swank Roof Garden of the Astor Hotel on Times Square does not sound like a smart thing to do. But that is what Paul Hilken did on the evening of 4 August. The champagne flowed freely, and Martha Held who kept a safe house for German agents at 123 West Fifteenth Street, supplied the ladies. The event was not a big affair, and the guest list was not more than ten people, not counting Martha and her girls. Among the invited guests were Hinsch, Carl Ahrendt (who was now Hinsch's assistant and "gofer"), Sir John Hamer (businessman and Swedish vice consul in New York), Paul Hoppenberg (EFCO's New York office manager), and Charles von Heimolt, the NDL general manager in New York. Hinsch, Ahrendt, and Hoppenberg knew what the celebration was really about, but the other guests probably did not, assuming it was just a matter of celebrating Germany's good fortune that so much ordnance, either through carelessness or by accident, had blown up.

Conspicuously absent were members of the German diplomatic corps, for whom any sort of public celebration of the incident would have been a very big mistake. The festivities on the Astor roof did not attract the press, but had the German diplomats attended the press would have attended too. Though the celebration was overlooked or ignored in 1916, it assumed great importance to Mixed Claims Commission many years later in establishing who had been responsible for the Black Tom explosion.

Also absent was Fred Herrmann, who was in Chevy Chase, Maryland, keeping a close eye on Carl Dilger. To Hilken and Hinsch's surprise and chagrin, Carl had returned to Baltimore in late July, just before the Black Tom explosion, and had brought with him a specially built steamer trunk that had new anthrax and glanders cultures and improved incendiary devices cleverly concealed in the sides. On the night of the roof-top party, the trunk and its hidden contents were sitting in Hilken's third-floor office in the Hansa Haus.

Another meeting in which the Baltimore cell's responsibility for Black Tom was clearly established took place the day after the celebration party. The meeting was held at the EFCO office in the Whitehall Building, overlooking the Hudson River.

Hoppenberg, Hilken, Hinsch, and Herrmann were in Hoppenberg's office, which still bore signs of the explosion—two or three cracked windows. Hoppenberg facetiously pointed to the broken windows and said, "Why, you fellows have broken my windows." To which Herrmann responded, *"Lieber Moltke, sei nicht dumm, Mach mal wieder bumm, bumm, bumm,"* which means, "Dear Moltke, don't be so dumb, make again boom, boom, boom," meaning cause more explosions.[1]

▲ Captain Karl Schwartz-kopf, who commanded the *U-Bremen* and was lost with her, along with his entire crew. The German term used to describe the unexplained disappearance is *verschollen*. *Claas Stöckmeyer collection*

Getting quickly beyond the Black Tom explosion, the discussion turned to the situation with Carl Dilger, who was no less a threat to them now than he had been when they sent him to Germany in May. The decision was to give him some of the money he was always demanding, in the hope that it would pacify him enough to reduce the threat he represented. It was also decided that Herrmann would continue to monitor Carl, but not as closely as he had been doing. Herrmann had other irons in the fire and did not want to become Carl's permanent babysitter. The discussion also included the upcoming arrival of the *U-Bremen,* tentatively set for on or about 17 September. There was much to be done, and it was decided to include Herrmann in the preparations, in order to provide him with the same cover that Hinsch enjoyed through his public association with EFCO. To provide Herrmann with even greater cover, he would be introduced as Hinsch's brother, Fred H. Hinsch.

While the *U-Deutschland* was still in Baltimore, Hilken had signed a six-month lease that included an extension option with the state of Connecticut for a large section of the newly constructed State Pier in New London. On Monday, 7 August, he contracted with the T. A. Scott Company to build two temporary warehouses, one to be 125 feet long and the other five hundred feet. Both buildings were to be framed with heavy timbers, sheathed in corrugated iron, and laid out so that when completed they would block all view of the submarine from the shore. Construction started on 9 August, and the Eastern Forwarding Company offered the T. A. Scott Company a "substantial bonus" for completing the job "on or before" 22 August.[2]

In order to complete the job within the deadline, the Scott Company dropped all other work and devoted itself full-time to the warehouses, hiring a large workforce to "work day and night." The "work day and night" claim turned out to be a press exaggeration, but the workdays were long, lasting from sunrise to sunset, and they included Sundays. While the construction was ongoing, Hinsch, who was to be the full-time superintendent in New London, bought a house and a large piece of property in Neptune Park.

Hilken insisted on secrecy about all aspects of the construction project on the State Pier whenever he dealt with a government official or Thomas Scott, whose company was building the new warehouses. One of Hilken's first conversations dealing with the project's purpose was with Waldo Clarke, the engineer in charge of the State Pier, whom Hilken cautioned to say nothing about the anticipated arrival of the *U-Bremen*. Clarke told F. Valentine Chappell, the secretary of the state's Rivers, Harbors, and Docks Commission, advising him "of the necessity for the greatest secrecy." Chappell gave the news to James L. McGovern, collector of customs at New London, also adding the need for secrecy, and McGovern told his boss, William G. McAdoo. It was not long before everyone in New London knew that a "merchantman of the *Deutschland* type" was coming to New London and was probably already on the way, which explained the need for speed in completing the warehouses.

On 16 August, Hilken, Hinsch, Chappell, and Clarke went to the customshouse to talk to McGovern. Hilken introduced himself as the Swedish vice consul at Baltimore and immediately made a point of telling everyone in the room that he wanted "no public mention made regarding the nature of his business." He told them in confidence that the *U-Bremen* was coming, that he did not know if it was already under way or not, but that he expected it to arrive in two or three weeks. The boat's arrival would signal the start of a monthly submarine freight service between Bremen and New London. He also told them that EFCO's company tug, *Hansa,* the ex–*Thomas F. Timmins*, would be bringing the four-hundred-ton barge *George May* to New London shortly. What he did not tell them was that an NDL passenger-freighter would be brought down from Boston to act as the accommodations ship for the *U-Bremen*.

The next day Hinsch, together with Georg Öding, went to Boston to look over the SS *Wittekind* and the SS *Willehad* as prospective accommodations ships for

U-Frachtschiff „Bremen"
Ausfahrt aus dem Kieler Hafen zur ersten Reise

▲ The *U-Bremen* setting out for her acceptance trials on 17 July 1916. Note the absence of the black skirt on her port quarter and the white coveralls in which the crew is dressed. Both were unique to the *U-Bremen* and serve to make positive identification in photos. *Jørn Jensen collection*

the *U-Bremen*'s crew and those of all subsequent U-freighters. Their first choice was the *Wittekind,* the *Willehad*'s sister ship; she had been launched in 1894 and lengthened (unlike *Willehad*) to 461 feet in 1904. The former Roland Line passenger-freighter was ideally suited to be the accommodations ship at New London.

But the superintendent of the Cape Cod Canal Company, E. R. Greer, would not allow the *Wittekind* to pass through the canal, because her displacement was too great, the canal having been "practically blocked by a vessel wrecked in the canal." But he did approve the *Willehad,* 383 feet long. She, like *Wittekind,* was a twin-screw passenger-freighter built in 1894, then used in the immigrant trade. After receiving a fresh coat of bottom paint, 373 tons of coal, and a three-month supply of provisions, her captain, Johann Jachens, took her out of Boston en route to New London, where he arrived at 0930 on 25 August.[3]

The *Willehad* was positioned and anchored so that she formed a solid wall parallel to the long side of the L-shaped State Pier, her stern toward the short foot of the L. The opposite wall was the five-hundred-foot-long warehouse that the Scott Company had built for EFCO on the pier. On the shore end of the State Pier, the smaller warehouse filled the space between the foot of the pier and the stern of the *Willehad.* The result was a U-shaped berth with the open end toward the harbor. As soon as the *Willehad* was anchored, a work crew from the Scott Company began the construction of a twelve-foot-high floating wall that could be drawn across the berth's opening.

At 1500 the day after the *Willehad* dropped anchor in New London, 26 August 1916, the *U-Bremen* left Helgoland. As it had been when the *U-Deutschland* had gone out through the same entrance two months earlier, the breakwater around the entrance to the naval fortress was lined with sailors, all of whom shared an interest in the boat's success. Outwardly, the *U-Bremen* looked exactly like the *U-Deutschland,* except for the absence of a black exhaust apron painted over her port-side exhaust ports. The same harbor tug, carrying the same cameraman, was on hand to record the boat's departure. In trail behind a minesweeper, the *U-Bremen* proceeded out into the North Sea, following the *U-Deutschland*'s route, and was soon out of sight. She was never seen again, and there is no clue as to what happened to her. The German word for that is *verschollen*—missing and presumed lost.

Outside of a few people in Germany, no one knew when the *U-Bremen* had put to sea, where she was bound, or when she should arrive, but there was a lot of speculation about what happened to her. Much of the speculation focused on her being captured or sunk. Though it was not reported that she was presumed lost until 1 October, two rumors had circulated in August that the *U-Bremen* had been sunk.

The first rumor came from "waterfront men" who said that U.S. warships off the Virginia Capes and merchant ships in the Atlantic had intercepted a radio transmission between HMS *Lancaster* and the French cruiser *Condé* stating that the British Admiralty had reported the destruction of the *U-Bremen* in the English

Channel on 2 August. The Germans quickly discounted the report, because they knew that the *U-Bremen* had been still in Kiel on that date. Within days of the initial report a new one, "brought in by merchant ships," popped up saying that a British patrol boat had caught her in a net and destroyed her but providing no date or details.

The first story on the loss appeared in the American press on 10 August, claiming that a "widely published report" was circulating that the *U-Bremen* had sunk. The report supposedly came from the Swiss newspaper *Tageblass* [sic] and said that it was "probable" that the boat had sunk due to "an accident with her machinery." Given the later mystery and opinions surrounding the boat's disappearance, the report has an eerie prescience, in that it was issued sixteen days before the boat left Helgoland. In fact, though, there is no way anyone can say with authority what caused her to vanish without a trace.[4]

On 11 August there was a report that a British cruiser had sunk the *U-Bremen* "off Nantucket." When reporters asked the British naval attaché about it, he answered that he was "unable to talk about it," giving a sort of left-handed confirmation to the rumor. A week later the *U-Bremen* was supposedly seen "in the tow of two British warships off Deal." According to the fanciful tale, reportedly given in New York by disembarking passengers of the Cunard liner RMS *Alaunia*, "two cruisers approached the *Alaunia* towing a long covered boat resembling a submarine that was slung on chains made fast on board the two warships." One of the *Alaunia*'s officers conjectured that the submarine they saw had been "captured by British patrol boats in the English Channel somewhere between South Foreland and Beachy Head." The problem with the story is that in 1916 RMS *Alaunia* was a troopship carrying Canadian troops from Canada to England. No civilian passengers disembarked from the ship in New York in 1916.[5]

Nineteen days later, on 5 September, real passengers disembarking in New York from the American Lines SS *Philadelphia* "declared positively" that a British destroyer had captured the *U-Bremen* and had taken her into Sheerness or Chatham Dockyard. The accuracy of this seemingly eyewitness account was reinforced by the assertion that "several British and American officials" were among the declarants.[6]

The reports of the *U-Bremen*'s loss or capture had little effect on the men in Germany who were responsible for the commercial submarine operation. All the reports published prior to 26 August were known to be wrong, because the *U-Bremen* had been still in Kiel or at Helgoland. But reports made after that date caused worry and concern. German naval intelligence gathered reports from wherever they could find them, including press clippings, diplomatic reports, and interviews with neutral seamen who still had access to the world's ports. On 20 September they received information that British sailors were openly talking about the *U-Bremen*'s having been captured and taken to Liverpool. The source was considered reliable, and the timing fit.

Misleading information in the newspapers was not limited to the United States. Acting on a report filed in Rhode Island by Reuters, Dr. Emil Leimdöfer published an article in the *Vossische Zeitung* that the *U-Bremen,* long overdue, had arrived in New York. The story was picked up by nearly every German newspaper, and editors wrote front-page editorials praising Captain Schwartzkopf, his crew, Germaniawerft, and Lohmann. The German people had been totally unaware that the *U-Bremen* was overdue and missing, a fact that the German censors had kept under wraps. The word was out now, but the problem had passed, and the nation rejoiced.

Doctor Leimdörfer had used the same technique to put together the report of the *U-Bremen's* arrival in New York that he had used to assemble his story about the formation of a cargo U-boat company. The earlier story had been surprisingly accurate, considering that he was working with unlinked bits of information. But in the earlier story he at least had several bits to work with. For the story about the *U-Bremen* he had no information other than a Reuters report that a tug had been dispatched to meet a cargo U-boat at Montauk Point.

What Reuters had neglected to say was that Captain Hinsch had been sending the tug *T. A. Scott, Jr.* out to sea to wait for the *U-Bremen* since 12 September. Later, when it became clear that something had probably happened to the *U-Bremen,* Hinsch recalled the tug but continued to send the *EFCO* to wait at night in the lower New London Harbor. The State Department closely watched the movements of both boats. When the *U-Bremen* did not show up in New York or anywhere else, the German government had to construct an explanation. Doing the only thing it could under the circumstances, it said the *U-Bremen* was undoubtedly safe, her delay caused by extraordinary measured taken to evade the British fleet. And everyone waited.

The other side of the speculation coin was when and where the *U-Bremen* would arrive. That sort of speculation started as early as 16 July, the day before she had even started her acceptance trials. While the *U-Deutschland* was still in Baltimore, the press was reporting that the *U-Bremen* was "now almost halfway across the Atlantic" and bound for New York. Paul Hilken and König had told the press that the *U-Deutschland* was the first in a fleet of merchant U-boats then under construction and that the *U-Deutschland's* sister, *U-Bremen,* would be arriving next. They had not given a date or place for her arrival, but the implication had been that it would be soon.[7]

On 22 July, Theodore Judson, the lighthouse keeper at Stratford, Connecticut, reported having sighted a large submarine on the surface at 0945 that morning, which led immediately to a report that the *U-Bremen* was already here. The large submarine turned out to be the U.S. Navy's *G-3,* which was a training boat based at New London and frequently seen in Block Island Sound and on Great Salt Pond Bay. The *G-3* was also about sixty feet shorter than the *U-Bremen* and not nearly as wide. The next day the press reported that König, Hilken, and Hinsch were visibly distressed over the "non-arrival of the *U-Bremen*." The truth was that none of those three men knew when the *U-Bremen* was going to start her transatlantic trip. In fact, as they were completely unaware, she had failed her first acceptance trials three days earlier and was being worked on in Kiel.[8]

On 10 August it was reported on the basis of unattributed authority that the *U-Bremen* was coming "directly to New London and is now expected any hour." Given the construction activity and accompanying rumors in New London, the assertion was logical, but in reality she was still in Kiel, having finally passed her acceptance trials on the 11th.

By 25 August it had become evident that New London was in fact where the next submarine freighter would tie up. The *Willehad* had arrived and was anchored just off the State Pier, both warehouses were complete, and the collector of customs was assuring the locals that New London would be the *U-Bremen's* port of call. The customs officials were already describing the *U-Bremen's* cargo as consisting of dyes and pharmaceuticals, which was also correct. That same day, Hilken met Hinsch in New York and gave him two thousand dollars in cash, which he was to divide with Herrmann for the "good job they had done at Black Tom."[9]

On 26 August, the date on which the *U-Bremen* left Helgoland, Captain Wade of the American steamer SS *Edward Pierce* told reporters that he had "passed and spoke to" a submarine fifty miles north of Cape Henry but had received no reply. At the time the submarine had been heading "south by southwest." Finally, on 27 August, the Overseas News Agency correctly reported that "the German submarine the *U-Bremen* is now on her way to the United States with a cargo of dyes." She was certainly carrying dyes, pharmaceuticals, and negotiable securities, among which might have been credits for Lake's plans to build cargo U-boats in the United States. The same day, Alfred Lohmann told the German press that the boat was on the way to Baltimore, a claim that was probably disinformation intended to mislead the Allies as to the boat's real destination.[10]

Based on the Lohmann interview, which had been published in American newspapers, and advice from the Krupp engineer Prusse, Hilken correctly estimated that the *U-Bremen* would probably arrive in New London on 17 September at the earliest. The first solid indication the New Londoners had that the boat's arrival was very near was Prusse's arrival on Thursday, 14 September, as a one-man advance party. He checked into the Mohican Hotel early in the morning and was then seen going into the EFCO warehouse at State Pier. Two days later, Paul Hilken arrived and also checked into the Mohican, followed that afternoon by Paul Hoppenberg and Sir John Hammar, who checked into the Griswold Hotel. The evening edition of the New London newspaper, *The Day,* told its readers, "The arrival of the undersea craft is now considered only a question of hours. Paul Hilken and other officials of the Eastern Forwarding Co. are here and all is ready for the big show. Collector of Customs James L. McGovern and numerous newspapermen and photographers came in on the early afternoon trains. No information is available at the terminal, but the impression was strong late this afternoon that the merchantman is near at hand."[11] With Hilken and his party in town and the assurance of the newspaper report, the stage was set for humorous crowd reactions.

Late Saturday afternoon cries of "The *U-Bremen* is coming!" were heard in the streets, causing "a grand rush in the direction of the waterfront." Other than the usual harbor traffic, the only thing to be seen was a 125-foot section of fence floating in the channel. A similar false start occurred the following evening, prompted in part by the arrival of the publisher John Wheeler and the marine artist Henry Reuterdahl at the Griswold Hotel on the morning of 17 September.

Reuterdahl was there to sketch the boat's arrival, and that evening someone started the rumor that the *U-Bremen* had positively been seen off Ocean Beach. As soon as the news reached the town, the telephone wires came alive with the message, which again sent a "wildly expectant throng" to the waterfront. This time customs officials, moving-picture operators, photographers, and newsmen joined the crowd, eagerly identifying every light "shimmering in the outer harbor" as the *U-Bremen.* The tug *T. A. Scott, Jr.* hastily got under way, followed by the *EFCO* with Hilken and Hinsch on board, which in turn was followed closely by the yacht *Whirlwind,* filled with cameramen and reporters.[12]

The two false reports did not dampen Hilken's spirits about the *U-Bremen* ultimately arriving in New London, since there were so many factors involved in an Atlantic crossing that could delay the boat. On the evening of Sunday, 17 September, he hosted a large party at the Griswold Hotel. An uninvited attendee was Charles Thorne, who was Hinsch's courier. Thorne had returned to New York at the end of his fourth trip to Liverpool, bringing a new supply of incendiary devices to Baltimore. When he learned that Hinsch was in New London, he took the first train and arrived there at the height of the party. The party was in full swing, and "there was great excitement and everybody seemed to be very happy and expectant." Thorne found Hinsch and told him he was through as a courier, because of the risk of arrest in England. Hinsch told him to go back to Baltimore and meet with the "Swede," who would give Thorne a new job. Hinsch got Thorne a room in the Mohican, and the following morning Thorne returned to Baltimore.[13]

By 20 September the truth was starting to sink in at New London. There were no longer expectations of an imminent arrival, even among the newspapermen and photographers, who were described as "getting weary." Over nine weeks had elapsed since the first unfounded report that the *U-Bremen* was at sea, more than enough time for the boat to have reached New London had she been at sea for the entire time. Though Hilken continued to publicly express confidence that the boat would soon arrive, he and the others who were close to the operation were having strong doubts. As the doubts hardened into certainty, another act in the drama was unfolding.[14]

When Captain König wrote his report to the Admiralstab upon his return to Bremen in August, he was still overly concerned with the threat the cruisers of the 4th Cruiser Squadron represented or were imagined to represent. He still believed that American fishing boats had been hired to report his movements and to do everything possible to interfere with his departure from Baltimore. In his report he said that upon his departure British warships had been patrolling close to the three-mile limit with the obvious intent of capturing or destroying the *U-Deutschland,* and he warned that the *U-Bremen* would face the same threats on her return trip.

On the basis of König's report, the Admiralstab looked into the feasibility of sending a war boat to the East Coast to attack British warships lying in wait for the *U-Bremen.* It was apparent to the Admiralstab that an operational U-boat would be completely unexpected and thus able to safely attack any enemy warship that threatened the *U-Bremen.* On the basis of that general idea, the Admiralstab developed a two-part plan—to protect the *U-Bremen* and to impress the Americans by demonstrating that the U-boat war could be brought to their doorstep.

The question was, would it be possible to increase the fuel load of a *U-51*-class boat to allow it to easily make a round trip of over eight thousand nautical miles? Refueling in an American port could, within limits, be authorized under international law. But given the situation with respect to the United States, there was a question as to whether or not that would actually be possible. The opinion was that a short visit to an American port without the need for refueling would drive home the point that German U-boats had the necessary range and ability to reach America's shores and return to Germany without outside assistance.

By converting ballast tanks to fuel tanks it would be possible to substantially increase the range of a boat of the *U-51* class. The firm of Augsburg-Nürnberg Diesels had proven reliable, and there was no doubt about the type's seaworthiness for such a trip. The engines would be completely overhauled, and the engine room crew increased so that there would be three watches instead of two. Furthermore, a second U-boat would be assigned to a station between the Hebrides and the Faeroe Islands to watch for the returning war boat and provide her any assistance she needed.

The boat selected to cross the Atlantic was the *U-53,* under *Kapitänleutnant* Hans Rose. The boat had been commissioned on 22 April 1916 and sent into service on 31 May, assigned to the High Seas Fleet. She was 172 feet long, had a surface speed of fifteen knots, and could dive in fifty-five seconds. She had two bow and two stern torpedo tubes with eight reloads and carried a 105 mm deck gun. When commissioned, the *U-53*'s estimated maximum surface range at eight knots had been just eight thousand nautical miles. By increasing her fuel supply the range was increased to nine thousand nautical miles at the same speed. That sounds like a safe increase, but in fact it was a narrow margin.[15]

Hans Rose was a rising star who would end the war with the *Pour le Merit* and be ranked as the fifth-highest-scoring U-boat commander in World War I. He had entered the U-boat service in 1915, in command of the old kerosene-burning

Körting-engine boat *U-2*. In 1916 he was assigned as an instructor at the U-boat officers' school in Kiel, where his students included Paul König and Karl Schwartzkopf. In April 1916 he was given command of the newly built *U-53,* which he took on one war patrol before the boat was selected for the transatlantic mission.

The Admiralstab issued Rose a four-point order. First, he was to attack any enemy warship he saw east of Long Island Sound, provided the target was outside the U.S. three-mile limit. Having accomplished his first assignment, Rose was to enter Newport News and provide American naval personnel an opportunity to visit and examine the *U-53*. He was to remain there for only a few hours; if it proved possible to refuel and take on provisions there, it should be done. The third point was that should he not see any enemy warships upon his arrival of the coast, he was to go directly into Newport News. Lastly, upon leaving Newport News, he was to attack merchant ships outside the three-mile limit, but only in accordance with the Prize Regulations. This last direction was to drive home the point that the U-boat war could be brought to the East Coast. The demonstration would accomplish its purpose but prove to be an enormous diplomatic blunder.

▲ The crew of the *U-Deutschland* on the boat's bow for the homecoming photograph. The man in the white sweater in the front row is Franz Krapohl, first officer. Next to him is Captain König (right), and over König's left shoulder is Paul Eyring, second officer. Showing between Krapohl and König is the steward Adolf Stucke, and directly behind him is the *Leitender Ingenieur* Klees. *Claas Stöckmeyer collection*

He left Helgoland on 17 September and immediately ran into heavy seas and strong winds, which lasted until he was well out in the Atlantic. The weather was so bad and the seas so high that a week after he left Helgoland he wrote in his war log that his rate of advance was just 185 nautical miles per day and the earliest date on which he could reach his assigned position off Long Island Sound was 7 October. He noted that if there was another delay, he would have to abort the mission and return to Helgoland.

After seventeen days of winds ranging from near-gale to strong gale force and mountainous seas with breaking crests, the weather cleared, and he made better time. He arrived on station on the morning of 6 October and began a search for the enemy warships that lasted until the following day without a sighting. It was evident that the British were not lying in wait, so Rose complied with the second and third parts of his orders and entered Newport News that afternoon.

At 1345 on Saturday, 7 October, he dropped anchor in the Newport News Harbor where he remained until 1710. During his three-and-a-half-hour stay he made an official visit ashore to Rear Admiral Austin M. Knight and got a look at several American warships. During his absence his watch officers gave tours of the *U-53* to U.S. naval officers and a few civilians. Rose learned that the *U-Bremen* had not arrived. Without taking on any fuel or provisions he left Newport News to attack commercial shipping off the coast.

Rose spent all day on Sunday, 8 October, carrying out the fourth part of his orders. He stopped seven ships—three British, two Norwegian, one Dutch, and one American. He sank five and released two, the American and one of the Norwegian ships. His total would have been higher, but he spent a good deal of time towing lifeboats from the sunken British freighter SS *West Point* to the Nantucket Lightship because he felt they were too far from shore to reach safety before nightfall. Returning from the lightship he stopped the Dutch SS *Blommersdijk*, bound for Amsterdam and carrying goods consigned to Dutch companies. Under a strict interpretation of the Prize Regulations Rose should have released the ship. Instead he sank her, on the grounds that she would have to put into Kirkwall for inspection, where the British would have seized the goods.

Rose started his return trip to Helgoland on the evening of 8 October. The trip back was not quite as messy as the trip out, but it still took him twenty days, and he ran into some very heavy weather with winds that at times reached strong gale force. Not taking on provisions in Newport News proved to be a mistake, because the boat's food supply ran short, resulting in diminished crew performance. Six days out of Helgoland Rose located *U-55,* which had been on station between the Hebrides and the Faeroe Islands since 19 October. The *U-53* obviously did not need assistance, and after she passed the *U-55* left her station and went south to continue her war patrol in the Irish Sea. The *U-53* reached Helgoland on 28 October.[16]

By the time the *U-53* returned to Helgoland, the German navy had already declared the *U-Bremen* lost with all hands on 1 October. But reports of her capture or sinking persisted well into 1917. Meanwhile, on 29 September 1916, as the Germans waited, a drama played out on a Maine beach called Maiden Cove, on the ocean side of Cape Elizabeth.

Ten-year-old Frederick Lakeman walked along the beach, head down, searching the sand. Little Frederick was not looking for anything in particular—anything would do. Suddenly he stopped, his attention fixed on a peculiarly shaped something half-buried in the sand. Freddie did not recognize it, but whatever it was, it was big, and he had found it. Excited to have found something really big, he quickly scraped the sand away and stood it upright. The thing was brownish-white and had rope around its edge. It was horse-collar shaped, but he did not know that, because he had never seen a horse collar. It was too heavy for him to carry, so he grabbed a short length of rope that was attached to the ring and started dragging it across the beach to where his parents were sitting.

His dad stood up and walked toward him, asking, "What have you got there, Freddy?"

"I don't know," the little guy panted, struggling with his treasure.

The elder Lakeman recognized it right away as a life preserver of some type and assumed it had fallen off a yacht or that someone had tossed it in the water. He reached down, grabbed it, and held it at arm's length to examine it. He did a double take: stenciled in black letters at the top was "Bremen." He turned the ring around and saw the same name in black letters on the other side. The German imperial crown was stamped on one side at the bottom, above which was written *"Schutzmarke"* (trademark). Beneath that in small letters was "V. Epping-Hoven, Wilhelmshaven," which he assumed was the manufacturer. "It looks like you have really found something, Freddy," he said softly. Convinced that Freddy had found a clue to the missing *U-Bremen,* Freddy and his parents rushed the ring to the nearest police station.

Quartermaster A. J. Martinson, from the Coast Guard cutter *Ossippe,* inspected the ring. It was well made, and it showed signs of wear, use, and exposure to the elements. It was the type used on German commercial vessels and ships of the Imperial German Navy. But there was something about it that bothered him. He moved it to a place where the light was better and studied the letters and the marks. The first thing that caused him to be suspicious was that the imperial crown was not a registered trademark but a symbol associated with, in this case, the German navy. Quartermaster Martinson looked closely at the letters in "BREMEN" and soon saw penciled outlines of the letters. The name was not stenciled, it was hand painted the way a sign painter would have done. He also knew that the ship's name should appear on only one side of the device, not on both. The ring was a fake.[17]

The life preserver was not the only hoax that was perpetrated in connection with the *U-Bremen*. Six weeks before Freddie found his treasure in the sand, a radio operator on the Jersey coast transmitted to ships messages purporting to come from the *U-Bremen*. The messages were sent around midnight on 10–11 August 1916, and in several cases the radioman knew the correct call signs for the ships he was addressing. Just after midnight he sent a message addressed to the Telefunken station at 47 West 47th Street in New York City, using the correct call sign, WNT: "Passing 35 miles southeast of Ambrose 4:30 A.M. Smooth seas. Expect to reach destination at 10 A.M. All's well." The phony message, which other stations copied, got the desired results, causing "a number of moving picture operators to flock to the Battery," at the southern end of Manhattan.[18]

For the next several months German intelligence continued to gather reports on what had happened to the *U-Bremen,* hoping to find the answer. The German attaché in Stockholm heard that the British had sunk the *U-Bremen* in mid-October. According to the story, the British were saying nothing about it because of the boat's popularity and the adverse effect the news might have on American opinion. But the most persistent rumors were that the boat had been captured

▲ The *U-Bremen* in the Baltic, 18 July 1916. *Jørn Jensen collection*

and was in a British port. Those rumors persisted until June 1917 and were often attributed to well-known people.

In December 1916 Lord Robert Cecil told a Norwegian friend that the boat had been trapped in nets and was at Leith, and in January 1917 a German agent in Stockholm sent the same report, attributing it to an English engineer. That same month they heard that *U-Bremen* had been towed from Liverpool to Chatham; she was also said to be in Avon and Newcastle. The Germans discounted most of the reports, but from March to June 1917 they received a series that they took more seriously. The first came from a German naval officer and was addressed to Alfred Lohmann.[19]

The report's author was working for German naval intelligence in Norway, posing as a merchant seaman aboard a freighter making regular trips to Britain. On his last trip a British sailor in a bar told him that the *U-Bremen* had been captured, which was nothing new, because everyone was saying that. But then the sailor added that the British had found 20,000 cans of Salvarsan among the *U-Bremen's* cargo of dyes. That bit of information got the German's undivided attention

The *U-Bremen's* cargo manifest had, like the *U-Deutschland's*, been a closely guarded secret. While it was true that there might have been a leak, there was no evidence to support that. The German agent knew that Salvarsan, a form of arsenic used in the early twentieth century to treat syphilis, was part of the *U-Bremen's* cargo. That the British had acquired a huge amount of the drug would have been news in any seaport, which explained how a common sailor might have heard about it.

The report seemed credible: How would the British have known that the *U-Bremen*'s cargo included Salvarsan unless they had captured the boat? The fact that the British sailor had said the drug was stored in *cans* should have been a tip-off that something was wrong with the report. The drug was stored in glass vials. But the only question the Germans had was, the *U-Bremen* having been carrying 32,500 vials of the drug, what had happened to the other 12,500. The report opened an entirely new area of speculation.[20]

In April 1917 a German businessman who had lunched with the British military attaché in Copenhagen reported that the *U-Bremen* was in Falmouth and that two crewmen were being held without any outside communication. On 27 April a German agent in Britain got word back that the *U-Bremen* was in Hampton Shire Bay, supported between two large wooden floats. Then, in May 1917, Marquis Cortina told a German agent in Madrid that he had just returned from England where, he had gone aboard the captured *U-Bremen*. Other stories included an account by a Swiss businessman who claimed to have seen the *U-Bremen* among forty U-boats that were on display in London, each identified by a sign, *Bremen*.[21]

Obviously, however, the *U-Bremen* was not captured, since she was never displayed during or after the war. And the British have never taken credit for sinking her. It is possible, but unlikely, that she hit a mine. She was escorted through the British minefield outside of Helgoland, and the North Sea was clear of mines until 1918, when the Northern Mine Barrage was created. The route north around Scotland was not mined, and the open Atlantic was free of mines, with the exception of the occasional floating mine that had broken free. The most probable explanation for her loss is an accident. We have already seen that the design was difficult to handle and easy to lose control of during a "crash dive" in heavy seas. Given her inherent stability and control problems, there were ample opportunities for a fatal problem to occur during her long voyage across the Atlantic.

The Layover

Most German civilians, including their prime minister, Theobald von Bethmann-Hollweg, wanted peace. The war had gone on too long, the casualties were staggering, and the economy was in ruins. But the German army did not want a negotiated peace, which was the only kind of peace that could have been achieved in 1916. What the army wanted was to crush the enemy and then dictate the terms. Barring that happy outcome the army wanted to dictate the terms of the peace from an overwhelmingly superior military position. But the war was not being fought only in the trenches on the western front; it was being fought on the home front too.

When the Germans had gone to war in August 1914, they had raised the army and fielded their troops according to a detailed and efficient mobilization plan that included an extensive reserve system. But they had had no economic mobilization plan. As a result, by the spring of 1915 they had to make a choice—feed the war industry or feed the people. They chose the former. The solution was to strip the civilian population of whatever it had that the war industry could use.

Initially the demands had no seriously negative impact on the civilian population, since the demand was only for old, expendable things. But by the time the *U-Deutschland* had returned to Bremen, the government was taking copper kettles, doorknobs, even the iron fittings from railroad cars and metal signs, including street signs. In fact, the government took anything that could be melted down and turned into munitions, including church bells. There was also a desperate hunt for rubber; bicycle rain covers and automobile tires were the first things to go.

German chemists tried to replace what was taken with substitutes made from nonessential materials. Leather was no longer used to sole shoes; cardboard was substituted. Cotton and wool vanished from the civilian market and were replaced with substitute cloth made from nettle, raffia, hops, and gorse. Paper became a critical raw material for the consumer market and was used in one form or another for many substitutions: paper instead of iron, paper instead of leather, paper instead of cloth. Eventually there was nothing civilians had that the war machine did not need.

Chemists were finding ways to take nitrogen from the air to reduce the need for imported saltpeter, they had created synthetic rubber, and they were extracting oil from shale. Pulp waste was used to make alcohol, sugar produced glycerin, and gypsum yielded sulfur. None of these solutions met the demand, but they made it possible for Germany's military to continue the war.[1]

The most serious problem the civilian population faced was a steady decline in food supplies after the British and French formally abandoned the 1909 Declaration of London on 7 July 1916. They made that move to increase the effectiveness of the blockade with respect to the neutral countries neighboring Germany. Freedom from having to find excuses and explanations for violating the declaration themselves gave them greater leeway to put pressure on Holland, Norway, Denmark, and Sweden with regard to reducing the transshipment of cargo from those countries to Germany.[2]

The effectiveness of the British move was demonstrated by the drop in American exports to Holland, Sweden, and Norway from the war's first year to the third year following the British abandonment of the London Declaration. American exports to Holland dropped 99 percent, exports to Sweden dropped 69 percent, and to Norway 82 percent. The dramatic reduction in exports to the neutrals neighboring Germany caused food supplies to Germany to steadily decline until well into 1919.[3]

Fearing a collapse of civilian support for the war, General Eric von Falkenhayn launched a massive offensive at Verdun in an effort to defeat the French and "break Britain's Continental sword." The assault opened at 0715 on 21 February 1916, supported by the heaviest preparatory bombardment since the start of the war. Three army corps, equipped for the first time with flamethrowers, rolled over the French in very heavy, savage fighting. But by the end of February the German attack, which had advanced beyond the effective range of its artillery, was starting to stumble. Fighting over ground that was by then a sea of mud and increasingly coming under French artillery fire from emplacements on the Meuse, the German advance became a crawl.

Flanking attacks were tried and continued into March but suffered from a lack of supply because of the mud and stiffening French resistance allowed the Germans only limited gains at an enormous cost in casualties. The battle was essentially stationary during May and June, until the Germans tried another push to take the city of Verdun on 12 June. The new effort lasted until 12 July and then stalled. On 21 July, while the *U-Deutschland* was in Baltimore, the Germans went over to the defensive. The battle of Verdun lasted until 18 December, by which time the French had regained most of the ground they had lost. General von Falkenhayn had failed to win a decisive victory. In the meantime, the Allies had opened the Somme offensive.

The battle of the Somme lasted from 1 July to 18 November, and was intended on the Allied side to draw German troops from the battle of Verdun. The tactic worked, but at a terrible cost to both sides. The offensive resulted in over one million casualties and, like Verdun, accomplished nothing approaching a victory for either side.

During the butchery at Verdun and the Somme, which killed millions of young men and boys, the previously easy relationship between von Bethmann-Hollweg and von Falkenhayn wavered. By the time the *U-Deutschland* returned to Bremen on 25 August, the relationship was nearing an end, as the chancellor came to believe that *Feldmarshall* (Field Marshal) Paul von Beneckendorff und von Hindenburg held the key to peace. The kaiser did not share the chancellor's enthusiasm for von Hindenburg, asserting that to replace von Falkenhayn with von Hindenburg would "be tantamount to his own abdication and the elevation of Hindenburg as popular tribune to his place." But on 27 August Romania declared war on Germany, and the kaiser's resistance to the command change evaporated.[4]

The following day Ambassador James W. Gerard of the United States sent a lengthy telegram to Secretary of State Robert Lansing:

> CONFIDENTIAL: FROM MANY SIGNS THERE ARE INDICATIONS THAT GERMANY IS CONTEMPLATING A RETURN TO RUTHLESS SUBMARINE WARFARE. PEOPLE LIKE [ERNST] BASSEMANN, LEADER OF NATIONAL LIBERALS AND [EUGEN] GUTMANN, DIRECTOR OF DRESDENER BANK, WHO FORMALLY OPPOSED IT, NOW FAVOR IT. THERE IS A TENDENCY TO STIR UP FEELING AGAINST AMERICA AS A FIRST STEP. I DO NOT THINK THE QUESTION WILL BECOME ACUTE UNTIL AFTER OUR ELECTIONS, AND POSSIBLY NOT UNTIL SPRING WHEN GERMANY WILL HAVE A GREAT NUMBER OF SUBMARINE BOATS WITH TRAINED CREWS. AM INFORMED THAT ONE SHIPYARD ALONE IS TURNING OUT TWO SUBMARINE BOATS PER WEEK, POSSIBLY ENTRANCE [OF] ROMANIA TODAY MAY ACCENTUATE SUBMARINE SITUATION.[5]

The change of command took place on 28 August 1916, and the chancellor thought he had finally created the winning command structure, one that would bring a negotiated peace. The truth was that von Bethmann-Hollweg had made a terrible miscalculation based on ignorance. He thought he was appointing von Hindenburg to the position, but he either failed to realize or simply did not know that wherever von Hindenburg went, his chief of staff, *Generalmajor* (major general) Erich Friedrich Wilhelm Ludendorff, went too.

The following day, a meeting was held at the Supreme Imperial Headquarters, at Pless in the duchy of Silesia (Poland). What to do about the entry of Romania into the war headed the agenda, but another item had greater long-term significance—the reopening of an unrestricted submarine-warfare campaign against commercial shipping. The Germans called it "commerce war." When the Pless war council convened, the *U-Bremen* had been at sea for three days.

The Chief of the Naval Staff, Admiral Henning von Holtzendorff, argued that the shortest route to total victory, or at least a favorable negotiated peace, was to turn loose the U-boats on all shipping, Allied and neutral. He acknowledged that the decision would bring the United States into the war, but he believed that an unrestricted assault on world shipping would end the conflict before America's presence was felt. He confidently predicted that the war could be won in six months. Von Bethmann-Hollweg and Foreign Secretary Gottlieb von Jagow were appalled. They argued that von Holtzendorff was using misleading figures with regard to the monthly tonnage that the U-boats could destroy and that America's entry into the war would be catastrophic for Germany.

For the time being, the politicians were able to shelve the implementation of unrestricted submarine warfare pending the resolution of the Romanian situation. But ultimately the decision to launch an unrestricted submarine campaign was turned over to von Hindenburg. Von Bethmann-Hollweg, still believing that Hindenburg wanted an end to the war, was not overly concerned. But he should have been.

The commercial U-boat project now became the best indicator as to which direction the German war effort would go. As long as the cargo boats were operational, the peace advocates held the high ground. At the end of August the future looked reasonably secure for the commercial U-boat project. The *U-Bremen* was at sea, and the *U-Deutschland* was in Bremen, most of her crew on leave. A few weeks earlier the RMA, using the DOR as a cover, had placed an order for six more *U-Deutschland*-class submarine freighters. The contracts were given to Krupp, but Germaniawerft had no available slipways, so the six contracts were parceled out to four other yards. Three of the boats went to the Reiherstiegwerft in Hamburg, and one each went to Stülckenwerft in Hamburg, Flensburger Schiffbau in Kiel, and Atlaswerke in Bremen.[6]

But four days after the Pless meeting, the commercial U-boat project began to look a lot less secure. On 2 September, the U-Boot-Inspection (UI) suggested to the RMA that two of the *U-Deutschland*-class boats that were under construction be converted for war use. The UI suggested three possible conversions: a fuel carrier (a type later known as *Milchkuh* [milk cow]), a minelayer, or a U-cruiser carrying heavy artillery. The suggestion was taken under consideration.[7]

On 29 August the *U-Deutschland* went to Wilhelmshaven under escort for repairs to correct an unexplained problem. Whatever the problem was, it was apparently serious, because she made the trip from Bremen to Wilhelmshaven in "a non-diving condition," which is why she had an escort.[8] In addition to König and a skeleton crew, Dr. Ernst Bischof was along for the trip. Bischof had been interviewing König and studying his charts and log while the *U-Deutschland* was in Bremen so that he could ghostwrite *Voyage of the* Deutschland, with König as the named author. Bischof had already outlined the book, on the basis of newspaper reports and the political slant the government had provided. The plan now was for him to remain on board the *U-Deutschland* until she reached Wilhelmshaven.[9]

The manuscript was completed on 12 September, and on the 15th Bayard Hale, representing William Randolph Hearst in Germany, acquired on behalf of

Hearst the American rights to the book in English and German. Hearst was to pay for the translation into English; Hale said he could cable a ten-thousand-word installment for a serialized version to be run in one of the Hearst magazines. Two complete manuscripts, one in English and one in German, would be sent to Hearst on board the *U-Deutschland* on her next trip.[10]

The profits from the book sales were to be paid to the DOR's Pension Fund, in care of Paul Hilken who was the fund treasurer. The fund was also described as being for the widows and orphans of the DOR's U-boats, which made it almost prescient inasmuch as the *Bremen* was then overdue in New London and probably already lost. The DOR Pension Fund was actually of a fund-raising scheme that Hilken set up to bring in funds for generally supporting the German cause in the United States other than his sabotage activities. When it became obvious that the *Bremen* was probably lost with her entire crew, the pension fund became the Fund for the Benefit of the Widows and Orphans of DOR Crewmen.

But somehow Joseph Pulitzer's *New York World* obtained a copy of the serialization of König's story and beat Hearst to the punch, essentially killing sales of the book. In 1918 James Moore, general manager of the Hearst International Magazine Company, told a congressional committee:

> In January 1917 James L. Perkins, the former General Manager of the Hearst International Magazine Company and Paul Hilken established the U-Deutschland Library, a publishing house. In March 1917, Hilken demanded full payment of the royalties he believed were due. When he learned that there were no royalties he tried to get Hearst to give him the remainders of both English and German editions of *The Voyage of the* Deutschland against the royalties and to turn over to him all rights for the book. Perkins had already set up retail outlets for the books and was preparing to publish an inexpensive edition, the profits from which would go to Hilken's phony charity. Hearst did not do what Hilken wanted and on 6 April 1917 when the United States declared war on Germany, all sales of the book were stopped.

Both editions of the book were outright propaganda. The American edition was slanted toward the American reading audience, featuring themes of Britain's multiple violations of the rights of the sea, its heavy-handed interference with free commerce, and the illegality of the blockade, which was aimed at starving German women and children. The German edition had a strong nationalist tone and offered the *U-Deutschland* as the solution to the blockade while depicting the ships of the Royal Navy as chasing their tails trying to locate the *U-Deutschland*. In both editions the *U-Deutschland*'s crew traveled in complete safety and comfort, enjoying a rest on the floor of the English Channel listening to classical music and drinking champagne. Because the *New York World* scooped Hearst's *New York American,* the book did not sell well in the United States. But in Germany it remained a strong seller until the end of the war, going to four editions.

While the *U-Bremen* was at sea and not yet considered overdue in New London, a rumor reached Berlin that the Americans intended to deny exit clearance to the next cargo U-boat that arrived, thus effectively interning the boat. The rumor probably stemmed from newspaper reports published in July when the State Department was determining the validity of *U-Deutschland*'s status as a merchant ship, and the French and British were doing everything they could to have the boat interned. The rumor probably stemmed from a combination of three elements that were widely reported at the time.

The first element was the Neutrality Board's 13 July suggestion that the State Department make the decision on the *U-Deutschland*'s status "subject to revision" in future cases. The second was the State Department's 17 July telegram to U.S. ambassador to Britain, Walter Hines Page, directing him to explain to the British government that the State Department would keep an open mind with regard to the status of the next boat to arrive. And the third was the earlier British reference to the Lafollette-Seams Act, requiring American-flagged passenger-carrying ships to be equipped with lifeboats and davits. Inasmuch, as we have seen, as the Lafollette-Seams Act did not apply to foreign-flagged vessels, there was no basis to the rumor. Nonetheless, it worried the Germans, who had no doubts as to which side the Americans favored.[11]

And there was plenty of distrust on the part of the Americans as to the *U-Deutschland*'s real purpose. The fact that the *U-Deutschland* had taken on twenty-eight tons of fuel on 17 July raised the possibility that she was going to become a floating fuel station for German surface raiders and U-boats. The fact that König had the extra fuel pumped into the *Neckar* did nothing to offset the idea. After the *U-53* stopped in Newport News before sinking five ships within sight of land, the prospect that the *U-Deutschland* would be used to refuel war boats at sea looked even more likely. On 13 October 1916, C. W. Taintor, a gadfly with an office in the Sears Building in Boston, wrote to Robert Lansing, "I would respectfully ask if you think there is any possibility of the German Unterseeboten [*sic*] *U-Deutschland* being a mother ship for *U 53* and *U 61* and the notice that she has returned to Germany is a masquerade to fool the American people, whom Captain von Papen is reported to have so courteously described as fools in one of his letters intercepted by the British Government."[12] The State Department simply referred him to the Navy Department, but his question was not as far-fetched as some people might think.

Six weeks earlier, Professor Doctor Franz Falk, a medical doctor in Berlin who specialized in anthrax and glanders, had written a letter to the Admiralstab suggesting that the *U-Deutschland* be used to lay a trap for Allied warships operating off the American coast. His plan was to send four U-boats, a sort of wolf pack, to wait off the port to which the *U-Deutschland* was bound and torpedo any

Allied warship that came along. He also believed the U-boats would find there a rich hunting ground, one in which they could do serious damage to commercial shipping, among the freighters leaving the American port en route to Allied ports. If the professor's plan worked as envisioned, the U-boats, having rid the area of Allied warships, would be able to operate without interference. The frosting on the cake was that after the *U-Deutschland* had taken on more fuel than she could use, she would depart loaded with raw materials for Germany and stop at sea to refuel the U-boats, which by then would be critically low on fuel.[13]

Following repairs in Wilhelmshaven the *U-Deutschland* returned to her Bremen berth, where she took on cargo and provisions for the coming trip. This time her outbound cargo consisted of 165 tons of dyestuffs, valued at approximately $6,251,418; three cases of semiprecious stones, valued at $3,500; securities valued at $4,538,403; diamonds valued at $56,000; and 131 cases of pharmaceuticals, for which no value was given. The total value of the cargo, including the pharmaceuticals, exceeded $10,000,000.[14]

Tight security is usually a necessity in wartime, but there are times even then when it seems unnecessary and excessive. Such was the case with information regarding the *U-Deutschland's* cargo. Keeping the British in the dark about when the boat would depart and where she was going was a sound precaution. But even if the British did discover the nature of the cargo, the knowledge would offer them no advantage. Nevertheless, the Germans classified the cargo and the consignees as *Ganz Geheim,* top secret, in bold letters stamped on all documents pertaining to the cargo.

The Germans' insistence on secrecy about the cargo rubbed off on American officials like William Fee, the American consul in Bremen, who on the *U-Deutschland's* first trip had not notified his government of the boat's departure or cargo. The State Department rapped Fee's knuckles for the omission but adopted a similar policy about the release of cargo information to the public after the boat departed Baltimore with her load of tin, nickel, and rubber. In a memorandum to William Ryan in Baltimore, the Treasury Department directed, "In accordance with the advice of the Secretary of State and the Secretary of Commerce, the details of the cargo of the German submarine *U-Deutschland* should not be furnished to the public until a reasonable period after clearance has elapsed. The Department regards thirty days as a reasonable period, but if the consignors should desire a longer period fixed, the Department will give due consideration to the request." To be fair to the Washington bureaucrats, the thirty-day nondisclosure policy applied to outbound Allied cargoes too.[15]

The German insistence on secrecy about cargo came from the navy, not the DOR managers. In fact, the navy's strict policy interfered with the normal commercial business practices associated with international shipments and made things difficult at both ends of the line. As the time for the *U-Deutschland's* departure grew nearer, Alfred Lohmann, representing DOR, was sending a flurry of messages to

EFCO and DOR's insurance carrier in Sweden regarding the outbound cargo and the consignees. Messages also went to EFCO giving directions on the cargo to be brought back to Germany. Those messages were being delayed because of the navy's overdone security, under which each telegram had to be submitted to German censors, who deleted much information that the recipients in Baltimore and Sweden needed to know. That and normal bureaucratic delays in processing the telegrams drove Lohmann to despair. On 25 September he sent a strongly worded letter to the navy: "I cannot understand the secrecy in regard to cargo. The Swedish company that provides our insurance will not insure the cargo if they do not know what it is. We have to tell them. We have to tell the various American Consuls whose districts provide the cargo, and in turn they report to their government. Once the boat reaches America, the manifests are made public; so why the secrecy?"[16] Documents related to the cargo continued to be stamped *Ganz Geheim*.

There was one piece of cargo about which nothing appeared in any of the telegrams, because it was included in the diplomatic mail. It was a new diplomatic codebook, called "0075," intended to replace the old code, "13040" (which the British could read, although the Germans were unaware of that). Changing codes is a good practice, but it helps if everyone involved receives the new codes. In this case 0075 went only to von Bernstorff, whose responsibility included Mexico. Any messages he received in the new code and wished to forward to the German minister in Mexico, Heinrich von Eckhardt, had to be reencrypted in the old code, 13040. The groundwork for America's entry into the war had been laid.[17]

By 1 October the insurance had been arranged, and the *U-Deutschland* was loaded and ready for sea. As she swung away from her berth, a small harbor tug accidentally rammed her on the starboard side just forward of the conning tower, damaging her forward diving planes. The damage was not terribly serious, but she was no longer seaworthy, and the next day she went to Wilhelmshaven once again for repairs. Lohmann sent a telegram to the Admiralstab saying that the damage was "trivial" and would cause a forty-eight-hour delay. The delay was actually a week.

On 8 October, Wilhelmshaven notified Kiel by radio, "COMMERCIAL U-BOAT U-DEUTSCHLAND DEPARTED JADE NORTH 1100." In London an officer in Room 40 picked up the transmission, opened a battered copy of the *Signalbuch der kaiserlichen Marine* (SKM), and flipped it open.[18]

The Second Crossing

Franz Krapohl ducked below the steel rim of the conning tower as a wall of water bore down on the *U-Deutschland*. The face of the wave exploded against the steel casing, causing the boat to shudder as the top curled and collapsed in a deluge that buried Krapohl and the seaman next to him. The U-boat heaved up onto the next wave and then dropped like an elevator into the trough, burying itself as the wave swept across the boat while the two men in the conning tower hung on. The Force 11 wind was out of the southwest, pushing against the prevailing North Sea swell, creating "exceptionally high waves" and filling the air with spray that reduced visibility to almost zero. The *U-Deutschland* was taking the seas on her starboard bow, which caused her to corkscrew through the wild seas, rolling to starboard as she fell down the back side of the wave into the trough and then to port as she rose up on the next mountain of water.

The next waves were slightly smaller and rolled over the decks, streaming past the conning tower like surf on a beach. But the "breaking wave on the beach" analogy is only half right, because the wave did not recede before the next one hit, leaving the boat half-submerged, with only the conning tower visible. Krapohl counted the waves, since, as mariners have recognized for centuries, every seventh wave is larger than its six predecessors. Right on schedule, the seventh rose up ahead and slightly to starboard, towering higher than the conning tower. Krapohl and the lookout grabbed the rim, ducked, and held their breaths as the wave broke.[1]

They had encountered the heavy weather as they passed Helgoland. The two torpedo boats escorting them had rolled so heavily that König was certain he would have to put about to pick up survivors. That did not happen, and when the group reached the outer picket line the escorts turned back; König was glad to see them go. Now the *U-Deutschland* was well into the North Sea, and the storm was at its maximum fury.

Conditions inside the hull were no better than atop the conning tower. The *U-Deutschland* was a terrible sea boat in any sea condition other than a flat calm. She rolled like a bottle, was almost impossible to get under the surface, especially in a really heavy sea, and the ventilation system was hopeless. Inside the hull, the temperature was always over 100 degrees Fahrenheit and the air was oppressively humid. In the course of a voyage, clothing mildewed, mold formed on the bulkheads, and condensation dripped from the overhead. There was no water or showers with which to get clean, and the stench of unwashed bodies combined with diesel and vomit was almost unendurable. All the talk in Baltimore about taking passengers had become a joke among the crewmen, who said that after three days in the *U-Deutschland* any passenger would happily opt for an open boat and a pair of oars.

The only advantage the foul weather offered was the near ineffectiveness of British patrols in the North Sea. They were certainly out there, but the visibility was so low that the *U-Deutschland* was virtually invisible, and the weather meant that the British were probably focusing more on survival than chasing *U-Deutschland*. Despite the weather, König had to dive twice to avoid patrols, once off Fair Isle and again off the Butt of Lewis.

From a point off the northern tip of the Orkney Islands to St. Kilda Island, west of the Hebrides, the weather remained foul but was not as severe, which allowed the *U-Deutschland* to make slightly better time. Reaching St. Kilda just before noon on 12 October, König came right, onto a track to pass south of Newfoundland. The weather remained miserable, the sky thickly overcast, and the seas high. But the situation had improved enough to allow König to make eight knots for the next four days, reaching a point in the open Atlantic about 1,800 nautical miles from the entrance to Long Island Sound. But during the afternoon of 16 October the weather began to deteriorate, and by dawn of the 17th the *U-Deutschland* was in the teeth of a full-fledged Atlantic winter storm.

The storm, already more violent that any they had yet experienced, continued to build in strength. The boat rolled and pounded, flinging crewmen from one side to another. There were several bruises and a few sprains, though no broken bones. The boat was pounding hard, rising up at an extreme angle and then slamming down into the following trough. König was navigating by dead reckoning, and it was all the helmsman could do to maintain a reasonably steady heading. The boat yawed left and right, corkscrewed, rolled, and pounded. Even the hardened salts were throwing up.

Once late in the afternoon, after the bow had come down hard, sending a shudder through the boat, accompanied by a deep boom, and the bow rose again, something slammed into the starboard bow with such force that everyone in the control room thought they had been rammed. Paul Eyring was officer of the deck and immediately ordered *Matrose* Fritz Humke and three seamen forward to investigate. The heavy crashing against the bow continued every time the boat lifted on a wave. Humke reported flooding in the forward compartment.

Eyring called for König, who was already coming into the control room, looking at Eyring for an explanation. At that moment one of the seamen who had gone forward with Humke came into the control room with word that the anchor had broken loose and was pounding the hull like a pile driver. Some of the pressure-hull plates had started, and water was entering the forward compartment. König relieved Eyring and sent him forward to handle the problem.

"The anchor has come loose," Humke said as Eyring entered the compartment.

"What caused it?" Eyring asked.

"The cable brake failed," Humke told him. "We are trying to fix it now." The anchor, normally held firmly in its housing on the exterior of the hull by the brake, tightly clamping the chain, had been allowed to pay out slightly and was now being flung back and forth; it would have to be hauled back into the normal stowed position and secured there.

The bow dropped, causing the men in the forward compartment to lurch forward, grasping for handholds. The bow rose, and the anchor slammed into the hull with a deafening crash. It did not take an engineer to realize that unless the anchor could be secured, it was just a matter of time before the section of the bow that was taking the beating failed. Eyring lifted a deck plate and saw water in the bilge. He dropped the plate into place and told *Matrose* Anton Born to go aft and tell the captain about it. A few moments later Eyring heard a low whine as the bilge pumps came on. When Born returned, König was with him.

"What's the situation?" König asked his second officer. His question was accompanied by a falling sensation as the bow fell into a deep trough, followed by a deafening crash and a violent shudder, followed almost immediately by a heavy blow on the starboard side. König visibly winced.

"Humke is working on it now," Eyring answered gesturing toward the burly seaman and a helper who were on their knees leaning into the chain locker.

König eased himself forward so that he was directly behind the two men. He crouched and tried to see into the chain locker over their backs. "How long will it take?" he asked Humke.

"At least an hour in this weather," came a grunted answer.

Another heavy thud sent shock waves through the hull, and a seam opened some more. König looked at the steady flow of incoming water and stepped closer to examine the joint where the transverse bulkhead joined the pressure hull. The water was entering along the seam. He placed the palm of his hand against the traverse bulkhead and waited for the next blow. When it came he nodded to himself and said to Eyring, "The bulkhead is taking the brunt of the blow." Then he crouched down and lifted a deck plate. The bilge below the forepeak deck was usually dry, but now there were several inches of water there. He dropped the plate back into place and stood up.

"Stay with it, Humke," he said as he turned to leave. "The bilge pumps are handling the water now, but if it gets much worse we might have a problem in the battery compartment," he said speaking to Eyring. "I'm going back to the control room. Stay here and move things along as best you can."

Everyone in the control room looked at König when he reentered. Krapohl had assumed the officer-of-the-deck position and was hanging on to the forward periscope to keep from falling down as the boat rolled. König lurched to his right and stumbled into a seaman manning the pump station as the boat rolled to port. König untangled himself from the seaman and grabbed an overhead pipe for support.

"We should dive below this stuff," Krapohl said.

König nodded agreement. "I wish we could. I'm not sure those hull plates would hold even if we were able to get under in this sea." He looked quickly around the control room and returned his attention to Krapohl. "Close the water-tight doors."

Two hours later the banging stopped, and Eyring returned to the control room with Humke and the three seamen. "The anchor is secured," he told the men in the control room, "but we are still taking water."

"How bad is it?" König asked.

"Nothing the pumps can't handle," Eyring reassured him.

The storm lasted four days. Unable to dive because of the damaged hull plates, König slowed the boat to the point that they were reduced to bare steerageway. The reduced speed eased the rolling and pounding, but the improvement was only marginal. In the meantime he looked ahead to New London. He had planned to dive and remain under until after dark, when he would surface and make a dash for the three-mile limit. But that plan was down the drain if he could not get the bow repaired. Also, Klees told him that because of the heavy weather they were using more fuel than normally. The report was not terribly alarming, however, because König was sure that he would be able to buy enough fuel to get back to Germany.

On 21 October, the storm passed and fog set in. But just before the fog rolled over them, König was able to fix his position with certainty. To his utter surprise, the distant made good since 17 October was less than one nautical mile. He was essentially in the same spot he had been in on the evening of the 16th. For the next ten days, though the sea was till rough and the fog greatly reduced visibility, he was able to run at eight knots. He was still worried about the weakened bow.

The moderately rough sea and persistent fog offered concealment that he and his crew needed. The boat's motion was reasonably comfortable, and the hatches could be left open, which helped to clear the foul interior air. The improved situation also allowed Klees and his engine-room crew to do something about the started seams, although the only immediate solution was to caulk the seams, use moderate speed, and keep an eye on things. On 28 October the fog thinned, the wind fell off, and the seas subsided. Since the seas were no longer rolling over the deck, König felt that he could increase speed to ten knots. Klees agreed, but he made frequent checks forward. The caulking held, but the real test would come when they dove.

Five days later the *U-Deutschland* passed south of Nantucket. It was hazy, and everything was gray on gray as König scanned the area to the north. This part of the ocean was usually heavily trafficked, but at the moment the *U-Deutschland* seemed to be alone. König was looking at the Nantucket Shoals, where a light-ship was anchored. Also British cruiser routinely patrolled there looking for ships coming out of New York. As he swung his Zeiss bridge glasses eastward he saw a vessel indistinctly through the haze. He focused on it. The ship definitely had four stacks, which meant it was probably a cruiser, but it was moving away. He continued to watch the ship until it disappeared in the haze. He swung the glasses left and peered intently through the haze. There on the horizon, barely visible through the haze, he recognized the tip of No Man's Land. To the right was the greater mass of Martha's Vineyard.

No Man's Land is a high, rocky island that lies five nautical miles south of Martha's Vineyard and is an important navigation waypoint for vessels going into Long Island Sound. It was 1500 on 31 October when the *U-Deutschland* was close enough to No Man's Land for König to positively identify it and come up with an exact position. He called Krapohl to the bridge and went below to lay a course into the Long Island Sound. He decided that when he reached a point where he could see the western tips of both No Man's Land and Nantucket Island, he would come to 273 degrees true and run in until he had Block Island's northern tip on his port beam. Then he would come left eight degrees and run up the Sound and through the Race. From his starting point off No Man's Land's western tip and until he had Block Island on his port beam he would have a straight, unobstructed run, because there were no obstructions along that heading and the water was deep.

His intention was to dive to eighty feet once he passed No Man's Land and run at maximum submerged speed, about six knots, until after sunset. Then he would surface and make a ten-knot run across the three-mile limit and into Long Island Sound. The depth between him and the Sound's entrance was over a hundred feet for the entire length of his intended track, and at eighty feet there would be no danger of being accidently rammed by a surface ship.

The *U-Deutschland* dove at 1600 and went down to eighty feet. As a precaution, König had ordered the watertight doors closed, sealing off the ship into five separate compartments. He had three men forward with tools and caulking. If the seams opened up, the men were to exit the compartment and close the watertight door behind them. Their sudden arrival in the control room would be König's signal to surface immediately. But that did not happen. The seams held.

The *U-Deutschland* surfaced at 2000 in total darkness. As König, a lookout, and a helmsman came onto the bridge, the running lights came on, the diesels fired up, and the boat began gaining speed. König shouted through the speaking tube to shift the helm to the bridge and lifted his glasses to his eyes. Just off the starboard bow was the Point Judith Light. He shifted his attention and saw the barely visible white-and-red flashing sequence of the Gay Head Light, at the western end of Martha's Vineyard, on his starboard quarter. He faced forward and scanned the blackness for the green buoy light off the north end of Block Island, but he was still too far out. But that did not matter, because the water was deep.

Only a light swell was running, and there was no wind. König decided that if the seams had held up for four hours at eighty feet, they would probably hold for an hour or so at ten knots. He called down for Klees to come to the bridge. The exchange was over in less than two minutes. König told his engineer what he was going to do, and Klees agreed. The engineer disappeared through the hatch, and König called down for full speed.

The turning point was farther away than fourteen miles, but Block Island had its own three-mile limit, which was fourteen miles away. Once the *U-Deutschland* was inside the Block Island three-mile limit, she was safe until she reached the western side of the island, where she would exit the island's safety zone. But there was only a four-mile-wide strip of international water separating the continental three-mile limit and the one around Block Island.

A little after 2100, König came abeam the lighted buoy at the north end of Block Island and turned to his new heading. All he had to do now was cross the narrow strip of international water, which would take about thirty minutes, and enter U.S. territorial water. There he would reduce speed to eight knots and run up the Sound, through the Race, make a right turn at the Race Point Light, and head toward the New London Harbor entrance. He checked his watch and figured that he would anchor outside the harbor entrance at about 2400.

An enduring myth about the *U-Deutschland*'s second trip to America is one that König started when he gave an interview to a newspaper reporter in New London. He told the reporter that he navigated in the Sound without a pilot, using a chart that had been published in 1860. It is true that he did not take on a pilot, but in 1916 no pilot was required, and none was stationed off the Sound entrance. As for the chart, König had made this trip many times as an NDL captain, and he knew where he was going. But he did have a chart. It was a standard-issue NDL chart, completely up-to-date and accompanied by a copy of the *United States Coast Pilot, Section B, Race Point, Cape Cod, New York, 1916.*

The trip up the Sound was uneventful until the *U-Deutschland* passed the Race Point light and came to a heading of 340 degrees to make the New London Harbor entrance. It was just a few minutes before midnight, and the river dredge *Atlantic* was coming out of the harbor entrance and into the Sound as the *U-Deutschland* was approaching the entrance. Both vessels were displaying the correct navigation lights, and they were closing nearly bows on, with the *U-Deutschland* pointed a little to the left of the oncoming barge. But the *U-Deutschland*'s lights were mounted on the sides of the conning tower and were considerably lower than the dredge's wheelhouse. The dredge's skipper had difficulty seeing the U-boat's lights and could see her green starboard light only faintly. It looked to him like the U-boat was passing obliquely across his bow from left to right. Since the dredge was exiting a channel (and so was restricted in its ability to maneuver), it had the right of way, and its skipper did not recognize the situation as a problem, figuring the other vessel was moving fast enough to get clear.

König saw the dredge but for some reason thought she was far enough to his left that the two vessels would pass each other port side to. But it was going to be a close pass. A moment later he decided it was going to be too close, and he told his helmsman, Anton Born, to move off to starboard. Born turned the wheel enough to swing the bow a few degrees right, which brought the *U-Deutschland's* port and starboard running lights into clear view. The barge captain suddenly realized he was looking straight down the other vessel's keel line. He sounded one short blast and turned hard to starboard.

The deep blast of the dredge's horn came at the same moment when König recognized the broad bow of an enormous dredge coming at him head-on. He shouted at Born to put the helm hard over to starboard and then called down the speaking tube, "Ahead full!" The barge—flat bottomed, broad beamed, and massive—responded slowly to her own rudder change. König ordered the lookout next to him to close the conning tower hatch, shouted down the speaking tube "Close watertight doors!" and hit the collision alarm.

Inside the boat two officers and twenty-three seamen felt their stomachs knot. Four watertight doors slammed shut, sealing the boat's five separate compartments. Then they all waited. On the bridge König was gripping the conning tower rim with both hands, staring at the barge's bow as it came closer. In his mind he ran a constant calculation as the situation unfolded. The seaman on his left was also gripping the rim and staring wide-eyed at the dredge. Born was looking straight ahead, watching the bow continue to swing away from the other vessel.

In the barge's wheelhouse the captain and his first mate stared down at the U-boat wondering what in hell he was doing here at the entrance to New London. The mate mumbled under his breath, "This is going to be close." The captain overheard him and without turning his eyes away from the *U-Deutschland* said, "Keep turning, you bastard, keep turning." The mate wondered whom the captain meant, the barge or the U-boat. The helmsman, also not knowing whom the captain had addressed, answered, "Keep turning, aye sir."

On the *U-Deutschland's* bridge, König was now nearly certain the barge was going to ram them near the stern. The boat's diesels were straining, and the boat was still turning, but she was slow in both accelerating and coming right. The engines were, after all, just four-hundred-horsepower generators, and the *U-Deutschland* was not a particularly maneuverable boat.

"We're going to clear," the lookout said.

König quickly looked aft and then at the dredge's bow, which was still very close. But they were going to clear. It was going to be very, very close, but they were going to clear. "Rudder amidships!" he shouted to Born, who was only about three feet away, to keep the stern from swinging in front of the barge.

As the bow settled on the new heading, the dredge plowed past the stern with almost no discernible clearance. When the ships were clearly separated by a widening space, König exhaled the breath he had been holding. He was badly shaken by what had been in fact a very near miss. The collision with the tug in Bremen had been embarrassing, but at least he had not been to blame. This, on the other hand, would have been a disaster in every respect. He took a deep breath, thanked the fates, and looked around for a place to anchor. Fifteen minutes later he was anchored on the west side of the entrance in twenty-six feet of water.

At 0035 on 1 November the *EFCO* came alongside and put Hinsch and the health officer, Dr. Walter Chipman, on board. The barge had found the launch near Race Light and told them about the near miss. Either the *EFCO* had been waiting in the wrong place or everyone on board had been asleep when the *U-Deutschland* went by. Doctor Chipman read the bill of health and asked if any of the crewmen were ill. Finding everything in order, he waived the quarantine regulations and released the *U-Deutschland* to proceed to the State Pier. At 0230 König laid the U-boat alongside the pier without any assistance and made her fast.

New London

A small crowd of not more than a hundred people clustered along the railroad tracks that led onto State Pier. It was a disappointed crowd. The people, mostly reporters, had come to get a glimpse of the *U-Deutschland,* but all they got was a solid, twenty-foot-high, corrugated-metal fence above which protruded the *Willehad's* funnel. There was no high ground near enough to allow someone to get a look over the top of the fence and no convenient pile driver, as had been available in Baltimore. A few enterprising souls had used their pocketknives to bore holes in the fence to peek through, but that small success came to an abrupt and painful end when New London Police Department's "one man strong arm squad," Officer Nelson Smith, showed up at 0800.[1]

Even without Officer Smith's intervention, the hole borers' efforts were doomed. From inside the already formidable fence came the sounds of hammering. Eastern Forwarding Company workers were erecting another fence inside the first one. The new fence, built entirely of wood, was parallel to, and set back twelve inches from, the corrugated-metal fence. The twelve-inch space between the fences effectively put an end to the peek-holes.

The people who had come to the State Pier in boats were equally disappointed. The *U-Deutschland* lay port side to the pier, her bow pointing toward land. The warehouse that had been built on the pier blocked any view from that side, and the *Willehad,* which was anchored one hundred feet away from the boat's starboard

▲ The *U-Bremen* in Helgoland, 21 August 1916. This is possibly the last photo taken of the boat. *Jørn Jensen collection*

◄ The *U-Deutschland*'s berth in New London, showing the *Willehad* and the floating fence, which, together with the purpose-built warehouses, completely enclosed the *U-Deutschland* and virtually prevented public viewing. Security in New London was even tighter than it had been in Baltimore. *Library of Congress*

side, completely blocked the view from that direction. A twelve-foot-high fence on pontoons was drawn across the entrance to the berth, making the U-boat secure and out of sight inside the box. The EFCO kept boats from approaching the floating fence too closely.

On the land side of the box was the two-story EFCO office building. Between the left side of the building and the corrugated-metal fence was a wagon gate with doors that swung out. The company's belated decision to build a second security fence inside the outer fence proved to be an unexpected benefit to the crowd. Having no materials on hand with which to build the new fence, EFCO had to order lumber from a local yard. As each wagonload of boards and posts arrived, the double gate swung open and the crowd pressed forward to get a quick glimpse through the opening.

Why such tight security? In part it was due to Paul Hilken's paranoia, which undoubtedly stemmed from his clandestine sabotage activities. The overdone security measures also stemmed from the Germans' belief that British supporters or even British agents would try to harm the boat in some way. Given Hilken's other activities and the realities of being in a country where the majority of the people supported the Allies, the need for security was genuine. But the visual secrecy was really Hinsch's doing. He hated the press, a feeling that Hilken shared. By making the *U-Deutschland* almost impossible to see or photograph, Hinsch was deliberately making life hard for reporters and cameramen.

Hinsch made no secret of his dislike for newspapermen, and over König's objection he placed an absolute ban on any newspapermen going on board the *U-Deutschland*. He would not even let them look at the boat. One reporter wrote that Hinsch had even strung barbed wire along the top of the security fence to prevent them from climbing to the top for a glimpse. Actually, the added topping on the fence was not barbed wire but a six-foot-high canvas screen. König told reporters that he and the EFCO officers, except for Hinsch, "would like to have correspondents go on board rather than take descriptions at second hand." Unfortunately for König's wishes and the newsmen, Hinsch was in charge of security.[2]

But the reporters were not entirely without an opportunity to get a glimpse of the boat, even if the opportunity was some distance away. Ruth Baker, who owned a small, two-story house on a bluff north of the State Pier, was doing a lively business "charging twenty-five cents for a peep at the submarine from the second story." She gave each customer a set of binoculars to use at no extra cost and by 14 November had reportedly made ninety-five dollars.[3]

Members of the press can be a pain in the neck under the best conditions, and a huge pain if they put their minds to it. But Hinsch overlooked the fact that one of the *U-Deutschland*'s primary roles was to create propaganda aimed at developing American sympathy for Germany's efforts to break the British blockade. Therefore, maintaining good press relations should have had a high-priority. Captain König certainly recognized that and tried his best to win the press' favor whenever the opportunity presented itself. But there was nothing he could do about the security measures on the State Pier.

To be fair to Hinsch, he was not entirely to blame for the poor press relations in New London. Many public-relations problems stemmed from German insensitivity, the actions of the *U-53* off New London in September being a good example. When the Germans decided to send the *U-53* to the United States to demonstrate that the U-boat's antishipping campaign could reach American waters, they knew that the State Department had been at odds with the British over Royal Navy cruisers stopping ships very close to the three-mile limit. Inasmuch as Germany's official diplomatic stance was to keep America out of the war, one has to wonder what the admirals were thinking about when they ordered Hans Rose to attack shipping as soon as he cleared the three-mile limit.

Insensitivity was not limited to the Admiralstab; Paul Hilken and Hinsch had enough to go around. The first example that appeared had to do with racism. The Eastern Forwarding Company sent seventy-five African-American stevedores to New London to handle the *U-Deutschland*'s cargo, the same men it had used in Baltimore. They arrived by train in New London on the afternoon of 2 November and were marched as a group from the station to the EFCO office building at State Pier. There each man was issued an identity card, which he kept with him at all times unless he left the pier for any reason. When all the cards had been issued, the men went on board the *Willehad,* which would be their home for the time they remained in New London. In keeping with the racial views of the early twentieth century, the African-Americans were not allowed off the EFCO property as long as they were in New London. Nevertheless, the word quickly spread that the Germans had brought a lot of blacks to town.

The issue took two directions. The first, and louder, was the white community's unfounded fear of an imminent crime wave. The second and more serious, insofar as EFCO was concerned, was the local white dockworkers' outrage over losing all those jobs. Not getting the jobs was bad enough, but losing them to what they viewed as a bunch of imported black workers was intolerable. They threatened to picket the State Pier. The last things EFCO wanted were an outraged community and a picket line across its gate.

Carl Ahrendt, who had come to New London as Hinsch's office assistant, arranged a public meeting for 3 November. Paul König was picked to present EFCO's side of the issue, and Ahrendt provided him with the speaking points the company wanted made. König was a good choice, but he should have tossed Ahrendt's notes in the trash.

Speaking to a large and attentive crowd of residents and reporters, König explained that the stevedores had been employed in Baltimore and were therefore experienced in handling submarine cargo. He told the crowd that the *U-Deutschland*'s cargo holds and handling equipment were different than those found on conventional ships and that the cargo itself was somewhat different and exceptionally valuable. He then assured everyone that the stevedores would live on board the *Willehad* and would remain inside the EFCO compound while they were in New London.

He then told them that EFCO used African-American stevedores for security reasons. First, he said, African-Americans were known to have "little power of observation" and were unlikely to recognize anything important. He was certain, he added, that even if one of them did learn some secret, his poor communication skills would prevent him from giving anyone else an accurate description of what he had seen. The explanation was blatantly racist but acceptable in early-twentieth-century America.

The residents were pleased with what they heard, especially the part about the stevedores being confined inside the EFCO walls. But the local white stevedores were not pleased with the implication that African-Americans could learn how to handle submarine cargo better than whites could. Everyone agreed that from the Germans' point of view the security argument made sense. The only people who were completely pleased with the EFCO decision to use African-American stevedores in New London were the British diplomats and attachés in Washington, especially the naval attaché, Lieutenant Guy Gaunt. One of those stevedores was a British spy.[4]

Having finished his explanation, König asked if there were any questions. There were. Did he expect to have any trouble evading the British cruisers when he left New London? The question had been asked countless times in one form or another in Baltimore, and König should have been ready with his stock answer. Instead, he changed direction and told the questioner that he expected to meet the *U-57* off the coast. Why he chose to specifically name the *U-57* is unclear.

The *U-57* had been commissioned on 6 July 1916 and had gone on her first war patrol in late September, so König might have heard about the new boat while the *U-Deutschland* was in Bremen. She was slightly larger and more heavily armed than the *U-53,* and her range was given as 10,500 nautical miles, which was 1,500 nautical miles greater than the *U-53*'s. But she could not have made an Atlantic crossing and carried out attacks on shipping without modification or being refueled on the East Coast. The possibility that the *U-57* would carry out the same destruction rekindled the question of the *U-Deutschland*'s real purpose and delivered a staggering blow to Germany's campaign to gain American support.[5]

That same day, at 1400, Commander Yates Sterling, five officers, and Customs Collector James McGovern went on board the *U-Deutschland* to conduct a neutrality inspection. But this inspection was far more detailed than anything done before. The navy officers were not just looking for weapons, they were looking at everything, for the purpose of learning all they could about the *U-Deutschland*'s construction and machinery. In the process they arrived at the same decision that Captain Hughes and his men had in Baltimore—the *U-Deutschland* was an unarmed cargo vessel. But their detailed inspection report's most interesting comments were found in the second and third paragraphs of the cover sheet:

> There was no evidence of weapons of war of any description. The construction of the ship would have to be materially altered to provide for the installation of torpedo tubes and torpedoes. The vessel could be quickly converted into a commerce raiding submarine by the mounting of several guns on the non-watertight superstructure; a certain amount of stiffening would be required. The vessel could also be readily converted into a mine laying submarine, launching the mines from the superstructure deck; the watertight hatches are large enough to pass a mine sufficiently large to do considerable damage.[6]

That was a substantial change from the opinion that Captain Hughes had written in Baltimore, simply that she could not be converted to a war boat "without large structural changes." But Commander Sterling's next assessment was even more revealing.

> Furthermore, the *U-Deutschland* could act to a limited extent with its present equipment as a tender for several submarines. The cargo space inside the pressure hull could be utilized for the stowage of spare parts and supplies. In addition to the 150 tons fuel oil carried in the fuel tanks, several hundred more tons could be carried in one or more of her ballast tanks. The *U-Deutschland* could act therefore in the capacity of a supply ship for war submarines within the limit of her oil capacity, thereby permitting war submarines to remain a longer time on operating grounds than they could remain with supplies and oil ordinarily carried themselves.[7]

Mounting deck guns and taking mines on board was out of the question in the United States. But the boat could easily take on spare parts, supplies, and fuel oil. In fact, she had taken on seventy-five tons of fuel oil from the *Willehad* the previous day. Two days later she took on another twenty-five tons from a tank car rolled onto the pier. The State and Treasury Departments got nervous.

According to the *U-Deutschland's* technical specifications, she carried a normal fuel supply of 150 tons, a figure that the naval inspections in Baltimore and New London confirmed. That amount of fuel gave the boat an operating range of about 7,200 nautical miles. Chief Engineer Klees told the navy inspectors in New London that the *U-Deutschland* burned four tons of diesel fuel per day under "ideal conditions," a figure that was in agreement with the boat's specifications.[8]

But ideal conditions meant running steadily at eight knots in calm seas. Higher speeds and rougher seas materially increased fuel consumption. Despite König's repeated claims that the *U-Deutschland* could easily make a round trip without refueling, the reality was that the *U-Deutschland* could steam for thirty-seven days and twelve hours in calm seas at eight knots, which made the round trip only marginally feasible even under ideal conditions. To explain why he took on supposedly unneeded fuel in Baltimore and again in New London, König again said it was because of the superiority of American diesel oil. But that, as in Baltimore, was just propaganda to make Americans feel good about the quality of their diesel oil.

The first round trip had taken forty-eight days. Using the four-tons-per-day figure, the *U-Deutschland* would have come up forty-two tons short had she not refueled in Baltimore. Still, she arrived in Bremen with fuel to spare, and it is safe to assume the remaining fuel went into a war boat about to depart. When he arrived in New London, König told everyone that he had left Bremen on 10 October. If that had been the case, the trip across would have taken twenty-one days. But the *U-Deutschland* had left Wilhelmshaven on 8 October and bypassed Helgoland on a crossing that took twenty-four days. Even under the best of conditions she would have arrived in New London with fifty-eight tons of fuel remaining. But the truth was that she arrived with closer to forty tons, which is why she took on another hundred tons in New London. The numbers Klees provided make sense, and they work out. But the repeated propaganda claim that the boat did not need additional fuel, coupled with Commander Sterling's report, convinced a lot of Americans that the boat was really a "milk cow."

In general, the subject of the boat's fuel consumption raised the question of her merchant status. If she did refuel a U-boat at sea, would she give up her rights as a merchant vessel and be subject to attack on sight? The answer was yes. The same law applied if she met a U-boat outside the three-mile limit to be escorted back to Germany. In that case, as the escorted vessel, she took on the character of her escort.

A more serious question stemming from taking on fuel in New London was the issue of American neutrality. If the *U-Deutschland* met a U-boat offshore and provided fuel that had come from the United States, would American neutrality be violated? If the answer was yes, American diesel fuel would be denied to the *U-Deutschland,* and that would jeopardize any future trips, because the boat did not have the ability to make a round trip without refueling in the United States.

Concerned over the refueling issue that Commander Sterling's report raised, the State Department tentatively said that American neutrality would not be compromised if the *U-Deutschland* provided fuel to a U-boat in international waters. But official doubt about that decision remained.[9]

On 9 November, Secretary of State Lansing wrote to Secretary of the Treasury McAdoo expressing his concern over Commander Sterling's opinion that the *U-Deutschland* could be "easily converted into a commerce raider or a mine layer." He asked that Treasury agents in New London be instructed to keep a close watch on the boat to ensure that no warlike modifications were made. He closed his letter by instructing that if "any circumstances arise showing that the *U-Deutschland* is being equipped for hostile operations *or laden for delivery at sea*," he wanted the boat's clearance delayed "until further consideration can be given the case."[10]

It was not only the government that was starting to have second thoughts about the Germans' commercial submarine cargo business. The rise of negative feeling toward the *U-Deutschland* and everything associated with her had begun in October following the *U-53*'s visit to New London. During October 1916 the State Department, Treasury Department, and the customs office in Bridgeport, Connecticut, were deluged with letters from citizens who saw evil intentions in the goings-on at the State Pier. One recurring theme was that EFCO's practice of sending a tug to sea daily to wait for the *U-Bremen*'s arrival was actually a cover for an elaborate U-boat resupply scheme.

New York attorney Anderson Price sent two newspaper clippings with headlines "U-Boats Have Base in America, Say Britons," and "New Hunt on for *Bremen*," to which he attached a handwritten note asking, "Is it possible that the tug which leaves New London so frequently is carrying supplies for German submarines? There does seem to be sufficient evidence to compel an examination."[11] (After the tug abandoned the offshore waits, Hinsch sent a thirty-foot launch every night to the lower harbor, from where the crew could view the Race.) But the best example of public paranoia is Bruce Ford's 31 October letter written to the secretary of state.

> At New London there is a large pier, a section of which has been rented by the Eastern Forwarding Company. They have built a galvanized iron storehouse and have put up a high board fence which conceals what is going on inside. A German steamship is moored alongside the pier, but spaced from it, forming an enclosed dock.
>
> It is said that there has been evidence of considerable activity there, and that small craft go in and out, and that a tug has been going out to sea and back again at frequent intervals for the alleged purpose of meeting the German merchant submarine Bremen.
>
> It is said that a short time ago a barge, whose mission is unknown, lay at anchor off the entrance of the harbor.

It has been suggested that any German submarine, such as the U-53, could easily have obtained supplies in this neighborhood, either by way of the tug or small craft, from the dock, or from the barge. It has even been suggested that a submarine could get in and lie concealed in the space between the pier and the German steamship. The fact that our own submarine base is just a short distance up the river [at Groton, Connecticut], and that our submarines are known to ply in and out in a submerged state with nothing but a periscope showing, is advanced as a reason that if a submerged foreign submarine were observed it would not attract special comment.[12]

Within four days of their arrival, Captain König, his crew, and his boat were already being viewed as "shady." So far, the public's growing negative attitude was the result of policies, statements, and actions formulated in Germany that caused the public to view the *U-Deutschland* in a poor light. The *U-53*'s actions were still a vivid memory, and despite what König had said about EFCO's need for security, the presence of so many African-American stevedores on the New London waterfront rankled.

Given the atmosphere of general distrust, petty grievances took on disproportionate importance, as happened in the case of Harrison Smith, of Auburndale, Massachusetts. Smith was outraged that when he had arrived back in America from Europe, his ship had been held in quarantine overnight, whereas the *U-Deutschland* was released in less than an hour. Then, in the early morning hours of 3 November, one of the *U-Deutschland* crewmen made a move on a woman in a local bar.

Two sailors from the *U-Deutschland* had been drinking in the Knickerbocker Restaurant on Bank Street and had become loud, boisterous, and belligerent. In the minutes after 2 November became 3 November, one of the sailors left his stool and approached a woman sitting alone at the bar. He said something to her, she said, "No," and he grabbed her. A noisy, ugly scene ensued as the woman struggled to free herself.

The lone waiter on duty, Lloyd Blanchard, intervened, while the few bar patrons watched. Blanchard was a big man who was accustomed to dealing with obnoxious drunks, which is why he worked the late shift. He grabbed the sailor by the shoulder, pulled him away from the woman, and sent him crashing into three empty bar stools. The sailor grabbed the edge of the bar, and as he rebounded he came up with a six-inch sheath knife in his right hand. He lunged at Blanchard, slashing with the knife from left to right trying to cut through the waiter's abdominal muscles. Blanchard blocked the attack with his left arm, and the razor-sharp blade laid his left forearm open from wrist to elbow.

Badly cut, Blanchard backed away, looking for something with which to defend himself. At the sight of blood most of the people in the bar decided it was time to go home, the woman among them. A noisy nuisance had suddenly turned violent, and the bar was not a good place to be. As the knife-wielding sailor pressed his attack, his drinking companion rushed forward and grabbed him in a bear hug. Pinning his shipmate's arms to his sides and pushing him out the door, he spoke rapidly to him in German.

As dawn broke, Lloyd Blanchard, two police officers, and a mob of reporters were at the EFCO gate. Blanchard's arm was thickly bandaged, and he was mad. The night watchman lost no time calling for Hinsch and König, who quickly appeared at the gate. Sensing that this was not the time to enforce the no–visitors rule, they asked Blanchard and the two policemen to step inside the gate and slammed it shut behind them, leaving the reporters outside. There was a time in America when this sort of crime was settled out of court, in a form of "curbside justice," and that is what happened now.

When the gate reopened and the three men came out, Blanchard was in a much better frame of mind. "The whole thing was a mistake," he now said. It had not been a crewman who cut him, and the weapon had been a harmonica rather than a knife. In fact, the wound was really "just a scratch." It is amazing in this day and age to learn what fifty dollars could accomplish in 1916.[13]

Circumstances that otherwise would have caused the Germans little concern individually were being brought together by a series of events. Some of the events were so minor, even petty, that they might have passed unnoticed were it not for the fact that the press corps was becoming increasingly irritated over being denied access to the *U-Deutschland*. One of those minor events occurred on 4 November.

Reporters had by then dubbed Hinsch "the bane of reporters." His no–press-visitors policy became more onerous as their daily vigil outside the gate dragged on. It seemed to them that anyone who was not a reporter could come and go through the gate as he pleased. That was not the case, but there were enough official visitors, mostly people with business inside the warehouse, coming and going to make it look that way. And there was one visitor who was obviously unofficial. The incident began on Saturday morning, 4 November.

An enterprising photographer slipped into a group of visitors and went through the gate unchallenged. His stay inside was short. He was busily snapping photos when a guard saw him and laid a meaty hand on his shoulder. Other guards came quickly, and one of them stripped the film from the camera and threw it in the water. While two guards held open the gate, the other two heaved the camera-man bodily out of the compound, tossed his camera out after him, and slammed the gate shut.

It was at this dramatic moment that a Packard touring car with Pennsylvania license plates rolled to a stop outside the gate. The lone passenger was Mrs. George L. Adams, a wealthy, attractive woman, "less than forty." Without stepping out of the car, she told an attentive gate guard that she wanted to see Captain König. Wealthy, attractive women, "less than forty," were rarely denied their wishes in that era, and the guard hurried off to summon the captain. The reporters pressed closer.

Shortly König came through the gate and went to the car. The two chatted, she talking about her summer home in Pennsylvania; she handed König a box of cigars and asked to go on board the *U-Deutschland*. Ever the gentleman, König opened the car's door for her, helped her from the car, and escorted her through the gate. The gate slammed shut, and an insignificant event became a scandal.

Reporters suddenly recalled that König had been frequently seen with ladies in Baltimore and had often dined in feminine company. That was all true, but what they omitted from the accounts was that in every case several males were included in the groups, and always as part of orchestrated publicity events. Now a woman had shown up alone at the EFCO gate and been escorted inside. It did not take a great deal of imagination to paint König as a ladies' man. No one ever accused him directly of being a womanizer, but the suggestion was enough in some circles.

From the moment the boat arrived at the State Pier there had been a general atmosphere of disenchantment and suspicion. The press was much more restrained than it had been for the first visit, and the gushy reporting that had been the norm in Baltimore was replaced by a more accusatory tone. The change in attitude was also evident in how the government dealt with the boat. The first indication of the shift in attitude had to do with the boat's radio.

International law and common practice allowed a foreign vessel's radio to remain unsealed for ten days after arrival. The term "sealed" meant that a naval radio specialist would go on board and render the radio inoperative by cutting out the brushes in the motor generator and disassembling the tuning set. The outer panels would be replaced and the seams sealed with special tape. In order to reactivate the radio, someone would have to break the seals. To ensure that the side panels were not secretly removed, the same naval expert would inspect the seals regularly during the vessel's stay in port.

Seven hours after the *U-Deutschland* tied up at State Pier on 1 November, Chief Petty Officer William Briggs went on board and sealed the radio. Hinsch immediately complained to Customs Collector McGovern "that when the vessel was in Baltimore she had been allowed to use her wireless for ten days." Hinsch, correctly, pointed out that neutral vessels routinely entered and departed New York Harbor without having their radios sealed. McGovern passed the complaint up the line to the Treasury Department, where it sat. In the meantime Assistant Secretary of the Treasury William F. Malburn sent the note to the Navy Department with the comment, "The Collector's attention has been invited to Treasury decision 37017 of December 24, 1915, showing the jurisdiction over such radio matters is vested in your Department."[14]

A Roxbury, Massachusetts, resident, Hugh P. McNally, spotted a brief reference to the sealing of the radio in a local newspaper and sent his own complaint to the secretary of the treasury:

> May I inquire why the Collector of the Port of New London, upon
> arrival of the merchantman *U-Deutschland* in that harbor recently

went on board and sealed her wireless outfit? I have never heard of the wireless outfits of the steamers docked at East Boston or at the Mystic docks here being sealed for the brief time they are in port to unload and load munitions of war, and if the *U-Deutschland* carried a six-inch gun on her after deck, a gun capable of effectiveness at least five miles, would she be permitted to enter and leave any port of the United States like any other armed merchantman armed "only for defense?"[15]

Alvey A. Dee, Second Assistant Secretary of the Treasury, dodged the radio question entirely but said in reply to the second, "The Department regrets to be under the necessity of adhering to its customary rule of not undertaking the discussion of suppositious cases in advance of their actual occurrence."

The State Department was starting to feel uneasy about the *U-Deutschland*. The *U-53*'s visit was still fresh in everyone's mind, and the implied threat was not forgotten, especially after the *U-53*'s dramatic demonstration. On 9 November, amid growing doubts about the *U-Deutschland*'s real purpose, the State Department asked the Treasury Department to withhold clearance until the State Department received another report from Commander Sterling. The plan was that as soon as König asked for clearance, Sterling would conduct a second inspection of the boat. Once the inspection was done, the Treasury officials in New London would keep the boat under close surveillance until she departed to ensure that no additional supplies went on board.[16]

Doubts about the *U-Deutschland* had been growing even before she arrived in New London. According to the German naval intelligence press office, most Americans did not believe the private-ownership story about the *U-Deutschland* and the other cargo U-boats. Experts in the shipping business were on record as saying that a submarine freight service could not make a profit even in wartime. They cited exceptionally high operating costs, as against extremely limited cargo capacity. And America's industrialists said that it would require a huge fleet of cargo submarines the size of the *U-Deutschland* to deliver enough raw materials to meet Germany's wartime needs. They were right on all counts.

And there was the nagging question about the crewmen. How was it that so many service-age men were available to man the *U-Deutschland* and the *U-Bremen?* Especially, how was it that here were young men who knew how to operate a submarine but had never been in the service? The status of the older crew members was even more questionable. Where did men like Klees, Johan Kissling, Karl Früchte, and Otto Wegener get the years of submarine experience required to hold leading positions in the engine room? König had addressed the public doubts in July, when the boat was in Baltimore: "It is foolish to believe that any of my men came from the submarine service. They have had their training in the shops at *Germania* in Kiel, where Krupp builds diesel engines. The crew occupies the same relative position as civilian experts in American submarine plants who continuously run the trials of their boats until they are turned over to the Navy."[17]

The reporters did not question König about the contradictions in what he had told them. For example, why would Krupp release valuable, experienced employees at a time when U-boats were being built around the clock? What possible advantage accrued to Krupp if fifty of his most important technicians were working as seamen on board DOR cargo U-boats? And both the international and American reporters missed another opening four months later when Lohmann told foreign reporters in Bremen, "They have been released to us until the end of the war. Their training was done exclusively on the *U-Deutschland* after she was launched in March." Not a single reporter asked Lohmann who had done the releasing, Krupp or the Imperial German Navy.

The failure of the press to expose the truth was largely owing to poor communications. Then as now, local news was here today and gone tomorrow; what was said in Europe rarely reached America in time to have any local news value. The biggest delays were results of the transatlantic cables having been cut and the fact that everything reaching the United States went through British censors before it was released. The third cause of delay was the primitive state of information recovery.

Today we are accustomed to retrieving archival information almost instantly using our own computers. Almost anything a person wants to know about can be found online, though the information is not always accurate. Nothing like that was available in 1916. Information recovery required time-consuming hand searches, aided only by reporters' memory of what they had seen and heard. And the information storage locations were often days apart. The whole problem boiled down to the inability to quickly gather information from several sources that were in a practical sense inaccessible.

Even without serious investigative reporting, the American people reached the general consensus that the DOR was a front, the boats belonged to the German navy, and the men who manned them were really servicemen. If there was a general consensus that the *U-Deutschland* crewmen were really members of the German navy, there was also a general consensus that it did not really matter. Nevertheless, the Germans carried on the pretense that the entire undertaking was a private-sector investment. Part of that pretense included the frequent claim that the *U-Deutschland* was paying her own way, which raised the mail issue again.

The problem in November was the same as it had been in July. The British were opening mail carried on board neutral ships bound for Scandinavian ports and Holland, and they were seizing the contents that they classed as contraband. The Germans still needed a secure, reasonably frequent way to send mail to, and receive it from, agents in the United States. Citizens in both countries wanted an open line of communications between their families and friends, and American and German financial institutions were in need of a regular, secure way to transfer funds back and forth.

The negotiators who were working on a mail agreement between Germany and the U.S. Post Office were slowly coming to an agreement, but they were hung up over the Germans' insistence that the U.S. Post Office put all submarine mail in hermetically sealed cans or waterproof pouches.[18] Despite the waterproof-packaging issue, however, everything else was in place, to the point that the German post office had already issued regulations for the sending of "submarine mail" and had printed the necessary forms and stamps. By December 1916, mail intended for shipment to the United States from Germany was being collected in Bremen, and an agreement was finally reached that set the starting date for submarine mail on 1 January 1917. But there would be no submarine mail route between the United States and Germany.

Meanwhile, even though the *U-Deutschland* would not be carrying mail back to Germany, the progress toward a mail-service agreement eased some of the doubts the public had about the boat. The important thing, insofar as the Germans were concerned, was that the postal issue highlighted the fact that the British were seriously interfering with the U.S. mail, and Americans objected strongly to that. The fact that relatively few Americans sent mail to Europe was of no matter, but the principle of the thing was, and if the Germans could get the mail through, so much the better.

The small public-opinion gains made with the mail issue got only a minor boost, however, from the boat's cargo. There was little fanfare associated with the boat's arrival in New London and almost no reaction to the cargo, which was in four categories. The first category was 165 tons of dyestuffs, most of which was consigned to five of the six big American dye companies: Farbewerke-Hoechst, Casella Color, Geigy, Berlin Aniline, and Bayer. The value placed on the dyes in Germany, $6,251,418, was much greater than its actual value, which was closer to $3,000,000.[19]

The *New York Times* business page remarked that the boat's arrival "caused much less stir" on this trip in part because the novelty had worn off and the loss of the *U-Bremen* had put a damper on the enthusiasm for a submarine freight link to Germany. More important was that the cargo of dyestuffs would "cut practically no figure affecting the supply or market value of dyes and chemicals here." The fact that most of the dyes were consigned directly to five of the six big American Dye firms went almost unnoticed. The exception was a small chemical company, Geisenheimer and Company, in New York City, which made and sold dyes.[20]

While it was true that there was little excitement evident among the buyers, the fact was that they needed those dyes and were prepared to pay for them. The advantage they had in this instance was that the dyes were already consigned to them and they would simply pay the amounts due on their orders, which the German dye makers, rather than the Hilkens, established. The most expensive dye in the lot was one called "Ink Blue BITN0," which was valued at $2.31 a pound. The least expensive was a dye called "Sulphur Brown 2G," at twenty-one cents a pound. In Baltimore the Hilkens sold nearly the same amount of dyestuffs for $6,180. The sales figures for New London are not available, but the price was probably not quite as high.

As for the pharmaceuticals, König and Hilken had erred by promising that the next boat to arrive would bring drugs for the treatment of polio, which in July was reaching epidemic proportions in New York. Instead, the next boat, which would have been the *U-Bremen,* was reportedly carrying Salvarsan, an arsenic-based drug for treating syphilis. Salvarsan was also what the *U-Deutschland* was reported to be carrying. But there was no Salvarsan listed in her manifest. Instead the 165 tons she brought were a mixed bag of everything from anesthesia to a veterinary medicine called Suprarenin Bitartrat, which was used for treating *Schweineseuche,* a disease affecting pigs.

The only pharmaceutical on the manifest that was directed at venereal disease was Albargin, which was used to prevent and cure gonorrhea and had been found to be effective as a prophylaxis against other forms of venereal diseases. When German sailors had gone ashore in China during the Boxer Rebellion, they had been issued vials of Albargin to take orally before sex; reportedly the venereal disease rate had dropped dramatically throughout the German East Asia Squadron. All 163 pounds of the drug were consigned to H. A. Metz in New York, who was hoping to sell it to the U.S. Navy.[21] The Farbewerke-Hoechst Company was the maker of both Salvarsan and Albargin, which were marketed through Farbewerke-Hoechst America in New York, of which H. A. Metz was the president. Basing their expectations on the widely reported promises made in Baltimore, the public and the press were disappointed when it was learned that there were no polio-fighting drugs on board the *U-Deutschland.*

The presence of a little over a half-million dollars in securities on board the *U-Deutschland* elicited an equally bored reaction from bankers, because there was no indication that any of those securities were going to American banks; instead, they would go to banks with specific interests in Germany. Whether or not it was sour grapes, many American bankers told reporters they were reluctant to risk shipping securities on submarines. In any case, given the unexplained loss of the *U-Bremen,* the bankers had good reason to be reluctant.[22]

In fact, of the seven banks, one investment firm, and one industrial company to which the securities were consigned, only three had German or Austrian backing or interests. The Deutsche Bank was consigned 1,004,000 marks for loans to Hugo Schmidt, who was the western representative for Deutsche Bank. The other two banks with German interests were Guaranty Trust Company of New York (where Hilken had an account for his sabotage operations), which received 1,600 marks, and the Transatlantic Trust Company (representing the Austrian and German governments), which received 25,240 marks. All three banks were deeply involved in funding the subversive activities of German agents in the United States, and Schmidt's role was to administer the funds held by those banks and several others. The manifest also listed three cases of "imitation precious stones" valued at $3,500, which were consigned to seven New York dealers, and one package of diamonds, without details.

The general lack of interest in the *U-Deutschland*'s cargo was reflected in the absence of any public hoopla over the crew and its captain. On one hand, there was not so large a German presence in New London as there had been in Baltimore, and on the other, the political climate in the United States with regard to all things German had shifted heavily toward the Allies. The German propaganda campaign needed those public displays of affection and support, and when those events failed to materialize, German public relations took a hit.

An official banquet for the officers and crew in New London received only local coverage, and when the Harvard German Club made König an honorary member, the notice ended up as a column filler in the *New York Times* want ads. Similarly, König's induction into the Order of the Hermann Söhne (the Sons of Hermann) went virtually unnoticed. The largest event in New London occurred on 8 November, when two thousand people attended a reception in the municipal building for König, his crew, and the crew of the *Willehad*. Mayor Ernest E. Rogers presented König with a gold watch bearing the city seal, and each man in the *U-Deutschland* crew received a silver match case and a fountain pen.[23]

Unlike in Baltimore, where nearly everything that happened on the EFCO Pier had been reported, analyzed, and blown out of proportion, in New London the coverage was unexpectedly sparse. As we have seen, the secrecy surrounding the boat's cargo was as tight as it had been in Baltimore, which, together with Hinsch's almost total concealment of the boat, turned the press against the German enterprise. Another result, aside from sparseness, was that reporting on the goings-on in New London was considerably more accurate than had been the case in Baltimore. Noticeably absent were the gushing accolades to Paul König and the predeparture hype about the threats that awaited the *U-Deutschland* when she crossed the three-mile limit.

The stevedores started loading the outbound cargo on 5 November. On the 11th, as the loading neared completion, Hinsch started laying off the stevedores. The last of the cargo went on board on the morning of 14 November, and the following afternoon König told Collector McGovern that he would be asking for clearance that evening. McGovern telephoned the New London naval base and arranged to have Commander Sterling make a final neutrality inspection, as requested by the State Department. Sterling, two other officers, McGovern, and "members of the customs force made a thorough inspection." The inspection was completed after dark, and McGovern issued König the clearance.[24]

By the night of 16 November the *U-Deutschland* was fully loaded and ready for sea. Her cargo consisted of 416 tons of crude rubber, 83 tons of tin in pigs, 207 tons of nickel, 160 tons of alloy steel, and 6.2 tons of silver. The silver, valued at $140,000, had arrived from San Francisco on 7 November and had been hauled in open wagons from the train station to the EFCO pier. There were no armed guards accompanying the treasure as it rolled through New London.[25]

The following morning, however, the *U-Deutschland* was still in her berth, and there were no signs that she would be getting under way soon. The press had been saying for two days that the boat was on the verge of leaving, and based on what had happened in Baltimore, most people assumed the *U-Deutschland* would go to sea shortly after sunup. A newsman in New London reported that there was "a conjecture that Captain König would leave the harbor awash in broad daylight." Thursday, 16 November 1916, passed without any activity on the EFCO pier. That evening, König, dressed in civilian attire, was seen "idling about town in the early part of the evening."[26]

13

The Not-So-Triumphant Return

In the waning minutes of 16 November, there was activity on the EFCO pier that indicated the boat was about to get under way. Reporters in a press boat stationed in the Thames River could not see what was happening, but they could hear the sounds of something being hoisted and later learned that the dock-workers had used a cargo crane to haul a huge steel net onto the pier. The net, the existence of which had been unknown to anyone other than the EFCO employees, was a surprise and a curiosity to the reporters. What kind of threat were the Germans guarding against that had caused them to hang a submerged net across the berth entrance? The question was never answered.

There was more open activity outside the EFCO office building, where a few reporters and late-night idlers were gathered. A dozen sailors from the *Willehad* joined the regular night security force to keep everyone away from the building and the wagon gate. Noises coming from inside the EFCO pier told everyone out front that something was up, and most of the watchers figured correctly that the boat was getting under way. In the excitement caused by the sounds of activity from behind the fence there were a few run-ins when individuals tried to maneuver to get a better look. A *Willehad* crewman threw a board at one man who got too close to the gate, and the regular security force turned a fire hose on others.

At about 0100 the reporters in the launch were rewarded with a clear view of the *U-Deutschland* as the floating fence was withdrawn and made fast to the outboard side of the State Pier. Two tugs stood off in the river, the *T. A. Scott, Jr.* and the *Cassie*. At 0115 the *U-Deutschland*'s lines were cast off and a line was passed to the *T. A. Scott, Jr.*, which started pulling the *U-Deutschland* away from the dock while the U-boat went astern on her electric motors. As the *U-Deutschland* cleared the end of the pier, the towline parted, but König was able to turn the boat around without the *Scott*'s help. As her bow swung to port, König cut in the diesel engines and started downriver, with the *T. A. Scott, Jr.*, a hundred feet off her port side and the *Cassie* a hundred feet to starboard. All three vessels had their running lights on, which surprised the reporters, who had expected the boat to depart fully darkened in order not to be seen.[1]

There was no need for such measures to get away unnoticed, because other than a handful of reporters and night-owl citizens New London was fast asleep. Unlike the Baltimore departure, which had been in daylight, this departure was made in the wee hours of the morning. There were no crowds, no hooting and honking steamers anchored along the way, and only one press boat, which maintained a respectful distance from the two tugs and the U-boat. The procession moved down the Thames at three or four knots until the vessels were off Pequot Dock, where the *Scott* increased speed, cut across the *U-Deutschland*'s path, and took a position ahead of the U-boat off her starboard bow. At the same time the *Cassie* moved to a position off the *U-Deutschland*'s port quarter.[2]

The morning of 17 November 1916 was a brilliantly moonlit night with "very light wind and almost calm sea." When the convoy passed the New London Ledge Light, the *U-Deutschland* increased speed to eight or nine knots and pulled away from the *Cassie,* which could not keep up. The *Scott* was still ahead on a parallel course "at a safe distance from the starboard side of the *U-Deutschland*." In fact the *U-Deutschland* was slowly closing the gap between her and the tug.

The only men on the *U-Deutschland*'s bridge were König and Krapohl; everyone else was below at their diving stations, and the helmsman was in the central control room. König had the boat and crew ready to dive the moment he sensed danger. The visibility was excellent, and König could clearly see the *Scott's* stern light three points off his starboard bow, and the Race Rock light two points (a little over twenty-two degrees) off the port bow, about a half-mile away. He noted that he had gained on the *Scott* and that the tug was now about four hundred feet away, off the starboard bow and still on a parallel course.

On the tug, Hinsch, megaphone in hand, was "at the bow, one foot amidships and the other on her port side near her forward bitts." Capt. John Gurney, who was helming the *Scott,* called down to Hinsch, "The *U-Deutschland* is getting too near Race Rock. You better sing out to her to port her helm and come closer to us." (Captain Gurney had used the old term for turning to starboard, a usage that stemmed from the days when ships were steered with tillers and turning to starboard meant pushing the tiller to port—thus "port your helm.") Hinsch raised his megaphone and called out across the water, "More to starboard. You are coming too close to Race Rock." (Hinsch used the term that was more common among steam sailors, whose vessels were steered with wheels.) "I don't think it's necessary," König shouted back. Hinsch shouted the message again and this time saw the *U-Deutschland* alter course slightly to starboard.

Capt. John Gurney was a longtime employee of the T. A. Scott Company and knew every inch of New London Harbor, the Long Island and Block Island Sounds, and the Race. Everything was in his favor—local knowledge, excellent visibility, and no traffic to contend with. All he had to do was lead the *U-Deutschland* through the Race, and his job would be finished.

Eugene Duzant, an able seaman was a newcomer to the Scott Company and was the only *Scott* crewman who did not live in New London. Duzant's background was crewing on fishing boats, and he was accustomed to long, miserable hours and backbreaking work. Despite several years at sea, he had never become accustomed to the cold, and right now he was freezing. He had taken refuge behind the deck-house, closer to the stern.

The only three people on board who were not cold were the cook, Clarence B. Davidson, who was making coffee in the galley, and the members of the engine-room crew—Ed Stone, the fireman, and William "Bill" Caton, the engineer. Stone and Caton were playing cards, something the two friends did regularly. If the engine telegraph jangled, Caton would deal with it, and if the fire needed tending, Stone would get up and shovel coal. The rest of the time they played cards.

The *T. A. Scott, Jr.* was a wooden-hull tug that had been built in 1888 and rebuilt in 1900. She was rated at thirty-six gross tons, was sixty-two feet, six inches long, had a sixteen-foot beam, and drew seven feet. She was powered by a single compound condensing steam engine that developed 228 horsepower and drove a single three-blade screw. When she entered the Race the tide was at full flood, a condition that Captain Gurney and the *Scott* had easily handled on many occasions. Being four hundred feet ahead of the *U-Deutschland,* the tug encountered the full force of the flood tide moments before the U-boat did. Hinsch was still standing on the bow when the *Scott* abruptly "swung against her helm," turning ninety-degrees to port. To fully understand what happened during the next brief seconds we need to examine the role of the tug's engine-room telegraph.

The *Scott*'s engine-room telegraph was a "gong and jingle bell system," the two signal types operated by separate levers on the telegraph stand. When she encountered the tide, the tug was running at half-speed. The correct command for increasing to full speed was one jingle. But in the gong-and-jingle-bell system, there were circumstances in which a single stroke of the gong also meant full speed ahead. And to make things more complicated, a single stroke of the gong could also mean stop. It all depended on the sequence of bell and gong signals that were used when the vessel got under way.[3]

When the *Scott* turned unexpectedly into the tide she moved directly into the *U-Deutschland*'s path at half-speed. Hinsch, whose attention was focused on the *U-Deutschland,* saw that she was going to ram the *Scott* unless the tug increased speed to get out of the way. The U-boat was about two hundred feet away when Hinsch shouted up to Gurney, "Ring her up!" and turned to the ladder that led up to the wheelhouse. As he was turning around he heard the clear sound of a gong, and the *Scott* immediately lost way. Apparently, Gurney rang down one gong thinking he was ringing for full speed ahead when in fact he was ordering stop. Engineer Bill Caton, correctly (in terms of the signal system) interpreting the gong as the stop command, would have closed the piston valve to the propeller shaft. Hinsch had one foot on the second rung of the ladder when the *U-Deutschland* plowed into the *Scott* just twelve feet forward of the tug's stern, about where Eugene Duzant was sheltering.

Atop the *U-Deutschland*'s conning tower both König and Krapohl were stunned when the *Scott* suddenly "sheered to port" and came to a stop. König exclaimed, "What is that boat doing?" A moment later he ordered the helm to starboard and then, seeing that a collision was imminent, ordered full astern. In the engine room Klees and his engineers knew immediately that something was wrong and clutched in the electric motors to reverse the propellers. König thought that the *U-Deutschland* had been slowed to about five or six knots when she rammed the *Scott,* but Krapohl thought the reversed power was "without much effect." He was probably right, because during the time it took to unclutch the diesels and clutch in the motors, the *U-Deutschland* was still forereaching and probably lost little way.

Hinsch had just enough time to jerk open the wheelhouse door and shout to Gurney, "Come out, Captain!" There was no response, and the tug had already rolled onto her beam ends. Hinsch stepped onto the side of the wheelhouse as the *Scott* "rolled right over and went down." In a blink Hinsch was alone in the frigid water struggling for his life. König said that the *Scott* "turned right over and then was gone"; he estimated that from the moment of impact until the tug vanished below the surface not more than fifteen seconds had passed. Krapohl said "She rolled down, lifted a little with her port side up, and down she went."

König immediately ordered the engines stopped to prevent injury to any swimmers who might be in the water. Krapohl dropped down onto the casing deck and ran aft, shedding his clothes in preparation to dive into the water if a swimmer needed help. Crewmen swarmed onto the deck and readied life rings and lines to throw to swimmers; others tossed life jackets into the water. On the bridge the crewmen searched the water with a powerful searchlight.

Hinsch was the only survivor; the *Scott*'s entire five-man crew had gone down with her. When the tug sank beneath his feet, Hinsch had gone under; when he popped back up the *Scott*'s lifeboat was close by, a line hanging from its stern in the water. He grabbed the line but let it go because he thought the boat was still made fast to the tug and would pull him down when it went under.

Hinsch, who described himself as a "poor swimmer but a good paddler," was wearing a "loose coat and had a pair of heavy marine glasses" around his neck. He was having a hard time staying on the surface, and the tide was carrying him westward, away from the collision site. He came close to the *U-Deutschland* and tried to paddle to one of the life preservers the crew had thrown into the water, but he could not reach it. Next he found a board, which he "rode for two or three minutes" before it rolled over and he fell off. He continued "paddling."

Ten minutes after the collision the *Cassie* arrived and started circling the area looking for survivors. One of her crewmen spotted Hinsch in the water and threw him a life ring with a rope attached. The throw was good, and Hinsch hooked an arm through the ring. The crewman pulled Hinsch to the side of the tug and told him to grab the life ring with both hands. The crewmen hauled him up until he was close enough for them to put a rope around his torso and drag him on board.

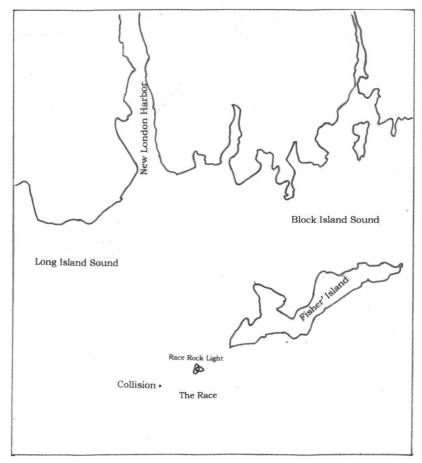

Long Island Sound

Block Island Sound

New London Harbor

Fisher' Island

Race Rock Light

Collision •

The Race

Map 5. The location of the 17 November 1916 fatal collision between the *U-Deutschland* and the tug *T. A. Scott, Jr.* in the Race off the New London Harbor entrance.

The *U-Deutschland* and the *Cassie* remained on the scene searching for survivors for an hour and a half before giving up the search. The collision had occurred at 0229. It was now obvious that there were no survivors other than Hinsch, who escaped only because he had been outside and very, very lucky. The *U-Deutschland* returned to her berth at the State Pier at 0500, and the floating screen was pulled back into place.

By sunup news of the disaster had spread through New London. Capt. John Gurney and his engineer Bill Caton had left widows and orphans; Ed Stone and Clarence Davidson had been single but with many friends in town. Only the deckhand, Eugene Duzant, had been an outsider—his home had been in Rhode Island. The flag outside the T. A. Scott Company office was at half-mast and a crowd of reporters, thrill seekers, and mourners gathered at the company's gate. Rumors were already rife.

The most popular rumor was that a strange boat had rushed out of the darkness in an attempt to ram the *U-Deutschland,* causing the U-boat to turn and collide with the *Scott.* The collision had caused the *Scott's* boiler to explode, which explained why none of the crew survived. According to that rumor, the *U-Deutschland* rescued Hinsch. The rumor about the mysterious boat trying to ram the *U-Deutschland* was so pervasive that the State Department asked the Treasury Department to look into it.[4]

In a variation of that same rumor, the *Scott* was cutting across the *U-Deutschland's* bow to block a strange boat that was menacing the U-boat. The crossing was so close to the oncoming *U-Deutschland* that she was unable to avoid the tug and rammed her in the engine room, causing the boiler to explode. In that version, Hinsch grabbed a life ring before jumping overboard just as the tug went down.

The boiler explosion morphed into a rumor of its own. According to that rumor, the *Cassie,* coming up astern, captured the mystery boat and found a man on board who was carrying explosives. The man reportedly told his captors that he intended to put the explosives on board the *U-Deutschland.* This implausible tale probably stemmed from an incident that may have occurred at the EFCO pier on Wednesday afternoon, 15 November.

On that occasion a man dressed like a worker and carrying a package had managed to get into the EFCO warehouse. Apparently his workman's attire and the package lulled the guards at the door into assuming that he had legitimate business in the warehouse, since "messengers had been arriving all day bearing purchases of the officers and crew." The man crossed the warehouse floor, heading for the door that opened onto the pier. As he neared the door, a phone rang and the guard at the door answered it; as the guard turned his back the stranger hurried past him and out onto the pier.

The stranger was going across the gangplank to board the U-boat when Franz Krapohl stopped him midway across. When he asked the man what he was doing there, he received only "a confused explanation." At this point three of the *U-Deutschland's* crew who were on the casing deck joined Krapohl on the gangplank and hustled the intruder back onto the pier. There they took the package away from him, opened it, and saw that it contained what looked like gunpowder. But that was all there was in the package. There was nothing that might have been construed as a detonator or fuse.[5]

Assuming the man was a crank, they had him thrown off the property rather than calling the police. Supposedly, they did not report the incident because they wanted to avoid a copy-cat incident that might be the real thing. But the story got out two days later and was reported in the press. König and Hilken denied that it had ever happened, but König referred to the incident in the report he submitted to the Admiralstab upon his return to Bremen in December.[6]

The collision had twisted and bent the *U-Deutschland's* stem, which was part of the casing rather than the pressure hull, and had deformed and loosened some of the pressure-hull plates. Fortunately, the casing had taken most of the impact, and the actual structural damage to the boat was relatively minor. The damage estimate, made on 17 November, was that the repairs would take at least a week to complete. But that estimate was shortened after a diver went down on the 18th and reported no damage below the waterline. A portable forge was brought onto the pier, and the after ballast tanks were flooded, lifting the bow clear of the water. The damaged plates were removed and set on the pier, where they were heated, reshaped, and refitted to the hull. The work was completed on 21 November, three days after the collision.

Probably more important than repairing the bow was preventing legal action from keeping the boat in New London for a long period. Investigations of accidents of this type were conducted by the Bureau of Marine Inspection and Steam Navigation, which in 1916 was a part of the Department of Commerce. At 1000 on 17 November Inspectors William Withey and Harry Rankin inspected the damaged bow and that afternoon convened a preliminary hearing in the customs-house. They took statements from König, Krapohl, and Klees. They also examined König's log and Klees' engine-room log. The only witness not questioned that day was Hinsch, who was not interviewed until 22 November.

During the afternoon hearing König was visibly shaken by what had happened. Witnesses described him as pale, his eyes "deep circled," and "his nerves entirely unstrung." Weighing on him were the facts that five men had died in the crash and that under most circumstances the following vessel, as his had been, was considered "burdened"—that is, with responsibility for avoiding collision. This was the second time on the same trip that he had collided with a tug, the first time in Bremen on 1 October when the tug rammed the *U-Deutschland*. He had been exonerated on the first occasion, but what had happened in the early morning hours of 17 November was an entirely different situation.[7]

The preliminary hearing established only the sequence of events; it could not move forward until Hinsch was well enough to testify. In the meantime, the civil process against the *U-Deutschland* started. On 18 November the T. A. Scott Company filed a libel action against the *U-Deutschland* for $12,000 in federal court in Hartford. That afternoon, U.S. Deputy Marshal Timothy E. Hawley served the papers on Captain König and took possession of the *U-Deutschland*. The petition that accompanied the action charged:

> That the *U-Deutschland,* which had been holding a parallel course on the port side of the *T. A. Scott, Jr.* suddenly sheered to starboard and struck the tug, causing her to fill and sink. At the time of the collision, the *U-Deutschland* did not have proper lookouts; did not display proper lights; did not have a competent officer on deck in command of the vessel; and did not have a competent helmsman. Further, the overtaking vessel approaching another at more than two points abaft

the beam she did not keep clear of the *T. A. Scott, Jr.;* did not give proper consideration to the force and action of the current being in the Race; and allowed her bow to swing suddenly to starboard.[8]

The same day the New London legal firm of Hull, McGuire, and Hull announced that it would be filing $90,000 in claims against the *U-Deutschland* for the deaths of John Gurney, William Caton, and Clarence Davidson. Paul Hilken immediately assured the parties involved that "all claims would be settled."

By Sunday, 19 November, the claims against the *U-Deutschland* totaled $162,000, and the number was climbing. That same day Hull, McGuire, and Hull announced that they would file claims totaling $80,000 on behalf of the heirs of Edward Stone and Eugene Duzant. In the meantime, the court barred the officers and the crew from going on board the *U-Deutschland* except when absolutely necessary for the maintenance of the boat, and then only in small groups. A private guard hired by the U.S. Marshall's Office was on board to enforce the court's no-boarding rule. On the deck just forward of the conning tower was a wooden sawhorse with the federal writ nailed to it.[9]

On Monday, 20 November, the Maryland Casualty Company, on behalf of EFCO, posted bond, and the U.S. marshall released the boat, only to have Sheriff J. H. Tubbs seize the boat in response to the claims filed by Hull, McGuire, and Hull. It was a formality, because bond had been posted. The claims against the *U-Deutschland* exceeded $200,000, but because the claimants were unable to show that the Deutsche Ozean Reederei, which had been named along with EFCO as the defendant, wholly owned the U-boat, the bond posted represented less than half the total claims.[10]

The boat was released on a legal technicality, but the suit was still pending, and the outcome of the ongoing Bureau of Marine Inspection and Steam Navigation investigation would figure strongly in its outcome and how much, if anything, EFCO would have to pay the claimants. The suit filed by Hull, McGuire, and Hull charged that Paul König had caused the collision by "negligently and carelessly operating the *U-Deutschland*." The charge rested on two points, that König had not had a competent pilot on board and that the *U-Deutschland* had been the overtaking vessel. The trial was set for Monday, 18 December 1916.[11]

On 20 November the boat was released, the crew went on board and resumed repairs to the bow. By midafternoon it was determined that the boat would be ready to sail the following day, and König went ashore to get clearance. There was no last-minute inspection to ensure that she was unarmed, and the State Department took no notice. That evening the last plate went into place on the pressure hull, the after ballast tanks were cleared, and the rubber cargo, which had been removed for the repairs, was restowed between the hulls.

König duly received clearance, and the word spread quickly through the town. Reporters stood outside the EFCO office, and others chartered a boat, waiting for something to happen. Shortly after dark two escort vessels arrived off the State Pier, the *Alert* and the steam fishing boat *Frank E. Beckwith*. It turned out to be a false alarm, and at 0230 the escort vessels went back to their berths. The press waited, not wanting to miss whatever was going to happen when it happened.[12]

It was not until midmorning on 21 November that things actually did start happening. In the first signs that the *U-Deutschland* was getting under way, the steel net was again hoisted out of the water and dumped on the end of the pier, and the floating fence was pulled clear. By now a crowd was starting to gather, and by noon "the waterfront was lined with spectators, housetops were crowded, and there was a rush for ferryboats and small craft." At 1400 the escorts *Alert* and *Frank E. Beckwith* returned.

The *U-Deutschland* backed into the Thames River at 1430, swung to port, and started downriver toward the Long Island Sound and the Race, her escorts following at a safe distance to prevent a reoccurrence of 17 November. The same men were on the bridge, König and Krapohl. Hinsch stood on the foredeck of the *Beckwith* with a huge megaphone in one hand. The ferryboat *Winthrop* stopped in midriver to allow her passengers a good look at the U-boat, and several tugs "edged near." Despite the crowds on shore and the people watching from boats in the river, no cheering, horns, or sirens marked the boat's passing. The *U-Deutschland's* off-watch crewmen were standing on the casing deck, but none of them seemed to notice the crowds. There was no waving back and forth between the shore and the *U-Deutschland*.

The *U-Deutschland's* escorts stopped following at 1545, when the *U-Deutschland* turned to port and proceeded past Race Rock Light and entered the Block Island Sound. In New London the crowds had long ago dispersed, the reporters were phoning in their stories, and the EFCO office was empty, except for Carl Ahrendt, who was cleaning out Paul Hilken's desk and putting the contents in a cardboard box. No one knew it at that time, but there would be no more cargo submarines coming to the State Pier in New London or anywhere else in the United States.

There is almost no information available on what the boat's final Atlantic crossing as a freighter was like. In his report to the Admiralstab König noted that steamer traffic seemed to have shifted to a more southerly track, which he attributed to a belief that the *U-Deutschland* was being escorted by a war boat. He wrote that on 22 November radioman Arthur Geilenfeld had heard the SS *Saratoga* broadcast a warning that "an armored [*sic*] submarine may be anywhere in the Atlantic. Take every precaution." He acknowledged receiving warnings of a new cruiser line off Kirkwall and nets deployed between Kirkwall and Udsire, but they had not been a threat to him, because they were not along his track. He mentioned, without going into detail, that when he was off Helgoland the *U-Deutschland* encountered some technical difficulty that caused a ten-hour delay.[13]

In November 1917, over a year later, a State Department employee, A. J. Buck, who had been stationed in Bremerhaven before the United States entered the war, sent a sketchy account to the secretary of state of what supposedly happened off Helgoland. According to Buck, he attended a dinner at the Hotel Behrmann in Hamburg during the week of 22 January 1917. Adolf Stadtländer, an NDL director, hosted the dinner for Paul König, who talked about his two trips to the United States in command of the *U-Deutschland*. König reportedly told his listeners that when the *U-Deutschland* had been off Helgoland, headed for the Weser mouth, both diesel engines had stopped and could not be restarted. At the same time, the *U-Deutschland* had started to settle by the stern, but fortunately the deck hatches were closed and secured, and the only people not inside the boat were the officer of the deck and one lookout, who were on the bridge.[14]

The boat settled steadily, causing the two men on the bridge to hastily go below and dog down the hatch behind them. Attempts to blow the after tanks failed and the stern reached a depth of twenty meters at a down angle of forty-five degrees. König reportedly told the audience that the pressure hull appeared to bulge inward as the boat hung by its bow from the surface.

But there is a problem with the account at this point.

The *U-Deutschland* was 213 feet long. If the stern dropped to twenty meters, about sixty-five feet, the down angle would have been just seventeen degrees, and in any case at that depth there would have been no inward bulging of the pressure hull. If the account Buck sent to Washington is accurate with regard to the forty-five-degree down angle, however, the stern would have been at 148 feet, very close to the boat's rated maximum depth. That the pressure hull would have bulged inward at that depth is doubtful, though not entirely impossible.

König, in Buck's account, did not offer any explanation for what happened but said that the crew members "despaired of success and had placed messages in bottles for release." They were even discussing finding a way to send a volunteer swimmer to the surface. At that critical moment, after ten hours without any progress toward starting the engines or bringing the boat to the surface, "the boat suddenly began to move and reached the surface." Back on the surface and apparently with power restored, the *U-Deutschland* continued on to the Weser mouth without further mishap, passing the Rotesand Light at 1400.

The fact that Buck wrote his report a year after the alleged event is odd, but even if he had submitted it when it was current, there would have been, beyond the noted problems, many holes in the story and a host of improbabilities. These might be owing to Buck's not being able to fully grasp what König had told his audience. If he reported accurately what he had heard, one must conclude that König had been spinning a tale.

Recall that König had a nearly fatal diving experience outbound on the first trip and an equally hair-raising experience in a deep hole in Chesapeake Bay. In both cases the stories he told had a basis in fact—something did happen. The same might be the case with his talk to the Bremerhaven dinner audience. Something delayed him for ten hours, and it could certainly have been an engine problem. But if both engines did stop simultaneously, why did the stern sink? There is nothing like a good tale, and König was undoubtedly an excellent storyteller.

Probably König was putting out disinformation. A decision to convert the six cargo U-boats then under construction to war boats had been made on 16 December, and there was little doubt that the *U-Deutschland* would also be converted. When he spoke at the dinner in January 1917 she had been in port since 9 December 1916, by when her return to New London would have already been expected. His tale, and the implied need for extensive repairs, explained why the boat had not yet sailed. The tale also provided cover for the boat's movements and absence for the next several weeks.

But something must have happened, because even König, who could spin a good tale on demand, would not have made up a story about the near loss of the *U-Deutschland* for no reason. Unfortunately, her log books were destroyed during World War II, as was König's written report to the Admiralstab for the second trip. The only suggestion that offers a clue is that the cargo in the after hold shifted, destroying the boat's trim. That sounds unlikely, though it could have happened. But even that suggestion has holes in it.

But despite the suggestion's implausibility, it does offer a clue as to what might have happened to the *U-Bremen*. Most experts believe she had a diving accident similar to what the *U-Deutschland* experienced on her first trip. She was in heavy seas for a good part of her trip, and if she had been forced to dive suddenly to escape a threat, it is possible that her cargo shifted, causing the boat to become uncontrollable. Such a scenario could plausibly explain her loss. We will never know.

The *U-Deutschland* completed her final Atlantic crossing carrying cargo in eighteen days, and her arrival in Bremen was utterly devoid of fanfare or celebration. The boat went directly to a berth in Bremerhaven, and her crew was put on board a receiving ship. The political situation in Germany was changing rapidly. Arthur Zimmermann had replaced Gottlieb von Jagow as foreign minister, a change that would have a profound effect on the *U-Deutschland* and the country whose name she bore. In just short of four months, the United States would be at war with Germany.

Back in the United States, the day after the *U-Deutschland* left New London Hinsch appeared before Inspectors Withey and Rankin in the New London customshouse. Given the testimony he later gave before the Mixed Claims Commission pertaining to his role in sabotage in the United States, one wonders if what he told the inspectors about Gurney ringing down "stop engines" was the truth. But he was the only survivor, and there was no one to refute what he told them.

Eleven days after the *U-Deutschland* returned to Bremen, Withey and Rankin released their final report, with the notation "Investigated and dismissed." In their opinion, based largely on Hinsch's testimony, "the collision was due to a mistake in the bell signals given to the engineer by Captain Gurney at a time when the vessels were in such position that this mistake proved to be a fatal error." The next day the Köln *Tagesblatt* reported that the *Scott* had been found at fault, because Captain Gurney had made an inaccurate "flag signal." Something had been lost in the translation, but at least the essence of the finding was there.[15]

The suit against the *U-Deutschland* never went to trial; it was settled for an unspecified amount on 22 August 1917. The claimants received restitution from the Germans, through EFCO. And it was German money they received—Hilken paid the settlement on behalf of EFCO and the DOR from funds provided to him by Sektion Politik for financing sabotage in the United States.[16]

14

The End of the Line, Part I

9 DECEMBER 1916–20 APRIL 1917

The writing was on the wall for the commercial submarine venture as the close of 1916 brought Germany to a crossroads in the war. Werner Beumelburg describes the situation as von Hindenburg and Ludendorff might have seen it.

> They saw in the joyless and haggard faces of their army commanders and chiefs of staff, the over-all decline in morale before they even spoke. Those faces spoke of chronic ammunition shortages for their artillery, unfulfilled promises for increased manpower, and the overwhelming Allied superiority in material. Their air commanders were desperate for aircraft and airmen in numbers that could match the enemy's strength.
>
> The message in the faces of the frontline troops was even grimmer. They needed artillery, grenades, and rifle ammunition to repulse the enemy. Many believed they were fighting to survive and tomorrow they would still be in it. In one week they would no longer be here. Others from the homeland or other fronts would replace them, and then they would disappear.
>
> The enemy, materially rich and in growing numbers, was to their front. But hunger surrounded them. Despite the greatest will, hungry men lacked the strength to fight. And there was the rising voice of Bolshevism. Could not the homeland provide more to eat? One heard that back "there" some have it very good. Was that true? They did not complain, but they believed it would be better for everyone if everyone got his fair share. They read in letters from home that this war was only for the Kaiser, the generals, and the capitalists, and that there would be peace if they were gone.
>
> The huge 1916 offensives had failed to break the deadlock, and it was obvious that the Allies would eventually win the war of attrition.[1]

In December 1916 Germany faced two enemies—the Allied forces and famine. Germany was in the grip of what became known as the "Turnip Winter," referring to the only sizable crop to reach the market. The critical fertilizer shortage had reduced grains production by 50 percent, livestock were starving, and the potato crop had failed. People were living at subsistent levels. As the food crisis worsened, a professor of nutrition and hygiene at the University of Bonn, Dr. Rudolf Otto Neumann, MD, tried the experiment of limiting himself to the legally allowed food ration for an average German. Six months later he had lost a third of his weight and was unable to work. The daily fare for the average German was boiled turnips and cabbage, with a piece of coarse, nearly indigestible *Kriegsbrot.*[2]

Kriegsbrot, war bread, which became the symbol of the food crisis, was a bread substitute made of whatever grains and meal were available. Originally *Kriegsbrot* consisted of about 20 percent potato flour. By 1916 the mix was 55 percent rye flour, 35 percent wheat flour, and 10 percent potato flour. As the grain shortages increased, ground turnips replaced rye flour, and other substitutes were found to replace wheat and potato flour. (Despite popular myth, sawdust was not one of the substitutes.) Because milk was a rarity, water was used instead. The daily adult war-bread ration in 1916 was two hundred grams, about seven ounces; it lacked any meaningful nutrition, was hard to chew, and did not satisfy hunger. The food shortage was even worse at the front.[3]

By the winter of 1916, German soldiers were the poorest fed on the western front. Their daily meat ration, when it was available, was four ounces of horse meat. German army cooks prepared a so-called stew from horsemeat, when it could be had, and ground nettles. In fact, a regular fatigue duty for rear-echelon troops was "nettle gathering." Meat of any kind was so rare that rear-echelon troops received a meat ration only nine days a month.[4]

As 1916 drew to a close, Germany was on the threshold of famine and defeat. It was obvious that the British blockade could not be broken by present methods and that the hopes for the cargo U-boat program were never going to be realized. The only apparent solution was to launch a ruthless unrestricted submarine campaign so savage that it would drive neutral shipping from the seas and fatally destroy Britain's merchant marine. It would have to be an all-out effort to end the war quickly. Only the civilian government opposed the plan.

The push for a return to unrestricted submarine warfare had been growing stronger since August, and it was now only a matter of when it would happen. For nearly a year, the U-boat arm had been gathering figures and writing papers on the effectiveness of such a campaign. The submariners believed that if the U-boats could sink 631,000 tons of shipping per month, Germany would win the war in six months.[5] Naval planners acknowledged that an unrestricted submarine campaign—in which any freighter, whether neutral or belligerent, would be torpedoed without warning—would bring the United States into the war. But the planners discounted that certainty on the grounds that the war would be over before American involvement would have any effect. They also believed that the U-boats would sink most if not all the troopships bringing soldiers across the Atlantic to France.

Sensing the momentum for a return to unrestricted submarine warfare, the RMA started dismantling the cargo-submarine project on 16 December, ordering that four of the six *U-Deutschland*-class boats still under construction be converted to "U-cruisers," *U-151* to *U-154.* The U-cruiser was a design concept that had been born in April 1916 when the Prize Regulations governed how the submarine war was fought.

A U-cruiser would be a very large, heavily armed U-boat capable of long-range patrols that lasted more than a hundred days, an endurance that made it possible for them to reach the U.S. East Coast. The boats would he sufficiently armored and heavily enough armed to hold their own in a surface battle with an armed merchant ship in areas that were not heavily patrolled. Since the first purpose-built U-cruisers, *U-139* to *U-141,* would not be commissioned until spring of 1917, the RMA elected to convert the seven *U-Deutschland*-class boats as a stopgap.

Meanwhile, unaware that the cargo-submarine program had been scrapped, work was under way in New London to receive the *U-Deutschland* again. On 5 January an advance force of twenty-five African-American stevedores showed up on the State Pier, having arrived that day by train from Baltimore. They were part of the original crew that had handled cargo in Baltimore and New London on trips one and two. There were no complaints from New London residents about their arrival, in part because their fears had proved to be unfounded the first time. And everyone in town accepted EFCO's overblown security concerns.

The stevedores were kept busy unloading freight cars that had brought tons of crude rubber and nickel to New London. Many of the cars had been sitting on the State Pier spur since December, and more had arrived in early January, all by the same kinds of roundabout routes used to deliver cargo to the EFCO plant in Baltimore. The continued arrival of freight cars at the State Pier and the new activity caused many people to assume the *U-Deutschland* was soon to arrive. The press was already hounding the EFCO office in New London, but again the reporters were dealing with Hinsch, and he would not have told them even if the boat had been due the next day. The tight-lipped policy created more rumors.[6]

When the British freighter SS *Clematis* docked in New London on 15 January, her captain, Joseph Williams, said that he had seen a large submarine east of the Nantucket Lightship. He acknowledged that he had never seen the *U-Deutschland;* what he had spotted was a "low-lying craft like a whaleback about a mile away on the port bow." Captain Williams had not waited around to see if the object had a conning tower or a fluke. The "sighting" and an unauthenticated report from Bremen that the *U-Deutschland* had left there on 2 January led to the assumption that the submarine freighter would put into New London in the next two days.[7]

On 16 January the Copenhagen paper *Ekstrabladet* reported that contrary to earlier reports, the *U-Deutschland* and *U-Bremen* had not been lost. The *U-Deutschland* had left Bremen on 2 January, and the *U-Bremen* was being used as an oceangoing supply station for U-boats in the Mediterranean. On 23 January an unattributed news flash from New London said "a German submarine is steaming into the outer harbor," which was soon found to be wrong.[8]

On 29 January the EFCO officers were reported to be "anxious over the non-arrival of the vessel," which was now reported to have left Bremen on 4 January and was scheduled to arrive in New London on 22 January. That same day two arriving merchant captains, one American and one British, both out of Liverpool, told reporters that the *U-Deutschland* had been captured and taken to a shipyard in Pembroke, South Wales. The capper for the month was that a "full-fledged war submarine had stolen up the New London channel under cover of darkness, and had taken on supplies from the *Willehad*." That same day a reporter asked Hinsch if the *U-Deutschland* was actually under way toward New London. Hinsch, true to form, answered, "Now, what is the use of asking me that question? You know I won't answer you." Finally a Reuter's dispatch arrived at the Tuckerton Radio Station on 6 February: "The *U-Deutschland* has not left her home port."[9]

While the first four *U-Deutschland*-class boats were being converted, the unrestricted U-boat war opened on 1 February 1917. That same day stevedores in Wilhelmshaven started removing the outbound cargo from the *U-Deutschland*. The work went on until the evening of 4 February, when the last of the cargo was removed. Two weeks later, on 18 February 1917, the *U-Deutschland* and the two remaining *U-Deutschland*-class hulls that were still under construction were ordered converted, the two still-incomplete hulls becoming *U-156* and *U-157*. The following day the navy commissioned the *U-Deutschland* as *U-155*, even though she was still configured as a merchant submarine and not ready for deployment as a U-cruiser.[10]

Despite the obvious operational drawbacks to using the *U-Deutschland*-class boats in an unrestricted submarine warfare campaign, the navy planners believed that they could be effective. Their strength was their extremely long range, 25,000 nautical miles at 5.5 knots, which meant they could easily operate off the Atlantic seaboards of Canada and the United States and remain at sea for longer than three months.[11] Until the advent of the purpose-built U-cruisers, no other U-boat could operate that far from home or for that long.

The fact that the enemy did not expect to encounter U-boats in waters so distant from Germany and therefore had only minimal antisubmarine warfare (ASW) measures in effect in those areas meant that the converted cargo U-boats would be able to operate as surface raiders most of the time. Unfortunately, the former cargo U-boats were so slow on the surface that almost any freighter could outrun them, and when confronted by an ASW-equipped warship, the boats' slow diving time would be a major drawback. But the Germans believed that the element of surprise and the absence of an effective defense against U-boats in North American waters would offset the clumsy boats' shortcomings and allow them to wage an effective anticommerce campaign.[12]

The conversion of the seven *U-Deutschland*-class boats to U-cruisers was a make-do proposition. As noted, their long-range advantage was undercut by their relatively low maximum surface speed of ten knots and their long diving time. But the engineers felt that arming them with 150 mm artillery would overcome their poor surface performance to some degree. The designers were able to increase the boats' maximum speed from ten knots to eleven by increasing the diameter of the screws from sixty-three to sixty-five inches and making it possible to run the electric and diesel power plants simultaneously on the same shaft. However, the electric motors could remain online for only a limited time, because of the need to have sufficient battery power left to operate submerged.[13]

The boats' interiors underwent major modifications. A new deck was added to each hold; the upper decks became quarters for the greatly expanded crews and the lower decks became space for stores and spare parts and magazines for ammunition and torpedoes. There would be two crews on board each *U-Deutschland*-class U-cruiser, the ship's crew, six officers and fifty enlisted men, and a prize crew of one officer and nineteen enlisted men. The most time-consuming job was redesigning the forward compartments to accept two torpedo tubes. There were no stern torpedo tubes because those compartments could not be altered from their original purpose. Each boat carried eighteen torpedo reloads.[14]

The casing deck had to be rebuilt, widened to nearly twenty-one feet where the deck guns were mounted, and strengthened to handle the guns. The 150 mm guns mounted on all the boats were the Utof-15L/45 type, designed and manufactured for use on U-boats, torpedo boats, and antiaircraft mounts. It was a six-inch gun with a barrel length of 22.2 feet. All the boats except the *U-155* and *U-156* also carried two 88 mm guns, Uk-8.8L/30s, which were designed for U-boats, 3.5-inch guns with barrels 8.75 feet long. The ready ammo for the deck guns was kept in watertight tubes beneath the wooden deck. Even with the holds divided by a deck, the storage space was enormous by U-boat standards. The boats could carry up to 1,672 rounds for their big deck guns and 764 rounds for the two 88 mm guns, plus stores, spare parts, and lubricants.[15]

The original one-periscope conning tower was retained in all the boats, but the casing around it was enlarged, creating a larger bridge. The periscopes used in all the boats, including *U-155,* were made by Zeiss, Jena, or C. P. Goerz, Berlin. The periscopes were built with two tubes, one inside the other, the inner tube being the actual periscope. The outer and inner tubes rose and descended together, but only the inner tube rotated. All the periscopes were electrically operated and equipped with a split-image rangefinder. The hoist motor was mounted in the well base, and the hoist cables were laid between the tubes. The hoist motor and cable winches were designed to rotate with the inner tube so that the cables were never twisted but ran true vertically.[16]

Conversion of the *U-Deutschland*, now known as *U-155,* began on 27 February, when she was moved from the loading dock back into the yard. Her conversion involved the same modifications as the other six boats with the exceptions that she did not receive a forward torpedo room and the two 88 mm guns were not added.

In order to get the *U-155* ready in the minimum time, she was equipped with six so-called lattice torpedo tubes taken from the old battleship SMS *Zähringen*. The tubes were mounted inside the casing, atop the tank deck, and angled fifteen degrees outward from the keel line. Four of the tubes were mounted in pairs, port and starboard, alongside the forward 150 mm gun. The other two tubes were mounted individually, port and starboard, facing aft alongside the after 150 mm gun. They were also angled fifteen degrees. Another minor variation in the conversion was that the *U-155* carried twenty-four reload torpedoes instead of eighteen as in the other boats. The problem with the exterior torpedo mounts was that they could only be reloaded when the boat was surfaced, and the preloaded torpedoes became unreliable after prolonged immersion in seawater.[17]

From the day that the stevedores started removing the *U-Deutschland*'s cargo, on 4 February, König and his crew were in a sort of limbo. It was obvious that there would be no third trip, at least not carrying cargo, but they were all in the dark as to what was going to happen next. When the *U-Deutschland* became *U-155* on 19 February, every member of the crew except König was returned to naval service, but all remained unassigned. Captain König was eventually also returned to naval service, as a *Kapitänleutnant,* and was assigned to the naval personnel office, where his job would be selecting former merchant officers for assignment on board U-boats as war pilots (merchant marine officers were on board to help the U-boat captain identify ships as to name, tonnage, and national identity). *Oberleutnant zur See* Eyring was assigned to the *U-155* as her second officer on 28 February. *Oberleutnant zur See* Krapohl became the first officer on the *U-155* on 10 March and reported to the boat—with the new skipper, *Kapitänleutnant* Karl Meusel—that same day. The boat's conversion was completed in fifty-two days, and on 20 April she ran her speed trials with the new propellers and power-train hookup.

15

The End of the Line, Part II

NOVEMBER 1916–MAY 1917

T he situation for Hilken and his saboteurs in Baltimore was similar to that of the cargo submarine project in Germany. By the end of 1916 there were obvious signs that the United States and Germany would soon be at war, but the sabotage operations went on as usual, and a new saboteur arrived from Germany. But in fact things were changing, as evidenced by the Bureau of Investigation's increased interest in Paul Hilken. While the *U-Deutschland* was still in New London, Paul Hilken was called to testify before a federal grand jury in the government's case against von Rintelen, and he took the stand on Wednesday 15 November 1916. At the time von Rintelen was still in a British prison, pending his extradition to the United States.

The prosecutor asking the questions was Raymond B. Sarfaty, the lead federal attorney in the von Rintelen case. Hilken testified that he had met von Rintelen in New York in April 1915 and that he knew him as "Hansen." When Sarfaty asked if he had ever asked von Rintelen why he was using an alias, Hilken said that it had not seemed important. He also testified that von Rintelen told him he was in the United States to buy as much artillery ammunition as possible, to prevent it from being sent to the British and French. He also told Hilken he was here to foment strikes among railroad and dock workers, indirectly for the same purpose. Hilken's testimony revealed that he had met with von Rintelen several times in New York and Baltimore and had received two thousand dollars from him for "travel expenses between Baltimore and New York" for their meetings. During those meetings von Rintelen used aliases, about which Hilken never questioned him. Hilken also told the grand jury that he and von Rintelen had never discussed the latter's plans to buy ammunition and foment strikes.[1]

Hilken's grand-jury testimony was probably the closest he came to being recognized as an active agent in Germany's clandestine sabotage operations in the United States. On the stand he was calm, evaded the questions deftly, and presented himself as simply a businessman whose advice on business matters von Rintelen had sought. But deft though they were, his answers were obviously framed to conceal what those meetings had been really about. When he stepped down, the impression he left was that he was probably up to something but there was no solid clue as to what the something was. He was admittedly associated with von Rintelen and several other pro-Germans who were under scrutiny, and his own reputation for being "rabidly pro-German" was well known in the Bureau of Investigation headquarters in Washington. His testimony left the authorities with nothing to work with. But on 27 November a man arrived in Baltimore who came very close to exposing Hilken.

When World War I started, Wilhelm Wöhst had been working for a Hamburg shipping concern, D. Fuhrmann, Nissle & Günther. He was in upper management, which afforded him the opportunity to visit the United States frequently, staying long enough each time to hone his English-language skills. When fighting began he was commissioned as a *Leutnant* (second lieutenant) in the army, but whether or not he served, as he later said he did, at the front is not clear. Given his shipping background and his English, he probably went directly to Abteilung IIIb and from there into Sektion Politik.[2]

Whatever his route to Sektion Politik actually was, Wöhst later created several stories to explain it. In one version he was wounded badly at the front and reassigned to Sektion Politik because of his English-language skills. In another version he fell ill while on active duty and was assigned to Sektion Politik after he recovered. As for the reason he had come to the United States, in one story Sektion Politik was sending him to either Spain or Italy by way of the United States, where he was to report to Hilken in order to obtain a U.S. passport and papers that would get him into either nation as an American. The other explanation for his presence in the United States was that he was to become either Hilken's codirector of operations or a free agent drawing funds from Hilken. The version he told depended on who the listener was.

There is one aspect of Wilhelm Wöhst's story that was entirely factual—he was a well-trained spy. The intelligence service (Geheimdienst) had trained him in all forms of spy craft, including working with codes and developing letters written with invisible ink. He also learned how to use various incendiary devices and make his own bombs. What the service did not do was train him to keep his mouth shut.

When he had completed his field training, he was given documents identifying him as Hermann Rupp, a Swiss citizen; $50,000, deposited in his name in the Transatlantic Trust Company, in New York; and a black suitcase. The money was to be used as necessary to carry out his assignments, and the suitcase contained the latest incendiary devices and fresh anthrax and glanders cultures to be delivered to Paul Hilken in Baltimore. He left Berlin on 2 October 1916, booked passage on the *Frederick VIII* under the name "Hermann Rupp," and arrived in Hoboken, New Jersey, on Monday, 27 November 1917.

The next afternoon, now *Oberleutnant* (First Lieutenant) Wilhelm Wöhst showed up at his sister's home at 716 Gladstone Avenue in Tuxedo Park, Baltimore. Wöhst was thirty-seven but looked ten years younger. He was five feet, nine inches, weighed 155 pounds, had a baby face and a "florid" complexion. When he arrived at his sister's door he was wearing a well-tailored "salt and pepper suit, light colored coat, a wide-brim, brown hat" and was carrying the black suitcase that contained the incendiary devices and cultures. He looked like a successful young executive, which is what he had been before the war.[3]

His sister was married to a newly minted PhD in geology, Charles Reeves; in keeping with the protocol of the times, she was identified only as Mrs. Charles Reeves. She and her husband were renting an apartment in the home of John Atterbury, who was a representative of the Ocean Accident and Guarantee Corporation and a good friend of the U.S. Attorney in Baltimore, Samuel K. Dennis. Atterbury's wife was the landlady at 716 Gladstone. Because the two wives were home most of the day while their husbands worked, they saw a great deal of each other and took coffee together every day.

Wöhst should be known as the spy who could not keep a secret. Immediately after arriving he told his sister he was working for German intelligence and showed her his counterfeit Swiss passport and the hollow heel in his shoe "where he kept secret messages." He told her that the German intelligence service had given him $50,000 to carry out his mission, which he did not describe. He also told her he was on his way to Spain and that he had brought important messages for von Bernstorff in Washington, neither of which was true. He told his sister that he had been wounded on the western front and had been sent to the intelligence service when he was sufficiently recovered. He did not go into detail about his injuries.

On Thanksgiving morning, Thursday, 30 November, Wöhst left the house to meet with Hilken in his third-floor office at the Hansa Haus. While he was gone, Mrs. Reeves and Mrs. Atterbury had coffee, and Mrs. Reeves told her landlady all the exciting news about her mysterious brother. She said he was in the German secret service, was disguised as a Swiss businessman named Rupp, carried a Swiss passport, and had a hollow heel in his shoe in which he had brought secret messages. She was particularly proud of the fact that "Willie" had $50,000, which in 1916 was considerably more than a king's ransom for someone renting a room. She also intimated that he had arrived on board the *U-Deutschland,* though she knew he had arrived on board the *Frederick VIII* at Hoboken, six days after the *U-Deutschland* left New London. But arriving on board the *U-Deutschland* made a much better story. Apparently Mrs. Reeves shared her brother's secret-keeping problem, with an added touch of embellishment. Mrs. Atterbury listened attentively and drank her coffee.

When Hilken met Wöhst that morning he thought that Wöhst had come to take up some of the load in Baltimore and speed up sabotage operations, which was in fact probably Wöhst's real purpose in the United States. But Wöhst presented himself to Hilken as a free agent who was willing to work with him but would remain essentially independent. He opened his suitcase and showed Hilken the anthrax and glanders cultures and the new incendiary devices. Seeing the cultures Hilken suggested that Wöhst acclimate to his new job by working with Carl Dilger making anthrax and glanders. Wöhst agreed but said that he also had another assignment from Sektion Politik to which he had to attend, which was not true. He offered no explanation about the other assignment.

Still believing that Wöhst was going to be his comanager, Hilken told him to use the EFCO office in New York as his own and gave him the responsibility of paying Fred Herrmann on demand from funds Hilken would provide. With the *U-Deutschland* gone from New London, Herrmann was operating independently out of New York. That fit Wöhst's plans perfectly, because he was going to New York anyway, something that he had not mentioned to Hilken (another was the $50,000 in a Transatlantic Trust Company account). During that meeting Hilken made Wöhst aware of the developing plan to blow up the Kingsland munitions plant, but what role, if any, Wöhst actually played in the matter is not known. At Hilken's direction, Wöhst left most of the incendiary devices for Hinsch to use and kept what remained to deliver to Herrmann in New York.

Wöhst returned to his sister's house, where he packed his few belongings in the black suitcase, then left for New York. He did not go there directly. He went first to Chicago, for some unknown purpose, and then to Rochester, where he had an aunt and an uncle, Heinz Jacobsen, who was a music instructor, violinist, and composer. Wöhst stayed with his aunt and uncle four days before going on to New York with his uncle Heinz.

At about the time Wöhst's train was pulling out of the Baltimore station headed for Chicago, Mrs. Atterbury was telling her husband, over Thanksgiving dinner, about the story she had heard from Mrs. Reeves. After dinner Mr. Atterbury called his friend U.S. Attorney Dennis and repeated what his wife had told him. Because it was a holiday, Mr. Dennis waited until the following morning to call the agent in charge at the Baltimore office of the Bureau of Investigation, Billups Harris. Dennis and Atterbury met with Harris in his office on Saturday morning, 2 December; Atterbury provided the federal agent with a complete and accurate account of what his wife had told him and gave Wöhst's description.

While the three men were discussing the presence of a bona fide German spy in Baltimore, Wöhst was already in Chicago. That same day Harris filled out a Form 417 detailing the information he had received and sent it to Washington. There is nothing in the Bureau of Investigation files to indicate that he went immediately to 716 Gladstone Avenue to follow up on what he had been told.

Wilhelm Wöhst and his uncle Heinz arrived at the Pennsylvania Station in New York on the morning of 11 December to find Wöhst's first cousin Hildegarde Jacobsen waiting for them. Hildegarde was a thirty-four-year-old aesthetic dancing instructor with a studio in the Three Arts Club on West 85th Street in New York. She was a tall, strikingly attractive blonde with the lithe figure of a gymnast. She and Wöhst were immediately attracted to each other.

Wöhst met Herrmann for the first time on 12 December in the McAlpin Hotel, where Herrmann was registered as "Fred March." Wöhst, now using the name Hauten, gave Herrmann the new incendiary devices and the anthrax and glanders cultures and told Herrmann that he would be Herrmann's paymaster. That suited Herrmann, who at that time had a crew spreading anthrax and glanders in Savannah. Wöhst said nothing about going to Chevy Chase to work with Carl Dilger, as Hilken had suggested, and there was nothing in the arrangement that even implied that Wöhst would take an active part in the group's sabotage activities.

Wöhst clearly had his own agenda, one that involved appearing to be working with Hilken without actually becoming involved. His real purpose seems to have been to remain in the United States for the war's duration or longer, living off the $50,000 in his Transatlantic Trust Company account and skimming off as much as he could of the money Hilken sent him to cover Herrmann's operations. Using the money from the Transatlantic Trust account would pose no problems, because there was no requirement that he account to Sektion Politik for withdrawals and expenditures, and Hilken did not know the money existed. And skimming off from what Hilken sent him would simply involve asking Hilken for slightly more than Herrmann needed. The day after Wöhst met Herrmann, Wöhst received five hundred dollars from Hilken, which he added to the $895 that Sektion Politik had given him for pocket cash. Hilken also required no accounting of how the money was spent, since the money was Sektion Politik's. During the nine weeks Wöhst was in New York Hilken sent him $3,900, only two thousand of which was actually paid to Herrmann.

Wöhst was successful in staying uninvolved actively, spending most of his time with Hildegarde or visiting his aunt and uncle in Rochester. In the course of his relationship with his attractive cousin he told her nearly everything about the Baltimore sabotage cell, including names. The only major players he did not tell Hildegarde about were Carl Dilger and Friedrich Hinsch, neither of whom he had met. He even went so far as to introduce Hildegarde to Herrmann, just before Christmas 1916. He was so successful in giving the impression of being fully involved, however, that the Mixed Claims Commission later lumped him in with Hinsch and Herrmann in accusations of "conducting a program of incendiary sabotage and of inoculating animals in America."

At the same time, he was so successful at staying uninvolved that the Mixed Claims Commission's final decision was to describe Wöhst as "not an important figure in comparison with Hilken, Hinsch, or Herrmann" and as having had a role limited to "aiding and abetting" Herrmann and Hinsch.

Herrmann, who at the time was actively involved in planning the attack on the Kingsland munitions assembly plant, had no objection to limiting Wöhst's role to that of paymaster; he preferred working alone. But he did not like what Wöhst had told Hildegarde about him. He never trusted her and would believe in the end that she was responsible for the Bureau of Investigation's flushing him out.

Meanwhile, he had been casing the Kingsland plant since October and had reached the conclusion that the plant was too heavily guarded to enter as had been done at Black Tom. Kingsland would have to be an inside job. In the mean-time, Hinsch, through Sir John Hammar, the Swedish vice consul in New York, had placed Charles Thorne in the plant as an assistant personnel manager with responsibility for hiring men and assigning them to various departments. One of the Kingsland employees was Fiodore Wozniak, for whom Thorne arranged a transfer from a laborer's position to a bench in the shell-cleaning shed, known as Building 30.[4]

Wozniak had been born in 1884 in the district of Rava Russka, which was then in Poland but is today in Ukraine. He had immigrated to the United States in 1912 and in June 1916 applied for Russian citizenship through the Russian con-sulate in New York. He needed work in any case, and the Russian vice consul, D. Florinsky, who was unwittingly involved in German espionage through a woman known as Baroness Ida Leonie von Seidlitz, got him a job as a laborer at Kingsland. How Hinsch got on to Wozniak has never been described, but Florinsky had ear-lier been involved with von Rintelen and through him knew Hinsch; that might have been the connection.

In early December, before Wöhst arrived, Hinsch took Wozniak to meet Herrmann outside the McAlpin Hotel in New York. Herrmann took one look at him and did not like what he saw: "He had a heavy thick mustache and dark eyes, looking sort of cuckoo—staring eyes." Herrmann did not trust him and asked Hinsch to find another man. The next day Hinsch showed up at the McAlpin with a man known only as Rodriquez [sic], a Puerto Rican who had been working for him in Baltimore; Herrmann approved him. Hinsch then had Thorne hire Rodriquez to work with Wozniak in Building 30. Despite Herrmann's misgivings about Wozniak, Rodriquez was not a replacement for him but was rather a backup player to ensure that the job was accomplished.

In the weeks that followed the initial meetings, Herrmann met frequently with Wozniak and Rodriquez to discuss the details of the operation and to pay each man forty dollars a week. Also, he showed them how to use the incendiary pencils that Wöhst had given him. Hinsch occasionally attended these meetings, and during one of them he suggested that the incendiary pencils might be too obvious to use in a closely supervised shop like Building 30. A discussion of alter-nate methods of starting the fire followed, in the course of which it was decided to use a phosphorus-soaked rag that would friction-ignite when placed inside a revolving shell casing.

Even after Herrmann decided to proceed with the plan, he continued to dis-trust Wozniak, who was unstable and certainly unreliable. But what Herrmann did not know was that since 13 December, Wozniak had been writing letters to a Major General Khrabrov, chairman of the Russian Artillery Commission in New York, warning him that "great negligence was being shown in the manufacture of shells at Kingsland." On 10 January, the day before the fire, General Khrabrov received a postcard from Wozniak that warned, "Things are getting worse with us. There will be a catastrophe." Wozniak was cleverer than Herrmann gave him credit for—with those letters he was building his defense against the charge that he deliberately started the fire.[5]

All the parts needed to make artillery rounds—casings, primers, fuses, projectiles, and powder—were shipped to Kingsland, where they were assembled. The first step in the assembly process was cleaning the empty brass casings, inside and outside. The work was done in Building 30, in which there were forty-eight cleaning stations, each with a workbench, a cleaning machine, rags, and a pan of gasoline recessed into the top of the bench. Because of the extreme danger of fire inside the plant, a sand-filled bucket was placed next to every workstation (some employees later told fire investigators that the buckets contained water).

The cleaning machine was a belt-driven turntable with a clamp in the center to hold the empty shell casing upright as it slowly rotated. The worker started the cleaning process by wiping the outside of the casing with a gasoline-soaked brush. He then dampened a rag with gasoline, wrapped the rag around a long stick, and inserted it into the shell. When the sides and bottom of the shell had been thoroughly wiped with gasoline, the worker took a clean, dry rag, wrapped it around another stick, and dried the interior. Bundles of fresh rags were delivered to each work station throughout the day. The used rags were thrown into pails beneath the benches, where there were also buckets for waste gasoline.

In Wozniak's statement, dated 15 January 1917, he described how he performed the initial step by wiping the shell casing inside and out.

> I then swabbed out the inside of the shell with some cleaning rags which were not very clean. I next placed a clean swab of cloth inside of the revolving shell. I noticed it was quite stiff and upon placing this cleaning swab in the shell, a flame burst from the interior of the shell which ignited the fumes from the pan immediately in front of it. I tried to put the flame out by throwing a cloth over it, but it spread so rapidly I could do nothing and in a moment the flames shot up along the electric light cord above the table to the ceiling and the interior of the ceiling blazed up. At the same time the flames spread along the table to the next pan and continued to run southerly along the table. There was a receptacle standing on the floor beneath the pan set in the table which had a small quantity of the cleaning solution in it, which had dripped through. This likewise took fire.

Witnesses gave somewhat different versions of what happened, the main differences being that some said the cleaning fluid was gasoline, others called it benzene, and some alcohol. There are also differences about who did what and when, but those differences simply reflect the utter confusion that reigned when the fire started and rapidly spread. The differences also stemmed from where each witness was when the fire started. The most reliable witness, from the point of view of where the fire started, was Maurice Musson, who was a crew foreman and was standing near Wozniak's workbench. Immediately after the fire, he told investigators,

> I noticed that this man Wozniak had quite a large collection of rags and that the blaze started in these rags. I also noticed that he had spilled his pan of alcohol all over the table just before that time. The fire immediately spread very rapidly in the alcohol saturated table. I also noticed that someone threw a pail of liquid on the rags or the table almost immediately in the confusion. I am not able to state whether this was water or one of the pails of refuse alcohol under the tables. My recollection however, is that there were no pails of water in the building, the fire buckets being filled with sand. Whatever the liquid was it caused the fire to spread very rapidly and the flames dropped down on the floor and in a few moments the entire place was in a blaze. It was my firm conviction from what I saw and I so stated at the time, that the place was set on fire purposely, and that has always been and is my firm belief.

Another witness, who was farther away from Wozniak's bench, later said that he saw fire burning in the cleaning fluid pan of the man next to him and then saw it spread to the next pan. This witness recalled that he poured water into his neighbor's pan and put out that fire but that the man next to him struck a burning pan with a board, spilling the liquid and spreading the fire along the whole bench.

The man who was working at the bench directly behind Wozniak told the investigators,

> A Russian was cleaning a shell with a brush and a spark from the shell fell on the table where there was gas and oil, which caused a flame. The Russian tried to put the fire out with a rag which caused the rag to burn. As soon as the fire started on the table the man at the machine tried to smother the fire with rags, and that set the rags afire and he dropped them and ran for a pail of water. I saw one man run for water and another man threw a pail of water on the flames spreading them more and then everybody ran.

Another witness who was close to Wozniak said, "The first I saw of the fire was burning rags on the floor, and the man at the machine, a Russian, was trying to stamp them out with his feet." Other witnesses also recalled seeing Wozniak trying to stamp out the fire on the floor. Based on the statements, it seems that the fire started inside the shell casing that Wozniak was "cleaning" with a phosphorus-soaked rag. As soon as the rag ignited, he jerked the stick out of the shell, causing the burning rag to fall on the bench top, where he had previously spilled gasoline.

When the bench top erupted in flames he made a pretense of trying to smother the fire with more rags, which predictably caught fire. He then dropped the burning rags on the floor and made a show of stomping them and in the process moved the fire to the pail filled with waste gasoline under the table, which "somehow" got knocked over. Rodriquez was active during this initial period throwing "water" on the fires, which caused the fire to spread rapidly from table to table. The "water" Rodriquez threw on the flames was undoubtedly gasoline, but in the confusion no one noticed that.

The fire spread throughout the entire plant with unexpected speed. Amazingly, all 1,400 employees escaped without injury, but the Kingsland plant was totally destroyed. The damage estimates ranged from $5,000,000 to $18,000,000. Three days after the fire, Herrmann paid Rodriquez five hundred dollars; Wozniak had fled to Mexico and was never paid.

The Kingsland fire was the Baltimore sabotage cell's last operation, not because the group was finished but because of Germany's decision to return to unrestricted submarine warfare—*Der uneingeschränkte U-Boot-Krieg*. The first element of that decision began to play out on 16 January 1917, when Arthur Zimmermann, Germany's new foreign minister, sent a coded telegram to von Bernstorff using code 0075, which the British (though they intercepted the telegram) could not read. The telegram directed von Bernstorff to forward the telegram to the German minister, von Eckhardt, in Mexico City.

The telegram said that an unrestricted submarine warfare campaign would start on 1 February and would end the war in a matter of months, and it directed von Eckhardt to invite Mexico to make war on the United States alongside Germany if the Americans went to war with Germany. If the Mexicans accepted the invitation, they would recover territory in Texas, New Mexico, and Arizona that they had lost in 1848 under the Treaty of Guadalupe Hidalgo at the conclusion of the Mexican-American War (1846–48). Following orders, von Bernstorff forwarded the telegram to Mexico City, using code 13040, which the British read.[6]

The second element of the decision occurred on 30 January, when von Bernstorff informed the U.S. secretary of state about Germany's intention to reopen unrestricted submarine warfare on 1 February, causing the United States to break off diplomatic relations with Germany. The rupture ended the Baltimore sabotage cell's operations by forcing all its key members, except Hilken, to flee to Mexico. Though not a key figure, Wöhst also fled, but not to Mexico. Instead, he returned to Germany on board the SS *Frederick VIII* on 14 February, together with von Bernstorff and his diplomatic staff. Wöhst was again "Hermann Rupp," a Swiss citizen of substantial means returning home from a business trip to the United States.[7]

Wöhst left with Bureau of Investigation agents right behind him, and had he not left when he did, they would have gotten him. It appears that during the final days before his departure he took out, in cash, all or most of the $50,000 he had in the Transatlantic Trust Company to take it on board the *Frederick VIII* in a "new black suitcase." As he went out the door he gave Herrmann the key to his apartment.[8]

Herrmann had been living with Wöhst in the apartment, on West 116th Street, in New York City, since 20 January. There he had met Raoul Gerdts Pochet, who became his "chauffer and bag carrier." Pochet, who used the name Gerdts, was only a bit player in the Baltimore cell, but he knew a great deal about the cell's activities. Herrmann kept the apartment just ten days before he and Gerdts fled to Mexico on 24 February. They too were just one step ahead of the Bureau of Investigation agents and only narrowly avoided capture. They traveled in considerably less style than Wöhst, departing on board the United Fruit Line passenger-freighter SS *Pastores* for Havana. The federal agents were so close behind that they were able to send a telegram to the Bureau of Investigation office in Havana on the same day the *Pastores* sailed, alerting its agents that "Fred Larssen" (Herrmann) and Raoul G. Pochet (i.e., Gerdts) would arrive in Havana on Wednesday, 28 February. They even knew the cabin they occupied and who had the upper berth. Herrmann and Gerdts successfully eluded the federal and Cuban agents in Havana, where they remained for two weeks before going on to Mexico.[9]

Hinsch and Carl Ahrendt left New London by train on 27 May 1917 headed for Mexico after a presidential warrant was issued for Hinsch's arrest as an enemy alien. They arrived in El Paso on 29 May and easily crossed the border into Mexico that same day. On 11 April 1930, Ahrendt described the ease with which they crossed the border:

> We left the train at El Paso, Texas, and I went across the border to see whether it was difficult or not to go across the border, and discovered that it was quite an easy feat to cross the border. They had sight-seeing cars that were transporting people around El Paso, and anyone that expressed the desire could stay in this car and ride across the border and see [Ciudad] Juarez. Hinsch and I got into an automobile for a sight-seeing trip around El Paso and when the guide asked if we would like to see Mexico we said, "Why, surely, if we could," and he drove us across the border. Captain Hinsch commented on how easily we crossed the border, marveling that a country at war was so lax at its border. At the border crossing the American officials simply asked whether we had any ammunition or firearms in the car. They did not look in the car or lift the seats, and we were asked for no papers, or our nationality. It was a very easy affair.

With the departure of Hinsch, the only key member of the Baltimore sabotage cell remaining in the United States was Paul Hilken. The Bureau of Investigation had opened an investigation of him in February 1917, but not for suspicion that he was an active German agent. The investigation lacked focus and became a hunting expedition that turned up a lot of worthless information and completely overlooked solid leads that would have revealed Hilken's sabotage activities. It would be more than a decade before he was revealed, and the revelation of his sabotage activities would be his own doing.

16

U-155

T he small, clean-shaven, man seated behind the large desk was the First Sea Lord, Admiral Sir John Rushworth Jellicoe, a man of great intellect and determination. The mufti-clad man seated in a chair across from him was considerably taller than Jellicoe and had a neatly trimmed beard and mustache. Though dressed as a civilian, Rear Admiral William Sowden Sims was the U.S. liaison to the Royal Navy and soon to become Vice Admiral Sims, commander of U.S. Naval Forces Operating in European Waters. Rear Admiral Sims had arrived in London that same day and had gone immediately to the office of the First Sea Lord to hear a candid report on Germany's unrestricted submarine campaign. What the First Sea Lord told him came as a shock and was completely different than what the British newspapers were reporting.

Sims learned that shipping losses in February had reached, in round numbers, 536,000 tons, followed by losses totaling 603,000 in March, and as of 10 April, the date on which he was listening to Jellicoe, the losses were projected to reach nearly 900,000 tons that month. Jellicoe flatly told his American visitor that if the losses continued at the current rate, the British could not "go on with the war." Sims later recalled that he was "fairly astounded; for I had never imagined anything so terrible."

"What are you doing about it?" Sims asked.

"Everything we can," Jellicoe replied, adding, "We are increasing our anti-submarine forces in every possible way. But the situation is serious and we shall need all the assistance we can get."

"It looks as though the Germans are winning the war," Sims said.

"They will win, unless we can stop these losses, and stop them soon," Jellicoe said, confirming Sims' opinion.

"Is there no solution for the problem?" Sims asked.

"Absolutely none that we can see," was Jellicoe's unhappy response.[1]

While Jellicoe was giving Sims the disquieting news about the submarine war, the *U-155* was preparing for her speed trials, and *Fregattenkapitän* Hermann Bauer, who at the time was the Commander of U-boats *(Führer der U-Boote),* was suggesting that the *U-155* be used as a radio-command boat stationed in the southern approaches to the British Isles. Her purpose would be to analyze radio traffic in order to plot the course of approaching convoys and to direct groups of U-boats to attack them. In effect, he was proposing what became known as the "wolf pack" tactic of World War II.[2]

But the Admiralstab was focused on deploying the U-cruisers farther west in the Atlantic to intercept ships approaching the Azores, known as the "Atlantic Crossroads," and rejected the suggestion. The Azores, nine volcanic islands in the central Atlantic, lay astride the major shipping lanes from the North American continent to Europe as well as the commercial traffic routes in and out of the Mediterranean. The islands belonged to Portugal, which was neutral and at that time had no Allied naval bases or airfields from which ASW vessels and aircraft could operate, making the island group a relatively safe operating area for U-boats.

The *U-155* departed Kiel on 23 May 1917 for operations in the waters south and east the Azores in an area roughly from 30° to 40° north and from 20° to 30° west. She did not use the Kaiser Wilhelm Canal to reach the North Sea from Kiel. She went east across Kiel Bay and up the Baltic to the Sund, a narrow avenue between Denmark's east coast and Sweden, passed into and across the Kattegat, hooked around Skagen on Denmark's northern tip, and crossed the Skagerrak into the North Sea. The route added extra miles to her trip but was deemed safer than entering the North Sea at Helgoland. Once she was in the North Sea, she took the long route around the Faeroe Islands and then southerly into the Atlantic.[3]

Karl Meusel had been commissioned in 1902 and promoted to *Kapitänleutnant* on 22 March 1914. He was thirty-six when he took command and had no combat experience in U-boats, but he had been trained as a watch officer in 1916 on board the *U-16,* an old Körting-engine boat, before reporting to the U-boat commanders' school in 1917.[4] Despite his relative lack of experience he was probably the best choice to command the *U-155* on her first war patrol, which was a test of both the long-range concept and the suitability of the *U-Deutschland*-class boats to meet the mission's demands. He was, above all else, tenacious and aggressive, character traits that were needed on board the *U-155.* He maintained a good rapport with his crew but was not lax. And he was not hesitant to express his dissatisfaction with the *U-155*'s shortcomings, which resulted from the construction cost-cutting and sloppy workmanship that stemmed from the rush to get her converted in the minimum time. The cause of his first complaint occurred on the second day at sea.

At midmorning on 24 May the *U-155* was in the Kattegat, off Anholt Island, when the motor that drove the main compressor burned out. The main compressor was critical, because it supplied the compressed air used to blow the tanks, and its motor ran almost continuously. The only other sources of compressed air were two smaller auxiliary compressors attached to the diesel engines. But running them continuously added extra strain to the engines, which were already seriously overtaxed driving the U-boat and charging the batteries. The extra strain caused the engines to overheat, which in turn revealed a design flaw in the cooling system and led to more serious internal engine problems. Remember, those diesels had been designed as auxiliary generators, not as propulsion engines.[5]

Repairing the compressor motor took nearly thirty hours, during which the diesels ran the small auxiliary compressors without stopping, causing the engines to overheat. As the engines overheated, the engine-room temperature rose to over a hundred degrees, even with the after deck hatch open and the boat's feeble air-circulation system pumping away at maximum effort. The patrol was not off to a good start, and it was about to get worse.

At 0820 on 26 May, when they were in the North Sea south of Stavanger, Norway, a lookout spotted a steamer, and the *U-155* went to surface battle stations, both deck guns manned and ready. Meusel laid a course to intercept the steamer and rang down for full speed. It would be an enormous overstatement to say that the *U-155* surged ahead, since on a good day the best speed she could make was eleven knots. But on this day she could not make even that speed. Shortly after the order for full speed was given the starboard diesel, coughed, sputtered, and quit. The engine had shed a valve head.

The chief engineer and his staff determined that the cause was a cooling system design flaw that allowed cold seawater to come into contact with a valve that was operating at four hundred degrees (Celsius), demolishing the valve. The culprit was the hand-operated system for opening and closing the through-hull valves. The system was composed of a series of wheels, cables, and pulleys that worked so slowly that some of the valves could be still be partially open during a dive, allowing the valve openings to be submerged. In this case the problem was the valve that closed the starboard engine exhaust stack.

In his postpatrol report, Meusel wrote that he had pointed out the problem during the boat's conversion in Wilhelmshaven but that it had remained unchanged. He added that the design flaw was a direct result of the rush to complete the conversion in the minimum time. As we shall see, the valve-control system was just one of several such problems.

It is probably safe to say that any other captain would have turned around and headed home rather than continue on one engine. Instead, Meusel doubled the lookouts, put the engine-room crew to work repairing the engine, and headed north on one engine. An attendant problem with one-engine operation was that the single engine could not provide the boat with all the electrical power it needed for surface running. A good share of the needed electrical power had to come from the storage batteries, which would be critically low if they had to dive. The only answer was to stop and remain dead in the water for three hours each day so that the lone operating engine could fully recharge the batteries. Having to run on one engine and stop for three hours every day meant that the *U-155* could advance only a little over a hundred nautical miles a day.

The temporary loss of the starboard engine was the reason that Meusel took the longer route around the Faeroe Islands instead of the shorter one that König had followed when the *U-155* had been the *U-Deutschland*. The shorter route would have meant encountering more British patrols and being forced to dive more often. And Meusel could not afford to lie dead in the water in a heavily patrolled area while he recharged his depleted batteries. So his only choice was the long, less dangerous, far northern route. The slow progress made on one engine put the *U-155* in a position that nearly got her torpedoed by the *U-19*.

The close encounter occurred in the evening of 27 May, when the boat was about ninety miles west of Stavanger. *U-19,* commanded by *Oberleutnant zur See* Johannes Spiess, had completed a twenty-four-day patrol attacking convoys between the Shetland Islands and Norway and was headed back to Emden. The sea was calm, and visibility was partially obscured by mist when a *U-19* lookout spotted a large submarine three or four miles away off the port bow, traveling north. Spiess sounded the dive alarm, and the old Körting-engine boat dropped below the surface.[6]

Peering through the periscope, Spiess saw a large submarine, which he vastly overestimated to be traveling at about fifteen knots. He also saw that the *U-19* would soon cross the target's path. Spiess ordered the electric motors reduced to half-speed and took another look. "Good God, what a mob of men on the deck," he muttered to himself and lowered the periscope.

Less than a minute later he again raised the periscope, took a quick look, and stepped back as the periscope slid down into its housing. "We are going to cross her path," he told the man who was with him in the conning tower. Running the targeting problem through his mind, he made the decision to continue across the oncoming boat's path and fire a stern shot.

When he next peered through his periscope, he was much closer to the target than he had been before, and the detail was clear and sharp. She was a very large boat and mounted two large-caliber deck guns with black gun tubes. Both observations bothered him. The size and armament of the boat was uncommon, and all German boats had black gun tubes. Was she German?

Just before he lowered the periscope he said to the man beside him, "Hold the stern tube." The periscope again slid down into the housing, and Spiess rubbed his chin in thought. The man in the conning tower was puzzled by the reaction and the stern torpedo room crew was equally puzzled. He took the speaking tube and called his first officer and navigator to the cramped conning tower. As the two men squeezed into the narrow space, Spiess raised the periscope and motioned them to look. "What is she, German or British?" he asked.

The first officer stepped back and the navigator had a look. "German," the navigator said, adding, "*U-Deutschland* class," as he stepped back from the lens. The first officer peered through the optic and nodded his agreement, saying, "*U-Deutschland* class." Spiess took another look and agreed. "Surface," he ordered.

When the *U-19* surfaced there was an initial scramble on the *U-155* to man the deck guns, since there was no time to dive and the boat was already making her maximum speed of five knots. To everyone's relief *U-19* hoisted the German naval battle flag and the correct recognition signal. *U-155* answered; the two boats were soon laid alongside one another, and the two captains exchanged information. Meusel got the better of the exchange, because Spiess was able to tell him about the Allied convoy system. Spiess warned Meusel to stay away from the coasts, where there were "only destroyers and cruisers waiting for convoys." He also passed along that he had found little use for his two 88 mm deck guns, because of strong convoy escorts and the large number of armed merchantmen he had encountered. He had relied almost entirely on submerged torpedo attacks. But making a torpedo attack was an ordeal, because of the difficulty in getting close enough to the target on the surface undiscovered in order to get a sure hit after diving.

Spiess had overstated the situation with regard to convoys; in May 1917 the transatlantic convoys had not yet been organized. The Scandinavian-trade convoys had gone into effect at the end of April 1917 but did not become fully effective until July, and the "War Channel" convoy system along the British east coast was just taking effect. Nevertheless, the problems that Spiess described to Meusel were a warning of what was to come.

After the meeting with the *U-19,* the *U-155* limped north, still running at one-engine speed. The following evening she was about a hundred nautical miles northeast of the Shetland Islands when a British destroyer forced her to dive. The destroyer passed over the U-boat and dropped two depth charges, which exploded very close. The boat shuddered, and the crewmen were badly shaken, since for all of them this was the first experience of being depth-charged.

Small, primitive depth charges had been in very limited service since January 1915, but the modern Type D, three-hundred-pound depth charge did not enter service until January 1916 and saw very limited service until after the United States entered the war. In May 1917, the depth charge was still a relatively new weapon, and British destroyers and patrol boats only carried two or four.[7] This destroyer had four, but the next two were dropped some distance away and had no effect.

Meusel called for damage reports; all compartments reported no damage and no leaks. Several hours later Meusel surfaced, clutched in the one working diesel, and discovered that the boat had in fact been damaged during the first depth-charge attack. When the engine room fired up the port diesel and opened the main induction valve, which supplied air to the engine room, water poured into the space. Not knowing the cause of the flooding, the engine room crew quickly closed the main induction valve. On the bridge Meusel was advised of the situation and ordered the after deck hatch and the lower conning tower hatches opened to supply air to the engine room. There was also a small air shaft in the after part of the boat that was unaffected and open.

The problem turned out to be a section of pipe that connected the main induction valve cap inside the conning tower casing to the engine room. The main induction valve *(Hauptluftschacht)* had the cap assembly at the top of a pipe that ran down into the engine room. The pipe had three sections. Starting at the top was a short, vertical section that included the cap. The second was a long section that ran diagonally aft to another short, vertical section that contained the valve and passed through the pressure hull into the engine room. The damaged section was the long diagonal pipe. The chief engineer told Meusel that though the depth-charging had contributed to the failure, the real culprit was shoddy workmanship in Wilhelmshaven. He told the skipper that he and his men could not permanently repair the damage; the solution was to cut away the damaged section and toss it overboard. That would leave enough of a stump on the pipe that contained the valve for his engine room crew to reattach the salvaged watertight cap. The control cables would be rerouted so that the jury-rigged cap would function properly.

Here was another example of Meusel's tenaciousness. Again, he had good reason to turn back. He had only one operating engine and a damaged main induction valve. The latter could still be made watertight, which meant the boat could dive. But if the temporary repair developed a sealing problem, the *U-155* would be in a very bad situation. Still, the cap problem was manageable, and his engine-room crew was working around the clock on the engine.

Despite his mechanical difficulties, during the period 27–31 June Meusel managed to stop three Danish steamers and the American SS *Texel,* all of which he examined and released. Releasing the three Dutch steamers is understand-able, inasmuch as they were neutrals bound for neutral ports, but the *Texel* was another matter. Built in 1913, she was a freighter of 3,210 gross register tons (GRT) operated by the Dutch shipping company Rotterdamsche Droogdok Mij. The Americans had seized her in New York Harbor in April 1917 under the Right of Angary (a tenet of international law allowing belligerents to seize and use neutral property) and put her under the control of the U.S. Shipping Board. Given that when Meusel stopped her she was in the service of the U.S. government, he had every right to sink her.

On 30 May, when the *U-155* was still east of the Faeroe Islands, the starboard engine came back online, and Meusel was able to increase speed to eight or nine knots. He made good time throughout the day of 31 May and passed the Faeroe Islands, but during the night a storm began to develop that became a whole gale on the morning of 1 June. For the next twenty-four hours the *U-155* was reduced to a crawl, and those who were new to the boat experienced for the first time what König had called "the hell below" that had developed inside the *U-Deutschland* during heavy weather. At noon on 1 June, in heavy seas and poor visibility, the U-boat was forced to dive when she encountered a four-stack vessel less than a mile away.

By dawn on 2 June the storm had passed and the seas had become moderate, providing Meusel the opportunity to fix his position. He was about two hun-dred nautical miles south of Vatnajökull, Iceland, heading west. That evening he stopped the SS *Hafursfjord* in 60° 25' north, 16° 20' west and scored his first success.

The *Hafursfjord,* built in 1882, was a 1,669 GRT freighter with a sixteen-man crew. Her captain, Martin Tygesen, had taken on a cargo of salt in Cadiz, Spain, and was en route to Haugesund, Norway, which is south of Bergen. He had taken the longer route, steaming north and well outside of the extreme boundary of the U-boats' four-hundred-mile-wide operating line.

Meusel sent a boarding party to set charges below the waterline while the *Hafursfjord's* crew took to their two lifeboats and rowed away from the ship. As soon as the boarding party returned, Meusel had the two deck guns open fire, both

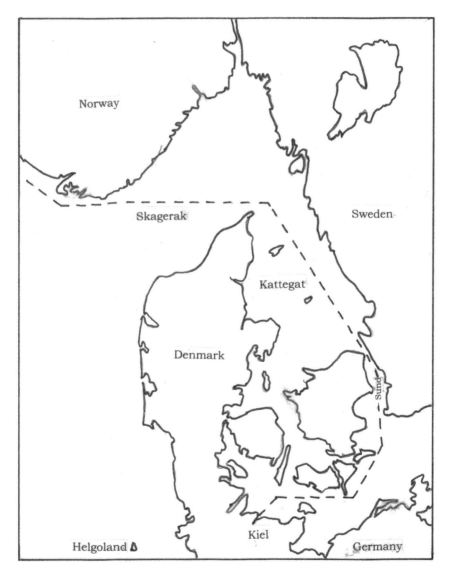

Map 6. The Scandinavian route used by the *U-155* on all three of her war patrols

to give the gun crews experience handling the guns and to speed the sinking. In the meantime, Krapohl talked to the freighter's captain and provided both boats with food and water. Then, shortly after 1300, the *U-155* got under way, leaving the two lifeboats and the freighter's crew adrift in the North Atlantic.

Though it is a fine point, the truth is that under what we now call "rules of engagement" Meusel was not required to sink the *Hafursfjord*. He had already stopped and released four ships, one of which was American, an enemy vessel. In every case, including the *Hafursfjord,* he had made a "stop and search," during which he learned that the ship was carrying noncontraband salt and was bound for a neutral port. The declaration of unrestricted submarine warfare was intended to give the U-boats a free hand to torpedo any vessel, neutral or belligerent, without warning, but it said nothing about what actions to take in a case such as that of the *Hafursfjord*. Meusel was free to exercise his own judgment in the matter, but given the state of the sea, the distance to land, and his prior practice, he should have released the ship, if for no other reason than humanity. As it worked out, both lifeboats were found on 5 June, and the crews were landed alive and well in Stornoway in the Hebrides.

The euphoria over the first success was quickly dispelled when Eyring reported that the torpedo tubes were badly damaged. Again, the damage was the result not of enemy action but shoddy construction and rough weather. The torpedo tubes, taken from the old battleship SMS *Zähringen,* had been modified to be mounted outside the *U-155*'s pressure hull. The modification consisted of welding short "legs" to the bottoms of the tubes and welding the legs to the flat tops of fuel and oil tanks also mounted outside the pressure hull. Large slots cut into the casing allowed the torpedoes to exit the tubes and the casing. But those same slots admitted seawater into the spaces between the casing and the pressure hull. Openings that allowed seawater to flow into these spaces and then drain out of them were common in all U-boats and necessary, but the presence of the *U-155*'s torpedo tubes in those spaces interrupted the normal flow of the water.

Heavy weather, such as the *U-155* had experienced on 1 June, had created a condition in which tons of seawater, coupled with the boat's violent motion, put enormous strain on the torpedo tubes' mountings. The strain was amplified, because a heavy steel bulkhead that had been built athwartships aft of the torpedo tubes to stiffen the gun deck acted as a dam that partially blocked the water from flowing aft and out through the drain slots along the side of the hull. The result was that the torpedo tubes were engulfed in a maelstrom of surging water that caused them to work on their short legs. The weld joints were the weakest part of the arrangement and the most likely to fail, which they did. But the worst, and very real, threat was that when the weld joints failed they would tear open the relatively light steel tank tops to which they were welded. The worst scenario had not yet happened, but the failure of several weld joints had loosened the tubes so that they were no longer properly aligned, and now they "wobbled."

On 10 June, Meusel had reached a point about six hundred nautical miles west of the Bay of Biscay and six hundred nautical miles northeast of his patrol area, and there he stopped the Canadian tanker SS *Scottish Hero.* The tanker, built in 1895, was carrying oil from Canada to Sydney, Australia, and was armed with a stern-mounted 120 mm gun. Upon sighting the surfaced U-boat the tanker presented her stern to the German, opened fire with her deck gun, and went ahead at twelve knots.

Meusel had intended to carry out a surface torpedo attack but decided the torpedoes were too unreliable and opened fire with his forward deck gun as he gave chase at his best speed—ten knots. During the thirty-minute chase and gunfire exchange, the *Scottish Hero's* rounds fell very close to the U-boat while the tanker opened the distance. But the *U-155's* gunners were on target and scored eight hits, one of which went into the tanker's engine room. The Canadian stopped, and her crew abandoned ship. Meusel brought the *U-155* close enough to question the survivors about the ship and to provide them with provision and directions to the nearest land. When he left the area the *Scottish Hero* survivors were adrift in open boats, hundreds of miles from land, with a storm approaching.

After sinking the *Scottish Hero,* Meusel laid a course that took the *U-155* southeast toward the Portuguese coast, crossing the forty-fifth parallel just before noon on 11 June. Once south of the forty-fifth parallel he was outside the effective war zone, the area in which British blockade and antisubmarine patrols were active. There was very little chance that he would encounter a hostile warship until he recrossed the forty-fifth parallel going north. In these southern waters, his active armed opposition would be armed freighters, which in most cases he would outgun.

Two days later a lookout sighted a large vessel several miles away, and the *U-155* turned to intercept it. As the U-boat was about to come within range to open fire, the vessel turned and ran. Meusel tried to close the widening gap and in the process shed another engine valve, forcing him to break off the chase and continue southeast at one-engine speed. A few hours later he fired on a freighter, believed to be the SS *Luckenbach,* that turned away and disappeared over the horizon. The starboard engine came online early the following morning, 14 June, shortly before another ship was sighted. Meusel hurried forward on both engines to get within gun range and opened fire. But the range was too great, and the intended victim, the grain carrier SS *Grainton,* simply put on speed, turned away, and fled safely out of range.

The *U-155* was too slow to overhaul most of the ships she met even under the best conditions, and she was completely outclassed running on one engine. Faced with the fact that many of his intended victims carried stern-mounted deck guns, Meusel devised a new tactic for engaging them. He would move across the target's path submerged, surface directly ahead of the ship at close range, and open fire with both 150 mm deck guns. The tactic laid him open to the possibility of being rammed, but Meusel dismissed that threat on the grounds that "no one in his right mind would try to ram in the face of such firepower." His first opportunity to try the new ploy and his theory occurred on 14 June, about 430 miles west–northwest of Cape Finisterre.

The SS *Aysgarth* was a "three island" (meaning superstructure forward, amidships, and aft) tramp of 3,118 GRT built in 1896 and now carrying iron ore from Aguilas, Spain, to Clyde. When the *U-155* surfaced three thousand yards in front of her, the *Aysgarth* put her helm hard over to bring her stern-mounted 120 mm gun to bear. The *U-155* was able to maneuver to remain ahead of the *Aysgarth* and opened fire with both deck guns. The Germans' fire was accurate and made several hits on the freighter's hull and superstructure. Unable to bring her stern gun to bear on the U-boat, the *Aysgarth* returned fire with a bow-mounted 76 mm gun. The freighter finally was able to maneuver so that her stern gun joined the action, and the gunfight grew hot. It lasted nearly an hour, with the *U-155* firing fifty rounds, scoring fifteen hits, and finally forcing the *Aysgarth* to stop and lower her boats. But the exchange had not been one-sided. One of the freighter's 76 mm rounds had scored a solid hit on the *U-155*'s port lubricating oil tank and had ripped open the adjacent fuel tank.

While Krapohl was providing the *Aysgarth*'s two lifeboats with water and provisions, the *U-155*'s boarding party planted charges below the freighter's waterline to finish her off. As the freighter's lifeboats rowed away, Meusel and his engineers examined their own damage. The *U-155* was now dead in the water, an expanding field of oil and fuel spreading from her port side. Meusel felt that the lubricating-oil loss was not terribly important, but the fuel loss was another matter, and he ordered the remaining oil and fuel transferred to other tanks. An hour after the *Aysgarth* had gone down and the two lifeboats had vanished from view, Meusel got under way, headed southeast toward the Portuguese coast while still transferring oil and fuel from the damaged tanks, forcing the *U-155* to travel at three knots to conserve fuel.

Ten hours after sinking the *Aysgarth* and thirty-eight nautical miles way, the *U-155* encountered the SS *Benguela,* a 4,612 GRT Norwegian freighter en route from England to New York in ballast. Instead of sinking her, Meusel took the four-hundred-foot-long freighter as a prize and put his prize-crew officer, *Leutnant zur See* Hild, in command. He intended to use the *Benguela* as a support ship to provide quarters for his twenty-man prize crew and any crewmen he took from ships he sank in the future. He also took stores from the freighter and used her to tow the *U-155,* mainly to conserve fuel but also to allow his crew to work on the boat's mechanical problems.

The most serious problem was with the torpedoes themselves, which were found to be "in very poor condition." The torpedo problems resulted from the tubes being mounted outside the pressure hull, which caused two negative situations. The first was that the *U-155* had no reload torpedoes; the tubes could only be reloaded when the boat was surfaced, and for that reason she had been issued just six torpedoes, all of which had been loaded in Kiel. The second negative situation was that because the torpedoes were fully immersed in seawater while they rested in the tubes waiting to be fired, they required periodic servicing. But the torpedo tubes' location made it very difficult to carry out the required work when surfaced; it had to be done in the cramped space between the hulls and in swirling water.

Three weeks of uninterrupted immersion in seawater had caused so much damage that three of the weapons were found to be inoperative. The problems were mainly faulty motors, but one was losing compressed air, and another had a damaged rudder. The torpedo problem was never fully resolved; of the six torpedoes that were loaded in Kiel, three sank targets, two simply sank when fired, and the sixth remained inoperative and was taken home in the tube.

From 15 to 25 June the *Benguela* and *U-155* headed slowly west, the U-boat under tow for varying periods of time. From noon on 15 June until 0800 on the 17th, the *U-155* and the *Benguela* lay side by side while the U-boat's radiomen jury-rigged a radio on board the prize. Meusel wanted to remain in radio contact with the ship while he was away hunting for targets. Since there were few if any enemy warships operating in this area, there was little risk that his men and the *Benguela* would be captured while he was gone. But to be on the safe side, he ordered that scuttling charges be laid in the hull.

After the trip west was resumed at 0800 on 17 June, Meusel broke off the tow to make sweeps ahead of the freighter, hoping to find a target, but he came up dry every time until midmorning on 25 June. Meanwhile the crew also continued to repair the *U-155*'s many defects, until in the evening of 22 June she was again fully operational, batteries fully charged, all repairs made, and the main compressor back online. Sixty-two hours later, at 0700, a freighter was spotted, and Meusel dove to maneuver into her path.

Instead of coming up directly ahead of the freighter, Meusel chose to surface off the freighter's port side so that both 150 mm guns could be brought to bear broadside. But instead of turning away, the freighter turned directly toward the surfaced *U-155,* firing steadily with a 76 mm bow gun. As the range rapidly dropped, the *U-155*'s gunners scored three solid hits on the freighter's superstructure directly below the bridge, causing the freighter to go about, unmasking a 120 mm stern gun.

The freighter's heavy-caliber deck gun came as an ugly surprise, especially when the rounds started falling very close to the U-boat. Two of those near hits opened a seam in a starboard-side fuel bunker and caused the starboard after lubrication oil bunker to lose five tons of oil and run dry. As the freighter pulled away, she made smoke from generators on her stern and continued to fire whenever the opportunity presented itself.

Meusel gave chase, increased speed to ten knots, and reopened fire as the freighter drew, notwithstanding, out of range. The chase lasted three hours, with the *U-155* pumping out round after round from her forward gun without effect, except maybe to cause the freighter to "bend on" more revolutions. During the next three hours, the *U-155* fired one hundred rounds without a hit. Disgusted with his boat's slow speed, which made overtaking most large ships impossible, Meusel ceased fire, broke off the chase, and returned to the *Benguela*.

The experience underscored the *U-155*'s single most serious deficiency—that she was too slow. The eleven knots she had achieved during her trials were rarely if ever reached during wartime operations, making her effective top speed just ten knots on a good day, more commonly just eight or nine. The problem stemmed in part from the relatively low-power engines that drove her and in part from the presence of two athwartships bulkheads that ran across the top of the pressure hull. They had been put there to strengthen the gun decks, but as already mentioned in connection with the trouble they caused for the torpedo tubes, those bulkheads also produced drag, by partially blocking the flow of water aft between the hulls.

The loss of speed was matched by a substantial increase in fuel consumption, because the engines had to work harder to make speed. And increased fuel consumption represented a corresponding decrease in range. When she completed her acceptance trials in April 1917, the Krupp engineers had estimated her range at 25,000 at 5.5 knots.[8] But experience caused Meusel to recalculate the boat's maximum range at closer to 12,000 nautical miles at three knots. He was probably underestimating the boat's maximum range, but the reality was that there was no way the *U-155* could cover 25,000 nautical miles on a war patrol unless she encountered only calm seas and could operate consistently at 5.5 knots, neither of which was a realistic expectation.

The recent action had produced another serious deficiency as well—the recoil from the 150 mm guns was beating up the casing. Every time the guns were fired, the gun deck worked, putting enormous strains on the steel struts that joined the casing to the pressure hull. The strain was passed down the deck from one strut to the next, so when a strut failed, the strut behind failed next. The immediate results were that the deck plates had loosened and the watertight ready-ammunition storage tubes leaked. On 28 June an inspection showed that forty 150 mm rounds had to be thrown over the side, the wooden deck was splintered and broken in places, and the steel flap covering the port bow torpedo tube had fallen off. In his log, Meusel wrote, "The recoil is an eternal well for failures."

The *U-155* was now almost directly north of the Azores, and the two-vessel convoy turned south toward the archipelago, arriving ninety-eight nautical miles northeast of Terceira on 29 June. There the *U-155* encountered the *Siraa*, an iron-hull, full-rigged sailing ship of 1,938 GRT that had been built in 1887. She was not quite a clipper ship, but she certainly resembled one, with her square sails set on her three masts and her long bowsprit. The *Siraa* was out of Buenos Aires bound for Le Havre with a cargo of *quebracho*, a wood-derived tanin used in the leather industry. Meusel sank her with gunfire after her crew took to their boats.

That same day the *U-155* stopped the SS *Joaquin Mumbru*, a Spanish 2,701-GRT freighter bound for New York with general cargo. Meusel put the crews of the *Benguela* and *Siraa* on board the freighter and released her. (Six months later, on 30 December 1917, the *Joaquin Mumbru*'s luck ran out when the *U-156,* under *Kapitänleutnant* Konrad Gansser, sank her a hundred nautical miles southwest of Funchal, Madeira.)⁹ The following day Meusel scuttled the *Benguela,* closing "phase one" of his war patrol. This period covered thirty-two days, during which the *U-155* sank five ships totaling 13,542 GRT. It was not an auspicious start.

Phase two opened on 4 July with an attack on the harbor at Ponta Delgada, on Sao Miguel, in the Azores. Meusel's intention was to torpedo any freighters he found in the harbor, but when he arrived off the harbor entrance he saw that a torpedo attack was impossible, owing to a huge stone mole that screened the vessels inside. Instead he decided to shell the harbor, doing whatever damage he could to the vessels inside the mole. It was a short-lived effort, ending abruptly when the coastal-defense batteries at Fort São Brás returned fire.

During the hasty withdrawal from Fort São Brás, a lookout spotted a steamer about five miles away, but the ship disappeared before the U-boat could get close enough to engage. Disappointed, Meusel noted in his log that had the *U-155* been faster, he would have chased the ship. He was then about thirty miles south of the harbor and decided to make another try at sinking the anchored ships inside the harbor.

When he arrived close to the harbor entrance he dove to periscope depth and started his approach, only to have the bow broach. Before he could order an adjustment, the bow dropped down, and the stern broke the surface. The U-boat was porpoising; she was out of control, impossible to hold at depth. Meusel went deep, came about, and sent the chief engineer to fix the trouble. As soon as he felt he was out of range of the shore batteries, he surfaced and headed off to the south.

The chief engineer returned to report that the trouble was no easy fix. The problem arose from the original decision to build the *U-Deutschland* on the cheap, using parts that were readily available and inexpensive, even for jobs they had never been intended to do. In this case the motor used to drive the after diving planes had been designed as a general-purpose motor for marine use. When installed to drive the diving-plane worm gears on the *U-Deutschland* it had been adequate for the job, but the rigors of war service were too much for it, and it had simply burned out. The real problem was that there were no spare motors on board, despite the copious room available for storing spare parts. The people responsible for outfitting the *U-155* for war service had seen fit to provide her with a complete machine shop, including a six-inch lathe, in what had been the after hold but had neglected to provide spare motors.

The solution was the one that is often used by combat units to keep equipment working—cannibalization. Since maintaining depth, especially periscope depth, was vitally important, the chief engineer unshipped the rudder motor and used it to drive the after diving plane. It solved the immediate problem but introduced another one, which while less serious was still a problem. Without a rudder motor the helmsman had a hard time turning the wheel, which was now very heavy. The best a single man could achieve against the hydrodynamic forces exerted against the unassisted rudder was ten degrees to either side. That meant that the *U-155* would be making very wide turns and would be nearly impossible to steer in a tight situation or one that demanded an immediate change of direction.

On 6 July Meusel spent four hours in pursuit of the British passenger-freighter SS *Glenturret,* fruitlessly, because the boat was too slow to catch her or even come within gun range. The next day was even more frustrating. When the *U-155* encountered the 1,338 GRT freighter SS *Coblenz,* Meusel dove, maneuvered to make a stern torpedo shot, and fired. He ordered the periscope raised and swung the optic toward the target, expecting to see a torpedo wake streaking toward the *Coblenz.* Nothing. There was absolutely no sign of the torpedo, which had exited the tube and immediately sunk like a rock to the bottom.

Housing the periscope, Meusel ordered the boat to surface, clutched in the diesels, and prepared to sink the ship with gunfire. The *Coblenz* should have been easy meat for the *U-155*'s 150 mm guns. The freighter was a slowpoke, with a top speed of ten knots, and she was unarmed. But when the *U-155*'s guns fired the first round, the *Coblenz* turned, made smoke from a stern-mounted generator, and steamed away. Unable to see the target because of the smoke, Meusel's guns ceased firing, and the *U-155* started another fruitless pursuit. The U-boat could match the freighter's ten-knot speed but could not overtake her. After firing a dozen ineffective rounds, Meusel broke off the chase. The failure was due in part to Meusel's newly adopted tactic of opening fire at extreme range, a result of previous experience with armed freighters.

By 8 July, Meusel had been ten days without scoring a victory. He had been run off at Ponta Delgada, had been unable to get close to the *Glenturret,* and had been eluded by the old freighter *Coblenz.* If for no other reason than morale, he needed the victory that he achieved that day in position 35° north, 17° west.

The SS *Ruelle* was a British three-island tramp of 3,583 GRT under lease to the French government, carrying coal from Cardiff to Algiers. Meusel made a submerged torpedo attack, firing at two thousand yards one bow torpedo that struck the freighter on the port quarter. As soon as the torpedo exploded, the *U-155* surfaced and moved toward the sinking ship to finish her off with gunfire, if necessary, and to question the crew about her identity, cargo, and destination.

The forty-four-man crew was already rowing away from the ship, which was now down by the stern and sinking rapidly. Following his usual practice, Meusel handed over food and water to the survivors and gave them a heading to the nearest land, which was Madeira, which lay two hundred nautical miles northeast. Sinking the *Ruelle* closed phase two of the *U-155*'s war patrol, which was even less auspicious than phase one. This period had lasted just four days, during which he had sunk just one ship of 3,583 GRT, and it convinced Meusel that he should be working south of the thirty-fifth parallel.

Phase three opened on 12 July with the torpedoing of the British ore carrier SS *Calliope* at 35° north, 17° west and the loss of the entire twenty-seven-man crew. The 2,883 GRT freighter was carrying ore from Seville, Spain, to Newport, Montreal, when a single torpedo struck her amidships, causing her to break in two and sink in less than five minutes. The *U-155* surfaced and moved through the wreckage looking for swimmers but found none. Meusel identified the ship from a life ring that was found floating in the debris field. The torpedo that sank the *Calliope* was the third fired and the second success, leaving the U-boat with three remaining, two in the bow tubes and one in the starboard stern tube.

Two days later Meusel stopped the Greek freighter SS *Chalkydon* carrying general cargo from New York to Marseille. The ship's cargo was a treasure trove of food for the *U-155* crewmen, who spent several hours transferring whatever they needed to the cavernous stowage room in their forward hold. Toward dawn on 15 July, explosive charges were detonated deep in the freighter's hull, sending her to the bottom.

On 18 July the *U-155* stopped the 3,877 GRT Norwegian freighter SS *Ellen*, which was carrying thirteen locomotives and 4,700 tons of coal from Philadelphia to Marseille. For some reason Meusel hung on to the freighter and remained in the same area until 20 July, when he finally sank her with gunfire and scuttling charges.

The disposal of the *Ellen* was prompted by the sighting of a large steamer coming toward them. Meusel dove, maneuvered for a torpedo attack, and fired one bow torpedo, which missed the target. When Meusel surfaced to sink the vessel with gunfire, he found himself faced with a fully alert, heavily armed merchant-man who proved more than a match for the *U-155*. Meusel broke off the attack and headed southeast.

▲ The ex-*U-Deutschland*, now the *U-155*, returning from her first war patrol on 5 September 1915. This rare photo shows the openings in the casing for her externally mounted torpedo tubes. The captured guns displayed on the foredeck are a 90 mm gun taken from the French sailing vessel *Marthe* on 2 August 1917 and a 76 mm gun taken from the British SS *Snowdonian* on 31 July 1917. *Jørn Jensen collection*

It was still daylight on 20 July when the *U-155* came upon the SS *Hanseat,* another Norwegian freighter, out of the Italian port of Civitavecchia bound for Hampton Roads in ballast. Once the crew was clear, Meusel had her sunk with scuttling charges.

Again the boat's success was followed by a setback. It was discovered that there was water in the starboard engine exhaust and that the boat's interior cooling system had broken down. The problems were unrelated, and the water in the exhaust system was easily fixed. The cooling system, however, was another matter. Inefficient as the cooling system was when working normally, without it the boat's interior became insufferably hot, and it was already 113° Fahrenheit.

While the repairs were being made, the *U-155* scored three successes in one day, proving that things were not as bad as they seemed. The first victim was the American *John Twohy,* which was stopped at dawn on 21 July 120 nautical miles south of São Miguel, in the Azores. The *John Twohy* was a four-masted, gaff-rigged, 193-foot, wooden-hull schooner built in 1881 and registered at 1,019 GRT. She was carrying sulphur from Philadelphia to Algiers. Meusel sank her with explosive charges.

The second victim that day was the Canadian three-masted, wooden schooner *Willena Gertrude,* 120 nautical miles southeast of Santa Maria, in the Azores. She was a 317 GRT sailing vessel carrying coal from Port Preston, in the United Kingdom, to West Africa. The day's third victim, also a sailing ship, was the Italian three-masted barque *Doris,* of 1,355 GRT, ninety nautical miles from Santa Maria. The steel-hulled ship was carrying wheat from Buenos Aires to Gibraltar. Meusel sank her with gunfire at very close range.

Five days passed before he found another target, on 26 July. When the ship was sighted she was out of torpedo range but within extreme gun range, and Meusel ordered the forward deck gun to open fire. The first round landed far short of the target and alerted the freighter, which returned fire, made smoke, and put on speed. The next two hours were a repeat of what the *U-155* crew had come to expect under these circumstances. The ship simply outran the U-boat while returning fairly accurate gunfire and making smoke.

But in this case a reality of which Meusel had already become aware was the real reason for the U-boat's failure to effectively engage the target. The wear and tear of wartime operations, combined with the already described design flaws in the boat's conversion, had reduced the boat's maximum speed to 7.5 knots in anything other than "best weather, flat sea, and no fog or rain." The encounter also revealed the arrival of another problem that had been in the making for some time.

More than once since the failed encounter with the *Glenturret* on 6 July, Meusel's log had contained references to the increasing inaccuracy of both deck guns. Now, three weeks later, the problem had become serious. An examination of the guns showed that they were in such poor shape that the muzzles could be pushed by hand as much as twenty-one degrees off the bore-sight line. At the time the forward gun had fired 435 rounds, which was hardly excessive for a gun of that type, and the after gun had fired only 288 rounds. The vicious recoil that was tearing the deck apart was the immediate cause, but the real cause was the engineering that had gone into adapting the guns to the *U-155*.

The pre-*Dreadnought* battleship SMS *Zähringen,* from which they had come, had been commissioned in 1902 and downgraded to training ship in 1916. The gun type was considered obsolete in 1916 but continued in use throughout World War I and would remain in service into World War II, frequently being converted to field artillery for the German army. The maximum effective range as mounted on the *U-155* was a little over five miles.

On board the *Zähringen* the gun had been in heavy mounts inside full shields that resembled small turrets. The total weight of the gun in its shipboard configuration was 5.5 tons, which was much too heavy for use on board a U-boat. The shield was removed and the gun was installed in a lighter mount, reducing the installation weight by about half. But the lighter mount was not up to the heavy recoil, with the result that the stress on the elevation and training gears that accompanied the firing of every round caused the gun's accuracy to fall off dramatically.

The *U-155* gunners tried to tighten the elevation and training gears by driving in lead stops, which worked for a while but made gun laying very hard work. The practice developed of hammering in new lead stops after every engagement, which was at best a stopgap; the guns became less and less accurate as the patrol continued. It got to the point where the guns were only useful at virtually point-blank range. Meusel accurately described the situation in his log, "The guns have ceased to be precision weapons."

But even the guns were not the only problems that showed up on 26 July. The two remaining torpedoes, one in a starboard bow tube and one in the starboard stern tube, were found to be defective. The one in the bow tube was leaking compressed air, which was a repeat of its earlier problem and fairly easily fixed—until it started leaking again. The stern-tube occupant was determined to be irreparable under the existing circumstances. Meusel decided to take it home in its tube rather than disposing of it over the side, because he wanted the torpedo engineers at Kiel to see firsthand what long immersion in seawater did to a torpedo.

A more immediate, and unresolvable, problem was the leak in the damaged port-side fuel tank. Using a jury-rigged bottle and string to sound the tank, Meusel discovered that the tank had already lost 10.5 tons of fuel. Since there was no way to stop the leak, he estimated that he could remain on station for another six days before starting home. In any event, the continued loss would result in a dry tank before he reached Germany.

When the *U-155* fired a warning shot and hoisted the "Stop" signal at 0700 on 31 July, the French sailing vessel she had met opened fire with two 90 mm guns. The *Madeleine* was a fifteen-year-old ship-rigged vessel, 289 feet long, with a steel hull and three masts. She had departed Bordeaux on 6 July bound for Sydney in ballast, under the command of Captain J. Lévèque and a thirty-one-man crew.

When the *Madeleine* encountered the *U-155* she had been in calm air and proceeding under power provided by a fifty-horsepower diesel engine. The gunfight lasted ninety minutes, with the U-boat scoring several hits, the last coming at 0830 when a round exploded in the *Madeleine's* stern, detonating her ammunition storage and setting the ship afire.

Only one boat got away, containing Captain Lévèque and five crewmen; other crewmen were in the water, and eleven had been killed during the fighting. Meusel moved into the sinking site and pulled several swimmers on board the U-boat before recovering an empty, drifting lifeboat. He had fifteen Frenchmen standing on the casing and one lifeboat that could hold twelve. The problem was quickly solved by calling the boat carrying Captain Lévèque alongside and putting the remaining three men in that boat. Shortly after the survivors had been placed in lifeboats, another ship was sighted, and the *U-155* pulled away to make the stop.

The new target was the British 3,870 GRT steamer SS *Snowdonian* out of Port Barry, Wales, bound for Freetown, Sierra Leone, with 6,700 tons of coal. Again the ships exchanged fire, the steamer being badly outgunned. After an hour, during which the steamer laid smoke with its smoke generator, she stopped and put out her boats. The *U-155* went alongside and sent a party on board to dismount the ship's 76 mm gum and put it on board the U-boat, after which charges were set and the ship sunk.

The following day another sailing ship was taken, the French *Alexandre,* a steel, four-masted barque of 2,671 GRT armed with two 90 mm guns. She was en route from La Pallice, France, to Iquique, Chile, in ballast. Despite being armed, she put up no resistance, probably because in light air she had no hope of outrunning the U-boat. Before sinking the barque with charges the Germans took both 90 mm guns, a task that took most of the day. That evening the *U-155* chased a British eleven-knot steamer, SS *City of Columbia,* for an hour before giving up due to the poor shape the diesels were in.

Still working the same area, the U-boat took another sailing vessel, the French four-masted schooner *Marthe,* which was also in ballast and bound for Chile. The Germans took two more 90 mm guns from her before sinking her. Meusel now decided to return to Germany and laid a course north. His engines were literally on their last legs, and his fuel supply was approaching critical. The day after he started for home he received an order sent from Nauen, Germany's international radio transmitting and receiving station, to hold a position off Madeira and waylay an American transport that was believed to be approaching the area. Grudgingly, Meusel changed course.

The following day the port engine quit, and Meusel broke off the effort to waylay the American. He again headed north while the engine-room crew tore down the diesel and went to work on it. The problem was the injection pump, but there were other issues as well. Three days later, 7 August, and not much farther north, the port engine was back online, and things were looking up again.

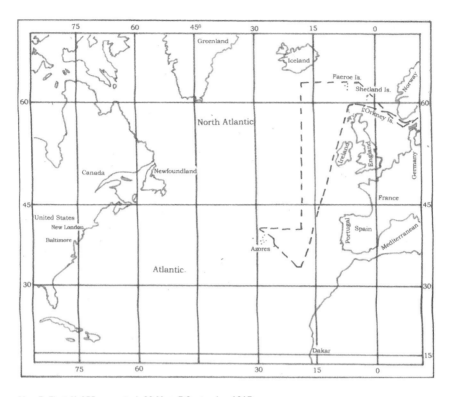

Map 7. First *U-155* war patrol, 23 May–7 September 1917

The port engine had only been running for an hour when a lookout spotted a ship less than three thousand yards away. The U-boat and the ship were about two hundred nautical miles southeast by east of Santa Maria. Their relative positions suggested that a torpedo would do the job, and Meusel dove. He had one good torpedo left, in the starboard bow. At 1123 he fired it at a thousand yards and watched the straight, foaming wake that pointed to the spot where the torpedo and the freighter would meet. The torpedo struck amidships, and the freighter immediately slowed, stopped, and started to list to port. The crew lost no time abandoning the ship, and there were no casualties. Meusel learned from the survivors that the freighter was the British SS *Iran,* out of Calcutta and bound for London with ten thousand tons of sugar, tea, rice, and corn.

Meusel sank the last vessel of the patrol on 8 August, 124 nautical miles north of where he sank the *Iran*. The unlucky ship was the small American barque *Christiane,* 946 GRT, en route to New York from London. The position where the Germans scuttled the vessel was approximately two hundred nautical miles east of São Miguel, in the Azores.

Meusel and the *U-155* had not done too badly, considering the technical problems the boat suffered. He had sunk thirteen ships totaling 36,836 GRT during the thirty-day period he called "phase three," and his total for the patrol was

▲ Not only was the security tighter at New London than at Baltimore, but the cargo handling facilities were much improved. The purpose-built warehouse was equipped with its own cranes, eliminating the need to use the *U-Deutschland*'s smaller and slower cranes, which had been left in Baltimore. *Claas Stöckmeyer collection*

twenty-one ships, totaling 52,370 GRT.[10] His score looks even more impressive when compared to the individual boat totals for the entire year 1917, in which the *U-155* ranks twenty-six out of seventy-one.

Meusel, his crew, and his boat returned to Kiel on 5 September 1917, and the boat immediately went into the yard for a complete overhaul and reconstruction. Among the changes made was to move the outboard torpedo tubes into a torpedo room, inside the pressure hull. Most of the crew remained with the boat, but Meusel was sent to the *U-79,* and *Korvettenkapitän* (Commander) Erich Eckelmann took over the *U-155* for her second war patrol.[11]

The End of the Line, Part III

K*orvettenkapitän* Erich Eckelmann had been commissioned in 1887 and promoted to *Korvettenkapitän* (commander) on 22 March 1914. He was thirty-eight when he assumed command of the *U-155,* and like Meusel, he had no prior combat experience in U–boats. He had spent most of the war in staff positions, starting with the Admiralstab in 1914 and then until November 1916 at the naval department responsible for the development and management of naval aviation, both lighter- and heavier-than-air craft. His first responsibility as commanding officer was to oversee the repairs and modifications that were being made to the *U-155.*[1]

In addition to the new torpedo room, which featured two tubes and space for eighteen reloads, the *U-155* received two new SK15cmL/45 deck guns. They were same type of gun as the Utof-15L/45 but a more recent design. The type was nonetheless an adaptation of a weapon originally designed for use on board battleships and cruisers, and it came with a single pedestal mount and casement that brought the total weight to 17.8 tons. The need to reduce weight resulted in again pairing an excellent gun with a make-do mount that was too light for the recoil.

Another improvement was replacing the larger propellers with the original *U-Deutschland* propellers, which were determined to be more efficient. Experience had shown that the original propellers could produce the same ten-knot top speed that the larger ones did but at thirty fewer revolutions per minute, which was more fuel efficient.

Not all the new gadgets were improvements, though they were intended to be. One change that failed the test was the new seven-meter-long secondary periscope in the control room that replaced the original six-meter stick. The original periscope had been so short that even when it was fully extended, half of the conning tower was out of the water. The one-meter-longer periscope did not materially alter that situation.

Another change that was a marginal improvement was something entirely new—a telegraph-cable cutter mounted on the stern. It looked complicated, and it was. The device worked on the same principle as a bolt cutter and was designed to be operated from inside the boat. The idea was to run close to the bottom, extend a grapple, drag until a submarine telegraph cable was snagged, pull it up, and deploy the cutter to sever it. To everyone's surprise it actually worked, and the through-hull fittings did not leak.

A totally useless device that was added was a bow-net cutter. It was a triangle-shaped unit with a forward-facing, saw-like blade that was intended to cut through antisubmarine nets. By 1918 every U-boat had one, but on the *U-155* and the other *U-Deutschland*-class converts they were unnecessary, because the boats were deployed in areas where no nets were laid. Eckelmann, who detested the device, had it thrown over the side after it was damaged in a storm during the outbound passage.

The *U-155* was in the yard in Kiel undergoing overhaul and repairs from 6 September to 13 December 1917. Her trials were run from 13 to 20 December, after which her crew went on holiday leave until 7 January 1918. From the day she entered the yard and until her crew returned from leave, the war passed through a period of mutual gloom and despair shared among the belligerents. In his book *A History of Warfare,* Field Marshall Viscount Montgomery of Alamein would write, "The 1914–18 war could not be won; it could only be lost in a final failure of endurance by the men of one or the other side."

The war had gone on far too long with no apparent gains for either side, and the scale of death and destruction had sapped the will of all. In his memoirs, Gen. John Pershing later wrote that when he arrived in France in June 1917, the Allies were nearing exhaustion; their "financial problems were becoming more difficult," and discouragement was rife among "not only the civil populations but throughout armies as well." He witnessed French army mutinies that "sprang up in sixteen army corps all at one time or at very short intervals."[2]

Pershing thought that the Germans still held the upper hand, noting that "practically all her offensives excepting that at Verdun had been crowned with success" and that the German battle lines were still in France, where they "withstood every attack since the Marne." In view of the situation at the front and the apparent success of their ongoing submarine campaign, he did not think that the Germans' "hopes of a final victory" were "extravagant."[3]

To Pershing's military eye the war situation in late 1917 appeared to favor the Germans, but things were not well in the *Vaterland.* The blockade had brought the civilian populace to the point of slow starvation, and Germany's economy was in tatters. But the most serious blow to civilian morale was the failure of the submarine campaign to achieve its promised goal of total victory by the end of summer 1917.

Von Hindenburg and Ludendorff saw the situation in a different light than Pershing. By January 1918 the U-boat campaign had become a secondary front, one that offered no hope for a victory, and the Americans, who were arriving in greater numbers, would soon bring their weight to bear at the front. Everything the German navy had said would not happen, had. German troops were still disciplined, but the signs of strain were evident, and both von Hindenburg and Ludendorff recognized that it was just a matter of time until the German army broke down. The answer was to win a victory on the ground before the American troops entered the fight and before the Germans collapsed. Ludendorff saw the solution in a three-part offensive that would start in March 1918. It would be Germany's final, all-out effort to defeat the French and British in the field and win the war. It was a case of "go for broke."

The *U-155* departed Kiel on 14 January to take the shorter north-about route over the Shetland Islands rather than follow Meusel's track around the Faeroes. The operations area was again the Azores. The moment he exited the Skagerrak into the North Sea, Eckelmann ran into heavy weather, and it lasted eighteen days without respite. It was not until 7 February that the weather cleared and the crew was able to open all the hatches for the first time to admit fresh air and help dry out the damp interior. The distance covered since entering the North Sea was 1,518 nautical miles at an average speed of 3.5 knots.

In many respects the second war patrol was a replay of the first, especially in that the *U-155* suffered repeated mechanical problems and equipment failures. Engine breakdowns continued to be a headache, the torpedoes were unreliable even after having been moved inside the pressure hull, and the boat was still too slow to catch anything that could make more than ten knots. The deck guns' mounts held up, but that was due to the fact that Eckelmann fired fewer rounds than had been fired on the first patrol, and the cable cutter was a success, but only until it broke beyond repair.

The situation in the waters around the Azores was not the same as when Meusel had been there. By January 1918, the Allies had adopted the convoy system, which meant that there were fewer ships sailing alone, and many, if not most, of those that were alone were sailing vessels. Eckelmann operated in an area southeast of the Azores that lay directly west of the Gibraltar Straits, so that the *U-155* could intercept traffic going toward the Mediterranean and coming out.

The first ship the *U-155* stopped was the SS *Arnabal Mendi,* which the boarding officer examined and released. Four days later she attacked the SS *Craonne,* a 4,264 GRT English freighter, west of Gibraltar. Eckelmann opened fire on the ship in heavy seas and at maximum range as darkness approached. After a few rounds Eckelmann ordered the gun crews below, because the heavy seas made remaining on deck too dangerous and visibility had dropped to zero.

Later that night he made a submerged torpedo attack on the SS *Tea,* a 5,395-GRT Italian freighter that was just three years old. The ship was carrying grain and flour from Portland, Maine, to Gibraltar. The torpedo functioned properly, ran true, and struck the steamer amidships but did not sink her. Eckelmann surfaced, sent a boarding party across, and sank her with scuttling charges.

The next two days were spent riding out bad weather that produced seas too high for the *U-155* to use any of her weapons. On 18 February the storm passed,

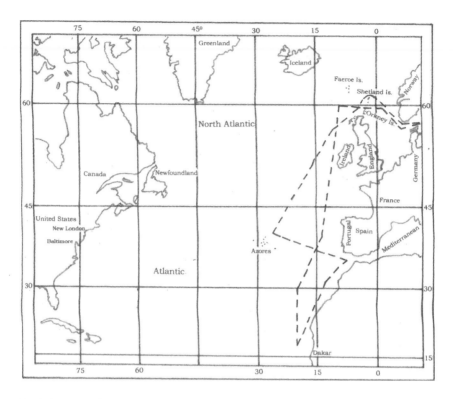

Map 8. Second *U-155* war patrol, 14 January–4 May 1918

the seas subsided, and the *U-155* found an easy kill in the same area where she had sunk the *Tea*. The victim was a small English sailing vessel of about 105 GRT, and the *U-155*'s gun crews made quick and easy work of her. She was the *Cecil L. Shave,* and none of her twelve-man crew survived.

Five days passed before the U-boat's lookouts spotted another ship—a gap that illustrates how effectively the convoy system had eliminated lone targets in otherwise heavily trafficked waters. The lone ship was the Spanish SS *Sardinero,* a 2,170 GRT, three-island tramp bound for Sette, France, with a cargo consigned to the Swiss government. Eckelmann followed a policy of releasing Spanish vessels in every case but this one; he sank the *Sardinero* with scuttling charges after the Spanish crewmen were in their boats. The only explanation he gave for the exception to his policy was "the misuse of neutral flag."

The following day he stopped and released the Spanish steamer SS *Villa Real,* which was carrying contraband cargo to France. This was a ship that under even the Prize Regulations was subject to destruction. Instead, Eckelmann spent most of the day alongside the steamer while his crew, together with the steamer's crew, tossed the cargo overboard. The next day he again kept to his policy, releasing the Spanish freighter SS *Ordunte Mendi.*

Eckelmann was off the Moroccan coast near Casablanca when he opened fire on an armed steamer at extreme range. The gunfire exchange was ineffective, and the steamer steadily increased the range until Eckelmann ceased fire and laid a course to put the *U-155* ahead of the steamer's projected track. Just after midnight on 3 March he fired a single torpedo that performed perfectly and sank the Italian 4,439 GRT SS *Antioco Accame.*

On 10 March the *U-155* struck gold. Shortly before noon she stopped the Norwegian 4,271 GRT freighter SS *Wegadesk,* carrying five thousand tons of brass, tarpaper, and lead from Baltimore to Gibraltar. The tar paper and lead were of no particular interest, but the brass was another matter. Brass was critical to Germany's war effort and worth its weight in gold, especially the amount on board the *Wegadesk.*

For three days the *U-155* and the freighter were rafted together while German sailors and Norwegian crewmen transferred forty tons of brass from the freighter's hold into the *U-155*. It was a coup that only a U-boat that had been originally designed as a freighter could have carried off. On 13 March, "after many difficulties, the transfer was stopped and the scuttling charges were detonated because patrol craft were seen approaching."

Eight days later the *U-155* attacked an armed Italian tanker, SS *Prometeo,* which was loaded with naphtha. The Italian returned fire with a stern-mounted 90 mm gun. A direct hit from the *U-155*'s after gun caused an enormous explosion and then fire on board the tanker, which came to a stop and lay dead in the water, oily black smoke and flames rising high above her. As the U-boat approached the burning tanker, lifeboats were seen pulling away, and Eckelmann altered course to approach them. Ten of the *Prometeo*'s crew were badly injured, some with serious burns. All ten were taken on board the *U-155,* and the rest were given a heading to Cabo de Sao Vicente, approximately 288 nautical miles east.

The *U-155* next moved 175 nautical miles northwest into an area fifteen nautical miles long and eight wide in which he spent the busiest week of the patrol. The period opened on 22 March with a gun battle with the British passenger-freighter SS *Chupra* at extreme range. The freighter's gun was no match for the *U-155*'s big deck guns, but the steamer was marginally faster that the U-boat. The engagement became a running gun battle, with the steamer slowly opening the distance while the *U-155* struggled to stay within gun range, hoping to score a hit that would force the fleeing steamer to stop. But before that happened, the submarine's port engine quit, and the steamer quickly disappeared.

That same day, limping along on one engine, the *U-155* attempted to close with what Eckelmann thought, due to its large size, was an armed auxiliary cruiser. At the time the mystery ship was spotted, she was well out of gun range, and Eckelmann was unable to close the gap with only one engine. The cruise in the new operating area was off to a bad start.

The following day, still with only one engine working, Eckelmann made a submerged torpedo attack on the 3,835 GRT Italian steamer SS *Ablak.* The torpedo either missed or failed to detonate; Eckelmann described the failure only as *vergeblich* (in vain) in his log. Since he was already well within gun range, he decided to surface and sink the ship with gunfire at what was for him relatively close range. The plan worked, and the *Ablak* was sunk very quickly.

The fact that the port engine was still being repaired seriously reduced the *U-155*'s efficiency as a surface raider and limited the sort of ships Eckelmann could attack, which is probably why only slower, more vulnerable sailing vessels were recorded in his log. The string of sailing vessels started on 24 March, when he sank the British *Jorgina* with gunfire. She was a small, 103 GRT, gaff-rigged schooner built in 1887. The sinking occurred 360 nautical miles northwest of Madeira. The following day he sank the Portuguese *Rio Ave* with gunfire just ten nautical miles away. The *Rio Ave* was another small, gaff-rigged schooner of 104 GRT bound from Lisbon to Madeira with beans. On 27 March the Canadian schooner *Watuaga* was sunk with scuttling charges. The last sailing vessel in the series was the Portuguese *Lusitano,* a 529 GRT, three-masted wooden barque built in 1873. She was out of New Orleans bound for Porto, Portugal, with a crew of twenty-seven. She was sunk with scuttling charges just two nautical miles from where the *Watuaga* went down. None of the crewmen, all of whom were left in boats, was ever found.

The port engine came back online on the same day the *Lusitano* was sunk, and Eckelmann headed south to Cape Verde, off the West African coast, where he sank the last ship of this war patrol. The victim was the SS *Santa Isabel,* a 2,023 GRT English steamer carrying coal from Cardiff to Dakar. Eckelmann made an unsuccessful submerged torpedo attack before he surfaced to engage the ship with gunfire. The freighter was armed, and a brief one-sided battle ensued, which ended when the *U-155* scored a direct hit close to the waterline that started a fire in the coal. The freighter's boats were set out and the crew was rowing away when several armed patrol boats were seen approaching. Eckelmann could not remain long enough to finish the job and dove. By the time the patrol boats arrived and took on board the survivors, the *Santa Isabel* was already lost.

Following the sinking of the *Santa Isabel,* the *U-155* started her long trip home, arriving in Kiel on 4 May 1918. The patrol had lasted 110 days, during which the *U-155* sank thirteen ships totaling 26,747 GRT. Eckelmann had sunk the same number of ships as Meusel but only about half the tonnage.

Eckelmann was replaced by *Korvettenkapitän* Ferdinand Studt, who at thirty-nine was the eldest of the three *U-155* captains and, like his predecessor, had no previous U-boat experience. He had been commissioned in 1898 and promoted to *Korvettenkapitän* on 27 January 1915. Prior to attending the U-boat commanders' school in late 1917 and early 1918, he had served on board the largely inactive ships of the High Seas Fleet as a watch officer. Because of the war situation during his period of command, the *U-155* was the only command he held in World War I.[4]

Immediately upon discharging her crew, the *U-155* started a complete overhaul that lasted three months. Included in the overhaul was the replacement of the

▲ In New London, as in Baltimore, the Eastern Forwarding Company hired only African-American stevedores and did not allow them to leave the EFCO compound while they were in New London. The stevedores, together with the *U-Deutschland* crew, lived on board the *Willehad*. The ladder, visible at the *Willehad*'s starboard quarter, was the stevedores' only way onto and off the pier. The only way to go ashore was through the warehouse, which was heavily guarded to keep the public out and the stevedores in. The two-story house in the background belonged to Ruth Baker, who allowed anyone to view the *U-Deutschland* from her second floor for a twenty-five-cent fee. She even provided the binoculars. She earned ninety-five dollars during the time the *U-Deutschland* was in New London. *Claas Stöckmeyer collection*

cable cutter with a mine rack that that guided eight mines over the stern and down a chute when they were dropped. None of the crew was happy working with mines using what was essentially a jury-rigged system.

By the time she started her overhaul the U-boat campaign was no longer considered essential to winning the war. On 27 May Germany launched the third drive in Ludendorff's three-part plan to win the war on the ground. Attacking on a thirty-mile front between Soissons and Rheims, the Germans drove west, crossed the Marne, and entered Château-Thierry on 31 May. Soissons fell to the Germans on 29 May. But from 3 to 6 June, U.S. Army troops and Marines stopped the German advance at Château-Thierry and Neuilly, just forty-two miles from Paris.

The fighting became a slugfest as the Germans tried to recover and push forward against stiffening Allied resistance. The Germans' worst scenario, that America's weight would tip the balance, was becoming a reality. The effort made to stop the German advance at Château-Thierry and Neuilly represented the beginning of American cooperation on a major scale. The Germans attacked again on the Noyon-Montdidier front from 9 to 14 June, with little success, and on 1 July the Americans took Vaux.

On 14 July the Germans opened their final offensive; the attack met against heavy resistance and faltered on the 17th. On 18 July the French and Americans launched on the Marne-Aisne front a massive counteroffensive that marked the beginning of the end for Germany. By 30 July the Germans were in full retreat to the Vesle. The French retook Soissons on 2 August, and the following day the French and Americans cleared the area between Soissons and Rheims, capturing the entire Aisne-Vesle front. On 8 August, three days before the *U-155* left on her third war patrol, the Allies launched a major offensive along the entire front. At supreme German headquarters in Pless, Ludendorff declared Thursday, 8 August 1918 the "Black Day for the German Army." The war would last just another ninety-five days.

On 11 August 1918, Studt took the *U-155* out of Kiel and across the Baltic to the Sund, from which he passed through the Kattegat and Skagerrak into the North Sea. He reached the North Atlantic by passing on 18 August around the Faeroes, where he ran into heavy weather that lasted until 30 August and reduced his advance to a crawl.

In his log Studt commented that the weather made his weapons mostly unusable *(Waffengebrauch meist ausgeschlossen),* but an opportunity did present itself on 27 August, when the American steamer SS *Montoso* was sighted and Studt dove to make a torpedo attack. But again the make-do, cost-cutting policy that had been used when the boat was originally built prevented the attack. The problem was not new. The after diving-plane motor quit, and it became impossible to hold the U-boat at periscope depth, with the result that she broached and exposed half of her conning tower. The *Montoso's* captain reacted to the sight of a U-boat abruptly rising from the sea by making a radical course change to starboard and ringing up full speed.

Studt recovered the initiative by surfacing completely and sending his gun crews to their battle stations. By the time the gunners had the guns in action, however, the *U-155* was already under fire from the *Montoso*. It was now that Studt got a nasty surprise. As his gun crews were finding the *Montoso's* range and the freighter's rounds were sending up columns of water off the U-boat's port side, two more rounds exploded to starboard. The *Montoso* had an escort, the armed auxiliary USS *Ticonderoga*. Fortunately for Studt and his crew, the escort's gunners had not found the range, and the *U-155* disappeared safely below the surface.

There was still the problem with the after diving-plane motor to be resolved quickly, but this time luck smiled on the *U-155*. The problem was nothing more than an electrical cable that, improperly installed, had come loose. An engineer reattached the cable, turned the nut down securely, and the *U-155* was again under control.

Unlike those of Meusel and Eckelmann, Studt's operations area was to be the North American East Coast from Newfoundland to New York, and the route he followed through the North Atlantic was almost devoid of shipping. The only vessel seen on the lonely trip toward the American coast was the unfortunate three-masted fishing schooner *Gamo,* out of St. Johns, Newfoundland, bound for Lisbon with a load of cod. Studt had the 128-foot sailing vessel scuttled. The *Gamo's* fishermen and crew, in thirteen open boats, rowed seventeen days, covering 440 nautical miles in "adverse weather," before arriving at the island of Faial in the Azores. Five of the men died during the trip.[5]

After sinking the *Gamo,* Studt made a 210-nautical-mile detour, traveling east and slightly south until 2 September, when he stopped the 3,560 GRT Norwegian steamer *Stortind* 360 miles north of the Azores. The 360-foot steamer, carrying railroad track and wire from Norfolk to La Pallice, France, was sunk with gunfire. Having disposed of the *Stortind,* Studt turned almost due west and headed for Newfoundland, which was the northern limit of his assigned patrol area. On 7 September, after traveling 1,084 nautical miles, Studt stopped and scuttled the fishing schooner *Sophia,* which like the *Gamo* had been carrying cod to Lisbon.

He then turned due south and on 12 September torpedoed the 3,245 GRT SS *Leixos,* the former Hamburg-America Lines SS *Cheruskia.* The next day he fired a torpedo at a steamer; he missed, causing the ship to alter course. Studt surfaced and opened fire at about four miles and was answered with accurate return fire from a large-caliber gun. The ship was steaming away on a zigzag course when Studt observed a hit at just over six miles. He was silently congratulating his gunners when a round from the fleeing ship struck the water right in front of the *U-155's* bow. The near miss had a mining effect on the U-boat, damaging the pressure hull to the extent that the boat's ability to dive was somewhat impaired.

After leaving the scene of the gun battle, Studt turned west toward Halifax, laying his eight mines in pairs in the approaches to Halifax Harbor on the nights of 17 and 18 September. Still south of Halifax on the 20th, Studt scuttled the American steam trawler *Kingfisher.* When the fishermen and crew took to their boats they were fortunately only eighty-five nautical miles away from Halifax, in waters heavily trafficked by fishing craft.

Nine days later the *U-155* engaged in another hot gunfire exchange, which ended when armed patrol boats were seen approaching. The same thing happened the following day, and Studt realized now that his presence in the area was known. Correctly assuming that the area was too dangerous, he turned southwest and headed for the coast of New York, arriving there on 3 October and torpedoing the Italian 3,838 GRT freighter SS *Alberto Trenes.* The following day he sank his last ship in American waters, the English schooner *Industrial,* which was engaged in the coastal trade carrying salt. She was scuttled 250 nautical miles off Nantucket.

From 6 to 8 October the weather was stormy, and the temperature inside the pressure hull hovered 105 degrees Fahrenheit. The air was stuffy and humid, and it reeked of body odor and diesel fumes. Studt wrote in his log, "The air-conditioning system was built for a crew of twenty-nine but is unable to cope with a seventy-two man crew."

On 11 October he was ordered to move into a patrol area east and south of the Azores, the area that Meusel and Eckelmann had worked. He laid a course that took the *U-155* generally southeast until he reached latitude thirty-six degrees south, where he turned due east. The following evening he was chasing a fleeing freighter while keeping up a continuous fire from his forward deck gun when, after firing 120 rounds, the gun overheated and would not go back into battery. He altered course to allow the after gun to bear, but the change in direction allowed the freighter to open the distance, and she was soon out of range.

On 17 October, while still east of his new operating area, he torpedoed the 6,744 GRT SS *Lucia*. She was Austrian and had been seized by the U.S. Shipping Board in April 1917 to be used for carrying troops and supplies to Europe. The Shipping Board turned her over to the army in 1918, but on the day she was torpedoed she had not yet been commissioned and was still the SS *Lucia*. She was in a convoy, with a single cruiser for escort. The torpedo hit her in the area of the engine room, bringing her to a halt, and she sank quickly by the stern. Since the convoy had scattered in all directions at full speed and the cruiser was steaming in circles around the site, Studt turned away and departed the area.[6]

On 21 October the Admiralstab issued an order to all U–boats at sea to cease all offensive operations and return to port. For Studt and his crew in the *U-155,*

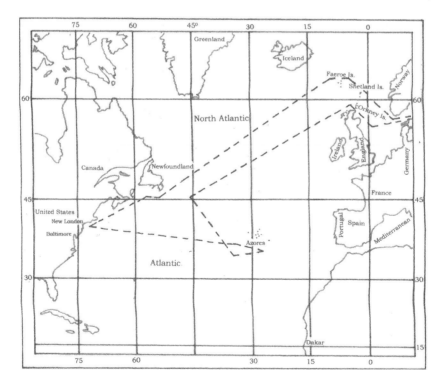

Map 9. Third *U-155* war patrol, 8 August–14 November 1918

the war was over. All they had to do now was get home in one piece, since there was nothing in the radio message about the Allies ceasing all offensive operations. Starting the homeward trip from 40° 15' north, 40° 15' west, the *U-155* had fifty-eight days of fuel remaining and three torpedoes loaded. She rounded the Shetlands on 6 November and entered Kiel on 13 November 1918, two days after the Armistice.

The *U-155*'s third and last war patrol had certainly not been spectacular, accounting for a total of 18,575 GRT—just eight ships, half of which were fishing vessels, three of them sail. Studt was not very aggressive, in part because of his inexperience and probably more so because of the war situation when the boat left Kiel in August. His log contains several entries about ships that were sighted but too far away to attack, or some problem, such as weather, that made it impossible to use the boat's weapons. His few surface engagements, coupled with the briefings Meusel and Eckhart had given him, caused him to resort to torpedoing rather than using the deck guns, which were in fact unreliable. His torpedoes were no better, however, half of them running wild or simply missing the target. The crew's morale was good, but the men were definitely not enthusiastic about pressing the war, and they were painfully aware of the *U-155*'s deficiencies.

The Germany they came home to was not the same Germany they had left. The economy was still in ruins, and the blockade was still starving the nation. The changes were nonetheless dramatic and not necessarily good. The kaiser was gone, the new government weak and ineffectual, and there were armed mobs in the streets of Berlin, Frankfurt, and all the rest of Germany's major cities. A left-wing revolution styled after the Russian Revolution was spreading, led by sailors' "soviets" (councils) in Kiel, Wilhelmshaven, and all the other naval bases. Germany's fleet was being dismantled, scuttled, and turned over to the Allies as reparations. On 24 November 1918, the former *U-Deutschland/U-155* was turned over to the Royal Navy at Harwich.

Epilogue

The *U-Deutschland*

The *U-Deutschland* was something of a celebrity during World War I. To German citizens she was Germany twisting the lion's tail and making a mockery of the blockade. She was the savior that would ensure regular deliveries of food and supplies from America. To the British she represented a potential threat to the blockade, if Germany built enough of the boats to be really effective. To the Americans the boat was either a cause for celebration or something to be roundly condemned and denied entry to U.S. ports. To the world press she was a story that made great copy.

Undoubtedly the press was the agency that catapulted the boat to international fame and assured her a place in history, even though her achievements failed to meet expectations. The press reported any story about her as though it was fact. She had been sunk, she had been captured, she was hiding in a pothole in the Chesapeake, or she was evading the might of the Royal Navy somewhere in the Atlantic. When König told the press that he and his crew had spent the night on the English Channel floor listening to classical music and drinking champagne, the press believed it and printed it. To the press, König, who had no previous submarine experience, was a sly fox who was able to time his movements with the precision of a trapeze acrobat. His boat dove to enormous depths, and it moved on and below the surface at tremendous speeds. The press believed that the submerged *U-Deutschland*'s battery life was measured in days. The press called her the "Super Submarine *U-Deutschland*."

Even after she went to war as the *U-155,* her combatant identity was rarely mentioned; she remained the *U-Deutschland*. Rare photographs of her taken during that period were impressive, usually showing her decks filled with crewmen and her two enormous guns, with very long barrels. She was regularly described as the biggest U-boat ever built, which by the time she went to war was hardly true. The fact that she was really an unwieldy white elephant, shoddily built and prone to serious equipment failure at inappropriate times was not reported. That, however, is not the fault of the press, for in fact the *U-155*'s shortcomings were a closely guarded secret.

There are dozens of silly stories about the *U-Deutschland/U-155* that were reported with a perfectly straight face in the world's press, but the most outlandish example, of which there are several slightly different versions, first appeared in June 1917 and was still being repeated twelve months later. Reuters put out the report under the headline "SUNK THE DEUTSCHLAND." The leading figure in the account was a "sturdy-built mariner of the old school," Captain John Thompson, who must have been a sort of nautical John Wayne with a British accent.[1]

According to the story, Captain Thompson's ship was stopped and examined by a U-boat in the Bay of Biscay in 1915. Keep in mind that Thompson was British, and so was his ship. According to Thompson, during the questioning about his cargo and destination, the German boarding officer called Thompson a liar and declared the cargo contraband. Thompson's response was to slug the German, knocking him down. At this point one could reasonably assume that Thompson's goose was cooked, but it was not. After the German boarding crew helped their officer to his feet, the German officer drew his sword—hardly a World War I boarding officer's weapon of choice—and, depending on which version you read, either ran the sword through Thompson's left hand or sliced open Thompson's left cheek. Then, apparently having salvaged his honor, the German left the ship and allowed Thompson, his ship, and the contraband cargo to continue their voyage.

Two years later, while on a voyage from Malta to Alexandria, Egypt, Thompson sighted an "exceptionally big" U-boat dead ahead. Since his ship was unarmed, the only choice Thompson had was to ram it. For more than an hour Thompson circled the U-boat, now somehow identified as the *U-Deutschland,* like a mongoose around a cobra. Thompson constantly kept his bow pointed toward the U-boat like a fencer's foil, an interesting maneuver while steaming in a circle. Finally Thompson saw his opening and lunged ahead, his bow cleaving "clean through" the U-boat and cutting her in two.

Positive identification was made when a lifebelt with the name *U-Deutschland* was fished from among the surface debris. For his bravery and determination the British government awarded Thompson five thousand dollars and the Distinguished Service Order. In another report the reward had dropped to one thousand dollars, but the DSO remained. Since then, Captain Thompson was known throughout the British merchant marine as "Deutschland Thompson."

Twenty-two days after the war ended, the British put the *U-155* on display as a war trophy, first at St. Katharine Docks in London, then in the Firth of Forth, and in January 1919 back to Harwich. Shortly after the boat returned to Harwich, Horatio Bottomley asked the Admiralty to sell him the *U-155*. His plan was to display the U-boat in various ports throughout the British Isles to raise money, which, after expenses, would be donated to the King George V Fund for Sailors. The offer was certainly worthy; the King George V Fund was a legitimate, registered charity whose mission was to "address the needs of seafarers and their families facing distress through unemployment, homelessness, or loss of livelihood through accident at sea." Bottomley's scheme—and it was a scheme—would be promoted through his weekly magazine, *John Bull,* and the revenue from the displays would be collected by his organization, the John Bull Victory Bond Club.[2]

The Admiralty agreed to the sale, on the provision that Bottomley paid for having the boat disarmed and certified that "all dangerous equipment had been removed from the ship, including bombs and torpedo heads." What the Admiralty did not know was that there were two bottles of compressed hydrogen in the engine room. With the forms all in order and signed, the *U-155* was moved from Harwich to the ship-repair yard of Glover, Clayton, and Company in Birkenhead, where the guns, torpedo tubes, and the mine rack were removed. The two compressed-hydrogen bottles were left undisturbed, because they were not ordnance and were therefore not considered dangerous.

Bottomley had been at one time or another a member of Parliament, a swindler, a financier, a publisher, and a populist politician. His magazine, *John Bull* had been around since 1820 in one form or another, but when he acquired it in 1906 it took on a nationalist tone that suited its name. The John Bull Victory Bond Club was based on the wartime savings bonds and postwar Victory Bonds programs, in which citizens in the warring countries essentially loaned their governments money to help pay for the war. The difference between Bottomley's scheme and the legitimate Victory Bond, other than that one was a private venture and the other a government program, was that Bottomley's Victory Club bonds paid no interest on the buyers' investment. Instead, the investors received "gifts" of dubious value.

At the time Bottomley asked the Admiralty to sell him the *U-155,* he enjoyed considerable prestige in Britain, despite his background, which included having been thrown out of Parliament for bankruptcy. His ownership of *John Bull,*

▲ The *U-155* at sea on either her second or third war patrol. The torpedo tubes had by this time been moved inboard, and the boat now had a regular forward torpedo room. There were no stern tubes.
Jørn Jensen collection

which had staunchly supported the war and strongly advocated harsh treatment for Germany after the war, served to gloss over his many defects. And the Royal Navy had discovered right away that the *U-155* had nothing new to offer in the field of submarine design and that its only value was scrap. The Admiralty sold him the boat for three thousand pounds, which in 2014 currency was about $14,000. The transfer of title described the *U-155* as a "converted mercantile submarine," an indication of what the Royal Navy thought of the boat.

The work of disarming the *U-155* was finished in April 1919, and the James Dredging, Towage, and Transport Company towed the boat to London for delivery to Bottomley's silent partner, Pemberton Billing, an arrangement that was probably part of Bottomley's scheme. Three years later, Robert James, managing director of James Dredging, Towing, and Transport Company told a British court that Bottomley was nowhere to be seen when the *U-155* was delivered to Billing, giving the impression that Billing was the actual buyer.

Before she went on her road-show tour, Bottomley had workers remove nearly everything that was made of brass, as well as the various bearings in the engines and equipment throughout the boat. The recovered metal was used to create a line of souvenirs that were sold wherever the boat was on display and could be ordered by mail from the John Bull Victory Bond Club.

The offerings included four types of brass cigarette cases, brass candlesticks, a tiny brass hinged table for calling cards, a brass brooch in the likeness of the *U-155* as displayed, and two versions of a round brass ashtray. The nonbrass items were made of Babbitt metal taken from the bearings. Those included a cast bust of Horatio Buckley, a metal wall plaque bearing his likeness, a bronzed Iron Cross pendant, and a statue of John Bull and his dog. The brass items bore the *U-Deutschland* logo, which was an embossed likeness of the boat as she appeared on display, with her tall radio masts extended. And nearly all the items bore a stamped guarantee, "GUARANTEED MADE FROM 'DEUTSCHLAND' METAL." A twenty-four-page brochure with illustrations, *The Official Guide to the* Deutschland, was sold dockside for six pence,

➤ The *U-Deutschland/ U-155* being readied for her showboat career in 1919. The odd fitting on the stern is a mine chute. This photo was taken in March or April 1919, when the boat was in the yard at Grove, Clayton, and Company, Birkenhead. *Author's collection*

and a smaller set of foldout plans, including a sectional elevation of the boat, was sold for "tuppence." The "John Bull Victory Souvenir Catalog" was a free handout.

Beginning in May 1919, the *U-Deutschland,* sporting her name in huge white letters on her sides, was towed to various harbors on the east and south coasts, where she initially attracted large crowds, who paid an admittance fee that varied with the port of call. The fee was generally twenty pence, but in London it was twice that. During the time she was on the road, she attracted over 150,000 visitors, which brings us to the question, did the *U-Deutschland* earn a profit that went to the King George V Fund?

Apparently not, according to Bottomley and his accountant, John Garloch. The account books showed profits only at the displays in London and the Isle of Man; losses at Yarmouth, Southend-on-Sea, Ramsgate, and Brighton; and no mention of any of the other harbors. Her last stop was at the Isle of Man in September 1920, and on 8 October she was back in Birkenhead in the Glover, Clayton and Company shipyard.

On 23 June 1921, the former *U-Deutschland* was sold at public auction to Robert Smith and Sons Ship Breakers, in Birkenhead, for two hundred pounds. On Saturday, 10 September, at 1100, an explosion occurred in the engine room, which six apprentices, three of whom were just seventeen years old, were dismantling. Rescuers who entered the smoked-filled space found the three seventeen-year-olds dead and the other three apprentices unconscious and badly injured. The autopsies revealed that the explosion had hurled the apprentices against the sides of the engine room with such force that they were killed instantly and "battered almost beyond recognition." Of the three severely injured men, two died later.

Several empty compressed-gas bottles, two of which had contained hydrogen, were found in the engine room. The other bottles had held oxygen or air. The cause of the explosion was found to have been that a mixture of oxygen and hydrogen in the air had been ignited by either a candle flame or a lighted cigarette. Other apprentices who had worked on the boat at different times said that they had been

➤ The *U-Deutschland/U-155* disarmed and ready for her first display under the auspices of the John Bull Victory Club, May 1919. *Gary McGee collection, New Zealand*

directed to open the valves on the compressed-gas tanks to empty them. Usually such tanks were removed from the hull before opening the valves, but it appeared that in this case some of the tanks had still been in the engine room when they were opened. It was learned that the apprentices were in the habit of playing cards by candlelight and smoking inside the engine room.

During the inquest, held in October 1921, the question was asked about the presence of filled compressed-gas bottles. It was learned that they had been there since the Germans surrendered the boat to the Royal Navy in November 1918 but that the presence of two filled with hydrogen had gone unrecognized. In any event, none of the navy officials associated with the sale of the boat had deemed the bottles to be a danger, and they had been sold to Bottomley along with the boat.

Several months after the explosion, the *U-Deutschland* was again in the news when Bottomley's ledgers dealing with his showboat operation came into question. According to his bookkeeper, the *U-Deutschland* business had lost £5,720, a figure that was greater than what Bottomley had paid the Admiralty and certainly left nothing for the King George V Fund. Given Bottomley's track record of going broke, the figure might have been right, but others did not think so.

According to the records, John Bull, Ltd., had bought the boat from Pemberton Billing for £17,000 and in turn sold the boat for £15,000 to Bottomley, who according to the navy records already owned her. The investigation revealed that Bottomley was running an enormous and complicated scam that involved buying a newspaper with worthless bonds and spending money he either did not have or that belonged to someone else. All the scams—the *John Bull* magazine, the Victory Bond Club, and the *U-Deutschland* charity—had been interwoven. In 1922 Bottomley was found guilty of fraudulent conversion of shareholders' funds in connection with the John Bull Victory Bond Club and was sentenced to prison for seven years.

In March 1922, Glover, Clayton, and Company won a judgment against Bottomley for £3,356, charges and fees that were due for the work they had done on the U-boat for Bottomley. By then Bottomley was broke and unable to pay anything to anyone. The final curtain dropped on the *U-Deutschland* saga in the Sussex village of Dicker, when the trustee in the bankruptcy of Bottomley sold whatever remained of the boat to "marine store dealers and souvenir hunters for £100."[3]

Persons of Interest

Alfred Lohmann

Alfred Lohmann was, first and foremost, a businessman, for whom doing business was not just a passion but a matter of life.[4] The war had literally stripped him of his overseas business interests and had greatly reduced his Bremen office. He tried to expand Germany's remaining business relations to the east (Austria, Hungary, the

Ottoman Empire), but this was only a downsized substitute for his lost worldwide enterprises. When the cargo submarine project came to life in 1915, Lohmann saw it and the Deutsche Ozean Reederei as a genuine opportunity to reenter transatlantic business in a meaningful way. He truly believed in the enterprise and wanted it to succeed. For Alfred Lohmann, the DOR was not a "straw" company but a viable, practical undertaking that he believed he could make successful.

In a perfect world, that might have been possible. But despite Lohmann's confidence and optimism, the practical truth was that the DOR existed solely as part of Germany's effort to break the blockade for the relief of the nation's war industry. The cargo submarine project might have appeared to be a civilian capital undertaking, but it was in fact just another aspect of the war effort.

Nevertheless, Lohmann's commitment to the company and its success was total, up to January 1917. The *U-Deutschland* was lying at her pier in Wilhelmshaven, fully loaded and ready to sail, when the navy ordered the sailing delayed while the decision to return to unrestricted submarine warfare was made. When Lohmann heard about the delay, he immediately traveled to Berlin to "convince the Admiralty he did not believe in a war with the USA." His effort failed; by the time he arrived in Berlin, the decision to resume unrestricted submarine warfare had been made.

The shutting down of the cargo submarine project, followed by defeat and the nearly total collapse of Germany's economy, took the spark out of Alfred Lohmann. The war ended on 11 November 1918, but the British blockade was not lifted until July 1919. Germany's defeat and the crushing of Alfred Lohmann's hopes were devastating to a man who lived for business and enterprise. Two months later Lohmann was dead, apparently from a severe hemorrhage.

Paul König

The man who commanded the *U-Deutschland* on both trips to the United States, Paul König, returned to active naval service at the end of the boat's second *U-Deutschland* voyage. Thereafter, he initially selected war pilots for newly commissioned war boats and helped select the officers to command the seven *U-Deutschland*-class U-cruisers. Near the end of the war he was assigned to command a half-flotilla of minesweepers, four former merchant steamers of around 3,700 tons that had been modified for mine clearance. He was released from service in 1918 as a *Kapitänleutnant* in the reserves and remained unemployed until June 1920, when he was promoted to a reserve *Korvettenkapitän* and returned to NDL in the company's Operations Division. Between 1921 and 1931, he held an enormously prestigious position in NDL as a *Prokurist*. There is no adequate English translation for the term or the position, but it signifies a very high ranking company official whose signature on a company document of any kind and for any reason is irrevocable and legally binding. At the same time he was the head of the Navigation Department, which handled technical development, a post he held until he retired in 1932. From 1921 to 1923 he was a member of the Bremen chapter of the Deutsche Volks Partei (German People's Party), which—despite its left-wing sounding title, actually a conservative party— existed from 1918 to 1933.

In 1926 he teamed up with *Vizeadmiral* Adolf von Trotha, postwar chief of the Reichsmarine, to write *Deutsche Seefahrt* (published by Verlag Otto Franke in 1928 and 1930). He had previously teamed with Edgar Freiherr von Spiegel von und zu Peckelsheim to write a thirty-two-page booklet for teenagers titled *U-Boot-Fahrten* (published by Jungendbücher, Heft 121). Von Spiegel is better known as the commander of *U-32* and *U-93* during the war and as the author of the fictional *Tagesbuch U-202* (1916).

König made several trips to the United States while he was employed by NDL, capitalizing on his name recognition to forward NDL's interests. His last trip, in 1931–32, was a speaking tour on the subject of his two voyages across the Atlantic in the *U-Deutschland*. The tour was a flop, in part because of the passage of time, but more specifically because of revelations in the press about Paul Hilken's Baltimore sabotage cell and its association with the *U-Deutschland*.

He retired to Gnadau, a village about twenty miles south and a little west of the Saxon-Anhalt capital, Magdeburg, and died there at the age of sixty-six on 8 September 1933.[5]

Franz Krapohl

Krapohl was selected for command in October 1917 and after completing the U-boat commander school at Kiel took over the *U-52,* where he served until the war ended. He was released from service on 31 December 1918 and returned to NDL in 1920. He was recalled to active duty on 26 August 1939 and given command of the nearly completed supply ship *Ermland,* which he commanded until she hit a mine off the French coast in 1943. She was towed to Nantes, where she was bombed and sank at the dock on 10 September 1943. The most notable assignment Krapohl had as the *Ermland*'s captain was an attempt to take the damaged *Bismarck* in tow. The *Ermland* did not reach the *Bismarck* in time and returned to port.

On 1 April 1945, after a long illness, he took command of the *Ermland*'s sister ship, the *Franken*. The war was in its last days when he took the *Franken* to Gotenhafen to bring out German soldiers and civilians who were trying to escape the oncoming Russians. As the ship was approaching the harbor, Russian bombers attacked and sank her. She went down with most of her crew, including Franz Krapohl.[6]

Paul Eyring

Eyring stayed on board the *U-155* as her second officer until the end of the war. He was released from service on 16 December 1918 and returned to his home in Bremerhaven, which was then in the grip of revolution. Fundamentally opposed to the politics of the revolutionists, who leaned heavily toward communism, he joined the Marinebrigade Ehrhardt, a Freikorps unit composed of former sailors and naval officers. He fought with the Ehrhardt Brigade until the collapse of the Kapp Putsch in 1920.

In 1922 he joined the Bremerhaven Police Department and the Nazi Party, a mix that did nothing to forward his police career. In 1923 he joined the party's paramilitary organization, the Sturmabteilung (SA), at the urging of his friend and former Ehrhardt Brigade comrade Hans Klintzsch, who at the time was the SA's commander. In 1928 he was dismissed from the police for "political activities." He survived on part-time work and whatever he could get for his activities with the SA until 1936, when he transferred to the Allgemeine-SS, of which he remained a member until Germany's collapse in May 1945.

On 25 August 1939 he joined the Luftwaffe, with the rank of *Oberleutnant* (first lieutenant) as an antiaircraft-battery commander. On 15 September 1943 he was promoted to major and given command of an antiaircraft group in Bavaria, where he spent the rest of the war. There is no record of what happened to him after that. He was fifty-nine years old when the conflict ended, and the postwar occupation laws governing employment for former party members and army officers would have made life very difficult for him.[7]

Wilhelm Karl Gotthold Prusse

Prusse was the only true civilian on board the *U-Deutschland* when she arrived in Baltimore in July 1916. Insofar as the record shows, he was not involved in any kind of espionage, and his sole function was to oversee the repairs to and loading of the *U-Deutschland* and any other commercial U-boats that came to America.

Prusse probably had active tuberculosis when he arrived in Baltimore, because in August he went to the Mont Alto Sanitarium in Waynesboro, Pennsylvania, where he remained for a month. How seriously ill he was at that time and whether or not he materially profited from the treatment we do not know. But on 17 September, Henry Hilken wrote to his son Paul that Prusse was returning to take up his duties in New London in expectation of the *U-Bremen*'s arrival. The senior Hilken wrote, "Prusse has recovered and is happy to go to New London."

Billups Harris, the Bureau of Investigation special agent in charge of the Baltimore office, opened a file on Prusse on 26 April 1917. The initial entry says only that George B. Page, who was in some way connected with the purchasing of munitions for the French government, had told Harris that Prusse came to Baltimore on board the *U-Deutschland* and was "somehow connected to the North German Lloyd people."

That information was certainly not news to Agent Harris, and why George Page felt it was necessary to report it to him is as big a question as why Harris even bothered to open a file on Prusse. At the same time, Harris put a "cover" on Prusse's mail at the local Baltimore post office. A cover was a log of the names and addresses of anyone who sent mail to a designated person, as well as of the names and addresses of anyone to whom he sent mail. In those days no court order was needed to place a cover on someone's mail.

Two weeks later, Special Agents Fred Chabot and William Doyas conducted a warrantless search of Prusse's room, at 3204 Winfield Avenue, in Baltimore; they found nothing of interest, except an account in German of the *U-Deutschland's* first Atlantic crossing. Agent Chabot returned to the bureau office, but Agent Doyas remained behind to interview Prusse when he came home. Earlier that day Doyas had visited the shipping district to ask around about Prusse. He had learned nothing, but a picture began to develop of a man who kept to himself and went about his work without attracting attention.

Prusse returned home at 2115 and was confronted by Agent Doyas, who demanded that Prusse "turn out his pockets." Prusse offered no objection to being searched and questioned, and he handed over to Doyas all the papers and letters he had on him. When questioned, Prusse said that he was not then working for, but remained connected with, A. Schumacher and Company and that he enjoyed the friendship of Henry Hilken, Paul's father. Doyas left, taking Prusse's papers and letters with him. He told Prusse they would be "examined" and returned.

The next morning Harris, Chabot, and Doyas read everything Doyas had collected and came up with nothing that would even hint at any sort of criminal activity. The letters and papers were mostly in German, which Chabot could read. There was one from a woman named Paula, who hoped that Prusse could provide information about her brother, who was in Germany. There was an invitation from a Mr. and Mrs. Kobrow to dinner, and an invitation from the Kobrows to join them on a trip to the Cascades. There was also an official notification that Prusse had been given a thirty-day membership in the Germania Club, at the request of Paul Hilken.

Five days later, Prusse applied for a permit to enter the forbidden zone along the waterfront, which was normally required of an enemy alien who had business that required his presence in such an area. Henry Hilken supported the application, noting that Prusse was a marine engineer whose employment with the Eastern Forwarding Company and the Deutsche Ozean Reederei made it necessary for him to enter and remain in the area for various periods of time. Since the United States was at war with Germany and the Deutsche Ozean Reederei and EFCO were no longer doing business in Baltimore or New London, the application was rejected.

Sometime around the middle of August, Agent Harris received information that a "mysterious German" was living at 3204 Winfield Avenue in Forrest Park, the home of a Mrs. Blank. He must have known that the reference was to Prusse, since agents from the Baltimore office had already been out there. Nevertheless, Harris sent Walter C. Foster, a civilian volunteer working in the Bureau of Investigation's Baltimore office, to look into the matter. Following his orders to the letter, Foster determined that the mysterious German was indeed Prusse.

On 24 August Foster saw Prusse board a streetcar. He knew where Prusse lived, and he knew that in order to get home Prusse would have to change cars to one that passed through a restricted zone. Foster boarded the car with Prusse, and as soon as Prusse got off to change cars, Foster "arrested" him and took him to the bureau office.

That afternoon Agent Harris and Assistant U.S. Attorney Jaraen A. Latane questioned Prusse and learned that he regularly rode the streetcar through the barred zone in order to reach a swimming beach. Both the federal agent and the U.S. attorney agreed that "Prusse's highly technical knowledge of submarines and kindred subjects render him undoubtedly dangerous potentially."

After agents made a phone call to the bureau headquarters in Washington, Prusse was booked into the Baltimore jail on a ten-day federal hold. In his report of sending Prusse to jail, Harris apparently felt it was necessary to again express his fears concerning Prusse's unique abilities: "I repeat that it seems to me that Prusse might be extremely dangerous as one trip along the neighborhood of forts, ships, etc. to a man of his skill would be equivalent to a photograph, etc."

On 27 August the Attorney General's Office ordered Prusse held indefinitely, "on the ground that his presence in your District at large is to the danger of the public peace and safety of the United States." But somewhere up the line cooler heads prevailed, and that same day Harris received another telegram from the Justice Department directing him to release Prusse in ten days "unless at that time in your judgment such action would be unwise."

Apparently Harris did feel it was unwise to release Prusse after ten days. On 18 September, twenty-five days after his arrest, Prusse was found hanged and dead in his cell. He had used his belt for the purpose and left no note. In his final report, Harris wrote that on the morning that Prusse hanged himself, a bureau agent went to the jail to collect Prusse's things, "none of which contained anything of interest."[8]

➤ Karl Gotthold Prusse, a Krupp engineer who was on board the *U-Deutschland* on her trip to Baltimore. He was the only true civilian on board. The Bureau of Investigation arrested Prusse in Baltimore on 24 August 1917 for being in a restricted area of the waterfront. He hanged himself in his cell on 18 September, leaving no note; his motive remains a mystery. *Author's collection*

The Baltimore Sabotage Cell

Paul G. L. Hilken

America's entry into the war ended the sabotage operations out of Baltimore. For a time, Hilken considered fleeing to Cuba but eventually decided to remain in Baltimore, where he still had paymaster duties to fulfill. For a short time he sent money, several thousand dollars, to Herrmann and Hinsch, who had fled to Mexico, and he continued to fund John Arnold in Argentina, where he was spreading anthrax and glanders.

The Bureau of Investigation continued to watch Hilken, thinking that he would continue to foment strikes and spread German propaganda. Agent Harris in Baltimore was sure that Hilken was using his position as the Swedish vice consul to somehow aid the Germans. The agency was successful in October 1917 in having Hilken's exequatur as Swedish consul in Baltimore canceled.

The bureau became particularly suspicious when Hilken went into the tire business in New York as an agent for the newly formed De Lion Tire and Rubber Company. Interest was aroused when the State Department sent a letter to Bruce Bielaski in August 1917 reporting that Hilken was in the rubber business in New York and was suspected of sending messages through the company to a German agent in Buenos Aires. The State Department was on to something, because at the time, Hilken was in frequent contact with Arnold in Buenos Aires. It was not the first indication that Hilken was communicating with a German agent in South America.

In April 1917, Harry E. Green, a Baltimore advertising agent, told the bureau agent in Chicago, Paul Berry, that he had been receiving mail from South America addressed to him with instructions to turn it over to Paul Hilken. The mail was sent to Harry Green because his company handled advertising for NDL. Another clue to Hilken's spy activities came from a Mrs. Cox, who had been a stenographer for NDL. She gave the bureau a statement about Hilken's communications with Germany and a clandestine courier system he ran using Swedish seamen. She also gave the bureau several pages of her stenographic notes on Carl Ahrendt, who had been a clerk at the Eastern Forwarding Company and was deeply involved in Hilken's spy activities. At the time she spoke to Special Agent Ralph Daughton, Ahrendt was the treasurer of the Seaboard Tire Company; in Mrs. Cox's notes was the cryptic notation, "He knows all of the *U-Deutschland*'s secrets."

Despite the clues connecting him to Arnold in Buenos Aires, the investigation remained focused on Hilken and his tire business. The only new information that resulted was that Hilken was actually doing business in Baltimore through his own newly founded company, Seaboard Tire and Rubber Company, and the bureau could find no evidence of wrongdoing. Nevertheless, the investigation went on until June 1918, when it died a natural death.

In the course of another investigation into Hilken's activities, the bureau received tips about more specific acts of sabotage in which he was allegedly involved. In June 1917, U.S. Attorney Harold A. Content gave Special Agent William Benham a copy of a letter written by Joseph J. O'Donohue Jr. According to O'Donohue, Paul Hilken had told an Ester Rice that "he had been personally involved in the destruction of the grain elevator in Connecticut." At the time, the bureau was searching for a Miss Frances Billings, who was closely associated with

Ester Rice and had a close connection to Hilken. Hard on the heels of that tip, also in June, came another that was connected with the same investigation.

The second tip came from a Mrs. Munoz, who had been Hilken's neighbor in 1909. During the summer of 1915 she had returned to Baltimore and reconnected with Hilken, who had taken her out on several occasions to cabarets and theaters in New York City. During one of their dates Hilken told her he had been personally involved in the destruction of a grain elevator in Connecticut. Mrs. Munoz also told agents that during lunch at Rector's Restaurant Hilken had told her that a five-inch-square package he was carrying contained "a powerful explosive sufficient to kill forty horses." On a third occasion, when they were attending a theater performance, he had told her he was a German agent and that "if the English knew what he was doing they would surely hang him."

The case that produced those leads was a sordid affair that Hilken was having with a woman who at the time was known only as Miss Frances Billings but was actually Mrs. George Reynolds. The case the bureau was trying to make on Hilken had nothing to do with espionage, despite the tips, but was an attempt to convict him of the White Slave Traffic Act, better known as the Mann Act, which had been passed in 1910. Like the tire company investigation, this one fell apart when the whole thing became public in November 1917.

Frances Billings' father, William Perry Billings, had been caught in a compromising situation with an actress, Mirian Burnadette. Following a raid by private detectives on William Billings' New York apartment, his wife, Mary, had filed for divorce and filed suit for $50,000 against the actress. Digging into the story, the press reported that Billings' daughter Frances had run off with the family chauffer, George M. Reynolds, in 1911. In a third scandal, an Emma Wood had sued Frances and her dad for alienating the affections of her husband. That case was still pending when this latest scandal hit the newsstands. The plot got thicker and more confusing when George Reynolds sued Hilken for $50,000 and requested a warrant for his arrest, on the grounds that Hilken might not remain in the state until the suit came to trial. At that point the bureau threw up its hands and walked away from the case.

After the United States entered the war Hilken continued sending money to German agents in Mexico, Argentina, and Japan. The amount he sent to Herrmann, Hinsch, and Dilger in Mexico was over $100,000; to Arnold in Argentina over $84,000; and to an unnamed agent in Japan, $50,000. It is almost unbelievable that, active and loose lipped as he was, the Bureau of Investigation never got on to him. There are two references in the bureau files about Hilken's being in the custody of the Secret Service but no details as to why or where.

The closest Hilken came to being caught was after the Kingsland fire in January 1918. Charles V. Merrick was a member of the American Protective League, an officially sanctioned citizens' group of unpaid volunteers—one might call them "official vigilantes"—who worked with the Bureau of Investigation to track down subversives. Merrick was deeply involved in finding out who was responsible for the many mysterious fires in defense plants, grain elevators, and railroad rolling stock. In the course of his "investigations" he stumbled onto the correct conclusion that Paul Hilken was the man behind the Kingsland fire. Exactly what evidence he had is not known, because whatever he had gathered was never recorded.

The problem was that in the months prior to the Kingsland fire Merrick started showing signs of being "unbalanced," and no matter what evidence he might have had, no one took it seriously. Something happened in August 1917 that caused the Bureau of Investigation to push for his expulsion from the American Protective League. Apparently the bureau's pressure finally paid off, because on 3 January 1918 Merrick wrote a letter of resignation from the league to Special Agent Roland Ford at the Albany, New York, office. He told Agent Ford that he was taking his case against Hilken to John Rathom, editor of the *Providence (Rhode Island) Journal*. Merrick also wanted Ford to write him a letter of recommendation that he could take to Rathom. Agent Ford demurred.

On 25 March 1918, Merrick sent a telegram to Paul Hilken, and the Western Union Telegraph office in Utica, New York, turned over a copy to the Bureau of Investigation. The telegram, which Special Agent James Tormey described as "incoherent," read, "In the Morse Code dash dot dot dash dash stands for good work. This same Message was published in the *Sun* after the Kingsland explosion in January 1917 see map with circles eight miles apart. Advise ex-Governor Martin R. Glynn of Albany that I stand ready with wife and two children to continue the good work on April sixth."

Chief Bielaski directed Agent Tormey to interview Merrick about the telegram's meaning, but Hilken's luck held again. Unable to find Merrick in Albany or Utica, he contacted Merrick's uncle in Syracuse and was told that on the day Merrick sent the telegram, he was committed to a sanitarium for the insane, where he was then under treatment. No further follow-up was made. Paul Hilken was never arrested, charged, or convicted of espionage or treason. His wartime activities remained unknown until 1928.

Hilken's sabotage came to light as the result of the 1921 Treaty of Berlin between the United States and Germany, which established what came to be known as the Mixed Claims Commission. The commission's task was to adjudicate all claims made by citizens of the two countries for financial losses stemming from the war. Among the cases heard was the Black Tom explosion and the Kingsland fire. The claimants were the Lehigh Valley Railroad and Foundry Company, which had that owned Black Tom, and the Canadian Car and Foundry Company, that which had owned Kingsland. In 1924 the law firm of Peaslee and Brigham assumed the lead in the two cases and was ultimately able to bring both to successful conclusions, in 1939.

In the course of the lengthy investigation, Amos Peaslee was allowed to examine still-classified radio intercepts that Room 40 had collected during the war.

Among the decoded intercepts were several that named German agents operating in the United States, including Paul Hilken. After great effort, Peaslee and the vice president of Canadian Car and Foundry, Leonard Peto, tracked down most of the major members of the Baltimore sabotage cell and convinced them to testify before the Mixed Claims Commission. Those who were U.S. citizens, Hilken among them, were guaranteed immunity from prosecution in exchange for their testimony.[9]

Fred Herrmann

Fred Herrmann, together with Hinsch, spent most of his time in Mexico feuding with another German agent, Kurt Jahnke, over who was to be the top dog among the German agents in Mexico. What he did with all the cash Hilken sent him is not recorded, but he certainly did not accomplish anything in the way of sabotage. Herrmann made some effort to carry out the firing of the Tampico oil fields, but the effort never got beyond the talking stage. When the war ended Herrmann went to Talcahuano, Chile, where he got a job in the National City Bank, married, and raised a family. He was still there when Hilken went to Chile on behalf of Amos Peaslee to convince him to return to the United States to testify before the Mixed Claims Commission in January 1929.

Herrmann refused to cooperate, on the grounds that if the bank found out about his sabotage activities he would be fired. Two months later his fear was realized when the bank fired him, having learned of his wartime activities. Some months after that his brothers Carl and Edwin went to Chile at Peaslee's expense to urge their brother to cooperate. They succeeded only after assuring him that he would be granted immunity from prosecution. He gave his testimony in April 1930 and returned to Chile.[10]

Friedrich Hinsch

Hinsch entered Mexico effortlessly on 29 May 1917. In fact, his escape from the United States had been so easy that he was still being sighted in various places on the Eastern Seaboard as late as September 1917. In July the press was claiming that Hinsch had escaped to Bremen on board the two-hundred-ton sailing vessel *Wanola,* with a three-man crew. That story folded when the vessel's owners, the Luna Shipping Company, informed the Commerce Department that it had owned the *Wanola* since 21 March 1917, had renamed her *Luna,* and had continuously employed her in coastal trade since that date. In fact, in July, when the schooner was reported to be in Bremen, she was en route to Nova Scotia from Philadelphia with a cargo of salt.

The *Wanola* story was replaced with one that Hinsch was still in the United States and would be arrested shortly. While that story was making the rounds, Hinsch and his new wife—his former housekeeper in Baltimore—were living comfortably in Mexico City. That story was in turn replaced by an admission that

Hinsch was in fact in Mexico but had crossed into Mexico from El Paso on 4 July 1917 "disguised as a laboring man." According to the story, a "girlfriend in New York" said that while he was hiding in New York he was in daily communication with German agents for whom she was the go-between. Those agents had concocted the *Wanola* tale, the story went, to cover Hinsch's run to Mexico and make it "comparatively safe for him to cross into Mexico whenever he felt inclined."

When Hinsch first arrived in Mexico he made a lot of noise about buying a used destroyer or other suitable vessel that he would arm and command as a commerce raider. The ersatz warship would be based in Mazatlán and would attack shipping en route to San Francisco. That was his basis for obtaining funds from Hilken in addition to the $24,000 he had brought to Mexico. Herrmann said that Hinsch thought "he might become the second Count Luchner [*sic*]" (in reference to the dashing Felix Graf von Luckner, who had commanded a highly successful German commerce raider during the war). He might have been serious at first, but then reality set in, and the idea went away quietly. After that Hinsch was not really involved in any serious sabotage discussions or plans. But he, Herrmann, and later Anton Dilger were fully occupied in feuding with Kurt Jahnke.

The issue was, who would be the designated sole "naval confidential agent" in Mexico, Hinsch or Jahnke? Hinsch had the navy rank and experience to hold the position, whereas Jahnke was a naturalized American citizen who had no German rank but did have lots of experience in sabotage on the U.S. West Coast. Hinsch started out holding the position by default and was confirmed in the slot on 4 January 1918 when the Admiralty withdrew Jahnke's commission for "sabotage undertakings."

But the German minister to Mexico, Heinrich von Eckhardt, favored Jahnke, and Jahnke was craftier and more devious than Hinsch. The decision was made on 29 April 1918 when Berlin designated Jahnke the sole naval confidential agent in Mexico, and Hinsch was out of a job. Job or none, Hinsch and his wife lived comfortably on Hilken's money until the end of the war, when the couple went to Germany, arriving there in January 1919. Hinsch went back to NDL and in the early 1930s testified on behalf of Germany before the Mixed Claims Commission. He died in 1936.[11]

Anton Dilger

In May 1917, Sektion Politik ordered Dilger to go to Mexico for the purpose of getting Mexico to go to war with the United States. His route would be from France to the United States, where he would deliver fresh anthrax and glanders cultures and new incendiary devices to Hilken, and then into Mexico. He obtained an emergency passport from the U.S. consulate in Zurich and departed from Le Havre on board the SS *Espagne* on 23 June. When the ship arrived in New York he went directly to Baltimore to deliver the goods to Hilken, who no longer needed them, because the Baltimore cell no longer existed. Having made the delivery,

Dilger went to his sister's house in Washington, D.C., and from there to his brother's house, three miles outside Front Royal, Virginia.

His arrival in Front Royal caused several citizens to write letters to the Bureau of Investigation about their suspicions of a man who had lived most of his life in Germany and had been in the German army. Not only that, but his sister was living in Germany and was married to a German army officer. On 29 July the bureau dispatched Special Agent George W. Lillard to interview Dr. Dilger in the family home in Front Royal.

Dilger freely told Agent Lillard about his education and his medical service in Bulgaria and Germany, explaining that he was on extended leave due to exhaustion. He told the federal agent that he had no intention of returning to Germany and was undecided about whether he should open a medical practice in Virginia. Agent Lillard was greatly taken with Dilger's gentlemanly demeanor and seeming truthfulness and reported that he "believed that Dr. Dilger is not a man who would be guilty of any traitorous acts towards this country." Two weeks later Dilger was in Mexico trying to carry out his orders from Berlin.

Dilger had no effect in Mexico and was tied up a good part of the time in the ongoing feud between Hinsch and Jahnke. When it became obvious that he was wasting his time there, Berlin ordered him to Spain, where he connected with the German intelligence service in Madrid.

Apparently he did not make a good impression on the people there, who seem to have distrusted him. On 17 October 1917 he was reported to have died in a German hospital in Madrid, apparently of influenza, though some say he was murdered. He was buried in a civil cemetery in Madrid, and his personal effects were sent to his sister in Germany.[12]

Wilhelm Wöhst

Wöhst was a small player—or, one might say, a "nonplayer"—in the Baltimore sabotage cell, but he was one of its more interesting personalities, and he remained so until he died in 1936, at about the same time Hinsch died. When Wöhst returned to Berlin in 1917, following the expulsion of the German embassy staff, he dutifully reported to Sektion Politik, where Hauptmann (Captain) Marguerre stiffly dismissed him, "because he was a failure in our eyes." If Hilken and company had failed to recognize that Wöhst was just along for the ride, the fact did not slip by the brass in Sektion Politik.

But being fired did not leave Wöhst badly off. He had no desire to go to Italy or Spain, where he was supposed to have been four months earlier. And he had most of the money that Sektion Politik had given him when he left for the United States, plus what he had skimmed off Hilken while he was there. And since Sektion Politik required no accounting for the cash, no one ever asked Wöhst about it. There is no record that Wöhst ever returned to the front. By January 1919 he was again a civilian looking for work, probably not too energetically.

In 1930 he was trying to recover $15,000 that he said Sektion Politik owed him for his work in America from October 1916 to February 1917. Since German intelligence had burned all its sabotage records in November 1918, there was no official record of what Wöhst was claiming he had been doing in the United States. So he turned to Hilken, asking him for an affidavit detailing what he had done while working with the Baltimore sabotage cell, to substantiate his claim. But Hilken interpreted the request as the opening ploy in a blackmail scheme, assuming that Wöhst wanted to use the affidavit as a way to lever more money out of him. He refused the request, even though the affidavit would be worthless to Wöhst for blackmail purposes. Hilken's past was already out in the open, since he was then cooperating with the Mixed Claims Commission.

The last thing heard from Wöhst was when he appeared before the Mixed Claims Commission in 1930 and 1932 to testify on behalf of the German government. His testimony, which was tightly scripted to make Hilken and Herrmann appear to be lying, was itself a collection of blatant lies, for which he was probably paid.[13]

Raoul Gerdts Pochet, aka Gerdts

Like Wöhst, Gerdts was a bit player in the Baltimore sabotage cell, a man who was happy being a bag carrier, gofer, and driver. He knew what was going on, but he did not take part. His closest approach to direct participation occurred in Mexico in April 1917, when Herrmann sent him back to Baltimore with a coded message for Hilken asking for $25,000. Hilken gave Gerdts a thousand dollars and told him that Hinsch would bring the remaining $24,000 with him to Mexico. By the time Gerdts returned to Mexico, with less than a thousand dollars, his relationship with Herrmann had changed.

The break had come when Herrmann offered him to $25,000 to set fire to the Tampico oil storage tanks. Gerdts refused, and Herrmann fired him. Gerdts returned to his home in Barranquilla, Colombia, where he found a job as an agent for the Sun Life Insurance Company. That is where Amos Peaslee and Leonard Peto found him on 11 January 1929. Always out for a buck, Gerdts told them he would appear before the Mixed Claims Commission but only if he was paid ten thousand dollars, which Peaslee was loath to do but did, because at the time he needed Gerdts' testimony. Gerdts testified in 1930 and then returned to his job, family, and home in Barranquilla.[14]

U-Deutschland Artifacts

Genuine *U-Deutschland* artifacts are rare, increasingly difficult to find, and becoming steadily more expensive, but they do occasionally show up on eBay in Britain, Germany, and the United States. There are probably still artifacts to be found in British antique shops, since the majority of the items were produced in Britain. Antique stores in the U.S. eastern seaboard states are probably sources for the artifacts produced in Baltimore and New York.

There are three *U-Deutschland* artifact categories: those made in Baltimore and New York in July 1916, those made in Britain by Horatio Bottomley under the auspices of the John Bull Victory Club in 1919, and those made in 1922 by the ship breakers Robert Smith and Sons. With a single exception, all the artifacts are made from metal removed from the boat. The lone exception is the group of dye samples that Herman A. Metz, president of Farbwerke-Hoechst in New York, had made up as gifts for favored customers in November 1916. The dye samples are without doubt the rarest of the artifacts.

The artifacts made in Baltimore and New York are all made from the boat's cast-iron ballast. The "John Bull Victory Souvenirs" are made from cast iron, white metal, gilding metal, copper, and brass taken from the boat when the armaments and engines were removed. There are no aluminum, lead, or pewter artifacts, and if you see something like that for sale, it is a fake. Robert Smith and Sons produced a single example, a copper ashtray, in very limited numbers.

The iron ballast that was donated to the Prisoners of War Relief Committee and the American Committee for the Relief of Widows and Orphans of the War in Germany arrived in Baltimore on board the *U-Deutschland* in July 1916. A second twenty tons of iron ballast was left in New London in November 1916 for use by the same two charitable groups, but there is no record that any of it was used.

U-Deutschland ballast souvenirs are not frequently counterfeited, except for the paperweights shown as examples 8 and 9 below. They started showing up on eBay in the United States and Germany in 1990; they are cast lead, pewter, and occasionally aluminum. Examples were still showing up on the collectors' market in 2013.

Artifacts made from the Boat's Ballast

▲ The Baltimore artist Hans Schuler Sr. designed both of these pendants for two wartime charities, the American Committee for the Relief of Widows and Orphans of the War in Germany (left) and the Committee for the Relief of Prisoners of War in Siberia (right). Interboro Badge & Medal Co., of New York City, die-stamped both versions. *Author's collection*

◄ Interboro also produced a much smaller stick pin and a lapel pin using the same design as the full-size pendant. Both measure 0.75 inch long and 0.5 inch wide. The wording on the front and back is the same as on the larger pendant. *Anonymous by request, private collection*

▼ One of the most interesting ballast items is this large cast-iron *U-Deutschland* cross, which Hans Schuler Sr. also designed. This design, done for the Committee for the Relief of Prisoners of War in Siberia, was cast in Baltimore by G. Krug and Son. The brass-plated-white-metal medallion embedded in the center on each side is made of metal not taken from the boat. The Iron Cross is 2.85 inches square, 0.5 inch thick, and weighs 10 ounces. One of the things that makes this Iron Cross interesting is that G. Krug and Son is the oldest ironworks in the

United States and has been doing business in the same location since 1810. Another interesting thing is that on one of the several trips that Paul König made to the United States on business for Norddeutsche Lloyd between 1922 and 1932, he acquired the entire remaining stock of these Iron Crosses and donated them to the Bremen chapter of the *Verein für das Deutschtum im Ausland* in Germany, a German cultural organization. As late as World War II, the group awarded the crosses to its members for loyal service.

There is also a rather dark and very little known fact about this cross. Not all of them were sold for charity. Paul Hilken acquired an unknown number and placed this advertisement in the pro-German magazine *Issues and Events*, 10 February 1917, "The above souvenirs are being sold for the benefit of the War Sufferers by the German Austro Hungarian Red Cross Aid Society of Baltimore, care of Messrs

A Schumacher & Co 2 East German Street for the Price of $1.10 postpaid Size 3 inches." The charity named was actually a Hilken front, and the money collected through sales was used to fund the Baltimore sabotage cell's activities. *Author's collection*

> This dye sample is undoubtedly the rarest of all the *U-Deutschland* artifacts. The four-inch-square box and its contents weigh seven ounces, which means that there are probably about five ounces of dye in the box. This particular dye, Indigo MLB 100%, sold for about forty-six cents an ounce before the war but went for

ten times that figure in 1916, $36.80 per pound. Herman A. Metz, president of Farbwerke-Hoechst, in the United States, had these sample boxes made up as gifts for his favored customers. Though not made from any part of the *U-Deutschland*, the dye sample qualifies as an artifact because the dye in the box came to New London on board the *U-Deutschland* as cargo. *Author's collection*

▼ There are two nearly identical versions of a flat paperweight, 3.24 inches by 2 inches, that Hans Schuler designed for two New York–based charities, the Committee for the Relief of Prisoners of War in Siberia and the American Committee for the Relief of Widows and Orphans of the War in Germany. Both were struck by Interboro in July 1916. The left example (5) was designed for the the the Committee for the Relief of Prisoners of War in Siberia, and the right example (5a) was designed for the American Committee for the Relief of Widows and Orphans of the War in Germany.

Both versions have been heavily counterfeited in lead, pewter, and aluminum since at least 1990. Because the counterfeit examples are cast, they do not have the crisp detail of the originals

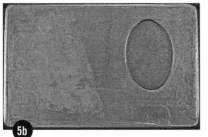

and do not have the sharply defined edges shown above (5c). Any example of these artifacts made of any metal other than iron is a fake. *5—Dave Schenkman collection; 5a, 5b, and 5c—anonymous by request, private collection*

John Bull Victory Souvenirs Made from Metals That Were Part of the Boat

◀ Horatio Bottomley thought highly of himself, and this cast-iron wall plaque featuring his likeness was one of the largest souvenirs offered. It measures 7 inches by 5 inches and weighs 2.5 pounds. In keeping with his ego, along with the plaque shown here an additional six identical in size and format were offered featuring the likeness of six wartime leaders: Admiral David Beatty, General Douglas Haig, David Lloyd George, President Woodrow Wilson, Georges Clemenceau, and General Ferdinand Foch. *Author's collection*

➤ This "specially modeled" Bottomley bust stands 4.33 inches high and weighs 3.25 pounds. *Class Stöckmeyer collection*

▼ The candlestick is solid brass, is 3.7 inches tall, and has a base 1.4 inches square. The candle hole is 0.4 inch in diameter. *Author's Collection*

◀ One of the rarest of the John Bull souvenirs is the figure of John Bull and his dog. It is iron, is 4.25 inches tall, and has a base 2.25 inches square. *Author's collection*

▼ This five-slot brass ashtray is 4.5 inches in diameter. *Author's collection*

▼ The pin-back brooch is made of gilded white metal and is 2 inches long and 0.5 inch high. These brooches were sold attached to the card. *Claas Stöckmeyer collection*

◄ John Bull offered four cigarette cases in small and large sizes, square, and in brass or silver plate. Shown is the square version, which is 3 by 2.5 inches. All the small cases are brass. *Claas Stöckmeyer collection*

➤ This brass table was described in the catalog as a "solid brass model of a hinged table." Actually, it is a tilting table, as shown in the right photo. It was also available with "fitted clips for menu cards or photographs." The table is 3 inches high, and the top is 2 by 2.75 inches. *Claas Stöckmeyer collection*

▼ This brass tray, 5 by 3.85 inches, is not shown in the John Bull Victory Souvenirs catalog, but it is a genuine artifact. *Claas Stöckmeyer collection*

▲ This brass teaspoon is 5 inches long and 1 inch wide. *Claas Stöckmeyer collection*

◄ These silver-plated brass napkin rings, which are described in the catalog as "serviette rings," are 1.25 inches long and have a 1.5-inch inside diameter. *Author's collection*

➤ A walking stick was offered in three colors—malacca, black ebony, and bamboo. All that is left today is the cap, shown here in side and top views. *Claas Stöckmeyer collection*

◀ This sixteen-slot ashtray is 4.3 inches in diameter and lacks the ocean waves beneath the U-boat logo. The catalog described it as "a useful present for a gentleman." It was offered in three metals—copper, gilding metal, and white metal. It was also offered in oblong form in either white or gilding metal. *Anonymous by request, private collection*

➤ This is the catalog illustration of an Iron Cross described as a "perfect replica of the notorious German decoration." According to the catalog, this item is bronzed, which suggests that it is made of gilding metal. *Photo by the author taken from his own collection*

▼ Nearly all the John Bull items have these guarantees stamped on them or cast into them. This cast warranty is found on the larger cast-iron items. *Photo by the author taken from his own collection*

➤ This stamped warranty is found on cast-brass souvenirs and ashtrays. *Photo by the author taken from his own collection*

▼ The machine-stamped artifacts, ashtrays, trays, and cigarette cases, bear one of the stamped logos below. The logo is stamped from the back side so that it is raised as you look at the front of the piece. As you can see, the sharpness and detail in the left example are much better than in the right example. *Photo by the author taken from his own collection*

Robert Smith and Sons

▼ After the *U-Deutschland/U-155* was sold for scrap to Robert Smith and Sons to be broken up, the company salvaged what copper was still on board and had it made into rectangular ashtrays to be given to customers and friends. *Author's collection*

The *U-Deutschland* Model

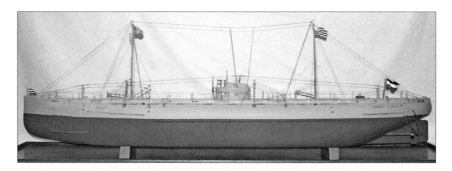

▲ The origin and builder of this model are unknown, but it is believed to have been built in Germany. The model is in 1:40 scale, sixty-four inches long, and very detailed. Below are some close-ups showing the detail. *Steve Zukosky*

▲ Port bow. *Steve Zukosky*

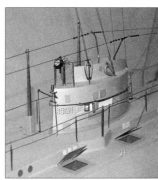

▲ Conning tower. *Steve Zukosky*

➤ Portside tank deck with open wet and dry cargo hatches. *Steve Zukosky*

▲ Port quarter. *Steve Zukosky*   ▲ Port empennage. *Steve Zukosky*

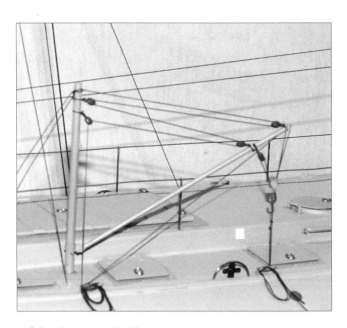

▲ Onboard cargo mast derrick. *Steve Zukosky*

NOTES

Chapter 1. The Blockade

1. C. Paul Vincent, *The Politics of Hunger: The Allied Blockade of Germany, 1915–1919* (Athens, Ohio, and London: Ohio University Press, 1985), 125.
2. Gordon A. Craig, *Germany, 1866–1945* (New York: Oxford University Press, 1978), 354–55.
3. Simeon D. Fess, *The Problems of Neutrality When the World Is at War: A History of Our Relations with Germany and Great Britain as Detailed in the Documents That Passed between the United States and the Two Great Belligerent Powers,* Sixty-Fourth Congress, Second Session, Document No. 2111, in Two Parts, Part 2, "Restraints on Trade Controversy" (Washington, D.C.: U.S. Government Printing Office [hereafter GPO], 1917), 291–96.
4. Louis Guichard, *The Naval Blockade,* 1914–1918 (New York: D. Appleton, 1930), 4.
5. Ibid., 4–6.
6. Craig, *Germany,* 354.
7. Ibid., 357.
8. Walter Görlitz, ed., *The Kaiser and His Court: The Diaries, Note Books, and Letters of Admiral Georg Alexander von Müller, Chief of the Naval Cabinet, 1914–1918* (New York: Harcourt, Brace & World, 1965), 129, 134, 142.
9. Paul G. L. Hilken was not responsible for all the German sabotage activities in the United States. But his Baltimore cell was unquestionably the most successful and the longest-running operation. The Baltimore cell was also entirely responsible for the spread of anthrax and glanders, an operation that extended to Argentina. No member of the cell was ever caught.

Chapter 2. The Beginning

1. Investigative Cases of the Bureau of Investigation, 1908–1922, Records of the Federal Bureau of Investigation, RG 65, Microfilm Publication M1080, National Archives and Records Administration, College Park, Md. [hereafter NARA], case 8000-174, "Paul G. L. Hilken Grand Jury Testimony," 15 November 1916 [hereafter cited as Bureau of Investigation, followed by case number].
2. Reports of International Arbitrator Awards, Mixed Claims Commission *(U.S. v. Germany),* Constituted under the Agreement of 10 August 1922, Extended by Agreement of December 1928, vol. VIII, "Lehigh Valley Railroad Company, Agency of Canadian Car and Foundry Company, and Various Underwriters (Sabotage Case)," 3 December 1939, Exhibit 771, 292 [hereafter cited as Mixed Claims Commission]; Franz von Rintelen, *Dark Invader* (London and Portland, Ore.: Frank Cass, 1997), x–xv.

3. Baltimore City Historical Society, *Baltimore: Its History and Its People,* "Henry Gerard Hilken" (New York and Chicago: Lewis Historical, 1912), 803–4.

4. *Technique,* yearbook (Cambridge, Mass.: Massachusetts Institute of Technology, 1901–4).

5. General Records of the Department of State, Record Group [hereafter RG] 59, Passport Applications, 2 January 1906–31 March 1925, Microfilm M1490, NARA.

6. Bureau of Investigation Case 8000-549, Paul G. L. Hilken.

7. Mixed Claims Commission, 87; Bureau of Investigation File, 65961, "Fire at B. & O. Pier, 30 October 1917: Probable German Matter."

8. Bureau of Investigation Case 8000-549, Paul G. L. Hilken.

9. Ibid.

10. Bureau of Investigation Case 8000-174, Franz von Rintelen et al.

11. Ibid., Hilken Statement, 11 September 1916, and Grand Jury Testimony, 21 November 1916.

12. Dieter Jung, Martin Maass, and Berndt Wenzel, *Tanker und Versorger der deutschen Flotte, 1900–1980* (Stuttgart: Motorbuch, 1981), 167–68.

13. Ibid.

14. Mixed Claims Commission, 303; Bureau of Investigation Case 8000-174, Franz von Rintelen et al., and William Benham Report, 2 November 1916.

15. Rintelen, *Dark Invader,* 95; Henry Landau, *The Enemy Within: The Inside Story of German Sabotage in America* (New York: G. P. Putnam's Sons, 1937), 45; John Price Jones and Paul Merrick Hollister, *The German Secret Service in America* (Boston: Small, Maynard, 1918), 157; Jules Witcover, *Sabotage at Black Tom: Imperial Germany's Secret War in Germany* (New York: Algonquin Books of Chapel Hill, 1989), 89.

16. Bureau of Investigation Cases 8000-925 and 8000-2423, Walter T. Scheele; 8000-174, Franz von Rintelen et al.

17. Mixed Claims Commission, 304, 310–11.

18. Ibid., 304.

19. Ibid., 311–12.

20. Bureau of Investigation Case 8000-174, Franz von Rintelen et al., William Benham Report, 2 November 1916; Mixed Claims Commission, 302, 303; Christopher Warner, "The Kaiser Sows Destruction: Protecting the Homeland the First Time Around," *Studies in Intelligence* 46, no. 1 (Spring 2002).

21. Jones and Hollister, *German Secret Service in America,* 169.

22. Ibid.

23. Patrick Beesly, *Room 40: British Naval Intelligence 1914–1918* (New York: Harcourt Brace Jovanovich, 1982), 229–30.

24. Guichard, *Naval Blockade,* 270–75.

25. Eberhard Rössler, *Die Unterseeboote der Kaiserlichen Marine* (Bonn: Bernard & Graefe Verlag, 1997), 50.

26. "Lake Threatens to Libel Craft," *New York Times,* 10 July 1916.

27. Simon Lake, *The Submarine in War and Peace* (Philadelphia and London: J. B. Lippincott, 1918), 251; "Could Feed Britain by Undersea Boats," *New York Times,* 18 July 1915.

28. James H. Belote, "The Lohmann Affair," *Studies in Intelligence* (Spring 1960).

29. Eberhard Rössler, *Geschichte des deutschen Ubootbaus* (München: J. F. Lehmanns Verlag, 1975), 67; Wilhelm Ehlers, *Deutschland: Was Wir vom Krieg nicht wissen* (Leipzig: H. Fikentscher Verlag, 1936), 266; Records of the German Navy, 1850–1945, RG 242, Microfilm Publication T-1022, Roll 631, PG62024, PG67334, NARA; Belote, "Lohmann Affair."

30. Christopher Kobrak, *Die Deutschebank und die USA: Geschäfte und Politik von 1870 bis Heute* (München: C. H. Beck, 2008), 260–61; Records of the German Navy 1850–1945, RG 242, T-1022, Roll 631, PG62024 and PG67334.

31. Rössler, *Geschichte des deutschen Ubootbaus,* 67.

32. Records of the Department of State, Passport Applications, RG 59, Microfilm Series M1372, 21 September 1915; Records of the Immigration; Naturalization Service, Passenger and Crew Lists Arriving in New York, 1897–1957, RG 36, Microfilm Series T715, Roll 2435, 131, NARA.

33. Mixed Claims Commission, 307.

34. Landau, *Enemy Within,* 72–73.

35. Bureau of Investigation Case 8000-549, Statement of Frederick Henjez Jr., 17 November 1915.

36. Bureau of Investigation Case 8000-549, Paul G. L. Hilken, Investigation of Paul G. L. Hilken, Alleged Neutrality Violation, 22 November 1915.

37. Landau, *Enemy Within,* 82.

38. Mixed Claims Commission, 294; Records of the State Department Records Relating to World War I and Its Termination, 1914–1929, Neutrality, 763.72114/5009.

Chapter 3. Sektion Politik and the Eastern Forwarding Company

1. Records of the German Navy, 1850–1945, RG 242, T1022, Roll 659, PG75196, PG 75197; Roll 660, PG75197.

2. Mixed Claims Commission, 345–47.

3. Landau, *Enemy Within,* 74–76; Mixed Claims Commission, 258–59.

4. Mixed Claims Commission, 352.

5. Ibid., 351–52.

6. Ibid., 307.
7. Ibid., 292–93.
8. Landau, *Enemy Within,* 74; Mixed Claims Commission, 309–13.
9. Landau, *Enemy Within,* 240–41; Mixed Claims Commission, 314–14.
10. Unless otherwise noted, all details about the Eastern Forwarding Company in this chapter are found in Bureau of Investigation Case 8000-1634.
11. Mixed Claims Commission, 310–11.
12. The details of the attempt to exile Carl Dilger to Germany are found in Mixed Claims Commission, 306.
13. Records of the German Navy, 1850–1945, RG 242, T-1022, Roll 659, PG75197; "Nails U-Boat Story," *Baltimore News,* 10 June 1916; Bureau of Investigation Case 8000-1634; William Lafferty, PhD, Wright State University via Walter Mather, Baltimore.
14. "Nickel from Canada for *Deutschland,*" *New York Times,* 11 November 1916; Bureau of Investigation Case 8000-1634, Eastern Forwarding Company.
15. Mixed Claims Commission, 403.

Chapter 4. The Crew and the Boat

1. *Telegramme der Deutschen Ozean Reederei, Bremen, an den Reichskanzler und umgekehrt, und Zeitungsartikeln über den Kapitän* Paul König, Juni–Oktober 1916, File 00423, Zentrales Staatsarchiv, German Democratic Republic [hereafter DDR]; Otto Weddigen, *Das ertse Handels-Unterseeboot, Deutschland und sein Kapitän, Paul König* (Leipzig: Wiking Verlag, 1916); Certified Copy of an Entry of Marriage: Paul L. König to Kathleen Marie Pennington, Nr. CAS886117/87, General Records Office, St. Catherine's House, Winchester, London, United Kingdom.
2. *Personalunterlagen,* Franz Krapohl, *Deutsche Dienststelle (WASt),* Berlin.
3. *Personalunterlagen,* Paul Eyring, *Deutsche Dienststelle (WASt),* Berlin.
4. *Personalunterlagen,* Karl Schwartzkopf, *Deutsche Dienststelle (WASt),* Berlin.
5. *Personalunterlagen,* Hermann Liebermann von Sonnenberg, *Deutsche Dienststelle (WASt),* Berlin.
6. *Personalunterlagen,* Gerhard Posse, *Deutsche Dienststelle (WASt),* Berlin.
7. *Deutsche Ozean Reederei, Zahl-Liste Handels-U-Schiff Bremen/Reise 1916/11 August 1916–10 September 1916,* in the possession of Claas Stöckmeyer, Bremen.
8. Commander Yates Sterling, "German Merchant Submarine *Deutschland,*" 14 November 1916, Secret and Confidential Correspondence of the Chief of Naval Operations and the Secretary of the Navy, 1919–1927, RG 80, M1140, NARA.

9. *Musterrolle der Manschaft des deutschen U-Handelsschiffes Deutschland, Kiel 9 Mai 1916,* in the possession of Claas Stöckmeyer, Bremen.

10. Paul König, *Voyage of the* Deutschland (New York: Hearst's International Library, 1916), 66; "Sailors Expect to Be Back," *New York Times,* 19 July 1916.

11. Hans Techel, *Der Bau von Unterseeboote auf der Germaniawerft* (Berlin: Verlag des Vereines deutscher Ingenieure, 1923), 96.

12. Arno Spindler, *Der Handelskrieg mit U-Booten* (Berlin: Verlag E. S. Mittler & Sohn, 1932), 1:171; "German Merchant Submarine *Deutschland,*" 14 November 1916, Secret and Confidential Correspondence of the Chief of Naval Operations and the Secretary of the Navy, 1919–1927. Unless otherwise noted, all the following technical information regarding the *U-Deutschland* is found in this document.

13. Techel, *Der Bau von Unterseeboote auf der Germaniawerft,* 96.

14. Secretary of State to Gerard, 12 July 1916; Gerard to Secretary of State, 14 July 1916; Gerard to Secretary of State, 15 July 1916, Records of the Department of State, RG 59, Microfilm Publication M367, Roll 179, 763.72111, NARA.

Chapter 5. The First Crossing

1. König, *Voyage of the* Deutschland, 16–19.

2. The 14 June departure date from Helgoland is found in *VDA Urkunde an Friedrich Tanger,* 13 März 1937, in the possession of Claas Stöckmeyer, Bremen. König provided the VDA the 14 June departure date, which is supported by the fact that since the boat could only make ten knots, it could not have crossed the Atlantic in sixteen days. It is a simple "time multiplied by rate equals distance" problem. The date of his departure from Helgoland that König gave the press, 23 June, was propaganda to make the *U-Deutschland* appear more capable than she really was. Her first return trip took twenty-two days; the second outbound crossing took twenty-four days; the second return took nineteen days, under improved sea conditions. Even the *U-53,* a much more powerful and streamlined vessel, required nineteen and twenty days to make the crossing.

3. Records of the German Navy, 1850–1945, RG 242, T1022, Roll 659, PG75196 and 75197.

4. Ibid., Roll 658, PG75195, Lohmann to Toussaint, 28 June 1916.

5. Francis Duncan, "German Commercial Submarines," United States Naval Institute *Proceedings* [hereafter USNI *Proceedings*] (June 1970), 1240.

6. Lohmann to Toussaint, 8 July 1916, Records of the German Navy, 1850–1945, RG 242, T1022, Roll 658, PG75195.

7. Hermann Bauer, *Als Führer der U-Boote in Weltkrieg* (Leipzig: Koehler & Amelang, 1940), 281.

8. Ibid., 276–81; Spindler, *Der Handelskrieg mit U-Booten,* 2:57; E. Keble Chatterton, *The Big Blockade* (London: Hurst & Blackett, 1932), 134.

9. Paul König, *Voyage of the* Deutschland, 35–120. Unless otherwise noted, the account of the first crossing that follows is found in these pages.

10. Johann Kirchner, *Das Boot bei der Arbeit* (Berlin: Verlag E. S. Mittler & Sohn, 1917), 13–22.

11. Beesly, *Room 40,* 3–7.

12. "Koenig Recalls Radio on the Deutschland," *New York Times,* 22 November 1931.

13. John Rogers, "Conversation with Captain König," 24 July 1916, Office of Naval Records and Library, Washington, D.C.

14. Norman R. Hamilton to Secretary of the Treasury, 10 July 1916, Serial 102574, Records of the Department of State, RG 59, M367, Roll 176, 763.72111/2974.

Chapter 6. Baltimore, Part I

1. Norman R.. Hamilton, Collector to Secretary of the Treasury, 10 July 1916, Serial 102574, Records of the Department of State, RG59, M367, Roll 176, 763.7211/2974.

2. König, *Voyage of the* Deutschland, 133–34.

3. "Mass of Machinery Inside," *New York Times,* 11 July 1916.

4. Bureau of Investigation Case 8000-1634, Eastern Forwarding Company, 10 July 1916.

5. Ferriday to Department of State, 10 July 1916, Records of the Department of State, RG 59, M367, Roll 179, 763.72111D48/8.

6. British Embassy to State Department, various correspondence 3–22 July 1916, Records of the Department of State, RG 59, M367, Roll 179, 763.72111D48/17.

7. Hayward to Ryan, 11 July 1916, Records of the Department of State, RG 59, M367, Roll 176, 763.72111/2974.

8. J. H. Klein, "Report on German Merchant Vessel SS *Deutschland,*" 10 July 1916, Office of Naval Records and Library, Washington, D.C.

9. Bureau of Investigation Case 180958, P. G. Wallmo, Re: A. J. Lamme.

10. R. Y. Cadmus to Collector of Customs, 18 July 1916; W. D. Ryan to F. M. Halstead, 24 July 1916; James F. Farrell and A. T. Rouse, "Submarine Report," 3 August 1916, Records of the Department of State, RG 59, M367, Roll 179, 763.72111D48/16.

11. Polk to Lansing and return, 10 July 1916, Serial 102574, Records of the State Department, RG 59, Roll 179, 763.72111D48/7.

12. "Navy Experts Say Giant Submarine Is Merchantman," *New York Times,* 12 July 1916.

13. Ryan to State Department, telegram, 11 July 1916; Capt. C. F. Hughes to Ryan, 11 July 1916, Records of the Department of State, RG 59, M367, Roll 176, 763.72111D48/7.

14. "Navy Experts Say Giant Submarine Is Merchantman."

15. Joint State and Navy Neutrality Board to Secretary of State, Serial No. 142, "Memorandum Re: Department of State Letter and Papers," 14 July 1916, Records of the Department of State, M367, Roll 179, 763.72111D48/29.

16. Hoppin to Polk, 12 July 1916, Records of the Department of State, M367, Roll 179, 763.72111D48/8.

17. "La Situation Diplomatique," *Le Temp,* 17 July 1916, Records of the Department of State, M367, Roll 179, 763.72111D48/21.

18. "Submarines and International Law," *Tanin,* 14 July 1916, Records of the Department of State, M367, Roll 179, 763.72111D48/25.

19. "Sees Threat in *Deutschland,*" *New York Times,* 15 July 1916; "Sees Value as Auxiliary," *New York Times,* 12 July 1916.

20. "Watching U.S. Decision on U-Boat Liner," Carl W. Ackerman Papers, Boxes 167–68, Library of Congress, Washington, D.C.

21. Werner Beumelburg, *Sperrfeurer um Deutschland* (Oldenburg: Gerhard Stelling, 1929), 189–90.

22. USNI *Proceedings* 40, no. 1 (January–February 1914), 1796–97; Records of the German Navy, 1850–1945, RG 242, T1022, Roll 659, PG75196; Philip K. Lundeberg, "Undersea Warfare and Allied Strategy in World War I," Part I (to 1916), *Smithsonian Journal of History* 1, no. 4 (Winter 1966), 49–72; "Submarine Blockade Runner: A U-boat to Carry Contraband Cargoes," *Popular Science Monthly* 89 (July–December 1916), 227–29.

23. "Plan Company Here to Build Subsea Boats," *New York Times,* 13 July 1916.

24. Gaddin Smith, *Britain's Clandestine Submarines, 1914–1918* (New Haven, Conn.: Yale University Press, 1964), 38, 46, 78–73.

25. "Where Germany Leads," *New York Times,* 5 May 1915.

26. "England to Refuse to Pass Dyestuffs," *New York Times,* 27 May 1916; "Despair of Getting German Dyestuffs," *New York Times,* 3 July 1916.

27. "New Plan to Get Dyes," *New York Times,* 18 July 1915.

28. "Dye Dealers Disappointed," *New York Times,* 16 July 1916; "Sell Deutschland Dyes," *New York Times,* 30 July 1916.

29. "The Cargo of the Submarine *Deutschland,*" *Journal of the Society of Chemical Industry* 35, no. 23 (15 December 1916), 1202; "Firms Here Expect to Get Dyestuffs," *New York Times,* 11 July 1916.

30. Inspectors James J. Farrell and A. T. Rouse to Surveyor of Customs, Baltimore, Maryland, "Submarine Report," 3 August 1916, 6 typewritten pages in the author's possession; *Information Annual: A Continuous Cyclopedia and Digest of Current Events, 1916* (New York: Cumulative Digest, 1917), 133–34.

31. The details of the price manipulations and ownership shuffles of the dyestuffs are found Records of the German Navy, 1850–1945, RG 242, T-1022, Rolls 631, 659, 711, PG67344, 75196, 75019; U.S. Senate, Hearings before the Committee on Finance, United States Senate, Sixty-Sixth Congress, Second Session, on HR8078, An Act to Regulate the Importation of Coal-Tar Products, to Promote the Establishment of the Manufacture Thereof in the United States, and as Incident thereto to Amend the Act of September 1916 Entitled, "An Act to Increase Revenue and for Other Purposes," 8–13 December 1919 and 12 January 1920 (Washington, D.C.: GPO, 1920); "Cargo of the Submarine *Deutschland*," 1202.
32. Ackermann Papers.
33. "Dampens Reventlow's Ardor," *New York Times,* 15 July 1916.
34. "Zeppelin Here Soon Says Capt. Koenig," *New York Times,* 14 July 1916.
35. Ibid.

Chapter 7. Baltimore, Part II

1. "Mailbags for von Bernstorff," *New York Times,* 11 July 1916.
2. Ibid.; Farrell and Rouse, "Submarine Report."
3. Chatterton, *Big Blockade,* 264.
4. "Mail and Dyes Coming Here," *New York Times,* 10 July 1916.
5. "U-Liner's Rates High," *New York Times,* 14 July 1916.
6. "Boat and Errand a Puzzle," *New York Times,* 10 July 1916.
7. Records of the German Navy, 1850–1945, RG 242, T1022, Roll 658, PG75195; Roll 569, PG75196; Roll 660, PG75196 and 75197.
8. "Navy Experts Say Giant Submarine Is Merchantman."
9. "Giant Submarine Unloaded Hastily," *New York Times,* 13 July 1916.
10. Charles F. Horne and Walter F. Austin, *Source Records of the Great War, Vol. IV,* ed. New York: National Alumni, 1923, "German Submarine *Deutschland*'s Atlantic Crossing by Captain Paul Koenig, 9 July 1916."
11. "Subsea Perils Bring Joy to Skipper; Wine Flows, Music Blares under Waves," *New York Times,* 11 July 1916.
12. Farrell and Rouse, "Submarine Report," 3 August 1916.
13. "Navy Experts Say Giant Submarine Is Merchantman"; "Giant Submarine Unloaded Hastily," *New York Times,* 13 July 1916.
14. "Zeppelin Here Soon Says Capt. Koenig."
15. "Decipher 201, 15 July 1916," Admiralty Historical Section, Packs and Miscellaneous Records, 1860–1924, ADM 137/12269, Public Record Office, Surrey, United Kingdom.
16. "Mystery in U-Boat Cargo," *New York Times,* 15 July 1916.
17. John M. Harper and Company to Department of State, "Allies Hurt U.S. Trade to Hurt German Business," 20 July 1916, Records of the Department of State, RG 59, M367, Roll 179, 763.72112/807.

18. "England to Refuse to Pass Dyestuffs."

19. "Mrs. Marshall Goes Aboard," *New York Times,* 16 July 1916; "Final Steps Taken for Dash of U-Boat," *New York Times,* 23 July 1916.

20. James L. Greenleaf to Robert Lansing, 17 July 1916, Records of the Department of State, RG 59, Roll 179, 763.72111D48/8.

21. Mitchell Ferriday to Frank L. Polk, telegram, 11 July 1916, Records of the Department of State, RG 59, Roll 179, 763.7211D48/8.

22. Farrell and Rouse, "Submarine Report," 3 August 1916.

23. "Subsea Trader's Dash for the Sea Only Hours Away," *New York Times,* 19 July 1916; "Sailors Expect to Be Back," *New York Times,* 19 July 1916.

24. "Aboard the Submarine *Deutschland,*" *Scientific America,* 10 February 1917, 156.

25. "Submarine Liner Rigs Up Wireless," *New York Times,* 22 July 1916; "U-Boat Tied at Pier Captain Awaits News," *New York Times,* 26 July 1916; "Warships Keep Vigil at Capes," *Baltimore Evening News,* 22 July 1916; "How Ships Patrol Sea in Search of U-Boat," *New York Times,* 24 July 1916.

26. J. Bernstorff to Frank Polk, telegram, 26 July 1916, Records of the Department of State, RG 59, M367, Roll 179, 763.72111D48/15.

27. See the thirteen pages of correspondence that constitute Records of the Department of State, RG 59, M367, Roll 179, 763.72111D48/31 and 763.72111/33; "Chesapeake Entered by British Cruiser," *New York Times,* 26 July 1916.

28. Commandant, United States Navy Yard, Norfolk to Secretary of the Navy (Operations), 25 July 1916, and Secretary of the Navy (Operations) to Secretary of State, 26 July 1916, Records of the Department of State, RG 59, M367, Roll 179, 763.72111/3886.

29. Norman R. Hamilton, Collector of Customs, Norfolk to Secretary of the Treasury, 25 July 1916, Records of the Department of State, RG 59, M367, Roll 179, 763.72111/3895; SS *Vinland,* Records of the Department of State, RG 59, M367, Roll 179, 763.72111V76/2 and 763.72111/3974.

30. Sir Julian S. Corbett and Henry Newbolt, *History of the Great War: Naval Operations* (London: Longmans, Green, 1920–31), 1:44–53.

31. "Submarine Liner Rigs Up Wireless."

32. W. P. Nolan to Secretary of the Treasury, 26 July 1916; Assistant. Secretary of the Treasury to Secretary of State, 27 July; W. P. Ryan to Secretary of the Treasury, 28 July, Records of the Department of State, RG 59, M367, Roll 179, 763.72111D48/20.

33. Landau, *Enemy Within,* 82–83; Witcover, *Sabotage at Black Tom,* 162; James Castagnera, *Counter Terrorism Issues: Cases Studies in the Courtroom* (Boca Raton, Fla.: CRC, 2013), xxvii–xxviii.

34. Mixed Claims Commission, 93; Castagnera, *Counter Terrorism Issues,* xxviii.

35. "To Furnish No Convoy," *New York Times,* 31 July 1916.

Chapter 8. The Triumphant Return

1. "*Deutschland* Off on Dash to Ocean as Warships Wait," *New York Times,* 2 August 1916; "*Deutschland* Out in the Open Sea Eluding Her Foes," *New York Times,* 3 August 1916; "Mystery Veils Course of the *Deutschland,*" *Fort Wayne Sentinel,* 2 August 1916; König, *Voyage of the* Deutschland, 164–69. Unless otherwise noted, the account of the boat's departure and movements until she passed beyond the Capes is from these sources.
2. König, *Voyage of the* Deutschland, 170–79.
3. National Oceanic and Atmospheric Administration [hereafter NOAA] Booklet Chart 12270, Grid 12; König, *Voyage of the* Deutschland, 170.
4. "Thinks U-Liner May Escape," *Washington Post,* 3 August 1916.
5. Mixed Claims Commission, 312.
6. König, *Voyage of the* Deutschland, 194–95.
7. König's Report to the Admiralstab, Records of the German Navy, 1850–1945, RG 242, T1022, Roll 658, PG75195.
8. Admiralstab to Kiel, 15 August 1916, Records of the German Navy, 1850–1945, RG 242, T1022, Roll 658, PG75195; Bodo Herzog, *Deutsche U-Boote, 1906–1966* (Herrsching: Pawlak Verlag, 1990), 126.
9. *U-200* to Helgoland, 22 August 1916; Helgoland to Kiel, 23 August 1916, Records of the German Navy, 1850–1945, RG 242, T1022, Roll 658, PG75195.
10. Arthur Brehmer, *Die Kühne Fahrt der Deutschland* (Berlin: Berthold Siegmund, 1916), 87; "Bells and Flags Greet *Deutschland*'s Arrival," Ackerman Papers.
11. "Bells and Flags Greet *Deutschland*'s Arrival," Ackerman Papers.
12. Eichberger family account, told to the author.
13. Brehmer, *Die Kühne Fahrt der Deutschland,* 92.
14. "*Deutschland* Gets Ovation," *New York Times,* 26 August 1916; "Bells and Flags Greet *Deutschland*'s Arrival," Ackerman Papers.

Chapter 9. The *U-Bremen*

1. Mixed Claims Commission, 314.
2. James L. McGovern to Secretary of the Treasury, 16 August 1916, Records of the Department of State, RG 59, M367, Roll 179, 763.7211B75/4.
3. "Memorandum for Mr. Bielaski," n.d., Bureau of Investigation File 8000-549, Paul Hilken, 35.
4. [Untitled item], *New York Times,* 10 August 1916.
5. "British Dodge Query on *Bremen* Sinking," *New York Times,* 12 August 1916; "Believe Submarine *Bremen* Is Captured: British Cruisers Seen Towing Strange Craft," *New York Times,* 18 August 1916.
6. "Insist *Bremen* Is Caught," *New York Times,* 6 September 1916.

7. "Koenig Awaits the *Bremen*," *New York Times*, 17 July 1916.

8. "Excited by Navy Submarine," *New York Times*, 23 July 1916; "*Bremen's* Delay Holds Up U-Boat," *New York Times*, 24 July 1916.

9. Mixed Claims Commission, 353.

10. Norman Polmar and Kenneth J. Moore, *Cold War Submarines: The Design and Construction of United States and Soviet Submarines* (New York: Brassey's, 2004), 225.

11. Mixed Claims Commission, 321–22.

12. Ibid., 321.

13. Ibid., 319.

14. Ibid., 332.

15. Erich Gröner, *Die deutschen Kriegsschiffe, 1815–1945* (München: J. F. Lehmanns Verlag, 1966), 1:348; Herzog, *Deutsche U-Boote*, 48.

16. Spindler, *Der Handelskrieg mit U-Booten*, 3:237–42.

17. "Life Buoy with Name of the Missing *Bremen* Is Cast Up on the Coast Near Portland, Me.," *New York Times*, 30 September 1916.

18. [Untitled item], *New York Times*, 12 August 1916.

19. Attaché Oslo to Admiralstab, 6 December 1916 and 24 March 1917; W.28e to Admiralstab, 13 January 1917 and 20 January 1917, Records of the German Navy, 1850–1945, RG 242, T1022, Roll 658, PG75195.

20. Lohmann to Admiralstab, 25 March 1917, Records of the German Navy, 1850–1945, RG 242, T1022, Roll 658, PG75195.

21. Generalstab des Feldherrs to Admiralstab, 3 April 1917; W29.c to Admiralstab, 27 April 1917; Madrid to Berlin, Records of the German Navy, 1850–1945, RG 242, T1022, Roll 658, PG75195.

Chapter 10. The Layover

1. Beumelburg, *Sperrfeuer um Deutschland*, 173–74.

2. Guichard, *Naval Blockade*, 69.

3. Ibid., 77.

4. Craig, *Germany*, 373.

5. Gerard to Secretary of State, telegram 4279, 28 August 1916, Records of the Department of State, RG 59, M367, Roll 0029, 763.72/2834.

6. Rössler, *Geschichte des deutschen Ubootbaus*, 67.

7. Ibid.

8. Deutsche Ozean Reederei to Toussaint, 29 August 1916, Records of the German Navy, 1850–1945, RG 242, T1022, Roll 658, PG75195.

9. Nachrichten Abteilung to Toussaint, 1 September 1916, Records of the German Navy, 1850–1945, RG 242, T1022, Roll 658, PG75195.

10. U.S. Senate, *Brewing and Liquor Interests and German Propaganda*, Hearings before a Subcommittee of the Committee on the Judiciary, United States Senate, Sixty-Fifth Congress, Second Session, Pursuant to S. Res. 307,

A Resolution Authorizing and Directing the Committee on the Judiciary to Call for Certain Evidence and Documents Relating to the Charges Made against the United States Brewers' Association and Allied Interests and to Submit a Report of Their Investigation to the Senate, 3 vols. (Washington, D.C.: U.S. Government Printing Office 1919), 2:520.

11. Lohmann to Admiralstab, 31 August 1916, Records of the German Navy, 1850–1945, RG 242, T1022, Roll 658, PG75195.

12. Taintor to Lansing, 13 October 1916, Records of the Department of State, RG 59, M367, 763.72111D48.

13. Falk to Admiralstab, 1 September 1916, Records of the German Navy, 1850–1945, RG 242, Roll 658, PG75195.

14. James L. McGovern to Secretary of the Treasury, 16 November 1916, Records of the Department of State, RG 59, M367, 763.72111D48/47.

15. Macado to Ryan, 27 July 1916, Records of the Department of State, RG 59, M367, 763.72111D48/47.

16. Lohmann to Toussaint, 25 September 1916, Records of the German Navy, 1850–1945, RG 242, T1022, Roll 658, PG75195.

17. Patrick Beesley, *Room 40*, 208–16.

18. Lohmann to Berlin, 2 October 1916; Lohmann to Admiralstab, 6 October 1916; Admiralstab to Wilhelmshaven, 7 October 1916; Wilhelmshaven to Berlin, 8 October 1916; Records of the German Navy, 1850–1945, RG 242, T1022, Roll 658, PG75195.

Chapter 11. The Second Crossing

1. The sources for this chapter are: König Report to Admiralstab, 3 November 1916, sixteen typewritten pages, Records of the German Navy, 1850–1945, RG 242, T1022, Rolls 658 and 659, PG 75195 and 75196; Malburn to Secretary of State, Records of the Department of State, RG 59, M367, Roll 179, 763,72111D48/49; "Deutschland Eluded Foe with $10,000,000 Cargo," *New York Times,* 2 November 1916; "*Deutschland* Here on Second Trip," *New York Times,* 2 November 1916; "Second Trip from Bremen," *New York Times,* 1 November 1916. Information on the storm is found in David Allen Glenn, "A Reanalysis of the 1916, 1918, 1927, and 1935 Tropical Cyclones of the North Atlantic," Mississippi State University, 2005, NOAA *Hurricane Database* (HURDAT), 48–52, http://www.aoml. noaa.gov/hrd/hurdat/Data_Storm.html.

Chapter 12. New London

1. Unless otherwise cited, the following account came from a collection of newspaper articles found in Records of the German Navy, 1850–1945, RG 242, T1022, Roll 660, PG75197.

2. "U-Boat Unloading under Strict Guard," *New York Times,* 3 November 1916.

3. "The Deutschland Loaded," *New York Times,* 14 November 1916.

4. Message 914, 17 November 1916, ADM 137/1262, Admiralty Historical Section, Packs and Miscellaneous Records, 1860–1924. He was probably the same unidentified informant who gave information to B&O Police captain John Danton in Baltimore during April and May 1916.

5. Spindler, *Der Handeslkrieg mit U-Booten,* 3:215; Gröner, *Die deutschen Kriegsschiffe.*

6. Commander Yates Sterling to Navy Department (Operations), "Examination of German Submarine *Deutschland,*" 3 November 1916; Robert Lansing to Secretary of the Treasury, 9 November 1916; Records of the Department of State, RG 59, M367, Roll 179, 763.72111D48/40.

7. Sterling to Navy Department; Lansing to Secretary of the Treasury.

8. Sterling to Navy Department; Lansing to Secretary of the Treasury.

9. Joint State and Navy Neutrality Board, Memorandum, Serial No. 142, "Status of German Submarine *Deutschland,* Whether or Not to Be Considered a Merchantman," 14 July 1916, Records of the Department of State, RG 59, M367, Roll 176, 763.72111/7321.

10. Lansing to McAdoo, 9 November 1916, Records of the Department of State, RG 59, M367, Roll 179, 763.72111D48/40 [author's emphasis].

11. Anderson Price to Secretary of State, 13 October 1916, Records of the Department of State, RG 59, M367, Roll 176, 763.72111/4165.

12. Bruce Ford to Secretary of State, 31 October 1916, Records of the Department of State, RG 59, M367, Roll 179, 763.72111/4204.

13. Paul König report to Admiralstab, *"2. November Vorfall u. Disziplinarmaßnahmen ergriffen,"* 3 November 1916, Records of the German Navy, RG 242, T1022, Roll 660, PG 75197.

14. Wm. F. Malburn to Secretary of the Navy, 1 November 1916, Records of the Department of State, RG 59, M367, Roll 179, 763.72111D48/40.

15. Hugh P. McNally to Secretary of the Treasury, 17 November 1916; Secretary of the Treasury to Hugh P. McNally, 6 December 1916; Records of the Department of State, RG 59, M367, Roll 179, 763.72111D48/51.

16. Lansing to McAdoo, 9 November 1916; Andrew J. Peters to New London Collector of Customs, 10 November 1916; Records of the Department of State, RG 59, M367, Roll 179, 763.72111D48/41.

17. "Crew Not Trained by Navy," *Baltimore Sun,* 12 July 1916.

18. "Submarine to Take United States Mail," *New York Times,* 2 November 1916.

19. "No Mail for *Deutschland,*" *New York Times,* 10 November 1916.

20. SS *Deutschland,* Summaries of Entered Value, Examination, and Appraisement; Frank H. Shallus & Co. Customs House Brokers,

"Consumption Compared and Liquidated"; H. A. Metz Credit
Memorandum, Hoechst A.M. *Rechnung;* Records of the Department of
State, RG 59, M367, Roll 179, 763.7211D48/42. McGovern to Secretary of
the Treasury, 13 November 1916; McGovern to Secretary of the Treasury,
16 November 1916; Records of the Department of State, RG 59, M367,
Roll 179, D763.72111D48/47.

21. "Not Excited over Dye Cargo," *New York Times,* 2 November 1916;
"The Merchants' Point of View," *New York Times,* 5 November 1916.

22. Thomas A. Berryhill, MD, "Venereal Prophylaxis in the Navy," *Long
Island Medical Journal* 7 (January–December 1913), 117–19.

23. "Give Watch to König," *New York Times,* 9 November.

24. Commander Yates Sterling, to Secretary of the Navy (Operations),
German Merchant Submarine "Deutschland," 14 November 1916,
Secret and Confidential Correspondence of the Office of the Chief of
Naval Operations and the Office of the Secretary of the Navy, File 123,
Submarines, German, RG 80, M1140, NARA; Secretary of the Treasury to
Secretary of State, No. 102574, 16 November 1916; McGovern to Secretary
of the Treasury, 16 November 1916.

25. McGovern to Secretary of the Treasury, 16 November 1916.

26. "*Deutschland* Off on Home Voyage," *New York Times,* 17 November
1916.

Chapter 13. The Not-So-Triumphant Return

1. "*Deutschland* Off on Home Voyage."

2. The details of the events leading up to the collision between the
U-Deutschland and the *T. S. Scott, Jr.,* and the accident investigation are taken
from Bureau of Marine Inspection and Navigation, RG 41, entry 47A,
Steamboat Inspection Service, Numerical Correspondence, 1905–1923,
File 733301 relating to the collision between the German submarine
U-Deutschland and the tug *T. S. Scott, Jr.,* 17 November 1916, Bureau Marine
Inspection and Navigation, Steamboat Inspection Service, RG 4, Numerical
Correspondence, 1905–23, NARA [hereafter File 733301].

3. Department of Commerce, Steamboat Inspection Service, *General Rules
and Regulations Prescribed by the Board of Supervising Inspectors* (Washington,
D.C.: GPO, 1914), 338.

4. Treasury Department to Secretary of State, 17 November 1916, Records
of the Department of State, RG 59, M367, Roll 179, 763.72111D48/44.

5. König Report to the Admiralstab, 10 December 1916, Records of the
German Navy, 1850–1945, RG 242, T-1022, Roll 647, PG75195.

6. "*Deutschland* Off on Home Voyage."

7. "*Deutschland* Rams Tug; Five Drown," *New York Times,* 18 November 1916.

8. *"Deutschland* Held by Damage Suits," *New York Times,* 19 November 1916.

9. *"Deutschland* May Get Away Tonight," *New York Times,* 20 November 1916.

10. Ibid. The bond was $97,250.

11. "Deutschland Held by Damage Suits."

12. "Submarine *Deutschland* Sails in Daylight," *New York Times,* 22 November 1916.

13. König to Admiralstab, 10 December 1916.

14. J. Y. Buck to Secretary of State, 26 November 1917, Records of the Department of State, RG 59, M367, Roll 179, 763.72111D48.

15. File 733301; *Tagesblatt* [Köln], 21 December 1916, Records of the German Navy, 1850–1945, RG 242, T-1022, Roll 660, PG75197.

16. Deutsche Ozean Reederei to Admiralstab, 12 September 1917, Records of the German Navy, 1850–1945, RG 242, T-1022, Roll 631, PG67344.

Chapter 14. The End of the Line, Part I

1. Beumelburg, *Sperrfeuer um Deutschland,* 227–28.

2. Vincent, *Politics of Hunger,* 124–26.

3. Rudolf Otto Neumann, MD, *Die im Krieg 1914–1918 verwendeten und zur Verwendung empfohlenen Brote, Brotersatz, und Brotstreckmittel* (Berlin: Julius Springer, 1920), 73–75.

4. John Ellis, *Eye-Deep in Hell: Trench Warfare in World War I* (New York: Pantheon Books, 1976), 127–29.

5. R. H. Gibson and Maurice Prendergast, *German Submarine War, 1914–1918* (London: Constable, 1931), 81–82.

6. "Expect the *Deutschland,*" *New York Times,* 6 January 1917.

7. "Thinks He Saw a Submarine," *New York Times,* 16 January 1917.

8. "Copenhagen Hears Merchant Submarine Is Not Lost," *New York Times,* 15 January; *"Deutschland* Starts for America," *New York Times,* 17 January 1917; "Submarine Reported off New London," *New York Times,* 23 January 1917.

9. "Hear *Deutschland* Has Been Captured," *New York Times,* 29 January 1917; "New London U-Boat Scare," *New York Times,* 30 January 1917.

10. Techel, *Der Bau von U-Booten auf der Germaniawerft,* 99–100; Rössler, *Geschichte des deutschen Ubootbaus,* 67.

11. Gröner, *Die deutschen Kriegsschiffe,* 2:359; Spindler, *Der Handelskrieg mit U-Booten,* 4:571.

12. Techel, *Der Bau von U-Booten auf der Germaniawerft,* 100.

13. Ibid.; Gröner, *Die deutschen Kriegsschiffe,* 2:359.

14. Techel, *Der Bau von U-Booten auf der Germaniawerft,* 100; Herzog, *Deutsche U-Boote,* 54.

15. Gröner, *Die deutschen Kriegsschiffe*, 2:359; Techel, *Der Bau von U-Booten auf der Germaniawerft*, 100.
16. Techel, *Der Bau von U-Booten auf der Germaniawerft*, 42.
17. Ibid., 100; Gröner, *Die deutschen Kriegsschiffe*, 2:359; Rössler, *Geschichte des deutschen Ubootbaus*, 67.

Chapter 15. The End of the Line, Part II

1. Paul Hilken Grand Jury Testimony, Bureau of Investigation Case 8000-174, Franz von Rintelen et al.
2. Unless otherwise noted, the information and the lengthy quotes that follow about the Baltimore sabotage cell and its members are found in Mixed Claims Commission, 273–96, 341–54, 395–96.
3. Bureau of Investigation Case 8000-2338, Woehst (Wöhst), Neutrality Matter, 2 December 1916.
4. Landau, *Enemy Within*, 202.
5. Ibid., 195–96.
6. Beesly, *Room 40*, 213–14.
7. Bureau of Investigation Case 8000-2338, William Woeh(R)st (Wöhst), Alleged German Secret Agent, 24 and 28 February 1917.
8. Ibid.
9. Ibid.

Chapter 16. *U-155*

1. William S. Sims, *The Victory at Sea* (Garden City and New York: Doubleday, Page, 1920), 9.
2. Philip K. Lundeberg, "The German Naval Critique of the U-boat Campaign." *Military Affairs* 27, no. 3 (Fall 1963), 1125.
3. Spindler, *Der Handelskrieg mit U-Booten*, 4:372.
4. *Personelunterlagen für* Karl Meusel, *Deutsche Dienststelle (WASt)*, Berlin.
5. Unless otherwise cited, the details of the 105-day patrol are found in the *U-155* log and Meusel's thirty-two-page patrol report, Records of the German Navy 1850–1945, RG 242, T-1022, Roll 21, PG61710.
6. The following account is from Johannes Spiess, *Six Years of Submarine Cruising* [translation] (Washington, D.C.: GPO for Office of Naval Intelligence, 1926).
7. See Dwight R. Messimer, *Find and Destroy: Antisubmarine Warfare in World War I* (Annapolis, Md.: Naval Institute Press, 2001), 76–81.
8. Gröner, *Die deutschen Kriegsschiffe*, 1:359.
9. Spindler, *Der Handelskrieg mit U-Booten*, 5:240–41.
10. Herzog, *Deutsche U-Boote*, 102, says 53,306.
11. Ibid.; Spindler, *Der Handelskrieg mit U-Booten*, 5:238.

Chapter 17. The End of the Line, Part III

1. *Personalunterlagen für* Erich Eckelmann, *Deutsche Dienststelle (WASt),* Berlin.

2. John J. Pershing, *My Experiences in the World War* (New York: Frederick A. Stokes, 1931), 1:66.

3. Ibid., 1:66.

4. *Personalunterlagen für* Ferdinand Studt, *Deutsche Dienststelle (WASt),* Berlin.

5. "FV *Gamo* 1918," Wreck Site, www.wrecksite.eu.

6. James L. Mooney, ed., *Dictionary of American Naval Fighting Ships* (Washington, D.C.: GPO, 1991), s.v. *"Lucia,"* 4:159.

Chapter 18. Epilogue

1. "Fate of the *Deutschland,*" USNI *Proceedings* (May 1919), 816; "Jockeyed for an Hour to Get *Deutschland,*" *New York Times,* 14 July 1918.

2. The account of the *U-Deutschland* (*U-155*) as a show-business venture is taken from *Explosion on the Submarine* Deutschland *in Dry Dock 1921,* www .old-merseytimes.co.uk/Deutschland.html, and is found in news reports taken from the *Manchester Guardian,* 11 September 1921 to 9 September 1933.

3. "Submarine Deutschland Broken Up," *New York Times,* 30 November 1922.

4. The information for this description of Alfred Lohmann is based on information provided by Dr. jur. Fritz Lohmann, his grandnephew, from an account written by his great-aunt, Elisabeth.

5. Bodo Herzog in *Neue deutsche Biographie,* 347, www.deutsche-biographie .de; *Personalunterlagen für* Paul König, *Deutsche Dienststelle (WASt),* Berlin.

6. *Personalunterlagen für* Franz Krapohl, Karl Meusel, Karl Schwartzkopf, *Deutsche Dienststelle (WASt),* Berlin.

7. *Personalunterlagen für* Emil Eyring, *Deutsche Dienststelle (WASt),* Berlin.

8. Bureau of Investigation Case 8000-1272, Wilhelm Gotthold Prusse, German Matter.

9. Bureau of Investigation Case 8000-549, Paul Hilken, German Matter; Bureau of Investigation Case 8000-1634, Eastern Forwarding Company of Baltimore; Bureau of Investigation Case 177344, State Department to Bureau of Investigation, 15 August 1915; Mixed Claims Commission, 343–44, 346; "Mrs. Billings Sues Broker for Divorce," *New York Times,* 17 November 1917; "W. P. Billings Named in Alienation Suit," *New York Times,* 20 July 1916; "May Arrest Hilken in Alienation Suit," *New York Times,* 23 November 1917.

10. Bureau of Investigation Case 21962, Fred Herrmann.

11. Bureau of Investigation Case 136207, Frederick Hinsch; Landau, *Enemy Within,* 183; Mixed Claims Commission, 387; "*Deutschland* Agent Escapes to Bremen," *New York Times,* 18 July 1917; "Capt. Hinsch Escapes from American Soil," *Baltimore Sun,* 18 July 1917; "Doubt Hinsch Escaped U.S.," *Washington Post,* 19 July 1917; "Capt. Hinsch Seeks Safety in Mexico," *New York Times,* 24 July 1917.

12. Bureau of Investigation Case 33415 and 277119, Dr. Albert Delmar (Anton Dilger).

13. Bureau of Investigation Case 8000-2338, William Woehst (Wilhelm Wöhst); Mixed Claims Commission, 273–96, 291–335, 341–54, 395–96.

14. Mixed Claims Commission, 354–58, 363–67, 370–72, 393–97; Landau, *Enemy Within,* 181–83, 243–57.

BIBLIOGRAPHY

Books

Asprey, Robert B. *The German High Command at War*. New York: William Morrow, 1991.

Baltimore City Historical Society. *Baltimore: Its History and Its People*, s.v. "Henry Gerard Hilken." New York and Chicago: Lewis Historical, 1912.

Bankers Trust Company. *America's Attitude toward the War*. New York: Rogers, 1919.

Bassett, John S. *Our War with Germany*. New York: Alfred A. Knopf, 1919.

Bauer, Hermann. *Als Führer der U-Boote in Weltkrieg*. Leipzig: Koehler & Amelang, 1940.

Beesly, Patrick. *Room 40: British Naval Intelligence, 1914–1918*. New York: Harcourt Brace Jovanovich, 1982.

Beumelburg, Werner. *Sperrfeurer um Deutschland*. Oldenburg: Gerhard Stelling, 1929.

Brehmer, Arthur. *Die Kühne Fahrt der Deutschland*. Berlin: Berthold Siegmund, 1916.

Castagnera, James. *Counter Terrorism: Case Studies in the Courtroom*. Boca Raton, Fla.: CRC, 2013.

Chatterton, E. Keble. *The Big Blockade*. London: Hurst & Blackett, 1932.

Craig, Gordon A. *Germany, 1866–1945*. New York: Oxford University Press, 1978.

Ehlers, Wilhelm. *Deutschland: Was Wir vom Krieg nicht wissen*. Leipzig: H. Fikentscher Verlag, 1936.

Ellis, John. *Eye-Deep in Hell: Trench Warfare in World War I*. New York: Pantheon Books, 1976.

Findley, James P. *U.S. Army Intelligence History: A Source Book*. Fort Huachuca, Ariz.: U.S. Army Intelligence Center, 1995.

Geisler, Erhard. *Anthrax und das Versagen der Geheimdienste*. Düren: K. Homilius, 2003.

———. *Biologische Waffen—nicht in Hitlers Aresenalen*. Münster: LIT, 1998.

Gibson, R. H., and Maurice Prendergast. *The German Submarine War, 1914–1918*. London: Constable, 1931.

Glenn, David Allen. "A Reanalysis of the 1916, 1918, 1927, and 1935 Tropical Cyclones of the North Atlantic." Mississippi State University, 2005, NOAA *Hurricane Database* (HURDAT), http://www.aoml.noaa.gov/hrd/hurdat/Data_Storm.html.

Görlitz, Walter, ed. *The German General Staff*. New York and Washington, D.C.: Frederick A. Praeger, 1965.

———. *The Kaiser and His Court: The Diaries, Notebooks, and Letters of Admiral Georg Alexander von Müller, Chief of the Naval Cabinet, 1914–1918*. New York: Harcourt, Brace & World, 1959.

Gröner, Erich. *Die deutschen Kriegsschiffe, 1815–1945.* 2 vols. München: J. F. Lehmanns Verlag, 1966.

Guichard, Louis. *The Naval Blockade, 1914–1918.* New York: D. Appleton, 1930.

Hadley, Michael, and Roger Sarty. *Tin-Pots & Pirate Ships: Canadian Naval Forces & German Sea Raiders, 1880–1918.* Montreal: McGill-Queen's University Press, 1991.

Hall, Clayton Colman. *Baltimore: Its History and Its People,* Vol. 3. New York: Lewis Historical, 1925.

Halpern, Paul G. *A Naval History of World War I.* Annapolis, Md.: Naval Institute Press, 1994.

Helfferich, Karl. *Der Welt Krieg.* Berlin: Ulstein, 1919. Vol. 1, *Die Geschichte des Weltkriegs.* Vol. 2, *Vom Kriegsausbruch bis zum uneingeschränkten U-Bootkrieg.* Vol. 3, *Vom Einggreifen Amerikas bis zum Zusammenbruch.*

Herzog, Bodo. *Deutsche U-Boote, 1906–1966.* Herrsching: Pawlak Verlag, 1990.

Jones, John Price, and Paul Merrick Hollister. *The German Secret Service in America, 1914–1918.* Boston: Small, Maynard, 1918.

Jung, Dieter, Martin Maass, and Berndt Wenzel. *Tanker und Versorger der deutschen Flotte, 1900–1980.* Stuttgart: Motorbuch, 1981.

Kirchner, Johann. *Das U-Boot bei der Arbeit.* Berlin: Verlag E. S. Mittler & Sohn, 1917.

Kobrak, Christopher. *Die Deutsche Bank und die USA: Geschäfte und Politik von 1870 bis Heute.* München: C. H. Beck, 2008.

König, Paul. *Voyage of the* Deutschland. New York: Hearst's International Library, 1916.

———. *Die Fahrt der Deutschland.* New York: Hearst's International Library, 1916.

———. *Die Fahrt der Deutschland.* Berlin: Ulstein, 1916 and 1917.

———. *Fahrten der UDeutschland im Weltkrieg.* Berlin: Ulstein, 1937.

Lake, Simon. *The Submarine in War and Peace.* Philadelphia and London: J. B. Lippincott, 1918.

Landau, Capt. Henry. *The Enemy Within: The Inside Story of German Sabotage in America.* New York: G. P. Putnam's Sons, 1937.

Manchester, William. *The Arms of Krupp, 1587–1968.* New York: Little, Brown, 1968.

Messimer, Dwight R. *The Merchant U-Boat: Adventures of the Deutschland, 1916–1918.* Annapolis, Md.: Naval Institute Press, 1988.

———. *Find and Destroy: Antisubmarine Warfare in World War I.* Annapolis, Md.: Naval Institute Press, 2001.

Nadolny, Rudolf. *Mein Betrag: Erinnerungen eines Botschafters des Deutschen Reiches.* Köln: Dme Verlag, 1985.

Neumann, Rudolf Otto, MD. *Die im Krieg 1914–1918 verwendeten und zur Verwendung empfohlenen Brote, Brotersatz, und Brotstreckmittel.* Berlin: Julius Springer, 1920.

Pershing, John J. *My Experiences in the World War.* 2 vols. New York: Frederick A. Stokes, 1931.

Polmar, Norman, and Kenneth J. Moore. *Cold War Submarines: The Design and Construction of United States and Soviet Submarines.* New York: Brassey's, 2004.

Rintelen, Franz von, *The Dark Invader.* London and Portland, Ore.: Frank Cass, 1998.

Robinalt, James D. *The Harding Affair.* New York: Palgrave Macmillan, 2009.

Rössler, Eberhard. *Geschichte des deutschen Ubootbaus.* München: J. F. Lehmanns Verlag, 1975.

———. *Die Unterseeboote der Kaiserlichen Marine.* Bonn: Bernard & Graefe Verlag, 1997.

———. *Die deutschen U-Kreuzer und Transport-U-Boote.* Bonn: Bernard & Graefe Verlag, 2003.

Schwerdtfeger, Hartmut, and Erik Herlyn. *Die Handles-U-Boote Deutschland und Bremen: Ein vergessenes Kapitel der Seefahrt.* Bremen: Kurze-Schönholz und Ziesemer Verlag, 1997.

Sims, William S. *The Victory at Sea.* Garden City and New York: Doubleday, Page, 1920.

Smart, Jeffery. *History of Chemical and Biological Warfare: An American Perspective.* Aberdeen Proving Ground, Md.: Chemical and Biological Defense Command, n.d.

Smith, Gaddin. *Britain's Clandestine Submarines, 1914–15.* New Haven, Conn.: Yale University Press, 1964.

Spindler, Arno. *Der Handelskrieg mit U-Booten.* 5 vols. Berlin: Verlag E. S. Mittler & Sohn, 1932–1964.

Techel, Hans. *Der Bau von U-Booten auf der Germaniawerft.* Berlin: Verlag des Vereines deutscher Ingenieure, 1923.

Tuchman, Barbara W. *The Zimmermann Telegram.* New York: Ballantine, 1994.

Tunny, Thomas Joseph, and Paul Merrick Hollister. *Throttled! The Detection of the German and Anarchist Bomb Plotters.* Boston: Small, Maynard, 1919.

Vincent, C. Paul. *The Politics of Hunger: The Allied Blockade of Germany, 1915–1919.* Athens, Ohio, and London: Ohio University Press, 1985.

Weddigen, Dr. Otto. *Das erste Handels-Unterseeboot, Deutschland und sein Kapitän, Paul König.* Leipzig: Wiking Verlag, 1916.

Witcover, Jules. *Sabotage at Black Tom: Imperial Germany's Secret War in America, 1914–1917.* New York: Algonquin Books of Chapel Hill, 1989.

Official Histories

Corbett, Sir Julian S., and Henry Newbolt. *History of the Great War: Naval Operations.* 5 vols. London: Longmans, Green, 1920–31.

Fayle, C. Ernest. *History of the Great War: Seaborne Trade,* 3 vols. New York: Longmans, Green, 1920–24.

Firle, Rudolf, Heinrich Rollmann, and Ernst von Gagern. *Der Krieg zur See, 1914–1918: Der Krieg in der Ostsee.* 3 vols. Berlin: Verlag E. S. Mittler & Sohn, 1922–64.

Groos, Otto, and Walter Gladisch. *Der Krieg zur See, 1914–1918: Der Krieg in der Nordsee.* 7 vols. Berlin: Verlag E. S. Mittler & Sohn, 1922–65.

Hurd, Archibald. *History of the Great War: The Merchant Navy.* 2 vols. London: John Murray, 1921.

Navy Department. *German Submarine Activities on the Atlantic Coasts of the United States and Canada.* Washington, D.C.: U.S. government Printing Office, 1920.

Palmer, Mitchell. *Alien Property Custodian Report.* Washington, D.C.: U.S. Government Printing Office, 1919.

Spindler, Arno. *Der Krieg zur See, 1914–1918: Der Handelskrieg mit U-Booten.* 5 vols. Berlin & München: Verlag E. S. Mittler & Sohn, 1932–66.

German Documents

Personalunterlagen für Emil Eyring, Paul König, Franz Krapohl, Karl Meusel, Karl Schwartzkopf, Hermann Liebermann von Sonnenberg, and Gerhard Posse. *Deutsche Dienststelle für die Benachrichtigung der nächsten Angehörigen von Gefallen der ehemaligen deutschen Wermacht (WASt),* Berlin.

Records of the German Navy, 1850–1945, Record Group 242, Microfilm Publication T1022, rolls: 021, 022, 095, 096, 558, 559, 560, 576, 596, 658, 659, 660, 711, 712. National Archives, College Park, Md.

Telegramme der Deutschen Ozean Reederei, Bremen, an den Reichkanzler und umgekehrt, und Zeitungsartikeln über den Kapitän Paul König, Juni–Oktober 1916, File 00423, Zentrales Staatsarchiv, DDR [German Democratic Republic].

Government Documents and Publications

Bureau of Marine Inspection and Navigation. Record Group 41, Entry 47A, Steamboat Inspection Service, Numerical Correspondence, 1905–1923, "File #73301 relating to the collision between the German submarine *Deutschland* and the tug *T.A. Scott, Jr.*," 17 November 1916. National Archives, College Park, Md.

Department of Commerce. *United States Coast Pilot: Section B Cape Cod to Sandy Hook*. Washington, D.C.: U.S. Government Printing Office, 1918.

Department of Commerce, Steamboat Inspection Service. *General Rules and Regulations Prescribed by the Board of Supervising Inspectors*. Washington, D.C.: U.S. Government Printing Office, 1914.

Department of the Navy, Office of Naval Intelligence. "Cruise of the *Deutschland* in the Region of the Azores 10 June to 16 August 1917." Naval Historical Center, Washington, DC.

———. "I.D. 1181, May 1917–April 1918." Naval Historical Center, Washington, D.C.

Fess, Simeon D. *The Problems of Neutrality When the World Is at War: A History of Our Relations with Germany and Great Britain as Detailed in the Documents That Passed between the United States and the Two Great Belligerent Powers*. House of Representatives, Sixty-Fourth Congress, Second Session, Document No. 2111, in Two Parts. Part 1, "The Submarine Controversy." Washington, D.C.: U.S. Government Printing Office, 1917.

———. *The Problems of Neutrality When the World Is at War: A History of Our Relations with Germany and Great Britain as Detailed in the Documents That Passed between the United States and the Two Great Belligerent Powers*. House of Representatives, Sixty-Fourth Congress, Second Session, Document No. 2111, in Two Parts. Part 2, "Restraints on Trade Controversy." Washington, D.C.: U.S. Government Printing Office, 1917.

Inspectors James J. Farrell and A. T. Rouse to Surveyor of Customs, Baltimore, Maryland, "Submarine Report," 3 August 1916. In the author's possession.

Investigative Case Files of the Bureau of Investigation, 1908–22. Records of the Federal Bureau of Investigation, Record Group 65, Microfilm Publication M1080, National Archives, College Park, Md.:

    A. J. Lamme, Case 180958

    Doctor Albert Delmar (Anton Dilger), Case 33415

    Dr. Albert C. Delmar (Anton Dilger), Case 8000-277119

    Eastern Forwarding Company, Case 8000-1634

    Fred Herrmann, Case 8000-21962

    Frederick Hinsch (Friedrich Hinsch), Case 8000-136207

    Franz von Rintelen et al., Case 8000-174

    Gotthold Prusse, Case 12727

    Gotthold Prusse, Case 75207

    Paul G. L. Hilken, Case 8000-549

    Walter T. Scheele, Cases 8000-925 and 8000-2423

    William Woehst (Wilhelm Wöhst), Case 8000-2338.

Records of the Department of State, Passport Applications, Record Group 59, Microfilm Series M1372, 21 September 1915.

Records of the Department of State Relating to World War I and Its Termination, Record Group 59, Microfilm Publication M367, Decimal Series 763.72111, National Archives and Records Administration, College Park, Md.

Records of the Immigration and Naturalization Service, Passenger and Crew Lists, 1897–1957, Record Group 36, Microfilm Series T715, Roll 2435, p. 131. National Archives and Records Administration, College Park, Md.

Register of the Department of State, 1918. Washington, D.C.: U.S. Government Printing Office, 1919.

Reports of International Arbitrator Awards, Mixed Claims Commission *(U.S. v. Germany),* Constituted under the Agreement of August 10, 1922, Extended by Agreement of December 1928. Vol. VIII, "Lehigh Valley Railroad Company, Agency of Canadian Car and Foundry, Ltd. and Various Underwriters (Sabotage Case)," 16 October 1930.

Reports of International Arbitrator Awards, Mixed Claims Commission *(U.S. v. Germany),* Constituted under the Agreement of August 10, 1922, Extended by Agreement of December 1928. Vol. VIII, "Lehigh Valley Railroad Company, Agency of Canadian Car and Foundry, Ltd. and Various Underwriters (Sabotage Case)," 15 June 1939.

Rogers, John. "Conversation with Captain König," 24 July 1916, Office of Naval Records and Library.

Secret and Confidential Correspondence of the Chief of Naval Operations and the Secretary of the Navy, 1919–1927, Record Group 80, Microfilm Publication M1140, "Submarines (German)," File 123, "German Merchant Submarine *Deutschland.*"

Spiess, Johannes. *Six Years of Submarine Cruising* [translation]. Washington, D.C.: U.S. Government Printing Office for Office of Naval Intelligence, 1926.

Treasury Department, U.S. Coast and Geodetic Survey. *United States Coast Pilot: Part V from Point Judith to New York.* Washington, D.C.: U.S. Government Printing Office, 1898.

U.S. Senate. *Brewing and Liquor Interests and German Propaganda.* Hearings before a Subcommittee of the Committee on the Judiciary, United States Senate, Sixty-Fifth Congress, Second Session, Pursuant to S. Res. 307, A Resolution Authorizing and Directing the Committee on the Judiciary to Call for Certain Evidence and Documents Relating to the Charges Made against the United States Brewers' Association and Allied Interests and to Submit a Report of Their Investigation to the Senate. 3 Vols. Washington, D.C.: U.S. Government Printing Office 1919.

U.S. Senate. Hearings before a Subcommittee of the Committee on the Judiciary, United States Senate, Sixty-Seventh Congress, Second Session Pursuant to Senate Resolution 77 (Alleged Dye Monopoly). Washington, D.C.: U.S. Government Printing Office, 1927.

U.S. Senate. Hearings before the Committee on Finance, United States Senate, Sixty-Sixth Congress, Second Session, on HR 8078, 8–13 December 1919 and 12 January 1920. Washington, D.C.: U.S. Government Printing Office 1920.

U.S. Senate. Hearings before the Committee on Finance, United States Senate, Sixty-Sixth Congress, Second Session, on HR 8078, An Act to Regulate the Importation of Coal-Tar Products, to Promote the Establishment of the Manufacture Thereof in the United States, and as Incident thereto to Amend the Act of September 1916 Entitled, "An Act to Increase Revenue and for Other Purposes," 8–13 December 1919 and 12 January 1920. Washington, D.C.: U.S. Government Printing Office 1920.

CIA Center for the Study of Intelligence

Belote, James H. "The Lohmann Affair." *Studies in Intelligence* (Spring 1960).
Warner, Christopher. "The Kaiser Sows Destruction: Protecting the Homeland the First Time Around." *Studies in Intelligence* 46, no. 1 (Spring 2002).

Private Papers

Carl W. Ackerman Papers, Boxes 167–68, Library of Congress, Washington, D.C.

Journals

Information Annual: A Continuous Cyclopedia and Digest of Current Events, 1916. New York: Cumulative Digest, 1917.
Information Quarterly: A Digest of Current Events 2, no. 1 (January 1917).
Journal of the Society of Chemical Industry 35, no. 23 (15 December 1916).
Thomas A. Berryhill, MD. "Venereal Prophylaxis in the Navy." *Long Island Medical Journal* 7 (January–December 1913).
Philip K. Lundeberg. "The German Naval Critique of the U-boat Campaign." *Military Affairs* 27, no. 3 (Fall 1963).
"To Strike Medals from Deutschland's Iron Ballast." American Numismatic Society Association *Numismatist* 29 (December 1916).
Popular Science Monthly 89 (July–December 1916).
United States Naval Institute *Proceedings* 40, no. 1 (January–February 1914).

Newspapers

New York Times, 1915–17
Toledo (Ohio) *Blade,* 1916
Baltimore Sun, 1916
New London (Conn.) *Day,* 1917
Gettysburg (Pa.) *Times,* 1917
Los Angeles Evening Herald, 1916
Tyrone Herald, 1917
Hartford (Ky.) *Herald,* 1917
Washington Post, 1916
Summary, 1916.

National Oceanic and Atmospheric Administration (NOAA) Navigation Charts

12208. Approaches to Chesapeake Bay
12221. Chesapeake Bay Entrance
12225. Chesapeake Bay Wolf Trap to Smith Point
12245. Hampton Roads
12256. Chesapeake Bay Thimble Shoal Channel
12264. Chesapeake Bay Patuxent River and Vicinity
12266. Chesapeake Bay Choptank River and Herring Bay; Cambridge
12270. Chesapeake Bay Eastern Bay and South River; Selby Bay
13205. Block Island Sound and Approaches
13212. Approaches to New London Harbor
13213. New London Harbor and Vicinity Bailey Point to Smith Cove
13218. Martha's Vineyard to Block Island.

INDEX

A. Schumacher and Company, 7, 8, 17, 27, 28, 31, 65, 66, 69, 209, 220

Ablak (Italy), 193–94

Abteilung IIIb (espionage section of German secret service), 20, 159

Ackerman, Carl W., 45, 62, 66

Adams, Mrs. George L., 132

Adlon Hotel, Berlin, 31

Admiralstab, 88, 101–3, 113–14, 126, 145, 148, 150, 170, 189, 198

Ager, Milton, 68

Aguilas, Spain, 178

Ahrendt, Carl, 17, 18, 28, 69, 94, 127, 148, 167, 211

Albargin (drug), 137t

Albert, Dr. Heinrich, 13, 19, 28, 72, 73

Alberto Trenes (Italy), 198

Alert (tug), 148

Alexandre (sailing vessel), 186

Allgemeine-SS, 208

American Agricultural Chemical Company, 24

American Protective League, 212–13

Anholt Island, 171

aniline dye, 64–65, 136

anthrax, 5, 11, 16–18, 20, 25, 86, 94, 113, 159–62, 211, 215; delivered, 94, 159

Antioco Accame (Spain), 193

Arlington Naval Radio Station, 59

Arnabal Mendi (Spain), 191

Arnold, John A., 20, 86, 211–12

artillery, 62, 158; ammunition shortage, 2, 4, 152; on U-cruisers 111, 156, 185; Russian, 163

Arundel Sand and Gravel Company, 26

Astor Hotel, 94

Atlantic (dredge), 121–22

Atlaswerke, Bremen (shipyard), 111

Atterbury, John, 160–61

Atterbury, Mrs. John, 160–61

Austrians and Turks to drop out of the war, 4

Aysgarth (United Kingdom), 178

Badger, Charles F., 60

Badische Company, 64

Baker, Ruth, 126, 195

Baltimore, 73

Baltimore and Ohio Railroad (B&O), 24, 26, 27, 29, 30

Baltimore Country Club, 9, 74

Baltimore Sabotage Cell, ix, 6, 8, 12, 29, 31, 56, 79, 162, 166–67, 207, 211, 216–17, 221; anthrax and glanders, 5, 11, 18–19, 20, 25, 86, 94, 113, 159–62, 211, 216; Black Tom, 17, 23, 79–80, 94–95, 100, 163–88; Kingsland, 11, 23, 163, 213, 161–64, 166

Baltimore Trust Company, 20

Barkhausen, Carl Georg, 92

Barranquilla, Columbia, 217

Bartlett, Captain, 6

Bartling, Wilhelm, 21

Bassemann, Ernst, 110

Bauer, Hermann, 5, 46, 169

Bayer & Company, 64, 136

Bell Syndicate, 76

Belvedere Hotel, Baltimore, 11, 72

Benguela (Norway), 178–80; sunk, 181

Benham, William, 211

Berlin Aniline Works, 64

Berliner Zeitung (*BZ*), 46

Bernstorff, Johann Heinrich Graf von, 15, 67, 72, 73, 115, 160

Berry, Paul, 211

Berwick (United Kingdom), 9, 78

Bethlehem University, 7

Bethmann-Hollweg, Theobald von, 4, 108; fires von Falkenhayn, 110–11

Beumelburg, Werner, 63, 152

255

About the Author

Dwight R. Messimer is a U.S. Army veteran and a former lecturer in history at the California State University at San Jose. His interests are U.S. Naval Aviation, 1911–42 and World War I with an emphasis on Allied POWs, escapes, and anti-submarine warfare. He is fluent and literate in German. He and his wife live in Northern California.